ASIA

Allahabad
Calcutta
Sundarbans
Akyab
Rangoon
Bangkok
Songkhla
Kota Bharu
Kuala Lumpur
Singapore
Semarang
Jakarta
Surabaja
Denpasar
Kupang
Darwin
Cape Londonderry
Katherine
Wyndham
Tennant Creek
Camooweal
Cloncurry
Blackall
AUSTRALIA
Bourke
Narromine
Sydney

London – Singapore – Sydney

ROBERT BAUDIN

FAKE

The passing fortunes of a counterfeiter

Methuen of Australia | Eyre Methuen London

First published in 1977 by
METHUEN OF AUSTRALIA PTY LTD

301 Kent Street, Sydney
225 Swan Street, Richmond
91 Elizabeth Street, Brisbane
First published in Great Britain in 1977 by
EYRE METHUEN LTD
11 New Fetter Lane, EC4P 4EE

National Library of Australia
Cataloguing-in-Publication data

Baudin, Robert.
  Fake.
  ISBN 0 454 00034 0.
  1. Baudin, Robert. 2. Counterfeits and
  counterfeiting – Biography. I. Title.
364.133

Printed in Australia by
Watson Ferguson & Co., Brisbane

CONTENTS

PROLOGUE

With father a conservative university academic and mother an unliberated housewife, the options open to a rebellious second child in a three-child family were somewhat limited. With an older brother early setting a shining example of how the young phase themselves into civilized existence, a middle-ground approach to life was not altogether feasible—nor particularly desirable.

The first indications that I was a burgeoning non-conformist caused only minor friction—compared to sparks that flew later when things really began to happen. Early behaviour that was mildly unacceptable evolved into a pattern that was to bring great humiliation to a family strong on respectability. After a few years home became untenable for a good number of strong reasons, and my only escape was to hit the road fast—as a teenage runaway.

What followed was a varied and exciting life. From the security and shelter of an American middle-class university-oriented background, I had to learn how to live by my wits as a drifter in depression-stricken U.S. This created a life-style that for a very long time did not encourage too much in the way of legitimate endeavour, but did provide many adventures in widely separated parts of the world. The climax to my protracted non-violent struggle against "the system" was a rather successful shot at beating them at their own game of MAKING MONEY.

In the telling of these many events there is little attempt to justify rebellious acts against authority, firstly parental and latterly legal, though some of it could be taken in the context of its time. Had the course set for me in my early years by others been followed, I might have been technically more proficient—but there would have been little to write about.

ROBERT BAUDIN

1

The shock tactics of childhood   masturbation
makes you mad   the friendly family alienist
versus the friendly downtown whore
academic failure and accomplished
shoplifter   in praise of bigger women.

LIFE WITH FATHER

Almost all my early recollections relate to conflict with authority. Shock tactics, I fast learned, could outrage adults, which meant anyone in power. Before discovering that words alone could be effective, I outraged some visiting ladies by farting loudly while being presented by my mother. I was violently hustled out of the room, but I thought it was funny and intended doing it again first chance. Next time was in Sunday-school, but the young girl teacher spoiled it by laughing instead of tossing me out.

It was a lot of fun causing histrionics, though harder smacks than those brought on by farting came from the use of certain badly chosen words. Retribution might have been held to a tolerable level if fairly mild words had continued to satisfy, but older kids used better-sounding ones. Coming out with the best of them in mixed adult company created such a violent scene that it seemed better not to try that stunt again until I was sure of the word's real meaning. Older kids explained it as a seemingly impossible thing men did to women, but I decided there must be something to it after experiencing the reaction over my asking a man if he ever fucked the woman standing beside him. Adults simply went too far over that word, and the less explosive ones were no longer worth while.

Then came stealing, with no desire to shock people by getting caught. Mostly I stole from stores and got away with it for a while, but a blow-up finally came. My place for stolen things was discovered and there were emotional outbursts from both my

1

father and mother, along with talk of reform school. This was a terrifying adult reaction, particularly as I thought I'd been so clever in hiding my loot. The lesson I learned was to be selective and not accumulate so much junk—and to pick better hiding-places.

My new methods worked well, except for suspicion over items that had gone missing. This meant lengthy questioning followed by a search of my room and other likely hiding spots. More often than not I emerged unscathed from those sessions, but some were lost. And when my defences crumpled there was a lot of ranting and raving from my father. Then I'd intend to stop stealing—for a few days.

With my father being a young, but to me old, teacher at Miami University in Ohio, my tendency to be near the bottom of the class at school made for a less than happy home relationship. No support for my feeble scholastic efforts stemmed from the marks achieved by my older brother and younger sister. These were highly praised, and I also had it rubbed in that these two never questioned rules laid down by others. Rules to me were acceptable only if their reasonableness was apparent, and they happened to fit in with my plans.

Sanctions against stealing weren't queried as such. In that field my objective was to acquire desired things, with the added challenge of not being caught. In time my techniques of theft developed more polish and I learned to explain "ownership" of items too big to be concealed as the proceeds of deals with other kids. Acceptance of those tales led to overconfidence, and a too ambitious theft.

For some reason a microscope became highly desirable, and I knew where to get the real thing rather than a junky toy made for kids. Where my father taught French at Miami, there wasn't much worth taking and I knew better than to work so close to home, but the science laboratory was a good source. Not yet had that ivy-covered old building yielded anything as big as a microscope. An overheard conversation, in which another professor told my father of the university's inability to prevent thefts from the laboratory, gave me confidence.

Before acquiring my instrument, I checked for a time when it could be taken from the building unobserved and worked out a route for getting it off campus and into a hiding-place where it

2

could remain until any hue and cry died down. At the chosen hour I crossed the university grounds with the heavy loot wrapped in a jacket, and was pretty sure I'd not been close to anyone who'd recognize me. For a nine-year-old that microscope was a fascinating acquisition, and I was determined to resist the temptation to return to its hiding-place until I was sure it was really mine. The passage of several days before whoever had spotted me from a distance got in touch with an outraged science professor lulled me into a false sense of security. Then it wasn't long until my father called me into his study.

Right away I knew there was trouble, but hoped this was only a routine general-principle questioning simply because the microscope had been missed. Casually and without giving reason, my father asked if I'd been in the science building recently. I'd survived enough of his quiz sessions to have a good idea of what slight admissions might make me appear truthful when the big denial was made. It seemed safe to admit to having been in the place within the past week. With an intense stare my father asked if I'd removed anything from the laboratory, and, assuming my practised look of innocence, I denied having done any such thing. Half an hour of grilling followed and I had repeatedly to detail all recent moves, but I had a good memory and each time the story came out the same way. Again my method of a slightly flawed tale seemed to be working, though I wondered how many times I'd have to tell the story. I also regretted having taken an expensive microscope, but what really mattered was not being found out. The session ended with my father appearing to half-way believe me, though in my own mind I'd already written the microscope off.

Next day the incident seemed in the past, my feelings had recovered from the hard slaps in the face that accompanied some of the questions, and I'd decided that the whole thing would soon be forgotten. That afternoon I learned that my troubles hadn't even begun, and there were no doubts in the minds of those concerned that I was the culprit. Again questions were asked, with memory-aiding slaps. I tried to evaluate the strength of the case against me. It seemed weak and I was standing up to it, until my father changed his tactics. He simply stated that the police would be brought in if the instrument wasn't returned, and there was enough proof to send me to reform school. At this point I caved in to superior strength. While I was telling where the microscope was planted, there was silence, but from past experience I recognized the lull before the storm. Before losing control, my father said that I'd lied like a hardened criminal. This caused me to use bad judgement in putting forward a defence. I said that only the state had been robbed. My father then launched into a tirade about my being an incorrigible thief. He wound up to a peak of fury I wouldn't have thought possible, and then all hell struck. The physical and hysterical part went on for a seemingly never ending half-hour, and from that time on relations between my father and me were not to be the same. Also I suffered further damage when the story spread all over town. It seemed the professor whose microscope I knocked off didn't like my father very much, so his kids made sure everyone at school knew of my disgrace. Even before this I'd not associated with other kids much because their interests seemed childish, but afterwards I became more of a loner. For a while my schoolwork picked up, but that didn't last until report-card time.

Instead of schoolbooks I favoured the university library, where owing to my father's position I could wander at will through the normally forbidden stacks. Nothing was ordered about my reading, though the case histories of Havelock Ellis were even more fascinating than the Civil War newspapers and articles on mechanical subjects. School was only a place to serve time, to watch freight trains in the distance and dream about being on one, and do enough last-minute study to save myself from the consequences of becoming the first faculty offspring to have to repeat a year.

When I was nearly twelve, my father and I had a heart-to-heart talk about another kind of misdemeanour, because I'd been caught playing with my prick. After my mother had unexpectedly come into my room and seen all four inches of the standing-up thing being stroked, I hoped she would keep it to herself, but she didn't. My erection, along with any erotic thoughts, vanished as she silently hurried out, leaving me to worry through dinner and a hushed parental discussion behind the closed door of my father's study.

His tone of voice when I was called into the room gave me hope that this might be a low-key discussion rather than the usual raving. As if finding it difficult even to mention masturbation, my

4

father began his talk. When it was clear there'd be no noise or violence, I barely pretended to take the session seriously. In the way of talking to an innocent who'd accidentally discovered the pleasure of jerking off, he started a pedantic lecture about how it would lead to insanity. Never before had we discussed anything sexual, and as he continued I wondered if my father could really be so out of touch as to think I wouldn't have some notion of these matters. For a minute I was tempted to air knowledge picked up at the library and say I had it on better authority that playing with my tool was harmless. Then I thought that this might change the atmosphere from bearable to downright unpleasant. Only when he persisted, did I wonder if by some outside chance his information could be more up to date than mine. That minor doubt was resolved by a silent resolution to do it no more than once a week, not counting the times I failed to spurt a little stream.

When my father was still lecturing long after the subject seemed exhausted, I gave in to temptation and said something that had to lead to disaster. During a pause to emphasize something, I simply asked my father if he didn't ever have to come up for air. Instead of taking that as meaning he was labouring his subject, the old man took my impertinence in his predictable way. As usual my brother was lurking outside the room, so when the slaps along with shouts about my being a disgrace to the family were finished, he was able to inform my sister that I'd been caught playing with my doodle.

We were living in Baltimore at the time, while my father completed his Ph.D. at Johns Hopkins. After the small Ohio town Baltimore was exciting, so in my spare time I wandered widely. School was still no place for work, but some of the kids were interesting, and it was possible to play hookey in the safety of a big city. With one or two other friends I took my regular days off, usually to go downtown and raid the stores. Baltimore shops were so easy we'd joke about anyone bothering to pay for things, but many must have because the clerks didn't worry about us and we were never caught. Our only trouble came in a department store where a big woman whose front was all tits grabbed me and another kid. She hadn't seen us steal anything, but being a truant officer took each of us by a shoulder and proceeded to march us out of the store. We exchanged meaningful looks, and at the

5

street door we both jerked free. With big tits shouting, we disappeared into the crowd. The woman hadn't our right names and did not know which school we should have been attending, so we didn't worry long. We decided that big tits would be easier to spot in a crowd than ourselves, so instead of staying away from the stores, we'd keep our eyes open. She never did catch us, though we saw her a few times.

The kid and I decided to run away and see New York. Both knew there'd be hell to pay later, but we were pretty confident of getting there and maybe even lasting a few days. Skipping school one morning, we went to the yards and boarded a freight train headed in the right direction. With food sneaked from our homes we ate lunch as the freight sped out of Baltimore. Then the train stopped, for a long time, and we stayed out of sight in the bottom of an open coal-car. Thinking the train mightn't be going any farther, we climbed out to see about catching something else, and that was when we were caught. In no time we were surrounded by gruff, but friendly railroad men who said we were too young to be riding freights, and should be sent home. The cops who collected us treated it as a joke, as did the photographer and reporter from a Baltimore paper during the interview at an outlying police station.

Everybody was good natured about it, except my father when he got me out of the cell. And that evening after he had seen our pictures and story in the paper his rage was boundless. He ranted for hours, and late that night I overheard a discussion between him and my mother. Both agreed that I had to be seen by an alienist, and next morning my father would get the name of one from the university. Alienists were psychiatrists before they'd learned to charge so much, and I'd read enough to know that I was headed for a nut doctor. Alienists meant insanity, and if that was suspected I might be in the sort of trouble that could lead to an asylum. My knowledge of alienists was that, besides sending people away, they appeared as expert witnesses in murder cases for whichever side paid them. This scared me and I tried to think what the alienist might ask, also how to make him think I wasn't crazy. I'd deny playing with my prick just in case there was anything to that, but it might be difficult if my father said I'd been caught at it. Otherwise I'd give answers that seemed normal and hope the doctor didn't know when I was lying.

6

My big hope was that all this would blow over, but that didn't seem likely when next day my father was still ranting about the publicity and how no university would want him after such notoriety. I thought it was a load of crap and couldn't really believe all that stuff about the family never recovering from the disgrace. My thoughts, when my father cooled down enough to let me think, were that he was acting like a lunatic and people would take the story the way those cops and railroad men did.

Days later when I thought the alienist threat had passed, my father said he was taking me to a doctor. I tried to show lack of concern. Masturbation was not mentioned by the alienist, so I decided afterwards that my father didn't know much about the subject. He asked of other matters, and I had to think fast to come up with what I hoped were the right answers. Quickly I learned that questions often related to earlier ones, so what might seem correct at a given time could easily make me out a liar. My way around this was to act as if considering everything carefully because of the importance of being truthful. After some talk about resentments I tried to prevent the doctor's sensing my realization that this was a sanity examination by asking why he wanted to know about these things. Saying these questions helped him to know me better, the man went on to discuss my feelings toward others in the family. Still giving answers I hoped fitted in with earlier stuff, I admitted to not being very fond of my brother, rather than really hating his guts because of his making the most of any situation where I'd appear in a bad light. Suddenly the alienist concluded the interview. What he had to say was to my father, while I sat nervously in the outside waiting-room. My father's expression conveyed nothing when he emerged, and there was no mention of further visits. Somehow my brother found out what sort of doctor I'd seen, which meant the matter was raised frequently.

The next major upheaval came when, back in Ohio, I was kicked out of school, but the sting was taken out of this by the timely offer to my father of an appointment to the New York University Faculty. This couldn't have materialized at a better time, because he had only just started to extract information about my expulsion when the registered letter arrived.

My respite came just short of the point where I'd have been compelled to admit breaking up some old maid's classes by letting loud bean-farts; in time a watered-down version would have to be told, but the effect of that letter on my father gave me hope.

In the evening, after a family discussion about moving to New York, my father returned to interrupted business. This time his emotions weren't so involved, though his sharp questions demanded fairly honest answers. My admission that what had upset the teacher was some accidental farting in class brought colour to his face. This I softened by saying other boys did the same, and I was unfairly blamed for bigger and louder farts than I'd actually let. When I saw how this went down, it occurred to me that possibly my father wanted to believe it rather than get worked up, and if that were the case I shouldn't have admitted letting anything. Blaming the lot, rather than just the big ones, on boys unknown might have worked, because the old maids at that school would have been quite unable to discuss farting with my father, let alone mention that I had the noisiest rectum around the place. Once it was clear to the school officials that I'd not be in attendance next year, they allowed me to complete and pass the current one.

The family moved into a big old house at East Orange, and a fresh start in a new school meant beginning the eighth grade as a cleanskin. By report-card time it was obvious I'd never do much beyond attending, and the ageing miss in charge of the grade started keeping me after school for lectures about the kind of adult I'd become if I didn't start working. She could put it over pretty well, so afterwards I'd have visions of breadlines, riding freight trains, or just slaving away to get enough to eat. Where she killed her argument for hard work was by laying it on too thick. So grim a picture of the price of success did she paint that I decided after one hearing of the lecture to find an easier way of making a living when the time came.

The first time the teacher wanted to see my parents was when a piece of my writing provoked her into calling me a foul-minded degenerate. A class assignment was to do essays on current events, with the students to make their choice from whatever was running in the newspapers. Several days were allowed and I hoped to manage a couple of paragraphs on some dull topic, when I stumbled on a juicy item in a New York Sunday tabloid. It rated a full page in the newspaper and seemed to me a damned good story—on a police whorehouse raid. What made the story so good was that the establishment catered for sadists and masochists. Using vocabulary I had acquired in that university library, I expanded on the theme of whips and flagellation, with examples. When my piece was handed in, I thought it wouldn't get much more than a cursory glance for neatness. From the way the teacher looked at me next morning I suspected she might have read it, and when asked to stay behind that afternoon—after a day of exemplary behaviour—I learned that my essay was in the hands of the principal, who would by now have duly noted its contents. In his own good time he would see me to discuss the matter. Then I was told I had a sick mind. I argued that there wasn't a word in my essay that was objectionable in itself, and within the meaning of "current event" I'd complied with instructions. Before the old girl really blew up, I got in something about my topic being of such interest that a major newspaper saw fit to give it a whole page.

Next day I did all the listening, in the principal's office with my father present. When the school people were placated by a promise of an end to such writing, my father wanted to know why I'd done it. He wasn't annoyed to the point of histrionics when I said it was done to get the old maid's reaction. I had then to listen without comment to a talk about how women generally, and neurotic ones specifically, disliked being confronted with such material.

Scraping into high school by attending special summer classes, I rapidly ran out of my head of steam in the presence of girls with tits rather than straight up-and-down figures. East Orange was a conventional place, and what little might have been going had eyes only for the football team rather than freshmen such as myself. The best I could do was mentally to undress different ones, and walk out of class holding my books to conceal my erection.

Approaching a big-titted girlfriend of my sister's was my first serious attempt at anything more interesting than my hand, although it ended disastrously. The girl refused when I suggested screwing, let me touch a tit, but not her pussy—and seemed willing to remain friendly. When my father called me into his study next day I sensed trouble, without connecting it with the girl. This time I was told, with slaps in the face, rather than asked. It seemed the girl had confided in my sister, who had passed the story on to my mother and it had not stopped there. Also I was considered perverted and lucky not to have been shot by the girl's father. Though I couldn't tell my father in the midst of his raving, I felt victimized for trying something normal, and later in the privacy of my room gave serious thought to an idea that had been in my mind a long time.

This was a plan to run away, and not as a half-cocked measure like that stunt in Baltimore. To get away with it, and not have to face any more of my father's sessions, I should have been a couple of years older, but in my favour were my height and a way of talking that made me seem older than I was.

The ruction over asking a girl for a screw failed to cool me down, so not long afterwards I visited a whorehouse. With considerable difficulty this was arranged by a third-year student, after refusals at a couple of places because of my age.

After closing her bedroom door in the sleazy whorehouse, the woman put her arms around me and placed my hand inside her dress and onto a bare tit. I felt like coming right then. Being well built and twice my age, she had soft tits I could move my fingers around without running out of softness, instead of the hard little things on schoolgirls. While my hand was tucked warmly under one of those tits—they hung a long way down—the whore reached into my pants to play with my prick and there seemed no way I couldn't come. The woman then told me to take off my clothes, and while I did so she lifted her dress over her head and flopped nude on the bed. Right away I was on top of her wanting to go straight between her legs; she told me to take it easy or I wouldn't last long enough to get in. My balls were hurting as they did when jerking off was prolonged by slowing down short of coming. Lying on her back, the woman looked old with her tits flopped onto her arms, but that didn't matter as I put my hand on her pussy. That thing, all hairy and soft and wet in the middle, was exciting to touch, and when I wanted a close look she spread her legs wide so I could see everything. Missing was the dead-fish smell I'd been told to expect, and I was fascinated by the pink mass with fleshy flaps.

When I'd explored the hole with my finger and decided it was big, I manoeuvred into position for action. A practised flip of the whore's hand moved my tool to the right place and it just seemed

10

to be sucked in. I managed no more than three strokes before it was all over. Rolling off, I had a let-down feeling, as though I wouldn't want any more for a long time. By the time I was home telling my father about being at another kid's house, my thighs were stirring and I was wondering about finding enough money to go again.

From then on I was hooked on mature women, and annoyed by the childish evasions of young girls. Finance was a problem, because my allowance didn't much more than cover movies, and my father was usually suspicious enough to ask what picture I'd seen. Whorehouse visits were probably the only activity the old man wouldn't suspect.

To get sufficient cash for more than one lay a week plus an occasional movie, my shoplifting had to be upgraded. This took the form of lifting to order for kids who wanted things cheap, but weren't inclined to do their own lifting. Boys without expensive habits, such as needing to get laid, were my customers and I obtained all sorts of things for them. Those with hobbies were good buyers, because they always needed items and had the cash if the price was right. My prices were always right and they never asked questions.

In moving around and mixing with strange company, I got to know a few shopkeepers who'd buy things on a no-questions basis. A man in a radio store provided funds for many whorehouse visits, also lesser luxuries such as cigarettes, which I'd been forbidden to smoke. He'd buy at quarter price all the radio tubes I could steal, after testing them to make sure they really were new. Wishing to deal direct and cut out my profit, he asked me where they came from, never guessing that my source was anything so simple as strolling through bigger radio stores and plucking tubes from sets when nobody was looking.

Those shops, together with radio sections of department stores, were easy, because at the time radios were large and open-backed—and nobody seemed to think a kid would carry the whole thing away. I would have loved to be around when they tried to demonstrate a radio and found it wouldn't work because half the tubes were missing. They might have suspected pilfering, cannibalizing by technicians—or anything but my visits. There were enough radio stores for me to spread my patronage, and not return to already clipped places with indecent haste.

11

A sixth sense usually told me when to act as an innocent kid interested only in radios. I often had a semi-erection from thinking about what lay ahead, but I could still concentrate on business. Those thoughts were forced out of my mind before I got down to the serious work of plucking radio tubes as if they were flowers. A couple dozen tubes a week meant at least three whorehouse visits, without cutting into my allowance. Such funds as my father provided were for movies and incidentals, while proceeds from shoplifting for other kids went into ever increasing savings. Haunted by fears of catching something, I thought my extra money might have to go on treatment, or anything else to keep my father from finding out; each morning there was the ritual of milking my tool to check for pus. Luckily there never was any, and I was able to put unpleasant thoughts out of my mind.

In my first year at high school I became friendly with only two kids: one a good shoplifter and the other a boy who liked to put my tool in his mouth. With what I was getting from my radio-tube business, that kid's performance was no great thrill, though I sometimes let him do it on condition he didn't bite. The boy who was more interested in our thieving activity than what was between my legs finally overcame his fear of clap and accompanied me to a whorehouse. Then a whore sucked me off much better than when the kid tried it, and this meant that at least some whorehouse visits weren't followed by fear of clap.

After the boy who was fascinated with my penis dropped out of orbit, the thieving boy and I were left to ourselves and came up with the idea of making fake quarters. My experience with mechanical things included some self-taught watch-repairing and the other fellow had done some radio work, but this was breaking new ground. To produce our quarters we made a plaster-of-Paris mould consisting of two halves in a hinged box, and poured molten lead down a channel to the reverse image formed by a good coin. After we'd cleaned up the edges with a file, they looked a bit like money, but they were heavy, soft, and quickly tarnished to their natural lead colour. We soon realized what bad business this was, apart from the risk of real trouble for counterfeiting, so we happily broke up the mould and threw the pieces away. We returned with renewed zest to the tube racket, and until the other kid's family moved away from East Orange

12

the radio stores within reach had to support the sex habits of two lusty boys.

My savings grew to where they burned a hole in my pocket, so I bought a motor cycle. I was years too young to ride legally, and kept it a dark secret until the cops caught me on it. My friend was on the rear fender when a police car headed us off in a quiet street, following the complaint of some busybody. We were both locked up until our respective fathers reclaimed us; the other kid's father accepted the whole thing as no more than his son's mixing with bad company, while mine put on one of his all-time best performances. When a beefy, red-faced, unpleasant detective sergeant learnt that I'd bought the ancient Harley with a wide-open exhaust from a backyard dealer and couldn't be charged with theft, his rage almost equalled that of my father. That irate Irish cop had to let me walk out of the station facing no more than a driving-without-a-licence charge, and for a moment it was a toss-up whether he or my father was the most outraged. Uncharged because he was only a passenger, the other boy faced no more than mild parental censure.

Lengthy questioning at home provided my father with no more information than that I had acquired the twenty dollars recorded on the receipt for my motor cycle by selling a few things I owned. In the matter of punishment my father acted like a judge, announcing that my allowance was cancelled for six weeks and for the same period I'd be allowed out of the house only to go to school. The remainder of his sentence was that, since I'd proved on so many occasions that I couldn't be trusted, my movements after the detention period would be supervised. Until I demonstrated trustworthiness, my father would have to be told my destination whenever I went out, with a phone number if I was at some kid's house, and otherwise I'd only be allowed out accompanied by my brother. From past experience I knew that this would only last until his rage cooled down.

The court appearance was only long enough for the judge to let me off with a warning, but on the way there my father's anger was rekindled to the point of again shouting about what a disgrace I was to the family. Afterwards the cops asked my father what he wanted done with my motor cycle and I talked him into letting me push it home for storage in the basement pending a sale. It was still there when I ran away from home, to be sold by my brother along with the rest of my stuff when I'd been gone long enough for him to be pretty sure I wouldn't be brought back.

While my freedom was curtailed, school attendance had to become less than regular. With no way of getting to the whorehouses at night, or collecting the necessary radio tubes at other times, I needed a day away from school every time I had to get laid. This coincided with my brother undergoing some sort of change, in which he ceased trying so hard to curry favour with our parents at my expense. No longer the perfect student, he began absenting himself from school to take some girl he was screwing on day trips to New York. He was afraid I'd reveal him by taking too many days off, and cause the school to check closely why two boys from the same family were away so much. Several times the school pressed for a note from home explaining some absence, and my brother would oblige by forging a letter; the notes were accepted because of his ability to imitate the writing of either parent. My part of the bargain was to limit my days off to one a week.

In time the school people were sending a steady stream of letters to our father, which thanks to an early-morning mail delivery were intercepted and appropriately answered. Illness requiring days at home and medical visits were the excuses given. Finally the school people did what they should have done in the first place, if they'd been clever. They phoned home on a day we were both at school, asking if there was some health problem, but fortunately there was no mention of letters sent and answered. Late that afternoon there was a lot of explaining to be done, but with my brother to take some of the heat off there was no major uproar. The old man seemed willing to believe our stories about going to movies together.

Serious trouble loomed at the end of the school year, when I realized I was so far behind in three subjects that there was no hope of passing. In this school it mattered not a damn who my father was, so I'd simply been warned a few times that if my work didn't improve I would fail most subjects. Those warnings only had effect until it was time for another whorehouse visit, and then they, like other unpleasant matters, were put out of mind. Things were finally catching up, with no way out but to face my father with the ultimate disgrace of failure at school. For the first time I took my brother into my confidence over something serious. He knew the situation was hopeless, but to my utter amazement he offered a solution. One of his friends had stolen some blank report cards from the school office and he could get a couple.

My final report of the year, with all its failures, would never see the light of day. It would be destroyed after my brother copied all previous data onto a fresh blank, with the last column showing improvements and passes in each subject. My brother's clever penwork would take care of various teachers' writings, as well as earlier parental signatures, and the card would be sufficiently worn to make it look like the one that had been going back and forth all year. Next term I'd take home for approval another stolen card showing all subjects as year two, while my brother signed the one to be returned to the school. The fake report card worked so well that I felt guilty accepting my father's compliments for improved schoolwork. We realized this procedure might become suspect if carried on to graduation time, but it was pretty obvious that I'd fly the coop long before then.

During the Christmas holidays I got my first free piece of ass with a woman three times my age and it was good. I had a schoolteacher aunt who stayed an old maid until her forties, when she married some weak-looking object years younger than herself. My brother and I agreed that a good screw would have killed the man. Periodically my brother and I, and sometimes our sister, would visit our aunt and her little husband for two or three days in the town where they lived about fifteen miles away. On this trip only my brother accompanied me, and I looked forward to it because the atmosphere there was not so tense as at home.

Part of the first day was spent seeing what the local shops had to offer and similar activity was planned for next afternoon, but things worked out differently. The others went off to a movie I'd already seen, leaving me alone in the house with my aunt's maid. She was a plump, friendly woman around forty-five, about whom I'd had few thoughts other than that she had unusually big tits and an easygoing manner. Once or twice I'd wondered what it would be like to hose somebody so big. Before I could go out after radio tubes, the maid invited me into the kitchen for a cup of coffee. Soon it was clear that there was more in this than just an older woman being friendly toward someone a lot younger, so I forgot about the tubes. The maid told me I wasn't like the rest of

15

the family and suddenly she became desirable, a bit old and hefty but soft, and her expression suggested plenty of feeling. Walking to where I sat with my cup of coffee, she put her arms out and hugged me close to her soft body.

With an erection like an iron pole, I stood up to put my arms around her and she squeezed and kissed me so excitingly that I almost lost control. I'd been tongue-kissed before, but hers was huge and seemed to fill my mouth entirely. My hand went inside her dress onto a tit bigger than anything I'd ever felt, causing her to move her tongue furiously, and I began to come in my pants. Somehow I regained control without losing more than a few drops and before reaching the peak that would have momentarily killed the urge. My underpants felt sticky, though not as if they'd copped the full load, and with some of the pressure off my sore balls I was able to press hard against her soft belly without adding to the mess I'd already made.

Because she didn't live in my aunt's house, we used the room my brother and I shared. Leaving me to get undressed, she went into the bathroom and I could hear running water. It ran longer than if she'd taken a leak and was washing her hands, so I decided that she was washing her pussy to make sure it didn't smell like a dead fish.

My first impression of her naked body was that everything seemed even bigger than I expected. Her pussy was out of sight under a belly hanging down over it, but the woman was so warm and passionate that her size excited me all the more. Lying on her back, her belly didn't cover her pussy, and when I got on top I felt as if all of me was sinking in. By raising myself up on my arms, I managed to clear that belly and get my tool into a hole that seemed enormous until she started gripping tightly with some muscle. Her tightening and loosening the muscle almost made me come, so she eased me off after saying it would be better to make it last. Cooling-down consisted of playing with those great tits I could roll back and forth over the woman's chest, sucking her big nipples which she enjoyed, and finally examining her snatch. Those breasts were absorbing and the pussy seemed unbelievable. It was warm and very wet, and my hand fell into soft, loose folds of skin. When I said I really wanted to see the thing close up, the woman spread her legs apart, and there seemed a lot more than I'd seen on whores, with deep wrinkles

16

running between what looked like large pieces of raw liver. Though my nose was close, there didn't seem to be much smell, so I put a finger in and brought it out for a sniff; the slight odour was nice.

Finally I got on top, not lasting many strokes before it was over.

Where the maid lived was all right, as long as I could get away at night and back home early enough to keep out of trouble. It turned out to be possible, using three buses and leaving immediately after dinner. I wanted to keep the relationship going at all costs, and found it flattering that a woman so much older could be interested in me.

From my aunt's and uncle's talk I knew the maid was married, had a couple of grown kids by a husband who'd cleared off, and that my aunt thought her rather crude. My uncle disliked her, but put up with her because she worked hard for little reward.

Next evening, the last at my aunt's, a movie nobody else wanted to see served as an excuse to get to the maid's place, and this time she took my tool in her mouth. I'd heard that women like this usually wanted their pussy licked—muffdiving, the older boys called it—so when she started sucking, I expected her to ask me to do the same. Had she done so, I would have tried it, because I was tempted.

My arrangement with the maid lasted for a few more visits—until her husband moved back home. My friend of whorehouse visits and radio tubes couldn't agree with me that what I had experienced was anything special; he simply could not understand my finding a fat older woman exciting. To him a woman should be slim and attractive, which to me meant complying with accepted ideas of sexual desirability.

2

Exposed at last   freight-riding the Depression   stemming the streets, juicing the fruits, and biting for tail   fugitive from justice   honestly collecting the price of a good used car.

THE STREETS OF SAN FRANCISCO

Less than a month after the end of the maid affair every underhanded pursuit in which I was involved blew up, and I was soon on a freight train headed for distant places. My need for radio tubes became insatiable when there was no more tail without cost, so one day I walked straight into a trap—and this was only the beginning. Nobody paid attention to me in the store that was to be my undoing, but as soon as I lifted a couple of tubes out of a radio, people began converging from all directions. In the manager's office, with my loot lying on the desk, I learned that a number of radio shops had got together and worked out my description. I'd been watched from the minute I walked into his store, the manager contemptuously informed me, and now they were calling the police. My talking had no effect, and after saying that the stealing had been going on too long, the man told me to shut up until the cops arrived.

After a terrifying wait with various people poking their heads in to have a look at the thief, two detectives walked into the room. There was a discussion between them and the manager, before one of the cops said to me in a hard voice, "Okay, kid, let's go." On the way to the station the cop beside me in the back seat of the police car asked questions about where I lived, who my father was and so on. Giving straight answers, since they'd find out anyway, I told them my address and caused one of the cops to remark that I came from a good part of town; it was now time to admit my father was a university professor. This brought an

18

immediate reaction, the car changing direction after the cop guarding me suggested consulting my father first.

My father was home when the conspicuous police car pulled up, and somehow all the neighbours seemed to be out watching as I was marched inside. I stood silently in my father's study while my wrongdoings were explained, until one of the cops intimated that perhaps the matter could be settled in some way; I had to wait outside while the actual pay-off was being negotiated.

When the cops emerged from the study, both looking happy, I was still waiting and not knowing whether I was going—or staying. The rest of the family was hovering around, barely concealing their anxiety to know what was happening, when one of the officers said in a friendly voice, "Don't do it again, kid", and then they both walked out. While the others still didn't know what I'd done, I was called into the study and told to shut the door. Before going further my father said that in case I was interested it had just cost him a hundred dollars to save the family the humiliation of my being sent to jail. A bad session followed, but luckily the cops hadn't mentioned the extent of my tube thefts, so I didn't have to explain why I wanted them.

The trouble might have been weathered, but what happened on the second day following was total disaster. My father's presence at home when I returned from school gave me a sick feeling that this was connected with some activity of mine. Without visible emotion he said he'd like to talk to me, so once more I went into that dreaded study and shut the door. Whether or not I'd lied wouldn't have altered the outcome, though the initial blast was made worse by my not having the sense to realize after my father's first question that he knew everything. He asked about my schoolwork, and if I'd pass all subjects, in a way that took away my confidence. Alarm bells seemed to be ringing everywhere, and I was bordering on panic as I tried to think what to say. Clearly he wasn't here at this unusual time because of normal interest in my progress at school. And he wanted an answer right away without allowing me time to think.

Hope prevailing over common sense caused me to say I was doing all right, and would pass. That answer opened the floodgates, leaving me with the horrible realization that any reply short of truth would be wrong. My father's initial reaction was physical, with open-handed belts across my face that I couldn't roll away from because that would enrage him even more. Talking came after he tired of the other, and I got the full story of how I'd been found out.

Someone at the school office had heard about the radio-tube thefts and had called the old man in for a talk about my scholastic efforts. Phone contact had been made the day before and he'd seen the school people that afternoon to hear the truth, as he put it, before listening to my lies. He expected to hear no more than a tale of some run-of-the-mill offence, instead of the major thing with which they hit him. Whoever told the story had done a good job, and I reaped the full benefit listening to my father express his feelings on hearing that there was some thought of sending me to a special school for the retarded. Making it worse was the school official's amazement that a university professor wouldn't even bother to visit the school when he was aware that his son had failed practically every subject.

Retaining some measure of control, he related his argument with the man: an insistence that I couldn't be doing too badly since my reports were favourable. When the official revealed that I'd failed three subjects last year and at present was doing no work at all, it dawned on both that something stank, so the records were consulted. My father was shocked when shown a report card from the files, bearing his signature and clearly indicating I was repeating first-year subjects. After he insisted he'd neither sighted nor signed that card, and the one I brought home showed good marks in second-year subjects, it didn't take long for the two to conclude that a forgery had been committed.

The forgery angle badly upset the school man, and he and my father agreed that there'd have to be an investigation. They decided I couldn't have done it because my handwriting was too atrocious, but I'd got somebody to forge the card. If that individual wasn't stopped, this could spread through the school, wrecking the report-card system. Theft was also involved, the school man said, because the card I used for showing at home, and possibly many more, could only have come from that office.

My father maintained that if I knew what was good for me, I'd tell the truth. Without taking time to think up lies, I was to tell where that card came from, and who did the writing. First lie was that some kid, whose name or appearance I couldn't remember, gave me a couple of blanks. That wasn't pursued, and when my

20

only recollection of the fellow who wrote up my cards was that he was older and no longer went to school I was called a liar. Being evasive on those questions left me on fairly safe ground as far as sudden physical reprisals were concerned, because my father had no great love for informers. Questioning still continued on those lines, until my father offered the startling suggestion that he had ideas about who might have done the penwork; this made it imperative that I have a conference with my brother before he could be quizzed. Inevitably came rehash of past major offences, with my father working himself into a state where reasonable talk was no longer possible. When he was at fever pitch, I decided that I'd have to clear out. He ordered me out of his study after saying the school authorities would want to see me tomorrow.

As always the rest of the family hovered about, and closing the study door I signalled my brother to follow me to my room. Wasting no time on details, I told him the report-card switch had been blown sky-high, that he was suspected of the forgery, that the school officials would create a stink, and that I hadn't implicated him and, finally, that he'd be questioned. Before telling him to clear off, or the old man would know we'd got our heads together, I warned him not to believe it if he were told I'd confessed.

When I was alone to think, it became obvious that unlike other jams this one wouldn't recede into the past after a blistering climax and reasonable punishment. I was too far behind at school ever to catch up, and each time my father thought about it or I brought a report card home there'd be a scene. The way things were I'd be subject to constant humiliation, since scholastic failure was one thing neither parent could tolerate. From the moment I started school, I'd never been allowed to forget that kids from families of our class did not flunk out; only offspring of people who produced quantity rather than quality did what I had done, as I'd been told many times on critical occasions. I concluded that my impending trouble at school could see me on the way to one of those manual-training places for not-too-bright kids. I was in an untenable position, and realized I should be gone before those people "who'd know what was best for me" became involved. Any move would have to be good because I was on thin ice, and getting picked up for running away might mean reform school. To avoid further scenes I was tempted to sneak out that night and head for the railroad yards.

Over a period of time I'd adjusted to the fact that my days with the family were numbered, my ways would never fit in with theirs, and staying on would only lead to endless trouble. I had hoped to last another year, but this latest blow-up ruled that out. A month, until warmer weather set in, might be managed by keeping out of everybody's way.

Next morning I was ready for school and what might have to be faced. But, leaving the house, I hoped never again to see the place. There might be another school, I thought, but it would be the sort where students arrive in custody. Whatever happened I'd probably not see home again, because if caught I would certainly be sent to an institution, and with a bit of luck I just might make a clean getaway.

My face was still stinging from the hard slaps I had got for being caught finishing a cigarette in my room before leaving for school, and I decided finally that I wouldn't take that from anybody. My father would know my decision when darkness came and I wasn't back from school, but by then I planned to be as far away as the fastest train I could catch would take me. Less than five minutes passed between the decision to go and leaving the house, so there wasn't much chance to gather any of my things. Other members were hanging around during that brief interval and all I managed to collect was about twenty dollars hidden in my room.

Going out of the house, I hurried so I wouldn't have to walk to school with my brother, but he soon caught up. He talked about my failures, along with what might happen because I'd been found out. I told him I wasn't particularly interested. He gave me a strange look, before saying he was pretty sure the old man had believed him the night before when he denied knowledge of the report-card forgery. We parted inside the main door of the school. I walked straight through the building and out one of the lesser exits.

I got to Newark's big freight yard, and there a train, headed by a Pennsylvania Railroad mountain locomotive and enveloped in clouds of smoke and steam, was pulling out. Before it gathered speed, I grabbed the ladder of an open coal-car, and with wind-driven cinders stinging my face I was forced to keep my eyes almost closed as the train roared at what seemed express speed

22

through the string of towns beyond Newark. After hours of racing across cold countryside with few stops, the train headed into the yard at Harrisburg. Here I had to pass through a major terminal without being picked up by the cops, and catch another train headed still farther away. I got through Harrisburg without trouble, by acting natural, as if it was normal for me to be travelling by freight train. The next ride took me on to Altoona.

In another wind-swept car, going through the western Pennsylvania mountains late that night, I felt my first regrets. Had it been possible to slip back without trouble I might have been tempted, but by now my bridges were burned, and there could be no turning back. Voluntary return rather than being escorted back in custody might have avoided a juvenile court, but after all that had gone wrong, living at home wouldn't have been bearable. By comparison I convinced myself that the coldness and desolation of the fast-moving freight train was something I could accept. As the black hills leading toward Pittsburgh raced past the train, with icy wind swirling through every corner of the car, I began to wonder why I had to let things go so far.

While the lights of a fair-sized town streaked by, I thought that by now the cops would have been notified of my disappearance. So vividly could I imagine the scene if I was dragged back that my determination again became as strong as on the final walkout that morning. No matter how cold or hungry I was, I resolved there would be no weakening of will or spirit. It helped, trying to get out of Pittsburgh next morning, to meet some others who were travelling the same way. I learned that they were waiting for a train to Columbus. The three of them, none over twenty, decided that I was new to the road, and offered advice on avoiding trouble with the police. Since I looked young to be riding freights, there was a danger I'd be spotted for a runaway, they said. The way around that was to insist my family were fruit-pickers, and I'd been on the road for months, but I was never to admit being under eighteen.

I passed through Columbus and Cincinnati without trouble, and in the latter I spent the night in a transient shelter without getting questioned. A fast Baltimore and Ohio freight put me into East St Louis after a good run from Cincinnati, and by then I wasn't so worried about being caught and sent back. I had even

23

gained sufficient confidence to speak to railroad men when I wanted information. At East St Louis a switchman pointed the way to the bridge over the Mississippi, but before reaching it I had my cock sucked at a cost of five cents. Bordering the yard was a street lined with houses almost black from the grime of engines, and in each doorway stood a coloured woman looking hungrily toward anyone coming off a train. One immense Negress called out, "Hey, white boy, you-all want to spend a quarter", while others were more forward in describing exactly what they'd do for whatever money they could get. Another got mad at me for not stopping to talk, and let everyone within earshot know that I was a no-account motherfucker.

After a night on a freight train I did not need a piece of ass, but then a lighter and quieter one offered to blow me for a nickel. I went inside. Though I was gritty from train cinders and even my prick wasn't too clean, the woman popped it into her mouth. When I spurted, she swallowed, and less than five minutes later I was again headed for the bridge leading to St Louis.

Leaving home my destination had been a bit vague, but having now made a thousand miles I reckoned it was California. Other travellers at St Louis advised me not to go over the Rockies at this time of year, because it would be too cold; instead I should go down through Texas, then follow the southern route to Los Angeles. The weather became warmer as my next train approached Little Rock. My first questioning came at Fort Worth, where a whole bunch of us were waiting for a train headed toward El Paso. Sneaking up in the dark, several cops took us by surprise and herded us into an open space. Looking everybody over and frisking a couple for guns, they began questioning us. The cop who asked me my name and where I came from didn't seem to care what my answers were, as long as I spoke respectfully. They left without taking anybody. A little while later the westbound freight came out of the yard, slowly, as if the engineer wanted to give all a chance to board before he put on speed. El Paso was another transient shelter stop, and at that government facility I had a clean-up and a couple of meals. There was minimal questioning by a clerk, who finally pointed to a chart of rules and asked if I could read; when I huffily replied that of course I could, the man said that they got a lot of Southern hillbillies who couldn't. Next morning I was on the road again, headed for Tucson, Yuma and Los Angeles, travelling by courtesy of the Southern Pacific Railroad.

Two weeks after leaving the family home, I unloaded from a train slowing down to enter the Los Angeles yards. Already I had learned enough to dodge the police that friendly city sent out to meet incoming freights. Known far and wide as a "hostile" town, Los Angeles wasn't considered too safe for anyone in off the road; where no offence was committed and the charge was only vagrancy, an arrest was good for a day in jail, plus thirty days suspended on condition the drifter left town. My first night was spent at the Midnight Mission on the city's skidrow, where a cop had referred me after brief questioning on the street. With a depression putting countless people on the road the police were obviously not interested in returning runaways.

The mission was clean but the food not worth the come-to-Jesus stuff that had to be sat through. During the night the man in the next bed woke me by sliding his hand under the blanket to play with my prick. He stopped when I objected, but later woke me again and this time I shouted. That brought someone in charge who ordered the fellow to "leave the man's cock alone", and I felt good because I'd been called a man.

Next morning a mission official referred me to the Boys' Home. He explained it was not a place of confinement, but was run by the government for road kids, and that it would provide room and board while I looked for a job. On the way there a police car pulled up and I was asked questions which sounded like the lead-up to a vagrancy arrest. My piece of paper referring me to the Boys' Home saved me a trip to the lock-up.

Length of stay at the Boys' Home was limited to a few days, because with every freight train bringing fresh arrivals the place would otherwise have been swamped. With jobs impossible to obtain, boys who'd stayed their few days were advised by the well-meaning people in charge to leave town before the cops got them. All across the country I'd been learning to survive on the road, but the Boys' Home was a finishing school. Here were kids older and more experienced, and all seemed eager to pass on useful information. I'd got free meals from cafés with offers of work which were never taken up, but I hadn't been doing it the right way. Correct procedure was to approach the manager when customers were present, so he'd look a real shit if he

25

turned you down, or by hitting good places where people who'd just eaten well might feel guilty and offer the cash to buy a feed. Though the manager might feel like kicking the bum in the balls for doing it in his place, a meal would have to be provided.

Few of the boys were short of money, and soon I was let in on the secret. Los Angeles was loaded with queers, which the boys called fruits, when not using terms descriptive of what they did. The trick was to get money from queers without giving anything in return, and the kids doing this insisted that they went no farther. Some were suspected of giving plenty for what they received from the fruits. Queers were generally of two types with "Greeks", who weren't necessarily of that nationality, to be avoided because they were "brown" men and often vicious; and simple fruits who were usually harmless and liked to suck tools or sometimes be on the receiving end of some browning—though none of the boys would own up to providing that. Some admitted to letting the fruits go down on them for a dollar or two, but the general idea was to get something out of them for nothing.

Queers were one of the main topics for discussion in the home. The boys tried to outdo each other with tales of those they'd encountered, and a rather incredible story was told by a kid who claimed to have encountered a fart inhaler. He went to the fruit's apartment when money was offered, thinking he was in for no more than a blow job. Besides money, a meal had been promised and while the queer prepared it he told the boy he wasn't interested in sucking or cornholing. Instead, he wanted to sniff his farts. Baked beans were the main dish, and to earn his pay the kid had to stay long enough for them to work. At the fruit's insistence there was a second helping, and about three hours later the things began working full blast. Only a couple of farts were wasted before the fruit had the kid undressed on the bed. Fart after fart was let, with the queer's nose only an inch from the source. After the beans exhausted themselves, the boy was talked into letting the fruit suck him off.

According to the experts, a fruit could usually be conned into buying a meal on the inference that he'd get his mouth filled later. Later never came, unless the boy was in the mood. Money could sometimes be obtained by requesting payment before going anywhere with the fruit, then ducking off at the first oppor-

26

tunity. There was a way of going to the pictures for nothing too. All you had to do was stand in front of a theatre, and in no time a queer would turn up with an offer to go inside and see the film. Once inside, it was up to the kid to lose the fruit in the darkness, if he wanted to enjoy the movie without the fellow playing with his tool.

During an evening walk through downtown Los Angeles I got two dollars from a queer without giving him anything. My judgement was bad enough to pick the wrong kind of queer, and create a minor street scene. The man was the sort I'd been warned to avoid, but I was strongly tempted to get something for nothing. He made no bones that he was a "brown" man, and there'd be two dollars in it if I'd go to his room. In looks and accent he was like the "Greeks" I'd seen in cafés, and I had no intention of going anywhere with him. Saying that I wanted payment in advance brought two dollars out of the horny fellow's pocket. Next was the problem of shaking my "Greek", and it didn't look too easy when he clung to me on my entering a drugstore to buy cigarettes. At a street corner where a crowd was waiting for a trafffic light to change, I saw my chance. While he looked at the light, I turned swiftly from his side and darted away. If my running had been the only action, people mightn't have stared, but the damned "Greek" was behind me shouting like a stuck pig. Then he must have realized how awkward it would be if a cop grabbed me and he had to explain the chase, for he suddenly broke it off. Once turned the first corner I slowed to a walk.

According to those in the know, things not to be caught doing in Los Angeles were stealing or "stemming". Although thievery brought automatic jail anywhere for those on the road, Los Angeles gave more of it, with near starvation thrown in. You stole only if something was really worth taking and the chance of getting away was almost certain. Stemming was also overlooked in almost any place other than Los Angeles, where stopping a citizen to ask for one lousy dime could mean sixty days, served rather than suspended. A trick of some plainclothes cops was to rattle change in their pockets—known as ringing the bell—in the hope of attracting a panhandler so they could make a pinch. Los Angeles also had a lot of young sneaky cops who didn't look like law, and they were death on moochers.

27

When my time at the Boys' Home was up, I had the urge to be on the move and to hear once more the roar of a fast freight. That night I caught a train from the Glendale end of the Southern Pacific yard, heading up the coast. In San Francisco I stepped straight into the arms of the law, in the form of a railroad bull. It wouldn't have happened if I'd stuck to the freight instead of climbing onto the tender of a passenger train at San José; the change was a smart-ass move to get right into San Francisco rather than land in a miles-out freight yard. Where I unloaded was near the beginning of the platform, when the train had slowed enough so that I wouldn't go end over end. Not ten feet from where I stopped was the bull, and nothing I said would talk him out of making his arrest. Slightly worked up, he said that the railroad didn't mind people riding its freights, but expected those travelling by passenger train to pay their way. Then he added that the judge would only give me a floater; at the precinct house the booking-officer questioned neither my identity nor age.

I spent a sleepless night worrying about being found out and sent home. When it came my turn, I said, "Guilty", as did all the others on petty charges. The two before me were given suspended sentences, while I trembled in fear lest the judge look down and question my age. Without raising his eyes, he heard my plea, then said, "Thirty days suspended on condition the defendant leave town within twenty-four hours." I made myself scarce around San Francisco by going across the bay to Oakland. I now felt confident of coping with minor trouble, and that no authority was interested in returning me to the mess I left behind. Although sometimes during rainy nights in West Coast cities, or on trains, I thought about my family and wondered if I'd ever see them again.

All that first year I was on the move, never spending more than three or four days in one place, and learning countless tricks for survival. Back and forth across the country I travelled, far up into New England when the weather was warm, and there were no missed meals. At worst a few were postponed, when I didn't want to leave a fast train. My appearance was maintained by carrying reasonably good clothes in a case and changing before going into towns. That way I avoided police attention to the extent that sometimes I'd venture a little shoplifting—in places without a reputation for being "hostile" and of things that could be sold. I had to dump stuff cheaply, but drugstore cameras, fountain pens and such were readily disposable. I once had the humiliating experience of being frogmarched past a crowd of shoppers to the manager's office in a small department store. They had caught me in the act of stealing a camera, but let me go after hearing my hard-luck story.

Queers made some contributions, though no more "Greeks" after the one in Los Angeles. A fruit in Seattle who intended only to provide a meal supplied me with a head-to-toe outfit of top-quality clothes. His giving wasn't voluntary, and afterwards I was ashamed of what I'd done, especially since the man never even got his hand on my cock. He had the misfortune to meet me when I badly needed new clothes. The fruit left me alone in his hotel room while he went out for something to eat, and that was a mistake. Right away I looked around, and the sight of a beautiful new suit in the closet reminded me that the fellow was my size. A further search uncovered a fine leather case to carry the suit in, and the shoes, shirts, socks, ties and underwear I hurriedly collected. Speed was of the essence once my new wardrobe was assembled. It was important on the way out that neither fruit nor suspicious hotel employee see me with my superb piece of luggage. All I could think of was, ironically, a rear exit. Not knowing quite what to do, I walked down a corridor, and spotted an open window overlooking a dark alley. Down three stories went the case, to land with a plop that should have been heard a block away. I went through the lobby without seeing the fruit. Hurrying around to the alley, I picked up my new outfit, and later that night was on a freight headed for Portland.

In later years I was to feel genuine regret over having taken advantage of perfectly decent people, whose sexual preferences happened to differ from what was commonly considered "normal". This does not extend to "brown" men, who in the course of their vicious lives probably damage a lot of young boys. I was no more capable of rational thought during this era than millions of others who regarded anybody "different" as fair game. Gays in those unenlightened times were objects of scorn—to be victimized by police, or anyone else, because they had no comeback. I would have liked it better if I hadn't perpetrated dirty tricks against members of the "gay" community.

With my new clothes I tried for a job in San Francisco, but all

29

that was offered was door-to-door sales, and I wasted half a day finding out that this was a waste of time. A crummy studio promised big money for selling photo coupons, so I took a book of them along with sample photos and began canvassing. When I hadn't sold enough to buy lunch by midday, I traded coupons with a face value of two dollars for a hamburger. When that was eaten, I tossed my sample pictures down a sewer grating, and that night swapped the coupon book for a piece of ass in a whorehouse. No longer willing to fall for ads promising "big-income selling to eager buyers", I gave up thoughts of work as a way of living.

Stemming was good if done the right way. A walk along almost any important city street would produce a pocketful of change, and brief encounters with such well-dressed male pedestrians as could be induced to listen generally brought forth a stream of dimes and quarters. An expert I met on a train going into Salt Lake City showed me how to do it. While I watched from across the street he collected nearly three dollars in half an hour. The secret was to be well enough dressed that people wouldn't expect a bite when stopped, and not to launch into an elaborate story. Whatever reason was given for the touch should be so short that the victim didn't have too much time to think about whether or not he wanted to contribute. It should also be explained that the touch of the moment would only partially alleviate the financial embarrassment of the one doing the biting; that cleared the way for further activity in sight of recent contributors and reduced the risk of having the cops called by some irate individual.

My previous stemming had always netted me the price of what I was after, but seeing an expert at work was a revelation. He impressed upon me the importance of approaching someone to be nipped as an equal rather than as a supplicant; in the few seconds it took for a brisk bite, they could identify with the one asking, and visualize him as one of their kind in temporary distress. I'd been furtive on the stem in the past, and now knew better. But picking the right people to bite was something I had to learn for myself. It was impossible for the expert to explain just what it was in the faces of some people that indicated they'd be good for a touch. It was bad to bite anyone who might be embarrassed into giving, because that created the kind of ill will that could lead to a pinch; men accompanied by women should not be nipped, though they'd generally reach into their pockets rather than appear cheap. When I got the hang of all this, I no longer stole or took down queers. It was at a time when there were twelve million unemployed, and stemming was as good a way as any, and more legal than most, of acquiring enough money to live.

Travel still played an important part in my life, for if it hadn't I'd have spent too much of it in jail. Not once did I serve a sentence for stemming, though I made the passing acquaintance of many a municipal court judge. In the course of time those petty court judges, and some really were petty, began to look like one or another. By looking at one, I could usually guess how he'd go about ordering me out of town.

San Francisco had a couple of judges who were a considerable cut above the usual ears-too-close-to-the-head, bottom-grade political accident. Appearing before them was never a worry, since they didn't talk about such unpleasant things as jail. They conducted lively courts rather than plumb the depths of some pretentious wisdom before passing sentence, and often dismissed crappy charges, such as stemming, without waiting for a plea.

On one of my San Francisco appearances the judge suggested that I'd only been taking up a collection and waited for the laughter to subside before dismissing the case. The same judge in a later case remarked that since my record indicated a fair amount of travel perhaps I'd like to consider taking another trip. In cities less sporting than San Francisco, I was often given nasty instructions about not coming back.

In a hurry to get through a string of towns leading to Buffalo I rode a passenger train rather than a freight. I climbed on top of the tender behind the engine, and was having a smoky ride when I was spotted by the operator in a signal tower. The train didn't slow down passing the tower, though I caught a glimpse of someone leaning out as I whipped by at about seventy miles an hour. Forty miles down the line the train made a stop for water at a tank town, and awaiting my arrival was a friendly young cop. He wasn't too concerned about my offence of riding on the outside of a passenger train, but the railroad people had instructed him to arrest me. He thought that, perhaps, he was on to a big-time pinch, and I was wanted by the F.B.I.; being a fugitive from justice might account for my urge to travel so fast. He'd have to check my fingerprints, he explained, but that shouldn't be any worry if I wasn't wanted. In any case their jail was unlike any other and I was certain to like the place. As I listened, my train became a smudge of smoke on the horizon.

The cop said the judge wouldn't be at the courthouse yet, so we drove to His Honour's home. In front of a pleasant old house the cop said he'd go and find out if the judge was ready to try me. If I'd promise not to run away while he was gone, he wouldn't use the handcuffs; I promised and away he went. Five minutes later he was back to tell me there'd be no need for a trial. The judge had already sentenced me to ten days in the county jail. When I said something about not even having made a plea, the friendly officer agreed I might have a point. Again leaving me in the car, he returned to the house, to emerge with the news that my sentence had been reduced to five days. He maintained the five days would do me good, and if I'd missed any meals lately, this would be my chance to catch up.

The County Sheriff was a real nice fellow, and the food was prepared by the sheriff's wife; apart from bars on the windows, the atmosphere was like that of a hotel. When my time was up, I was almost sorry the judge hadn't stuck to his original ten days. A third of a century later, and half-way around the world in Australia, that term of imprisonment was raised as a matter of importance in a court more formal than the judge's house.

Three days later and a thousand miles away I tumbled into another pinch. This time my offence was walking along a Minneapolis street towards the yards to catch a freight for Seattle. Two plainclothes bulls questioned me on what I did for a living, and when I told them I was on my way out of town, one of them arrested me for vagrancy. Minneapolis fed its prisoners only twice a day, on slop. The judge dealt exclusively with drunks on Fridays and as my arrest was on a Thursday, it meant four days of starvation. From other prisoners I learned how lucky I was to be facing only a vagrancy charge and not something serious such as getting drunk. It appeared His Honour was a sanctimonious Bible-thumper and sudden death on anything sinful. Seated in court waiting for my floater, I heard the judge, with the look of a zealot performing a pleasurable duty, dispose of two years of

32

other people's lives.

Bad luck ran in threes on that cross-country trip, and in normally easygoing Seattle I was locked up again. Though I'd been stemming earlier I was picked up for vagrancy, by a cop who probably needed a pinch to prove he'd been working. With the timing of my arrest I had to spend a weekend waiting to see the judge, and found Seattle didn't treat prisoners too well; I was in a huge cell called a bullpen, with nothing but a bare concrete floor, and fed twice daily along with eighty other prisoners jamming the place. Each morning the floor was hosed down, but by night only a lucky few could find a space where some drunk hadn't pissed or vomited. Within hours of the judge telling me to leave town, I was on a southbound train.

Most of my pinches occurred before I'd been on the road long enough to learn how to keep away from skidrow, or which towns to avoid. On skidrow the big danger was police, especially late at night when they'd made their quota of arrests and the more sadistic of them liked to flex their muscles. For nothing more than being unemployed, men were knocked down and sometimes kicked in the face. On rare occasions when somebody took his revenge, there'd be newspaper stories about a brave officer being attacked on patrol in a dark part of his beat.

After a couple of weeks' hard work, fast talk and nimble cop-dodging in San Francisco, I managed to bite the price of a car. Not once while I was collecting enough to buy a pretty good Ford did I appear in front of one of the city's friendly judges. By trial and error and application I discovered something new and useful about stemming: the best way to get people to kick in was to be completely honest. Much of the public was fed up to the eyeballs with tales of hardship, and were ripe to be pursued by something different. When I'd stop a business man and tell him I was collecting the price of a car because I was tired of riding freight trains, he'd be amazed at my effrontery. If I'd correctly sized up someone by their facial expression, amazement usually turned to amusement, and a hand would reach into a pocket. Misreading faces led to frosty turndowns. In a city of such worldly people as San Francisco, it was piss-poor stemming to ask for the price of anything so uninspiring as a meal; everyone knew that a feed could be had for ten or fifteen cents on Howard Street and that would be the size of their donation. Much better was to set a

33

higher target, relying on breezy chatter to milk worthwhile slings from people who appeared susceptible to that kind of treatment.

Long before aiming for a car, I discarded the old worked-to-death, belly-filling routine. Very profitable was telling a man being bitten that I'd already had a meal, but could use the price of a piece of ass. While the subject was laughing at what he was being asked to contribute to, he'd generally cough up at least a quarter.

It was impossible to remember faces of the many people with whom I'd previously discussed my financial problems. Often a man would remind me that he'd helped out towards my piece of nooky only a day or two before. This was easily handled by explaining that what I'd had couldn't sustain me for ever, and I needed more of the same.

Twisting what at first sounded like a high-level appeal for some unnamed assistance into a blatant bite for an unworthy purpose really worked. Few people capable of laughing could resist when the sudden switch came, and in such a frame of mind they almost always contributed.

Using my Ford for clean and comfortable transport, I worked a number of cities across the country. Arrests were unavoidable, and looking like anything but a down-and-outer I ran the risk of harsh treatment from a judge. Though my offence was good for sixty days in some places, bail was usually around ten dollars. Cops get commissions from bondsmen, and hidden inside my shoe I always carried more than enough to cover bail; quite a few bails were lost when I evaporated.

3

Confessions of a seagoing tramp   exploiting
man's lust for gold   something like a real
relationship   a crotchful of crabs   life in the
Shanghai police force   randy in Rangoon.

THE CRUEL SEA

At the end of a long trip I was resting in San Francisco when an
opportunity to go to sea came my way. A clappy whore had cost a
British freighter a member of its crew, and through someone I
knew in a shipping office I was offered his job as an ordinary
seaman. A month's pay equalled two days' stemming, but the
ship was bound for Valparaiso, with a lot of interesting ports in
between; the idea of distant travel down the west coast of South
America had much appeal. Food on that ship was terrible, the
English officers were haughty as hell, and the crew seemed
strangely subservient. I would have preferred a civilized
American ship, but a closed-shop union arrangement made that
impossible. After my first British meal I doubted the strength of
my resolve to sail the sea.

While the ship loaded more cargo in Los Angeles harbour, I
noticed something that could be useful later. Topping the aft
hold were a lot of cases of canned fruit, vegetables and meat; that
hold could be reached through the mast house when the hatch
was covered. I resolved to do something about compensating for
my dietary deficiencies. Late the first night out of Los Angeles I
sneaked a case containing small tins of high-quality ham, and
next evening a case of asparagus and one of peaches. With all
safely hidden in the steering-engine compartment, I was set to
make up the difference between American and English eating
habits.

At a little port in Nicaragua I learned that the local boss
stevedore would buy cans of paint and coils of rope, if the price

was right. Finding out at the next port that more paint could be sold suggested this could be done wherever the ship called, as long as I didn't run the supply too low. Very quickly I ascertained where every saleable item was stowed, also the best way of getting it out unseen. Some of the things I sold had to be removed from their storage places while the ship was at sea. In port there were precautions against shore-based thieves, but by then my merchandise was stashed where it could easily be reached when there was a buyer. In Costa Rica it turned out that there was a market for tins of ham. Apart from what I needed for my own use, I planted three more cases before that cargo could be unloaded at some port.

Another source of money for spending ashore was a large tank of linseed oil, bolted to the forward bulkhead of the steering-engine room. Listening to the broken English of another boss stevedore, I accidentally discovered that this oil had value ashore. While haggling over the price of paint, the man used a Spanish word sounding like linseed, so I explained that I was also in the oil business. After sniffing a sample, the fellow became anxious to buy. When we agreed on a figure, he wanted to purchase every drop I could supply. All the time the ship was in the port of Guayaquil, Ecuador, I kept taking the swarthy cargo boss bottles and cans, to be sent over the side in slingloads from the holds. Toward the end of the voyage, when the ship was approaching San Francisco, the bosun went to the tank for some oil. A couple of other crewmen and I were present to hear the bosun's lurid language when all he could manage was a slow trickle. The chief officer was summoned, and he thought the disappearance of an entire tank of linseed oil most extraordinary. In his refined English voice he remarked that it probably had something to do with those villainous natives who came aboard. Out of hearing of the chief officer I told one of the English seamen that I thought it was amazing how any motherfucker could get away with all that oil. Looking at me with disgust, he asked if it was really necessary to use such expressions.

Much of the money I picked up in those Central and South American ports was ploughed back into the girls of the local whorehouses. Within two days of leaving the ship I was on the streets of San Francisco and in due course had a much better car, to replace the nearly worn-out one I sold before signing on. With

36

clothes to match the quality of my car, I was ready to try something I'd had at the back of my mind for a while. At that time the public was gold conscious, because the government was buying it. People were urged to drop into their jewellers with anything from old watches to tooth fillings. Since most people would believe any heavy jewellery with a carat imprint was gold, I'd obtain a suitable stamp and put the right markings on some stuff.

A wholesale junk-jewellery dealer sold me a gross of heavy "gold" men's rings at fifteen cents each, and for three dollars supplied a stamp to mark them fourteen carat. This was merchandise made especially for what I planned, with plenty of lead in the alloy to give weight. The dealer warned the gold colour would last for about twenty minutes' wear, so if selling off my finger I shouldn't put the rings on too soon. To make them look more valuable, each had a small glass diamond in the middle of a flat facing. The idea was to sell these quietly on the street, as "found" or "warm" valuables. I decided I'd stop people who looked right, explain a need for funds, then offer for a few dollars the ring I'd acquired but was "nervous" about selling in the normal way. Following my long experience at "interviewing" the public, I trusted my ability to spot people likely to snap up a bargain without wanting to know where it came from.

Starting east from San Francisco, I sold eight rings at Sacramento, averaging four dollars each. All my victims were told that their rings were of local origin, so it wouldn't be advisable to take them to pawnshops or jewellers for a few weeks. To prevent finger-blackened buyers looking for me while I was still in town, I emphasized the danger of wearing the jewellery openly too soon. Not trusting the customers to heed my warning, I was in and out of Sacramento within two hours.

My gross of rings lasted to Chicago, and then I switched to watches, known as "blocks". Costing three dollars, these were of little more value than the rings, but were impressive "solid gold twenty-one jewel" specials that looked like railroad watches. Inside were lots of little red glass jewels that screamed quality, to anyone knowing nothing about watch movements. Besides two dozen blocks I bought a gross of "hoops", as the dealer called his rings. While wrapping the stuff, he offered a couple of bits of useful information: that I could wire a money order for merchandise to be expressed to wherever I might be working, and that peddling these wares in the South was good for a stretch on the chain gang.

Never did I claim that anything was gold. If caught, my story would be that somebody had sold me the junk as genuine, but low-priced, merchandise. The cops would still regard it as a racket, so my real defence was always to have enough money for bail. Using one story or another, all of my stuff was sold by the time I returned to San Francisco and I had to obtain further supplies. Each selling trip was followed by a rest period while my nerves settled down.

As a result of this nomadic existence, my sex life was overly dependent on luck. Whores no longer satisfied me, because I'd outgrown the stage where the mechanics of intercourse were fascinating, so during my spells off the road I tried to form more lasting relationships. Young girls still had little appeal, and I usually found myself with women twice my age. Often I was gone too long to re-establish contact on return, though there was one woman in San Francisco who was an exception. She lived in the less than élite Fillmore district, had a couple of kids by a husband who'd done the disappearing act, and was permanently on relief because she was unemployable. Weighing around three hundred pounds, the woman didn't do much beyond waddle down to the relief office, but she did like sex.

We met in a café, and possibly detecting a response when our eyes met, she started talking. Right away I knew that this was nooky—my aunt's hefty maid's word for it—if I was willing to go to the trouble and I was. My thoughts were that this would be by far the biggest piece I'd ever had, and while she spoke I built up images of what she'd be like in bed. Instead of just getting on top, I thought looking at her immense heftiness, I'd be able to wallow in it, and the prospect of that was exciting. The possibility occurred that with such huge thighs and overhanging belly there might be trouble getting in, but then I remembered from other experiences that it could be done. Preliminaries began with a drive to Golden Gate Park, where I stopped the car in a quiet place. Aside from our agreeing on her flat rather than my hotel not much happened, other than my hand going between the woman's legs. I expected a lot of snatch odour and after working past the wrinkles of fat was pleasantly surprised to find so little.

38

While my hand was up there, with the woman putting a great arm around my neck and kissing me, I discovered that it could be difficult with someone that size to feel just where leg fat ended and crotch began. I seemed to feel more of everything than I'd ever felt before; all was so wet and slippery that I wondered if something wasn't wrong until my hand came up near my nose. Not wanting to be obvious about sniffing to see if her box was clean, I did my check while changing hands. When I put my free hand down the front of her dress onto some gigantic thing I supposed was a tit, the woman suggested driving straight to her place. It was mid afternoon when we reached the flat, so she told the kids to go out and play and they took no more notice of me than they likely did of other uncles.

Never would I have thought that such a huge woman could get much out of what I had to give, but she knew all sorts of positions where the fat wouldn't interfere. For nearly an hour I wallowed in that big, wet pussy. Then the woman said we'd better finish, because it was time to cook dinner for the kids. Inviting me to eat with the family, she gave promise of bed again when the kids were asleep. Staying all night would be risky, because neighbours seeing me leave in the morning might report her to the relief officials. Mention of relief prompted me to toss in for the groceries, so I handed her a couple of dollars which she reluctantly accepted.

I visited that woman regularly, without even thinking of trying to meet someone more presentable. Going for that big pussy the way I did convinced me I was peculiar, especially since all the men I knew who weren't queer raved about women with good figures. I wasn't against anyone young and attractive, but they did little for me; most of them seemed shrewd and calculating rather than easygoing like the plump ones I favoured. After I'd been going with my big friend for a while, the subterfuges necessary with more attractive women seemed less worth the effort than ever. And as for the sex part, the little things between their legs weren't nearly as exciting as the well-developed boxes I was acquiring such a taste for. Each trip back to San Francisco I spent much time with that big woman, and never bothered how many other "uncles" the kids met in my absence.

On a hoop-and-block trip I met an older woman in Portland, and stayed there for a while. She wasn't small, but she was no match for the San Francisco woman. Her love-making made up for anything else lacking, and her way of life afforded me certain opportunities. Instead of being on relief she had a poorly paid job in a department store, but compensated for it by taking all she could get. She was a Catholic, surrounded by practising relatives, and couldn't have me staying overnight. But much could be done by midnight, though I hated leaving her place at that late hour. After I knew her a while, she explained how her apartment came to be loaded with so many expensive items. Aided by relatives whose morals were only sexual, she had a practical way of getting things out of that department store. As a relief saleswoman she always changed departments, and had been clever enough to find a way of faking sales slips. Relatives—or occasionally a trusted friend—would go through the motions of shopping until it was time to walk out with a good-sized package, complete with sales docket. Soon I was a trusted friend, splitting fifty-fifty with her—which was much less of a strain than selling blocks and hoops. What I got was saleable merchandise, and after the first dozen profitable purchases I hoped that this might keep right on going, but it was too good to last.

One day I was leaving the store with a package under my arm when I was stopped by the strong arm and authoritative voice of the law. I acted innocent, but all the store dick would say was that I'd have to go with him. I tried to show him the sales slip for what I'd "bought", but he wouldn't even look. He allowed me a few seconds to resign myself to the fact that I'd been caught, and to realize just how bad this situation could be: planned theft, good for six months. My woman friend was probably already in the manager's office.

The door to the street was only feet away, the store detective didn't look very powerful, and he was alone. Heaving my parcel over the dick's head and back into the store I shot out the door, almost bowling over a couple of people on their way in. With him shouting at me to stop I sailed between parked cars to take an awful risk crossing the street. I couldn't shake him off and soon the noise he was creating would attract some cop to the chase. I ran into a big movie theatre with the next non-paying customer close on my heels. I made for the folds of a curtain under a red exit sign. Sounds of pursuit were well back. I pushed the exit open hoping the streak of light wouldn't draw my pursuers too quickly, but I didn't wait to find out. Afraid to run fast for fear of attracting more to the chase, I hurried out of the alley behind the theatre, and rounding the corner into a busy street, slowed to a walk. I headed for my hotel, gathered my hoops and blocks, along with store loot from other visits, and was clear of the Portland city limits in well under an hour. As far as the woman was concerned, I hoped she'd be in a better position if I skipped; the incriminating sales slip in her handwriting was still safely in my pocket.

Then followed a sales trip through the Pacific northwest, ending in Vancouver's Washington jail with a crotch full of crabs by courtesy of a friendly waitress in Tacoma. I made a mistake thinking I could work Vancouver, and, as the judge said, I was lucky I didn't make a sale. My downfall came at a gas station. I had almost sold a hoop to a mechanic when the boss suddenly appeared, took one look at it and advised against the proposition. I started walking off down the street, but within minutes a police car containing the manager and two cops pulled up, and I was taken in. Two rings were taken from my pocket at the station, and I was closely questioned by a young cop panting to have me on a theft charge. A more intelligent sergeant decided to send my hoops out to be valued while I was taken straight to the judge's office. The valuation arrived in the middle of the judge's recital of my deeds, and I was told I could plead guilty to peddling without a licence. Obviously I'd attempted a swindle, he said, and sentenced me to two days' jail. On that kind of a deal I wasn't going to argue a plea, so I thanked His Honour and went to the cells.

Not having much to occupy me, I found myself obsessed with the crabs in my crotch. The itching grew worse by the hour. With two days to serve, it seemed pointless to incense my captors, so the little beasts were tolerated until my release. A bottle of some chemical then soon fixed them.

By the time I returned to San Francisco, I was in fair shape financially. So for weeks I relaxed in my favourite city and went to bed with the fat woman every night.

When my funds ran low, I started stocking up for another road trip, but an unexpected opportunity to sail for Shanghai came my way. My large lady didn't like it when I said I wouldn't be seeing her for some time; but when I explained that the firm for which I'd been selling was broke, she accepted the inevitable. That evening, my last in San Francisco, I went down on her. She'd just taken a bath, and although I had always been intimidated by the contemptuous way people spoke of "muffdivers", I decided to give the thing a good suck. When I suggested kissing it, the woman's excited response dispersed any doubt. I put my face between her fat legs, and was immediately smothered in great soft, wet masses of flesh. There was a pleasant salty taste to the warm fluid she exuded, and it was so exciting I had to force my mind to other things, such as the little lipless box of a young girl, or I would have come. While this went on, the woman showed pleasure by making little sounds, and rhythmically pushing the back of my head. After controlling urges to let go the lot, I threw my leg over her shoulder, dropping my sticky tool close to her mouth. She took it instantly, sucking as if to drain me for all I had. Finally, when I could hold on no longer, I came. I stayed with her till daylight.

The captain of the British ship explained during signing-on that the voyage to Shanghai would be a one-way trip for me, since the vessel would be returning to England. Luckily I had a proper passport, rather than a useless seaman's card, so there'd be no trouble over landing at Shanghai; the passport had been obtained in anticipation of such an event. I decided to leave my fate to the future. After hearing stories of people who'd lived by their wits in Shanghai, I wasn't apprehensive. Besides the low wages I'd get from the ship, there was what my car brought on a quick sale. Also I had my stock of hoops, and two dozen blocks. That stuff should be saleable in the Orient, if salt air didn't eat the plating off and turn it into junk.

Thirty days out of San Francisco the ship was steaming up the Whangpoo River, and I was ready to get off. I had no intention of remaining aboard, even if asked. A break in the voyage had been a call at Yokohama, and from there I went to Tokyo, without reporting back for work until the ship was due to sail. While the chief officer grumbled about my absence, there was not a word of complaint from the bosun, despite the fact that I'd resisted his advances all the way across the Pacific. The brilliance of Tokyo was enough to sell me on staying in the Orient for a while. Having to leave my shoes outside certain establishments seemed a strange custom, but the girls were more friendly than others I'd encountered.

The first night out of Yokohama the bosun made his final attempt to talk my pants down. Instead of being forceful, the man seemed hurt each time I refused him a little cornhole. What upset him was my relationship with one of the stewards, and every time he tried to persuade me to bend over he brought that up. On his first stupid try at cracking it, he said he'd use plenty of vaseline, so it wouldn't hurt.

The steward was a fruit, poofter to the Limeys, and he tended to reserve his favours for the officers. Because the bosun thought that letting me off as much work as possible might be a way into my brown, I was half-way between seaman and passenger. In view of his status, the steward was able to bridge the gap separating officers from lower orders. To get choice food from the officers' pantry, I had only to let the steward put my penis in his mouth.

Unless I wanted to work like the others, the bosun couldn't simply be brushed aside. To prove to him that I wasn't playing favourites, I offered to let him do what the steward did. As a dyed-in-the-wool turd-pusher, the bosun was not going to take me up on that. To limit my labours to such pleasurable things as standing wheel-watches, I had to explain my aversion to browning, and how I might overcome it before the ship arrived at Shanghai. After Yokohama, with Chinese boys not too far ahead, the bosun accepted defeat. As the ship moved slowly past the lower reaches of Shanghai, and the tall city buildings came into sight, I had the feeling that this was a place I would like. Where the ship made fast to some buoys was a little way downstream from the famous Bund. Within an hour of tying up I was told that a replacement was available, and instructed to go to the British Consulate later in the day for paying-off. At the Customs Jetty half-way down the Bund I was prepared to explain my blocks and hoops, but there was no inspection.

I walked around the city, and after changing some money I had a good meal at a café called Jimmy's, in Nanking Road, for less than the price of a hamburger on an American skidrow. Most of those eating at Jimmy's were Europeans, and soon I was talking to an Englishman who suggested that where he lived would be a good place for me to stay.

After a long rickshaw ride along Nanking Road to where it

became Bubbling Well Road, then around a huge racecourse, and finally to a laneway lined with houses that looked right out of England, we came to a Salvation Army hostel where I could have a room and board for ten dollars a month. The hostel was for Europeans of good character who were not too financial. The welcome mat was definitely not out for bums or seamen. I was to tell the woman commanding officer that I'd arrived in Shanghai as a passenger and expected to find a job with a company. The only resemblance to other Sally establishments I'd seen was the crowding of beds into large rooms, but everything was kept clean by white-jacketed Chinese houseboys who glided silently about the place. There were Bibles handily placed for those who might require them. The large dining-room with its white-covered tables was like something in an old country hotel that had seen better days.

I was accepted as a resident by the English commanding officer, a stern-looking but pleasantly spoken woman with the rank of major. The House Rules were basic Christianity: no liquor, women, or unseemly language. The hostel was an adult version of the Boys' Home in Los Angeles; the transients were older, more sophisticated, and very international. Some had jobs, but most lived by their wits. It was a hotbed of information on how to survive in the city without working and how to avoid the police. Shanghai was one of those rare cities where trouble would only come if you did something really outrageous. Vagrancy laws did not exist, and as a United States citizen I was subject only to American Federal statutes, which were lightly represented by a resident United States Marshal, who would not be stirred into action by trivialities. It also turned out that, once accepted into the Sally, it was just about impossible to get thrown out.

Two other Americans in the hostel openly admitted to having escaped from a stateside prison, where they'd been serving long sentences for robbery, and though the United States authorities were aware of their presence in Shanghai, they weren't troubled. The official attitude seemed to be that when they'd had enough of the town, free transport to where they were wanted would be available. These two were into a refined form of stemming, more dignified than street panhandling, involving visits to offices of United States and other foreign firms. Three or four touches would take care of a month's living at the Sally, and a dozen or so

44

more paid for such necessities as women and liquor. The best people to nip were those of one's own nationality or at least of common language.

The Sally was in Shanghai's International Settlement, which was rather British, but much of the real action took place in the adjoining French concession, where many White Russian women—girlfriends of Europeans and whores—lived. As I learned after visiting a few cafés along Avenue Joffre, those who were not hustlers were very approachable, and not expecting much out of life. They were satisfied by the simple pleasures of a meal and going to bed. The first thing most asked of new acquaintances was whether they'd be around for more than one meeting. Such were the economics of Shanghai that, unlike other foreigners, local Russians were poorly paid and tended to live three or four to an apartment. Before I'd been in town a week, I had visited enough of those apartments to learn that these women didn't allow communal living to interfere with their continental love-making.

After my third week of wandering around the International Settlement by day, and making love to a well-built Russian nurse, about twice my age, in the French concession by night, I began to think about my finances. They were far from depleted, but I thought they should be boosted. An American ship tied to the buoys in the Whangpoo inspired me, and with my U.S. accent there was no difficulty in striking up conversations with crew members waiting to board water taxis at the Customs Jetty. I was an American stranded in Shanghai without funds, but wouldn't entertain the idea of biting anyone. I'd explain that rather than approach the consulate for help I would sell my watch for enough to keep on eating until a job turned up. There'd be the usual interest from someone hoping to pick up a bargain, and even more interest when I'd place my valuable timepiece into the hands of an intended victim nervously complaining that I was parting with it only because this was an emergency. I sold two to crewmen off a ship that was sailing in an hour, so there was little risk of them getting together in time to return ashore looking for my blood. The following week there was a repeat performance with another U.S. ship in the stream.

Then came the impractical notion that if I could talk my way into a job with one of the U.S. firms, I'd live like other Americans in Shanghai. They had a good life, and never seemed to do much work. I envied their apartments, along with enough money for the best of everything, and wondered if in some small way I might be able to crash their circle. Not too many approaches were necessary for me to get the message that these people were a closed corporation. When someone suggested I'd probably be accepted in the police force, my initial reaction was that surely he must be joking. Nobody could think of me as cop material. But then I gave it some thought.

The International Settlement cops, called the Shanghai Municipal Police, had European members. They did not look as officious as their counterparts in other places, nor did they appear to do much work. Employment of European cops was part of maintaining white prestige in the East. Keeping order in that huge city was left largely to the Chinese, and a force of Sikhs capable of frightening anybody who wasn't European. To one who'd never been a lover of police, the notion of becoming one seemed preposterous at first, but after discussing it with some Sally people and hearing that others from the hostel had gone into the force it sounded less improbable. Another American staying in the place had joined up, only to leave a bad impression with the authorities when he disappeared complete with gun and uniform. What happened was that while on duty along the Bund, representing powerful law and order to teeming hordes of Chinese, the captain of a ship outbound for San Francisco offered him a job. Forgetting duty and also that it was dishonest to leave without turning in police department property, the officer marched straight aboard with the captain.

Even the American jailbreakers, who knew all about me, considered it a good idea. Still thinking it out of character, I went to the recruiting office, and after creating a reasonable background and telling outrageous lies I was told my application would probably be approved.

My feeling about joining the enemy was eased when I was introduced to some off-duty European cops in the central station's recreation room. As they proceeded to pour drinks into me, it soon became obvious these were unlike any cops I had ever encountered. After drinking a little too much, I quietly told another American that I'd been arrested too many times to want

46

to do it to others. He replied that this was probably the only police force in the world where it was possible to get by without ever making a pinch; his method was to look the other way when anything happened, and if necessary disappear in pursuit of some imagined miscreant. Most of the work, he explained, was done by non-white lower orders; in theory, the Europeans were to be an example to them.

A week later I was notified of my appointment as probationary sergeant, and given a date to report to the training unit. There were half a dozen other recruits, but none from the Sally; most had been in Shanghai longer than I, and had made better living arrangements. An instructor whose job it was to make cops out of this improbable lot informed us that he wouldn't be surprised if half didn't ship out before completing the course. Within three days the new officers had been supplied with uniforms, but no guns since these were issued only when going on duty. Accommodation at the training depot was better than the Sally, with smaller rooms and less of a flophouse atmosphere; food was very good, and there were plenty of houseboys around. The recruits were allowed into town only three nights a week, and with compulsory return by midnight it was difficult to lead a normal love life. My Russian nurse didn't like short visits any more than she liked cops, and to account for my weird hours I told her a story about working part-time in an International Settlement gambling joint.

Within three weeks the idea of becoming a cop was running cool, although a few more weeks had me almost accustomed to pre-breakfast physical training and drilling to the orders of an ex-British-Army sergeant major. Each morning I seriously considered not staying much longer, but there was the thought that in time this might become interesting. Part of the later training was putting in shifts at various police stations, to learn procedure. At a station near the centre of Shanghai the sergeant showed me the paperwork. An item of some interest was the periodically updated list of undesirable Europeans; these lists were compiled by the detective division, for the purpose of identifying all suspect foreigners in the city. Practically the entire population of the Sally was on the current list, with such details as age, nationality, and suspected misdeeds. The previous circular had my details with no suspected activities, and when I pointed this out to the sergeant he said it meant nothing. The lists were got up by the detectives when they had little else to do, and tended to be a catalogue of all Europeans hanging around Shanghai without visible means of support. I appreciated their courtesy in deleting my name from the current suspect list after I joined the cops.

My first few times on the streets in uniform I felt conspicuous, as if all eyes were staring, and I was scared that if anyone turned up with a problem, I could only suggest that they call the police. However, as it turned out, the Chinese were in awe of European cops and tended to approach constables of their own race in times of trouble.

Membership of the Shanghai police force conferred no social acceptance among that class of foreigner sent to Shanghai on the pay rates of home countries. Officially the term "recognized foreigner" applied to all who weren't stateless for political reasons, but, unofficially, recognition was withheld from such as myself who were not members of the business or consular élite. Our acceptance was among the Russians and other refugee groups, where a lot of the women hoped to get married and acquire a visa for some worthwhile country.

The time I did know what to do while in uniform was when I spotted some American seamen. Sight of them near the Customs Jetty made me think that as an officer of the law I could sell blocks and hoops better than ever. My pitch was that in the course of handing in the proceeds of a robbery I'd somehow neglected to turn over a valuable watch. As it was too late to correct my oversight without embarrassment, the best way out was to let someone leaving Shanghai take the watch with them. Before resorting to selling my first block as a cop, I'd learned from other officers that there weren't many worthwhile graft possibilities; there were opportunities for the Chinese and Indian police, but few good bites for the Europeans. The only consistent fringe benefit was that some establishments didn't charge for meals or entertainment.

Two months of being a cop of sorts was enough. But telling the inspector who'd approved my application a tale about family problems in America was not the way to resign. He made that very clear when I said I'd like to give notice and would leave whenever it suited him. As far as he was concerned right then was the most appropriate moment. After offering to hand in my

48

equipment immediately, I was told how he'd accepted me against his better judgement; obviously I was not the desired type for the work. He said he'd appreciate it if I would give thought to leaving Shanghai and not hanging around to become a nuisance like so many other foreigners.

Taking seriously the inspector's advice about not staying in town, I remained only long enough to take up a juicy collection from officials in various American firms. One of the jailbreakers worked up a list of people worth biting, with the result that I did very well. My next move was to buy a ticket on one of the coastal ships sailing for Hong Kong—and bid my Russian nurse farewell.

As a British colony, Hong Kong had more law and order than Shanghai, but it still took a week for my profitable work among business houses to come under official notice. Instead of using the distressed seaman tale, I had come up with something more sophisticated and was getting results. Then an English inspector of the Hong Kong Police called at my hotel one morning, to ask a few polite questions. The interview was on a more dignified level than any encounter with American police over solicitations, though the inspector did want definite answers on my future travel plans. The fact that I was staying in a part of Kowloon loaded with whorehouses, and not at the Seamen's Mission where I might get a ship, did not go amiss. He asked what funds I had, and when these were modestly understated by three quarters, he proffered the bright suggestion that I might buy a ticket to some other place. Shanghai was eliminated, but Singapore was a distinct possibility; in fact, there was a ship headed that way in three days, the officer said, and he'd be most obliged if I'd make a point of being on board. I felt he was taking a perverse delight in sending me on to the British in Singapore. I put it to him that the more funds in my possession on arrival the less likely I'd be to encounter "difficulty", so with his kind permission could I, in the time before sailing, arrange conferences in the offices of a few firms I needed to visit? At first a look of outrage crossed his face, but then he began to laugh. I gave him my word to be on that ship and to restrict my activities to Americans, who could better afford that kind of touch. I bought my ticket right away and bit Americans only, but raced like hell to get through as many as possible before the ship sailed.

Office work differed greatly from street stemming, but to produce good takings it also required practice. Since each bite was a sit-down affair, rather than a rushed sidewalk conference, time could be taken to tell a good story. As I learned in Hong Kong, the trick was to put across something that suggested social equality with the individual being touched. Though I looked a bit young, my Hong Kong story was that a small American firm had sent me to Shanghai to open a branch there, and, while I was crossing the Pacific, had gone broke. I had arrived in China with neither job nor prospects, and, after failing to find employment, had used the last of my funds to come to Hong Kong. Lying that I had searched for a position unsuccessfully in the colony, I said that the only solution was to borrow the price of a ticket back to America. An extra flourish that probably fooled few, but increased the size of my bites, was my intention to repay the debts, which I was at that moment recording in my notebook, when I had a job in the States. Despite my best efforts there was the occasional hard-core non-giver, and it was a challenge to see how many of these could be turned. Some would expound at length about it being against their principles to contribute to non-organizational agencies; the smug way those people reacted sometimes provoked me into saying that in their position I might also be tempted to adopt such a money-saving philosophy. That would either shame them into a belated donation, or very quickly wear out my welcome.

Questioned eventually by a police inspector, I phased out the concept of collecting donations and, for the sake of self-respect, bites became "loan applications". The inspector highly recommended a ship soon sailing for Singapore.

In the three days it took to reach Singapore, I developed the idea of loan applications to finance my "tour" of the Orient. As an individual who talked things over with business men, rather than a white-collar hobo nipping people, I felt more equal with other passengers; the result was an affair with an Anglo-Burmese widow.

Inadvertently I used the expression "Eurasian" in our first conversation; she very promptly said she was Anglo-Burmese, and I apologized for my lack of familiarity with the East. As the plump and friendly woman was going on to Rangoon, there was no early suggestion of a longer-range relationship. She was happy to be temporarily involved, although concealment from other people would be a problem. On a ship with only a couple of dozen cabin passengers, segregated from coolie hordes travelling on deck, there was no place to go other than one of our cabins. Even then it would have to be a late-at-night sneak job, or the story would quickly go the rounds of the European officers and passengers. When my friend suggested her cabin I thought it would only be for a short time, but instead she let me stay the night. Waking up when the steward brought morning tea, I felt a perverse pleasure in being with someone who valued her reputation no more than I did mine.

Some of the English married couples who'd been friendly toward me chilled after my first night in the woman's cabin. So pointed was the snubbing that I wondered if the underlying cause on the part of the men mightn't be envy, turned to dislike by their wives' carping about the disgraceful conduct of that dreadful American and his woman friend. The twisted delight I derived from the stupid attitude of these people was heightened by thoughts of what different ones must be thinking. I could easily imagine those English women, who didn't look as if they'd be much use to any man, thinking that the Anglo-Burmese woman and I were a pair of animals. Also I had the idea that if one of the husbands would lower himself to speak, he'd say something such as, "Look here, old boy, one just doesn't openly do this sort of thing in the East, especially with a woman who is, after all, half native." My friend enjoyed this situation as much as I did, and we further flaunted convention by having meals in her cabin rather than the dining saloon. Her thoughts about the English were coloured by her father's return to London years before, leaving his family behind. In the final hours of the voyage she gave me an address in Rangoon, and asked me to get in touch some time.

Singapore didn't take so long to work, and without interference from the constabulary, I made loan applications in most of the worthwhile places within five days. By coincidence a ship was sailing for Rangoon just after I completed my deals, so I bought a ticket. My friend was surprised when I arrived on the next ship, and insisted I stay at her place. She suggested the family farmhouse a few miles up the Irrawaddy River from Rangoon, in preference to the room she had in town to be close to her job in a steamship company. I was to be a friend she'd met in Singapore the year before, and was on my way to India. My misgivings, expressed on the launch heading up the muddy Irrawaddy, were eased when the woman said she'd have no trouble explaining me to her family. Our concession to their sense of morals would be a pretence of sleeping in different rooms. As well as the influence of the English in members of the family, there was evidence of further foreign influence in the big, old-fashioned tropical-style farmhouse: bleeding hearts, sickly religious pictures and appalling plaster statues, of the sort I'd seen in New York slums. When the family were in bed, I asked her about those religious objects and how Christianity came to influence a family in Burma. I was told it was due to some Portuguese ancestry, and that the old people were the believers.

Four days later we were back in Rangoon, and with two more to wait for a ship to Calcutta I held conferences with members of the European community. I hoped that in a small place such as Rangoon my friend would not hear gossip about how I picked up a living. If she heard anything up to the time the ship sailed, she never mentioned it, and before going aboard I promised to try to return to Rangoon.

4

My philosophy of life   what's going on in the
world   back home to face the family   working
on the railroad   marriage never, older women
for ever   first flight.

AROUND THE WORLD IN SHADY WAYS

I liked travelling by passenger ship and getting a good living from loan applications. Travel by liner was a much more pleasant way of life than going by freight train, or driving with the thought that a sheriff might be waiting for me in the next town. Compared with America, where the struggle to exist by work or wit was fierce, and the legal system sometimes vicious, the Far East was rather pleasant. Worthwhile employment in either place was out, but in the Orient European dignity was something to be maintained. Face-saving was all important, and those from whom I borrowed were generally obsessed with upholding the national image. Out there it was my entitlement, by virtue of nationality, to maintain a civilized manner of living, and if someone from whom I'd arranged a loan saw me eating or drinking in the best places, he'd appreciate the reason. The worst that could happen might be an encounter with an official such as the gentlemanly Hong Kong police inspector, but there'd be no nights or weekends in local lock-ups, because the authorities just didn't do such things to Europeans.

What did trouble me was that with a major war shaping up, this good life in the East couldn't last much longer. Soon I might have to go back to America, and adjust to the idea of working for a living. Employment was rising by leaps and bounds in the U.S., so like it or not I might have to fit into a new way of life. Living by work would be a novel experience, but what I dreaded was that it might be boring. I had moved around far too long not to feel restless at the sound of a train whistle, or the sight of a ship. It could be hard to settle down to a routine job, where most of my time would be used up just making a living. Another worry was that I had no qualification for anything better than dull, repetitive labour.

Up to now full employment, to me, was only something older people talked about, but if there was to be a change I'd have to learn to do something. Being too much of a loner to fit into any group, or function without blowing up in a situation where I was controlled by others, my choice would be limited.

My scant knowledge of watch-repairing, gained through tinkering, could possibly be upgraded. That would still be tedious work, though there were a couple of things that fascinated me. Photography could be a possibility, because I had enough of an interest to have done a fair amount of reading on the subject. The other thing that intrigued me was learning to fly.

Of the two, the first seemed more practical, because I felt I'd have an aptitude for it, and it would be individualistic. Flying had also interested me for a long time and, given the chance, I didn't think I'd have great difficulty in learning. What use it would ever be might be doubtful, though it could provide a sense of accomplishment. With photography, there could be a chance of picking up a living doing something I'd like. For the first time in years I remembered being ridiculed by my father and brother, because I mentioned these subjects as occupations in which I'd be interested.

Calcutta was big enough to offer many opportunities for loan applications, so I planned to stay for a while. My habit of using fairly good hotels was varied and, on the recommendation of the English chief steward on the ship from Rangoon, I stayed at the Y.M.C.A. It contained people not normally found in a Christian institution and was run by an English manager who was an avid heterosexual. So many Anglo-Indian women turned up at the dances he organized that it would have been difficult not to score. During my three weeks in Calcutta I had half a dozen little affairs. As a concession to Christian morals, the friendly manager suggested that it might be an idea to be discreet about screwing these women on the premises. Not encouraging whores or too obvious gays, the manager ran his hostel as a pleasant hotel rather than as the usual depressing hangout for queers. Before I left he presented me with a collection of little stone figure groups representing most known forms of sexual intercourse.

Since Calcutta was like other Eastern cities for Europeans learning the doings of each other, it wasn't long before the Y manager knew all about my loans. His mention of my biting as something amusing brought the explanation that I was only making loan applications. After laughing about that, he gave me the names of some people not to be missed. One person I mustn't fail to interview was a U.S. consular official, and though normally I avoided such people I decided to make an exception.

The official listened to my story and made a loan, after saying that according to the rules he shouldn't do this. A few days later he contacted me at the Y on a matter of urgency. An American ship was sailing next day for New York via Cape Town, and it was short of a crew member. Before I could say whether I wanted to be on board when she steamed down the Hooghly, he explained that my lack of experience or union membership wouldn't matter. In a case of this sort the captain was entitled to sign on anybody available.

Calcutta had been a lot of fun because of its unusual Y, and I'd enjoyed being there, so I thought before giving an answer. The town was almost borrowed out, but, more important, the war threat was getting really serious. Finally I decided to take this opportunity to return to America, and possibly learn flying or photography.

Having claimed no sea experience, I kept up the pretence by signing on as an ordinary seaman—for as an American I was expected by the crew either to have total lack of sea experience or to be a member of their militant union (one was in real danger with these men if any suspicion of losing membership through scabbing in one of their strikes were aroused). Too late to change my story, I realized that an admission of experience on foreign ships would have been more credible.

In my first wheel-watch, instead of steering the zigzag course of the inexperienced, I very soon had the feel of the ship and held it to within a degree either side of the heading. The damage was done when the officer of the watch looked aft from the bridge wing to see the straight wake behind us. Coming back to the wheelhouse he suggested that this wasn't the first time that I'd been to sea. I maintained that the helm seemed somehow easy to manage, but neither he nor the crew was convinced. For the rest of the passage to Cape Town I was suspect, but after our five days there I seemed to have gained a degree of acceptance.

Half-way up the Atlantic on the long haul from Cape Town to New York I made up my mind to establish contact with my family. I'd been thinking about them since Calcutta, especially during early-morning wheel-watches. While there were still a couple of weeks before arrival in New York, I reached the point of resolution. My thoughts till then had been very mixed, particularly as I recalled the events leading to running away and to my intention of never seeing my family again. After leaving Cape Town my feelings mellowed, and I saw my determination never to return as a defence against guilt over the mess I'd made of my life. I'd previously tried to avoid thinking about the effect of my vanishing without trace, leaving my parents to wonder if I was still alive, but during the weeks at sea it became increasingly difficult to erase these thoughts from my mind. Sometimes I'd think that perhaps their lives were now organized on the basis that I no longer existed, and it would be best left that way. But as the ship made its slow way to New York, my resolve to contact my family strengthened, and I set about trying to plan how I could see them without creating the emotional scenes I'd find so hard to handle.

About a month out of Cape Town the ship arrived at New York, and as it moved up the river I realized that I hadn't yet decided how to make the approach. I thought of trying to contact my brother, and then remembered how much time had passed since I parted company with him at the school; he'd be nearly through university. And I had no way of knowing which one. He would probably regard my reappearance as disruptive, and suggest in his inimitable manner that I just keep travelling. In my search for a way around unbearable emotional stress I considered waylaying him near the house, at least to find out which way the wind blew. I dreaded confrontation with my father, and the recriminations that would follow. I could cope with the others, although there would be reproaches from my mother. But I was sure my father would be bitter, and unforgiving.

By mid morning I'd been paid off and still had no definite plan, apart from feeling that my approach would have to be made from the cover of darkness. I took a hotel room in Newark, went to a movie and then fortified myself with a couple of strong drinks before catching a bus for East Orange.

I'd checked the phone book to make sure my family still lived at the same address. Leaving the bus only a few minutes' walk from the place, I could think of little beyond the need for another drink. Had I left the bar after one drink, all might have remained clear. With each drink my mission became less important and urgent—and more hazy. I remember walking out of the bar, leaning against a parked car and vomiting; and then a cop came along and didn't seem to approve of the mess. And somewhere near him was an obnoxious character demanding to know who'd pay for cleaning the puke off his car. None of this appeared to be any concern of mine. On being bundled into a police car, I felt relief that I now would not have to go through with something I had been dreading. Then everything went blank.

Coming to, slowly, I realized the room and the people made no sense. I'd been pinched and should be in a police station. I closed my eyes again. Then my shoulder was shaken by someone bending over the lounge I was sprawled upon, and I heard a voice asking, "Don't you know where you are?" My eyes opened, and with a jolt like an electric shock I recognized my surroundings. Fully back to my senses, a feeling of horror struck me as I stared into the faces of my family and couldn't think of anything beyond that this wasn't the way I'd intended things to happen. Since nobody would come to my rescue with words instead of disconcerting stares, I asked how I'd got here. In a voice showing none of the rage I expected, my father explained that the police had somehow found out who I was and contacted him. I then became aware that the front of my good Hong Kong suit was encrusted with vomit, and I felt embarrassed. Sparing me the ordeal I was so sure would eventuate any minute, my father suggested we all went to bed and talked things over the next day.

Welcoming this respite from the tension I'd been expecting, I asked, rather vacantly, just where I'd sleep. In the first words I heard my mother offer, she said that I'd sleep in my old room, of course. My brother's look of bewilderment was something with which I could cope, but my father's gaze seemed inscrutable, as if something was ready for release when the time was ripe. Going towards my room, I felt relieved that none of the dreaded scenes

57

had yet taken place.

In the morning I realized that the previous night had shocked them more than it did me, because I'd been building up to it, while they hadn't. Feeling vulnerable with my armour of intoxication gone, I dreaded the moment I'd have to go down and face them. Listening to household sounds, I gathered my father was getting ready to go to the university, and decided to lie low until he was gone. Finally I came downstairs, to find that my brother was having the day off. He made it easy to slide into conversation by asking about places I'd visited, while my mother and sister were content to listen. Avoiding issues close to home, I talked about distant places and going to sea, but none of the other things I'd done.

When I was able to get away from the house alone with my brother, I learned about the events following my disappearance. Evidently the school officials sent for me to discuss the report-card irregularity, and this was the first anyone knew something was wrong. When I was not to be found, the phone began running hot. My father was still at the university at the time and when he got home there was talk of drastic action. The police believed I'd never get out of the New York area, and would be picked up by morning if I hadn't returned voluntarily. My father went on with much raving about punishment and reform schools, but as time passed his anger cooled, and he as well as the rest of the family became worried. It was thought I'd be caught eventually, and then something would have to be done. My prolonged absence became an embarrassment when the cops failed to bring me back. All were aware of likely gossip over an unhappy home situation, but the humiliation had passed and the family adjusted to numbering one less.

Last night's episode had, my brother told me, caused a greater furore than I realized. While I lay drunk in the lounge, there'd been a lengthy emotional discussion on what to do or say when I sobered up. Finally they decided it would be best to act as if I'd returned from a long trip, and not refer too much to the past. There'd be no recrimination, because it would only make me leave again; they would simply try to fit me back into family life. When I told my brother that reference to the past was what I dreaded, and fear of it had prevented earlier return, he said he felt sure our father would stick to his resolve not to resurrect old stuff.

During the first talk in my father's familiar old study I sensed that he was holding a lot back, though the only matter discussed was a plan for my future. He thought my education could be picked up, and I couldn't find a way to say that things weren't so simple. Trying not to provoke a scene, I hesitated to remind him that I had no base from which to start building. It was a touchy interview, and I had to be evasive rather than say I didn't consider myself university material, and in any case I was too restless to settle down into his plan. That talk was the first of several, leading to a final blow-up and rehashing of my past in one of those oldtime emotional uproars.

It didn't take my brother too long to get around to admitting my return had upset family life. One evening in a bar he suggested it mightn't be a bad idea if I were to take another long trip. Building up to what was really on his mind, he said that home life had been pleasantly stable after the shock of my departure, so it might be better if I were to go and allow things to return to normal. No sooner had I agreed with him than he spelt out what had obviously troubled him since the night of my return. Putting it very simply, my brother said that there wasn't enough money for two of us at university. I knew that this was not true, and when he got me to promise never to relate a word of this discussion to others, I realized that what I'd believed about him for years was correct. He'd always shown an abnormally close attachment to our mother and enjoyed the position of number one son. Obviously he now felt threatened. Though he was the only one I could talk to, I had no illusions about his real feelings. He could be interested in me to the point of wanting to know details of some of my far-out experiences, but given the right situation I suspected he'd still show me up badly in front of the others. His admission that he'd sold my things when he'd needed money didn't even annoy me.

But since I was going, and posed no threat to his pre-eminence in the family, my brother and I got along better than ever before. He even introduced me to the sister of one of his close friends, who had something going with our sister; this was frowned on by parents on both sides because of the Christian-Jewish factor.

In no time the sister and I were hitting it off well, on the basis

59

that our friendship was sex and nothing else. Our venue for love-making was her brother's accountancy office at night after he'd gone home. Though my brother told me he'd never screwed her because she was too fat, their conversation together was uninhibited to the extent that anything I offered to do might be reported back. As I'd heard my brother refer to muffdiving as disgusting and perverted, I didn't want him to know that I was an expert in that field. When my brother pumped me for details, I made the mistake of telling him that I'd been stimulated orally and omitted to say that my own particular desires had been frustrated, because for some perverse reason the girl would not let me go downstairs for lunch. My assumption that this would not be discussed in other quarters proved false, in a way to cost me for ever the friendship of that plump Jewish girl. I saw her last in the midst of a hysterical, miserable bust-up with charge and counter-charge, including the nature of our affair, between the two families over the impending marriage of my sister and her brother. The marriage did not take place, but later I heard my sister did marry into another Jewish family.

Not long after that, there occurred the emotional scene that speeded my departure. Late at night, after experiencing a breach of my father's no-recrimination vow, I informed my brother that I'd depart in the morning. Next morning I carried my suitcase, unseen, out of the house and headed for Chicago in the old car I'd bought a few days before. I left my brother to tell the rest I'd gone someplace where I wouldn't be constantly reminded of my failings. Out of it all, I had learnt that the personality clash between my father and me could never be resolved.

At Chicago I planned to pick up some hoops and blocks for sale on the way to California, but coaxing the car across Indiana I realized it wasn't going much farther. With water by the bucketful and plenty of oil I managed to roll the heap into Chicago, where it was dumped with a dealer. My finances would have run to another car, but my urge to get to San Francisco fast found me on the tender of a passenger train pulling out of Chicago's Northwestern Station.

Next morning I was in Omaha, but only long enough to catch, on the fly before it could pick up too much speed, a fast westbound Union Pacific freight train. That got me to Ogden, and a connection with the Southern Pacific. Since a freight train seemed a hell of a way to complete the last miles of a trip that had taken me right round the world, I got on behind the engine of a passenger train at Sacramento.

It was more obvious in San Francisco than in New York that there was truth in what I'd read in South-east Asia about employment possibilities. Of more immediate need was the big woman with whom I'd been going before starting out across the Pacific. Wanting company such as hers to offset what I'd experienced with my family, I hurried to where she'd lived, only to learn that she had departed for parts unknown.

With a little effort I managed to get a job as a news agent on the Santa Fé railway. For this I needed a life history that could only be a work of fiction, so I had to create a suitable background. Since lengthy periods out of work disqualified applicants for employment by the Fred Harvey Company, which ran the dining cars and news service on the Santa Fé, I never admitted to such a state. Since money would be handled during my runs along the Santa Fé, these details had to be recorded on a form for some bonding company. The job involved no more than going up and down the aisles of trains hawking a range of stuff supplied by the company, but for this they insisted on a bond. During a twelve-hour run to Barstow, on the southern California desert, quite a few dollars would be collected. After an overnight layover another train would be worked back to Oakland, where the take for the round trip, less a generous commission, was handed in at the Santa Fé Terminal. For the first couple of weeks I worried over whether my bond application would be approved by the head office in Chicago. What the job paid depended on how hard an agent was willing to hustle at selling magazines, soft drinks and endless other items. As soon as I'd worked long enough to think my bond application might have gone through, I began learning to fly. Through the tunnel from Oakland to Alameda was a small field impressively named San Francisco Bay Aerodrome, and from there I did my first flight sitting beside an instructor.

In a two-seater Luscombe I was whipped down the runway into the air, and right away I thought I'd never be a pilot. Facing me was a set of controls I didn't dare touch because the instructor hadn't told me to, and also they looked frightening. Over San

Francisco Bay I was ordered to put my feet on the rudder pedals and take hold of the stick. At a thousand feet things outside weren't moving so fast, and the controls seemed to be objects I could touch without bringing the airplane to a sudden end. What appeared awesome was the way the instructor achieved his aims with only slight movements of his hands and feet. I'd read enough to know which way stick and rudder were moved for certain effects, but in trying to deal with them my reading didn't seem to relate to doing. To prevent the stick getting away from me, I had a grip on it more suited to boarding a freight train. I wasn't even controlling the airplane yet, because the instructor had told me only to follow his movements. A resounding hand-slap against his stick travelled down it and up mine, making the airplane roll in a frightening way; then he shouted at me to relax my grip, for Christ's sake! Airplanes required a sensitive touch, he said, and I was hanging on as if this were a ten-ton truck. When I relaxed and followed him through a few medium turns, the instructor explained that I'd have to get used to flying with my left hand on the stick. When I began doing take-offs and landings, my right would be needed for the throttle.

Casual mention of landings and take-offs as things I'd be doing came as a shock after such a short time in the air. I quickly found that even simple turns required co-ordination, with many movements having to be done simultaneously. The airplane could be manhandled from one heading to another with experimental stick and rudder pressures, but the result wasn't quite what the man wanted; he liked the little black ball in its curved glass tube to stay in the middle right through the turn, and also expected these changes in heading to be accomplished without gain or loss of altitude.

An hour of instruction had me thinking I might learn to fly after all, but then it was time to land. This I was to watch closely without touching anything. The way the instructor levelled off just above the ground, then eased his stick back to put the wheels in contact at exactly the right instant, did not appear to be easy. Taxiing toward the hangar I had the feeling I could become a reasonably good pilot, provided somebody else came along to do the take-offs and landings. Then I was out of the airplane, listening to the instructor explaining much that didn't seem possible to grasp all at once. When he said I'd be capable of learning to fly, I believed him.

Before my next flying period I did a run or two on the Santa Fé. This was an era when trains were still pulled by steam locomotives and carried passengers. For an agent who'd walk swiftly along the aisles and not gaze at the scenery, there were good commissions. From the start, my trains were worked for all they were worth. Besides scoring the highest sales in my first month, I got a kick out of going through the cars shouting whatever nonsense would make the passengers buy. Because there was a limit to what a trainload of people would buy, I had to reach my position as top salesman by other means. Instead of sticking to my own territory, I'd do a sneak run through another train at Barstow. My train arrived there late at night, and during the twenty minutes it took to couple its cars onto a much longer Los Angeles to Chicago express I'd do my unofficial work. Realizing that the agent on the other train went to bed earlier, when the lights were switched off, I snapped up the opportunity to work off extra stock. Turning on the lights in each car on my way through, I loudly announced my wares to the half-awake passengers, adding that because stocks were getting low this would be the last call this night. As the passengers wondered if there'd be much left next day, they bought up big. The first time that was done I worked off so much stock that there wasn't nearly enough left for the return trip to Oakland.

In those first weeks on the Santa Fé I acquired a car, an apartment where I could take anyone without question, enough photographic equipment to begin learning the other subject in which I was interested—and my flying showed signs of improvement. I had no illusions that my job was more than crude hawking, or that it called for intelligence beyond low-level wit, but it was serving a purpose. It brought in more money by legitimate means than I'd have dreamt possible, and there were plenty of free days for the pursuit of my "higher studies". At long last I felt I'd really come in off the road.

Now that I was settled to where life could be planned more than a week in advance, there appeared the ugly cloud of "Selective Service". To me that term was a mealy-mouthed government way of saying "draft", and my reaction was less than enthusiastic. From what I'd read of the First World War and the following years of mass unemployment, a replay had little appeal. The only hopeful thing about Selective Service was that, if I could fly, I might enter as an officer and gentleman. Being the non-violent type, I had no desire to take the controls of a fighter, to shoot down other aircraft or to play cowboy in the sky for whatever number of minutes was the life expectancy of a fighter pilot. There would be slow aircraft used and so, still liking the thought of being in the air, I decided to concentrate on learning to fly the sort of little airplane I might be able to manage.

My second time up in the air the ball stayed closer to the centre, and back pressure on a less tightly gripped stick aided me in a turn of sorts. Stalling the airplane was a strange sensation when demonstrated by the instructor, and its initial juddering effect was startling. Stalls were never to be done at low level, the instructor explained, because they usually ended in violent contact with the ground. To show me what a stall could develop into he eased off power, brought the stick back and applied full left rudder. Instantly the airplane went into a spin toward the ground, with the landscape in front turning at a dizzy rate. This left me helpless, weightless and terrified, until the instructor did things to get us out of our spin. Afterwards he explained about stopping the spin by using opposite rudder with stick a little bit forward, and said I'd have to learn to do this before going solo.

More trips on the Santa Fé and additional periods in the air led to the day I was fired. Word came from the bonding company after all those weeks that my employment record wasn't satisfactory, and I must be dismissed immediately. Although I was something of a white-haired boy with the terminal manager, he had no choice. There existed an agreement between the fidelity people and the Fred Harvey Company covering money-handling employees and there was no appeal. As a result I vowed to screw a bonding company, if ever the chance came my way. Because the manager liked me and thought I got a raw deal, he helped me to a more lucrative job on the rival Southern Pacific Railroad. That line was putting on agents without bond requirement, he said, and he'd personally recommend me to their terminal man.

That same night I was working a train to Portland. The Southern Pacific was a fast hustle, carrying greater numbers of passengers to be treated as common herd. Rather than have its agents wear uniforms that might tempt them to tone down their

64

pitch, the Southern Pacific supplied half a dozen white jackets at the start of each trip; white cap with dark trousers completed the outfit, and at the end of the run they didn't mind how filthy things were, as long as the sales sheet made good reading. I found that on a run to Portland or Los Angeles I could generally coax enough unrecorded coffee from the dining-car crew to pay for an hour's flying instruction.

The Southern Pacific gave me my first contact with the penitentiary system. Local jails were familiar places, but the prison car coupled onto the night train out of Los Angeles every Friday for the run to San Quentin was a frightening object. Because of its law-enforcement methods in those times Los Angeles was a dangerous place for anyone knocking around, and the prison car was a reminder. That city was famous for its hanging judges, its police who'd fake evidence against anybody who was nobody, and its elderly juries notorious for paying little attention to defence-lawyer talk. Not long before my first encounter with the prison car, the Los Angeles district attorney proudly announced that he jailed more people per capita than his counterpart in more easygoing San Francisco. Anyone from out of town and not well off was fair game for the police, especially in the railroad end of town, so in my layovers between trains I never felt easy. To make their quotas the cops could use any one of several dozen kinds of vagrancy charge. Even having a job was no guarantee of immunity. Several times I was stopped in the streets and saved by my railroad-employee identification. But it was always made clear that one word out of place was good for a missed train and night in jail.

On my first trip with the prison car I assumed that I wouldn't be allowed near it, until told by the conductor to see if the prisoners wanted anything. A bull-necked guard unlocked the door, and walking to the front I turned to face the twenty or so men the Los Angeles courts had sent to the penitentiary in a week. Handcuffed to each other were people such as myself, and it just wasn't possible to put across a sales pitch. Where these men were going was for years, and I felt a deep loathing for the guards who seemed to be enjoying their train ride. The few prisoners who obviously had money paid for their purchases, and the others were told that theirs were on the house and I got out of that car quickly. For the remainder of the run I thought of people such as myself guarded in a barred railroad car, and wondered if this was the sort of institution the government was telling the public it must fight to preserve.

One result of my new off-the-road life was a decision to normalize further by taking an interest in women nearer my own age. I met a nice one on a train coming back from Los Angeles, and I took her out three or four times before she'd come to my apartment. Going with a respectable girl was a new experience, though the shock was tempered by a plump forty-five-year-old waitress I had tucked away in the background. Had I not started to like the girl, and suddenly developed a conscience, I could have gone on enjoying her company. Our love-making amounted to seeing how the other half lived, though the waitress was always available for something more imaginative. To that girl, our going together was meant to lead to something permanent, so I had to think of my own limitations. She would have wanted a conventional life with kids and all, but nothing in my background made me want to indulge in reproduction. I had little choice but to bring the association to an end. In future I would stick to women who'd accept me without change. But at present I had the problem of extricating myself from a situation that could only hurt someone I liked. First I told the girl I'd be in the army in a couple of weeks and then admitted that the sort of family life to which most people aspire would bore me to death. The last was said in a fit of annoyance at my inability to come up with something less blunt. I saw her a couple of times before the affair phased itself out.

That ended all thoughts of women my own age, so when I met the middle-aged aunt of another student at the flying school, nature took its course. From then on I had no intention of worrying about whether things were normal. When our meeting took place I'd reached the point where I could actually land the airplane, or was pretty certain I could. Spin recovery had been gone through enough times for me to lose my fear; also take-offs and landings were practised by the hour. Taking-off seemed easy after I'd done it a few times, but landing was a different proposition. Levelling off at the right height and maintaining that while the stick was eased back to stall the airplane onto the ground on three points was tricky. With patient instruction my landings improved to where they didn't quite so much resemble semi-controlled crashes. Photography was less of a strain; instead of spectacularly embarrassing failures, such as bouncing along the runway in a manner to let all know I couldn't fly an airplane, my darkroom mistakes never had to see the light of day.

My meeting with the student pilot's aunt was the result of going with him to a café. When we met I had the feeling it was going to be interesting. She was fortyish and well built and the look she gave me suggested that we were both thinking the same thing. When my friend went for a leak, the woman gave me the all-clear to drop around. From that visit a red-hot affair developed, and her only concern was that she didn't want her nephew to suspect. Somehow he found out, and from then on he wouldn't talk to me when we met at the flying school.

While that freeze was on, I did my first solo flight, as the final circuit in an hour of practice.

My only warning was when the instructor got out and shut the door behind him. With the airplane pointing down the runway, there was no time to think about whether I was capable of doing what the man wanted. Take-off wasn't much worry because I was busy, but on the climb to cruising height I had time to realize that the airplane had to be put back onto the ground without help. On the downwind leg I felt all alone in the world, until it was time to turn base and start easing off power. Concentrating on doing things exactly as I did when the instructor was in the other seat, I still had the feeling that the airplane rather than I was in charge. With proper coaxing, I hoped it might be got onto the runway. My only consolation was that if this approach didn't seem right, I could go around and try again.

At three hundred feet the beginning of the runway was too far ahead, so power had to be used whether the instructor liked it or not. To him, a proper landing was one so well judged that cutting power at a thousand feet turning base, and trimming for best glide angle, would position the airplane for touchdown just past the start of the runway. That wasn't quite the way I was doing this one. Since I let myself get low, and glides can't be stretched without disastrous results, I had to do what the instructor didn't like and apply power. Then the airplane passed over the beginning of the field, and suddenly I felt as if I had it under control. At what seemed the right height I levelled off, trying to hold it exactly there until flying speed was lost. My landing became two landings when the wheels touched before stalling, and I overreacted. The airplane went a couple of feet into the air before settling on the ground and staying there. No rude remarks were made about the quality of my landing, though the instructor did say he expected as much when I told him about using power on approach.

As student pilots completing first solos are prone to the dangerous thought that they know how to fly, those in charge have rules for protecting them against themselves. My shaky circuit was the end of flying for that day, and for two more because I was going out on a train that night. The instructor's parting remark was that with the relatively unimportant business of first solo out of the way, he'd now try to teach me how to fly.

In the following weeks I got some idea of what my instructor had in mind. There were more solo circuits, but the point the man was trying to make was that flying involved a lot more than just getting an airplane off the ground and back on again. With passing time, I realized how right he was. Cross-wind landings had to be learned, and the instructor assumed that at some time I might want to fly to distant places. With that in mind he insisted that I become able to map-read, use the compass and calculate wind effect. On the less serious side there were solo flights over San Francisco that were sheer pleasure. At the legal minimum of fifteen hundred feet that city was so spectacular that I wondered if it mightn't be possible to photograph what I viewed through the airplane's open window. Most enjoyable was the effect from lower down, though there was also something about flying at eight or nine thousand feet with the cabin of the airplane seeming remote and detached from all below. At low-level, buildings and bridges seemed to reach a long way up to where I circled, causing an exhilaration I'd never known before.

Dodging the draft by joining the War Effort   a
paid holiday in wartime London   forgery as a
future   the life of an LA taxi pimp   the wildcat
bus business.

MERRY ENGLAND

Several fellow agents had already been pulled into the army, and
from a happy individual at the draft board I learned that my call
wouldn't be too long in coming. Each run I thought of as possibly
my last, though weeks went by with no order to report. Finally I
managed to pass my private pilot test. Just before that I had a
real fright in the air, but didn't report it to the instructor.

This happened over San Francisco Bay, when I was paying
more attention to the scenery than my flying, and luck prevented
a mid-air collision. The United DC3 would have appeared
small in the distance had I been looking where I was going
instead of out the side window. Almost too late I saw the aircraft.
It was big and scary as it flashed past directly ahead of me. For a
horrifying instant it seemed to be frozen in one position. I made a
violent turn left as the monster vanished from sight—and waited
for the scare to wear off.

Within days of passing my licence test I walked into an army
office to enquire about becoming an officer and gentleman. Half
an hour later I was out in the street smarting from the knowledge
that I'd never be accepted as a trainee pilot; and if I didn't like
the idea of being a private, I was in for five years' jail for draft
dodging. I'd done fine up to a point. Wearing a good suit and
having a private-pilot training seemed to be getting results—
until the interviewing officer began asking all the wrong
questions. University requirements might be waived since I
could fly, but the officer assumed I had completed high school; I
realized evidence of scholastic achievement would be required,
so I admitted that economic circumstances had forced me to drop

out before graduation. Something the officer said about less qualified pilots for light airplanes sounded right up my alley.

Next came the question I dreaded. Before asking if I'd ever been in trouble, the man said that all applicants were checked by the F.B.I. and those with records of more serious offences than traffic breaches were unacceptable. It was clear which way this was headed, so I told all. Admitting to twenty or thirty arrests in different parts of the country, I flippantly said that I hadn't bothered to keep count of the exact number. To a professional officer and gentleman my admission was outrageous, so I was treated in a military manner. Telling me that the army was quite capable of training from scratch the people it wanted, the man worked himself up to where he was almost shouting, and others were turning to look. They wanted men of good character, the man barked, not jailbirds who'd somehow learned to fly.

My first reaction was resentment against stupid rules disqualifying someone who'd seen the inside of a few jails. Then I became furious at the way the stupid bastard spoke, and thought that life in the army under people like him would be worse than prison. Cooling down, I thought it might be possible to stave off military life by getting into something the "Selective Service" would accept as "essential". Trains were getting crowded and there'd be a fortune in commissions if I could last the distance, but I figured that the selective officials wouldn't see the job in the same light.

It was during this period, sweating out the draft, that I made my first crude attempts at aerial photography. I tried a few shots over San Francisco, knowing full well that I'd need a lot more skill at flying and camera work before much could be accomplished. What showed up in the darkroom only confirmed that I had a lot to learn. The buildings in downtown San Francisco that had looked so crisp from the air were blurry on film. The next time I managed a couple of negatives that stood some enlargement.

During a layover in Los Angeles I saw a newspaper article that suggested something much better than the army. The British were recruiting tradesmen in America for service in England, and those signing up would get draft deferment. Speeding me to the address given was mention of watch-repairing, among other acceptable qualifications. I hoped my self-acquired knowledge of that basically simple craft might be just enough to get me past any test. At the office, in a second-rate building, I was greeted by a man so enthusiastic that he would have signed me up on the spot had rules permitted. When I explained about living in Oakland, the recruiter gave me an address in that city and said they'd arrange a qualification test. It was very carefully explained that while those recruited would be under military control, they'd remain civilians. Conditions of service sounded all right, and at least I'd be in England where things were happening, instead of buried in some grim southern U.S. army camp. Members of the Civilian Technical Corps received six pounds a week, and were provided with distinctive uniforms.

The trade test was merely a simple paper on mechanics, with questions suggesting their own answers. Three days later it was with great relief that I took my acceptance notice along to the draft board. I was now on standby to await transport to England. After a string of runs to Los Angeles I began thinking about the interesting possibility of the Civilian Technical Corps having forgotten me, while at the same time being legal with the draft board. An end was soon put to that thought when a telegram instructed me to pick up a ticket for Montreal. As a rest from the long train ride two lazy weeks were spent in Montreal, in a big old mansion overlooking the city. A daily trickle of new arrivals filled the place, and then all were loaded onto a train for the Canadian seaport of Halifax. A military transit camp in that depressing town was jammed with people of different services awaiting shipment across the Atlantic. The camp officials, at a loss to occupy a mob of uniformed civilians, decided to march them to the rifle range and teach them to hit a target. It was fun deciding who was best with the Lee Enfield rifle, but then came Sunday and the British "church parade". Free choice extended only as far as deciding whether to fall in with the Catholics or Protestants, and one hundred per cent attendance was assured by an army sergeant marching along with each group. This put the finishing touches to any hope we had of enjoying some kind of special status.

Finally the Corps was marched aboard the nearly new passenger ship *Andes*, and allotted fairly good cabins. When we reached England, in September 1941, nobody seemed to know what to do with us. Lend Lease was such a big thing then, it seemed possible that the Civilian Technical Corps was merely something the English had gratefully to accept. We were billeted comfortably in the south coast resort town of Bournemouth, and would probably have been forgotten altogether if somebody hadn't been there to see we were fed and paid. Drinking and whoring became the main preoccupation for most of our oddly assorted bunch, with London as the focal point. This was the period after the big blitz, when England was fairly quiet. Though London was badly battered, it offered endless opportunity; for those who like the hard stuff there were tolerant police and plenty of pubs, and for womanizing the capital was the ultimate. Very soon most of us forgot why we were in England. Bournemouth was just a place to go when money was running short. There was still no threat of military discipline, but occasionally the head man blustered a bit and demanded that some particular absence be explained. All of this was like water off a duck's back, once we'd collected our pay and were safely on the train to London.

The time everybody was present without the inducement of money was the occasion of the royal inspection. Saying he'd like to be able to present the entire Corps for inspection by some very important people, the chief asked if all would defer their trips. Word soon got around about who was coming, though the group was only told that various military units around Bournemouth would be inspected.

Looking military in their R.A.F.-style uniforms, everybody stood neatly to attention in a large open courtyard. Then a huge old-fashioned Daimler with gleaming brass fittings pulled to a stop in front of a group of officials. Out stepped King George and Queen Elizabeth, and after a few words between their Majesties and the waiting officials there was a sharp command. The order stiffened any shoulders that had begun to slouch, and brought all eyes forward.

There was obviously a publicity angle in a group of Americans who'd volunteered to do something or other for England while the U.S. was still neutral, so the inspection was photographed by a newsreel outfit. While their camera recorded the event, the King and Queen walked slowly past the first of the two ranks comprising the Civilian Technical Corps. As though it were impromptu, their Majesties paused to exchange a few words with one of the better-type technicians; we had been carefully briefed before. When the royal car departed, the man in charge complimented the group on its smart appearance—and all were free to go about their usual business.

Then Pearl Harbour happened, between pay days, when most of us were up in London. Some attempt to round us up and bring us back to Bournemouth was made, but didn't get far, especially when it was rumoured that we'd be drafted into the American forces in England. Like many of the others who needed extra money for London living, I picked up a part-time job, repairing watches in a shop off Oxford Street. The shop had a supply of tools and parts left behind by one of the owners who'd gone to war, so I managed without too much trouble. My working hours were from about ten in the morning to half-way through the afternoon, except on days I put in my regular appearance at Bournemouth.

Instead of remaining for ever in limbo the Civilian Technical Corps was repatriated, in twos and threes, as transport became available. My turn came when I was handed travel orders for Montreal, by way of the night express to Glasgow, local train to Greenock and then a small passenger ship looking like something from the turn of the century. In a slow convoy to Halifax there was nothing more exciting than a great racket one night when the escorting destroyer dropped depth-charges. At Montreal everyone was given a rail-Pullman ticket to wherever they'd signed up.

As required, I informed the draft board of my return from England. With a war on I thought they might be less fussy about pilots, but this time a more sympathetic officer explained that higher authority would consider me a constant conflict-with-the-law type.

So close did the army seem that instead of worrying about a job I resumed my affair with the student pilot's aunt. Then I met somebody from the distant past. When a man spoke to me on Market Street in San Francisco I thought that either he was a queer out for a pick-up, or we might have met briefly someplace. When he gave his name I still wasn't certain, but then he mentioned the high school at East Orange and my running away from home. He was the kid who'd arranged my first whorehouse visit, and soon we were seated in a café having a long talk.

Ed Lanning had also failed to complete high school, and cleared out to go on the road, but he was a couple of years older so

73

there wasn't much fuss. His family were easygoing and placed no great store on formal education, so Lanning never made a definite break. He was welcome home whenever he felt like coming in off the road for a while. To the point of riding freight trains across the country when he first cleared off, and staying at the famous Los Angeles Boys' Home, Lanning's experiences paralleled mine. After leaving the Boys' Home Lanning travelled different paths, beginning with a move into the apartment of a moderately well-off fruit. Before I could make crude remarks about getting his brown stretched, Lanning said he only let the fruit suck him and apply mild flagellation with small whips. Introduced into a prosperous circle of queers, Lanning did the rounds for several months before going back on the road.

When he did go, it was in better style than my departure from Los Angeles on a freight train. In the company of two older fellows who had their own way of making money, Lanning hit the road in a good car. Their way of remaining financial was to use a set of moulds capable of turning out reasonably good silver dollars. Since Lanning had no technical qualification, he had to serve as passer.

Bearing metal was the main ingredient of the coins they cast, in hotel rooms or wherever their work wouldn't be interrupted. Their biggest piece of equipment was a blow-torch arrangement of the kind plumbers use for melting lead on the job. As long as the fire didn't get smelly, they could make a few dollars almost anywhere. It was a fair depression racket, but it was a Federal offence carrying a good, stiff sentence. Lanning functioned well as a passer, but one day he found himself in strife.

The metallurgist of the outfit wanted to improve his alloy, so the coins would give a good ring rather than a dead thunk. A little ground glass in the mixture gave encouraging results, but too much was added to one batch and Lanning had to run for his life when a storekeeper, dropping a dollar into the till, shattered it into little pieces. With the man bellowing in pursuit, Lanning ran around a couple of corners, managed to lose him, warned the others at the hotel, then severed his connection with them. Rather than risk riding out of town in their car, he slipped onto a freight train.

After telling Lanning about my loan applications in the Far East, and other ways of getting by, I said that in my opinion his

74

only smart move in the coin deal was breaking loose. Lanning seemed disappointed over my attitude, so I explained that he had risked a Federal penitentiary sentence for peanuts while my more profitable rackets would never attract more than thirty days.

Mention of Federal jails led to the matter of Selective Service. There was nothing backward about Lanning's admission that he had no urge to die for his country, or to perform lesser labours. After telling about the army's reluctance to accept me as a pilot, I owned up to similar reservations about serving in ways chosen by others.

Rather than dodge the draft, Lanning was keeping ahead of it. In his registration Lanning called himself a travelling salesman, as by coincidence did I, and he remained legal by informing draft boards in different places of his latest "address". At present Lanning worked as a taxi-driver in Los Angeles, but he'd come to San Francisco to register a local address as a move from San Diego. The Los Angeles office wouldn't know he was in their city until he'd registered at a number of other places. Using various friends' addresses, Lanning would be advised of the arrival of anything official. With papers being sent from one office to another, there was some hope that his file might get lost in the confusion and that they'd never catch up to him.

In Lanning's opinion my problem could best be solved by a quick move out of the San Francisco area. He had taken the trouble to learn the workings of the draft system, and thought that the de-activating of my file by going to England could cause some delay in tracing me. Lanning's suggestion was that I register a transfer to San Diego, then come to Los Angeles with him and start driving a taxi. When I told Lanning that I thought Los Angeles was only good for getting arrested, he brought me up to date. All that was in the past, he told me, and the place was now loaded with opportunities for different kinds of hustling. There was nothing about Lanning's appearance to suggest that the two to three hundred dollars a week he claimed to be making wasn't real. Neither was there any reason to think he made that kind of money driving people to their destinations. When it was settled that I'd be a taxi-driver in Los Angeles, Lanning promised to show me the ropes.

Then he told me more about his exploits before becoming a hard-working taxi-driver, including the time he was fired from the Salvation Army. One of his homosexual playmates wangled him a job driving a Sally truck, with the result that Lanning went into the salvage business for himself. The meetings he was forced to attend failed to make him honest, and secondhand dealers rather than the Salvation Army got the best items from his collections. A major who wondered why one of his trucks brought in so little followed it one day, and that was the end of Lanning's "military" career.

Through his association with queers Lanning managed to depart from several cities nicely outfitted with just about everything portable. Instead of leaving behind taken-down homos, he left a trail of merchants lamenting credit losses. After getting a job through one of his better-connected gay friends, Lanning used him as a credit reference, buying and paying off items in two or three stores. With a rating finally established at the local credit bureau, Lanning went like a dose of castor oil through as many stores as possible, before heading out of town.

From San Francisco we drove to San Diego in Lanning's almost new Oldsmobile, and, after registering with the draft board as a transfer, doubled back to Los Angeles. So hard-pressed for drivers was the city's Yellow Cab monopoly that walking in the door was enough to get a job.

I spent a couple of weeks learning my way around the city before switching to Lanning's night shift and the more profitable aspects of taxi-driving. Female companionship ranging from five minutes in the back of a taxi up to all night was the most desirable commodity in Los Angeles. Within the broad limitations of our jobs, Lanning and I helped to overcome a general drought among the teeming numbers of civilian and military men in the downtown streets. Taking sex-starved people to where they needed to go brought riches for the ambitious taxi-driver.

Neither company nor vice squad approved of this activity. The cops could be bought off, but so many from other squads tried to horn in that it wasn't worth while. Like other cities, Los Angeles in wartime was supposed to be closed tighter than a drum. This was to placate religious groups and others who wanted to ensure our boys remained pure before they got their asses shot off, but it made the vice cops meat in a sandwich. Pressure was on them from above to make arrests, while at the same time their appetites

76

for money had to be satisfied, so their actions could be unpredictable. They'd collect plenty from a whore or hustling driver for a while, then set a trap and make an arrest that would stick.

With all the military activity, even an honest police force couldn't have coped, but the Yellow Cab Company would fire drivers who were too obviously hustling. Its meters with their little rolls of paper recording paid mileage, empty driving and so on could be a dead give-away to whether a driver was working or pimping. This led to a conflict of interest because the company wanted money run up on its meters, while the get-rich-quick drivers couldn't afford to waste time running people around the suburbs. Their presence was required around certain downtown corners, and though any pimping driver would gladly have handed in normal takings for a shift, the company still wanted its rolls of paper to read right. The only way of handing in enough money while making the meter read right was to put down the flag leaving the garage, switch on and off constantly to record several trips, and put it on waiting-time even during meal breaks.

A constant threat to business was the passenger who, seeing an empty taxi, jumped in and demanded to be driven somewhere. Having the meter on waiting-time wouldn't discourage those smart enough to know what was going on. Threats to report us to the company often trapped Lanning, myself or other drivers into long profitless trips to outlying suburbs of Los Angeles, until I came up with a solution. Since nobody could demand an already engaged taxi, the easy way out was to hire a "passenger" for the night; Lanning and I were soon driving to the Midnight Mission at the start of our shift, to each "employ" a bum for the night. With a reasonably dressed drifter in the cab, we could sit on any corner and be legal to the moment of making a deal.

There were plenty of girls in the business, but with some judges handing out jail sentences they had to be careful. They set up in twos and threes in apartments for a week or so, let a few trusted taxi-drivers know where they were, then lay back in wait. For their fat commissions, drivers were expected to vet the clients and not land the vice squad on the girls' doorstep. A trick of the vice cops was to follow suspect taxis, so it was always necessary to make sure there was no tail before dropping someone off to get laid. When a doubtful car couldn't be shaken, as occasionally happened, the customer was simply dropped off somewhere without a fare being collected.

For rougher trade there were a couple of drinking joints miles out on Central Avenue, featuring what were euphemistically referred to as "Spanish" girls. Nobody even attempted to get commissions from the various-shaded coloured women passing themselves off as Spanish, who did their screwing in cars parked out of sight. Profit on Central Avenue deals came from as many sex-hungry men as could be crammed into the cab, paying double the fare they'd see on the meter. As the bum hired as a "passenger" couldn't be allowed to occupy a revenue-producing seat on these trips, he was left at the starting-point, to be picked up later.

Very worth while were the girls who wanted to make a fast couple hundred dollars, working on the back seat of the taxi. They'd wait in a hamburger joint until the driver drummed up a full load of seven or eight customers, then service the lot while the cab was parked in an alley. Those girls were rough and tough, and they could polish off a whole cabful with barely a wasted movement. No time for niceties existed in a situation where the driver remained behind the wheel ready to roll at the sight of a police car.

Sex began with the girl lifting her dress while the customer dropped his strides. Then there was rapid insertion, fast pelvic movements to make the john come quickly, and finally a hurried wipe with a towel before taking on the next one. After the third or fourth, the cab was smelly and the seat slippery, but there was no stopping until the last client had been relieved. When her work was finished, the girl was dropped back at the hamburger joint to wash her thighs, douche herself out and wait for more business.

Lanning and I had to make frequent trips to change draft boards, but we didn't expect this method to work much longer. He had an interesting idea about seeing a psychiatrist, after hearing that this kind of doctor could suggest ways of highlighting inadequacies that might result in rejection on the grounds of emotional instability. As Lanning had earlier studied draft-board methods, he now intended to pursue this further.

By this time gas rationing was well established, though any amount was available at a slight premium. Even wildcat buses operating outside the law got all they needed, but a few far-seeing owners converted their vehicles to burn butane gas. Those buses which were mostly eight-seat limousines or station wagons did a lively business transporting servicemen to and from bases far and near. To Lanning and me they were of more than passing interest.

Many of the owner-drivers had been forced out of taxi-driving, before taking up the lucrative wildcat bus business. What cost them their jobs in most cases was activity similar to ours. Working hot as we were, neither regarded our jobs with the Yellow Cab monopoly as more than opportunities to make hay while the sun stayed out. We did not expect it to shine for ever.

Inevitably the ranks of pimping cab-drivers were infiltrated by a member of the vice squad, so a bunch including Lanning and I were fired. By this time petrol rationing was well established and from it grew a lucrative wildcat bus business with eight-seater limousines or station wagons. Lanning and I bought a Cadillac and a huge Lincoln V12 respectively and started hauling illegal passengers. From the first day it was profitable. With a little squeezing we could seat ten passengers plus driver. Civilian seating was restricted to eight because they tended to scream about overcrowding, but on shorter runs with servicemen it was often possible to fit in fourteen. Good-natured cajoling was the way to get those first in the bus to hold still while extra passengers were laid across their laps. With servicemen stuck in tens of thousands at bases hopelessly served by public transport, peak activity was endless.

Wildcat bus fares weren't cheap, but neither were they outrageous on an individual basis; collectively they amounted to a fantastic rate on a full load. Even when the driver was shoe-horning passengers in, as if hoping to pay for his car in one trip, there weren't many complaints. The stock answer to protests at fares or overloading was that these practices were necessary because of frequent fines.

Those Lincolns and Cadillacs were so strongly built that they couldn't be overloaded, and with passengers wherever they'd fit the cars remained manageable on the road. Basic traffic laws were not violated, but the police still posed a threat and survival depended on passenger participation. All were told at the start of a trip that while this form of transport provided a service, and was an example of American free enterprise, it violated city, county, state and Federal law, so precautions would have to be observed.

That speech was rattled off when all fares were safely in my pocket, and the car was rolling. As if it happened nearly every trip, I'd say that when the cops stopped us, everyone must say they were hitch-hikers. Rarely did anything happen, though the big Lincoln jammed full of servicemen stuck out a mile away as a wildcat bus. Often the passengers seemed disappointed when we weren't stopped, and they were cheated out of their chance to thwart the police.

One of the most lucrative runs was Los Angeles to San Diego, with heavy loadings of sailors both ways. Also it was the most dangerous as far as the law was concerned, but rare was the report of a sailor admitting to paying a fare. Occasionally different branches of the law joined forces to war against wildcat buses, and set up road blockades.

My first encounter with such a trap was on a night run to San Diego with fourteen sailors, who'd each paid five dollars. Going into a slight dip in the road north of Oceanside, I was confronted by flashing red lights, too late to do more than slow down from a legal fifty-five miles an hour. Hardly was there time to remind my passengers they were hitch-hikers, when the car doors jerked open and everybody was roughly ordered out. From the diversity of people manning the barricade, and the military way my passengers were lined up by Marine M.Ps under instructions from a snotty young officer, I was sure this would end in a trip to the lock-up.

Half an hour later the Lincoln, full of sailors, was again rolling toward San Diego, and in appreciation of the way they stood up to questioning I offered to buy my passengers a feed at Oceanside. Those sailors were bullied by Marines and questioned by men in plain clothes, but not one cracked. After failing with the sailors, the Marine lieutenant suggested to an officer of the California Highway Patrol that they tear up my draft card, then hand me over to the F.B.I. for not having one. That officer coldly rejected the idea, before leading me aside for private questioning. At the start I sensed the Highway Patrol attitude of not bothering wildcat buses too much as long as they were driven safely. This cop was clearly willing to let me go if I showed enough sense to continue my denials, so I did not disappoint him.

When I was brought back to where the rest were, the Marine

80

officer was complaining that my passengers wouldn't admit anything; the cop interrupted him to say that they might as well let me go. While the sailors shivered in the cold night wind waiting for permission to reboard the bus, a plainclothes man asked me where I got the gas for the trip. I could only insist that to run my huge twelve-cylinder car just this once I'd saved my ration for weeks. Showing impatience with the other members of the law, the highway cop took the line that there was no reason to further delay the bus. On the frequent occasions when our cars passed after that, the officer never failed to give me a friendly wave.

Trouble came again later in a somewhat different form. On a return evening run from San Diego with a light loading of eight sailors, I pulled up at the Marine camp gate to fill up my extra space. The result was a long and noisy highway chase. As the last of four Marines for Los Angeles squeezed aboard, a vehicle with flashing red light shot out the camp gate and was alongside by the time I had the Lincoln rolling. One of two Marine M.Ps in a weapons carrier shouted at me to pull over, while my passengers yelled at me to give them a run for it.

With that encouragement and the thought of going for three hundred dollars in front of a notorious Oceanside judge, I pointed the Lincoln down the highway and poured on the coal. That caused a siren to be turned on, with both cars neck and neck while I tried desperately to prevent the other getting in front. As the siren screamed and the red light blazed into the side of the bus, my passengers urged me in full cry. At the top end of second gear the enemy was not in a position to cut us off. Into high with all the Lincoln's twelve cylinders working hard, we still had the other vehicle alongside. Then oncoming traffic forced it to fall in behind. Clear of traffic, the military car tried again to head us off, but lacked the power. At well over sixty, the M.Ps could only hang behind with their siren blaring, but with the noise of my passengers it didn't come over very loud. More throttle put our pursuers a bit behind, though coming up to San Clemente the bastards were still there. Luckily no other form of law was on the road that night, because I had to barrel through the town like a bat out of hell before they finally dropped off.

Months of wildcat bus operation passed, with the variation of countless trips to San Francisco and a few to New York. The cross-country ones were mixed civilian and military loads willing to pay a good price for a fast trip, rather than fight the airline priority system. For that class of trade, numbers had to be limited to eight.

New York was a quick turn-around to get back to normal business, so a call to my brother on the first trip was my only family contact. What he said about the reaction to my last departure convinced me that fast turn-around was best. Running light to St Louis, I picked up a load of cheap travel-bureau passengers for Los Angeles.

After a Seattle trip Lanning suggested that we do something about the worsening gas situation. His idea, which had already occurred to me, was that we print counterfeit tickets. Ticketless gas was becoming hard to get, since most of the tickets on the market came through ration-office leakages or robberies; with tightening security their price was rising by the day.

Lanning had taken the trouble to learn the inner workings of rationing. Handling procedure began with tickets taken from the public being pasted onto large sheets by the retailer. From him they went to the distributor and then the ration office, where before being destroyed they were credited to their correct accounts. After crediting but before burning was where most leakage occurred, with the tickets being steamed off their sheets. Some had been recycled so many times that they looked like bad fakes.

As an argument for going into the gas-ticket business for a quick killing, Lanning said that neither board switching nor psychiatry would keep us out of the army for ever. Admitting he wouldn't be technically capable, Lanning suggested that I would, and offered to finance the project by doing enough wildcatting for both. Not yet committing myself, I bought books on printing and photo-engraving, for study between trips.

About this time I discovered that a good way to contact the sort of women I liked was through lonely hearts clubs, rather than relying on luck. Young "sailor gash" abounded in Los Angeles, but older women who weren't whores or barflies weren't always easy to meet when I was on the road so much.

Before joining the club with the biggest ad., I had an idea these places might be top-heavy with older women. I was not disappointed. Writing my details on a card, the woman running the club broke some news in a way she obviously hoped wouldn't cause me to walk out without joining. She explained that it might take time, because women in my age-group were in short supply.

The woman's tune changed when I said I liked them plump and around forty, so suddenly the club could do a lot right now. No longer justifying the fee, she told me how welcome someone with my tastes was. Her files were loaded with my kind of women, who could usually be referred only to men who were "personality defectives". While I waited, the woman culled a stack of cards for a collection of about twenty names with phone numbers and addresses. Reading descriptions together with her assessment notes, the woman wrote only names I thought interesting. Handing me the list, she said that if what I wanted wasn't among this lot there were plenty more.

I regretted not having joined one of these clubs before, because from the start the arrangement worked. All I had to do was to call and introduce myself as a fellow club member. From then on, it was only a matter of sorting out such things as age difference, and if a woman's way of talking caused me to visualize myself sliding in, I'd set up a meeting. Quickly I learned to separate wheat from chaff over the phone and not waste time on fruitless meetings.

I soon found out that these clubs had their share of mental cases. One was a rather pleasant woman who willingly took me to bed, then complained to the club that she'd practically been raped. When I told the club woman what really happened, she said that, if in doubt, I should go easy.

Most of the women I met were divorcees or widows, often with places of their own where little affairs could ripen. For ones not living alone but worth following up, there was the apartment that Lanning and I shared. In the atmosphere of prevailing transience it seemed natural to be in and out of these affairs with no emotional involvement. Most club women lacked personality, but there was always the hope of striking a really good one, while meantime there were many and varied nights in bed.

6

Psychiatry as a secret weapon   forgery as a
nice steady job   do I advocate Communism for
America?   no homos in the army   the
psychiatric ward at last and assisted-passage
escape.

MR LONELY HEARTS

Half-way through my second lonely hearts club list Lanning
developed the draft horrors and saw a psychiatrist. He confessed
that his feelings of inadequacy caused him to fear relationships
with people in military service. Empathy was established when
the doctor revealed it had been his practice to reject potential
misfits when he worked at the induction centre. I guessed that
such an advanced rejection policy probably accounted for the
doctor's removal from that position. Lanning was advised to
speak to the psychiatrist at the induction centre about his difficulties with group situations, and hope for the best. If he landed
in the army there'd be something on the record, which could
result in the desired psychiatric discharge in case of trouble. With
the thought of establishing a prior psychiatric record I visited the
same doctor and learned that either I told a better story or really
was in worse shape than Lanning. Long before my hour ended,
the therapist said that I must stay out of the service. After hearing
more about family troubles, running away, my liking for older
women and so on, he suggested that I might benefit from
therapy. He advised me to speak to the induction psychiatrist and
tell the whole story. If the army man was half-way reasonable,
I'd be rejected.

Returning from a San Francisco trip I found Lanning highly
excited, because he had a firm order for five thousand dollars'
worth of gas tickets from a former street ticket supplier, now
turned wholesaler. We'd have to produce a hundred and fifty
thousand gallons for the first order, and the same for the second if

the product was of good quality. The tickets would be used by our customer in such a way that the Office of Price Administration would routinely destroy them as used and genuine, while his connection in the O.P.A. would steam the actual genuine ones off the sheets on which they were pasted, for him to peddle to the public. Spurred on by success, Lanning aroused the interest of some used car dealers we knew. For the gallonage we intended to produce, it seemed best to have movable plant that could be set up for short periods in places rented for the purpose, leaving our apartment cool if things went wrong; though it could be used for the preliminary job of making the plates.

Our first acquisition was a press with a chase only big enough to print twenty tickets each stroke. So small was that well-made little platen press that it could be packed into a suitcase. Next came zinc plates, nitric acid for etching, bichromated solution for plate sensitizing, an old five-by-seven camera and other items detailed in my book on photo-engraving. Photographic, printing and art material stores provided all without question.

With my limited knowledge I was attempting a crude photo-engraving job and frightened it might be just that. Fortunately gas tickets bore no intricate design, as did money, so, following book instructions and hints, I finally produced a set of quite good plates. There was some trial and error in photographing the original design and getting it onto metal. Suitable high-contrast negatives had to be made from retouched enlargements of tickets, which was easy enough, but I struck trouble with the background. For some perverse reason the government printed that in pale blue against the grey of the paper. This was difficult to photograph and enlarge with any usable contrast, so in the end I had to do some freehand artwork.

Plates were easy to make once everything else was done. Zinc coated with bichromated fish-glue was exposed to sunlight through my negatives, developed in water to remove non-light-hardened emulsion, and then baked to further harden the acid-resisting enamel over the printing portions. Etching caused a little trouble because of nitric acid's tendency to undercut the image. When I learned to do it in steps, using powdered resin and further applications of heat, that final stage of preparation became simple.

Apart from providing moral support with tales of the fabulous sales he'd make, it was Lanning's job to find paper such as that used by the government. He was present during the first part of the test of my newly made plates, and, using his more promising paper samples and the carefully mixed blue for the background, we printed a number of sheets. Each grouping of twenty tickets looked as if it should pass anywhere—except for lack of perforation. Our book on printing obligingly outlined a simple method of doing this essential job in a platen press. Its writers advised lengths of steel printers' rule sharpened to a knife-edge, notched with a file and finally locked up in a chase with suitable spacing. Perforating was done by "printing" the sheets with the ink rollers removed, so they wouldn't be cut to pieces. Out of all paper samples procured by Lanning we decided to use a stationery named Crillon Grey. It seemed at first that, with a war on, it might be difficult to get all we wanted, but, before going to press in a newly rented apartment, Lanning quietly bought enough paper for three hundred thousand gallons. ("Going to press" was an expression Lanning and I worked to death, after hearing Walter Winchell use it on his Sunday-night broadcasts.)

With everything incriminating removed from our own apartment, we went into the temporary quarters arranged with so much difficulty by Lanning. Housing was very short in Los Angeles, so a premium had to be paid even for short-time use of a place that could only be classed as a dump. Our entire printing outfit was streamlined to fit into a single suitcase. Into that case went everything necessary to start production at short notice, even if it had to be done in a hotel or motel room. Topped off by a radio for killing sound whenever we might start a run, there was the press together with stacks of paper, inks, perforating blades and all ancillary equipment. Platemaking items and other things not needed for a press-run went into the safe house of a friend.

The first hour of printing barely made a dent in our mountain of cut paper. Gathering speed we settled down to a rate of six hundred prints an hour, but as each little sheet of paper had to go through the press four times there was a long job ahead. Half an hour of feeding sheets, operating the printing handle and watching the ink didn't run light or heavy was the most either could stand without a rest period, so we took turns at it. The one not printing got his rest spreading sheets for air drying and making endless pots of coffee. When all the backgrounds were

86

printed and the press loaded with black ink, we saw real results. Working late into the night, with the radio on to kill clicking sounds, we finished the main black printing at the end of the fourth day. All that paper now had to go through two more times, to give both horizontal and vertical perforation. As soon as the second perforation run was started, it was possible to tear a few tickets from their surrounds, and compare them, complete with serrated edges, with the official product. We agreed that whoever designed the tickets had done an appalling job, but what did please us was that both kinds looked the same. Our delight was tempered by the realization that tearing the half-inch border from four sides of five thousand sheets of tickets would be one hell of a job.

In a sudden inspiration Lanning and I got the idea of letting our customer perform this tedious task. We could put it to the buyer that borders had been deliberately left on to prove that our tickets were genuine forgeries, and not hot loot from some ration-office robbery. When we showed him how easily our perforations tore, he probably wouldn't worry about having to rim all those sheets, until he got home and tried a few.

Lanning met our customer in a coffee shop, handed him an unrimmed sheet for inspection, and the man was happy with quality. Since the fellow was a known black-market operator, we didn't want to conclude the sale without being certain that he wasn't followed by Office of Price Administration investigators. Before taking him by a roundabout route to a drive-in café where I waited with the goods, Lanning explained that all the tickets were in sheet form as per sample. Then to avoid an in-depth discussion of rimming he casually mentioned that to compensate for the slight inconvenience, we were throwing in a couple thousand free gallons.

Two days later Lanning spoke to our client, expecting to hear a woeful tale of less than half the tickets being done. Instead of strong remarks about not falling for that again, the fellow amazed Lanning with a story of how the work was completed in one evening. The buyer told how he and his wife organized a rimming party. Arriving home, he tried a few tickets, realized that single-handed it would take for ever, then put his wife to work until both decided it was too tedious a job. The wife suggested inviting a few trusted friends, feeding them and providing drinks, and then putting them to work. With three other couples the rimming party was a great success, continuing for hours after the last of the tickets had been freed of their borders. This social event brought the host's assurance of future business.

As expected, our car-dealer connections were becoming mercilessly demanding on price, so, in a Hollywood motel, we ran our ticket reserves to four hundred thousand gallons. Lanning and I talked about this profitable business probably being spoilt before long by some draft board, and at one stage talked ourselves into going into smoke. Realizing that the F.B.I. would be on our trail for draft evasion, we decided it might be safer to comply with Selective Service orders.

For security reasons one or the other always slept in the work flat, and nobody was ever brought there or told of its existence. On alternate nights each had sole use of our living apartment. This gave Lanning an open go with the younger women he seemed to favour. On the nights he minded the shop, I was free to sleep with whichever lonely-hearts friend was in favour. With such a good place to work, we launched an ambitious production program of both A and C series tickets. Passenger hauling was suspended, and resumed as a cover when stocks were built up to where we could have a run of sales without having to go to press at short notice.

It happened on a rest day, when I was entertaining a plump lady from the lonely hearts club. There could be no mistaking the identity of two plainclothes men wearing hats to whom I opened the apartment door in response to an insistent ring. All I could think, while owning up to being the person asked for, was that there wasn't anything incriminating in the place, and I probably needed a lawyer. When the man showed his F.B.I. card, I hoped this might only be a routine check-up. Very politely the special agent asked if I could spare a little time for discussion. Trying not to show relief I told the agents they'd be welcome to come in, but they declined the invitation and suggested I drop round to their offices in a couple of hours' time. I tried desperately to think of a reason other than draft for the F.B.I. wanting to see me on a drop-in-and-chat basis. In no way could it relate to fake gas tickets, because their approach would have given me time to destroy evidence.

Without contacting Lanning, who was at our operational apartment, I went to the F.B.I. office. The two agents proceeded to lead me through the itinerary of my Far Eastern travels. Their questioning about people I knew in Shanghai, Hong Kong, Calcutta and Rangoon alarmed me. It would seem I was politically suspect. Quite truthfully I explained that my contacts in the East had been extremely casual, but they then diverted their curiosity to connections I might have in other countries. People and places as such were not their concern, they explained, but political belief in the context of subversive activity was. They asked me first for my views on Fascism, then on Communism. I felt safe in saying that no form of extremism had the slightest appeal. I asked their reason for all this, and was informed there'd been a report which they had to check out. Now they were interested in my views on one of America's allies, Russia. I explained my opinion of Russia's government by saying that it might be all right for a country with its historical background, but that answer meant very little to them. This was followed by direct questions. Did I belong to any organization, attend meetings, advocate Communism as a form of government for America? Somehow I felt a straight answer would lack conviction, so I just started talking my head off until I ran out of words. I pointed out that anyone as keen on travel as I was would hardly favour a government that might curtail it. I went on a lot about freedom, until I realized it might give the impression I wasn't overly keen to get into the army either. Parting advice was that I keep in touch with my draft board. Everything I told those F.B.I. men about my belief in the American system was true, though I hoped they'd never learn just how liberal was my interpretation of "free enterprise". Whatever led them to my doorstep could only remain a mystery I'd never solve. For the sake of his nerves, I did not intend to mention this to Lanning.

Switching boards did at long last let me down, and I was landed with a notice to report for induction. On a dreary Monday morning I was one of several hundred who presented themselves at the induction centre in Los Angeles's grimy old Pacific Electric Building. From the start of processing it was obvious that the military doctors took little delight in rejecting people. Half-way through I began to wonder if there even was a psychiatrist in the place. After more pokings and probings I was certain that in the interest of efficiency the army had dispensed with such fripperies, or else this happened to be the man's day off. The doctors worked like assembly-line inspectors not paid to find fault, and the only people enjoying this were the soldiers in charge of herding and mustering.

At the end of the line a doctor sat behind a table stacked with papers—and two rubber stamps on it. It seemed that none of the men filing past was invited to sit down on the chair in front of him. Rubber-stamping was the name of the game, and out of twenty or so thumps before my turn all were with the one stamp. The other seemed to be a spare, in case the one in use broke or wore out. Chancing a bad start in the army, I spoke when it was my turn to pause in front of the table. When I asked if he was the psychiatrist, the man pointed to the chair. Taking that to mean that it would be all right to sit down, I did so and began talking. I poured out the tale of trouble with father, inability to relate to people, and all the rest, as though the man really wanted to hear about it. That the doctor wanted to listen no longer became clear when he suddenly barked his first word. The way he said "homo" gave no clue to whether he was questioning me or stating a fact. It arrived in the middle of something important I was saying, and all I could do was to look wide-eyed at the man and ask what he meant. As if explaining facts of life lay beyond the call of duty, the doctor said that what he meant was, did I like to make love with men rather than women, and was I a queer? More wide-eyed than before I said I definitely wasn't one of those and continued talking.

Suddenly I didn't seem to be doing too well. The sheet of paper in front of the psychiatrist was obviously more interesting to him than anything I was saying. He turned sideways, reached toward the two rubber stamps and picked up the "spare" one. The stamp remained poised six inches above my sheet, and I wasn't even thinking of the blow about to fall. My mind was made up that the use of the other stamp could only mean I'd go into an outfit for misfits. The stamp crashed down onto the sheet. As if he hated what he was doing, he let it rest there a full second before lifting the thing off.

The time for anxiety had passed, and with little further interest I noticed that, without re-inking his stamp, the doctor pressed it onto a tiny slip of paper. Now that the interview was over, I felt

90

safe in leaning forward slightly to see exactly what had been stamped on my medical sheet. Spelt out, upside-down, in big letters was the word REJECTED in the most beautiful shade of red I'd ever seen. The small slip of paper was held toward me in the doctor's outstretched hand. In pale pink, because the stamp hadn't been inked a second time, was a repeat print of that exciting word. With pointed finger the psychiatrist silently indicated a door guarded by a soldier. To reach the door without recall, I slunk towards it dejectedly, frightened that joyous bounding might be disastrous. The soldier looked at my little paper before releasing me to freedom. Nothing in sight suggested the army now, but I didn't want to hurry lest a voice from somewhere might bid me return.

Splashed in all the papers was a government announcement about the introduction of a new type of gas ticket that could not be counterfeited. Nobody in the business thought the authorities would make such a claim unless they had something to tax the skill of a master engraver. Lanning and I had stashed away a good few thousand dollars, so that we could look upon the operation as a success. We decided to keep our equipment for the moment. A week before release of the new tickets, our man with the Price Administration connection brought us a sheet of them. I looked at them with disbelief. They looked like giveaway coupons, and, on turning them over, I saw only a blank Crillon Grey paper surface instead of the intricate design approaching currency standard I'd expected.

Two days after the government's release our own version of the "forgery-proof" ticket hit the market. So well did they sell that three weeks later we were into a second big pressing. Then the authorities caught onto the fact that someone was imitating their new issue, and suddenly a dealer who knew Lanning and me as suppliers rather than manufacturers was arrested by Price Administration agents. As some of our tickets were found in his pocket, they charged him with possession of fake ration coupons. Within hours the man was out on five hundred dollars' bail, and his lawyer reckoned on stalling the case for a year before beating it entirely. The dealer assured us that he hadn't talked, and from the way he was questioned the law didn't seem to regard him as a very big fish. All we could learn was that the Office of Price Administration seemed to think there was a big counterfeiting operation based in southern California.

After lengthy discussion Lanning and I decided that our best cover lay not in flight. Instead we should continue as before, but with more emphasis on transporting passengers. Also we could shed a few lesser customers, keeping only our big man plus the better car dealers.

Since both of our cars had seen a lot of service, we replaced them within weeks of going back to part-time wildcatting. Lanning bought a big Chrysler, while I was lucky enough to locate a little-used eight-seat Dodge. Then to make ourselves a bit scarce from the local scene, we each took a load of passengers to New York. By the time we returned to Los Angeles everything was very quiet on the legal front, but another problem was beginning to emerge. Legitimate gas, or at least genuine authorization to buy it, was becoming hard to obtain. No longer was it safe to rely on en-route fuel for longer trips. Other than breaking the rule about using our own product, the only solution was to get our cars converted so they'd burn unrationed butane. During the conversion I had overload springs and truck-type rear wheels fitted to my Dodge; this compensated for the heavy steel pressure tank filling up just about all the boot space.

The next thing we knew was that the authorities were moving to restrict the use of butane by issuing permits for "essential" cars only. Lanning thought there'd be so few applications that the Office of Price Administration could be talked into issuing a permit; but it didn't work, so we concluded we'd concoct our own. We were able to get some official letterhead and, using a typewriter from one of my lonely hearts girlfriends, I composed a couple of paragraphs of what seemed very good official terminology. In capitals appeared the title, Special Permit for Purchase and Consumption of Liquefied Petroleum Gas. We had no idea how the director signed his name, so we assumed the service-station attendants wouldn't either. Lanning's handwriting was better than mine, so he produced something we both agreed was a masterpiece of flourishes, and well suited to such an important man. Soon the other wildcatters wondered why we were not plagued by fuel problems, and we ended up in the butane-permit business too. To make it sound good, I told of men in top positions who often needed a little tax-free cash. Executives such as the director or his assistant couldn't be bribed, I explained, but a consideration helped them to see merit in an application. As with one voice the drivers wanted to know how much it would be for a permit. Being quite honest, I said we expected something for placing applications in the right quarters. Fifty dollars seemed fair for us, I said, before adding that the director and his assistant would each receive a hundred. To convince these drivers that we could deliver, both of our Special Permits were passed around for inspection. Everybody was impressed, and there was no questioning of their authenticity. It took two days for the regional director to "consider favourably" eight applications, and in that time we obtained more letterheads and typed up twenty more. Sooner or later we expected a rumble over those permits, but it never happened.

Instead of publicity over dubious butane permits, there was plenty about fake gas tickets a few weeks later. A car dealer close enough to the makers to obtain unrimmed tickets had been tricked into selling some of our product to a pair of Office of Price Administration agents. When Lanning and I heard the news, we split for parts we hoped would remain unknown. He headed for New York, while I took the remainder of our tickets to San Francisco to be dumped for what they'd bring.

Through our big man I learned that the dealer was out on bail, and probably hadn't talked. What didn't look good, the fellow told me over the phone to San Francisco, was that Federal investigators were turning over practically everybody with whom Lanning and I had dealt. Apparently they were certain that the source was somewhere close to that group, and there were questions about where we might have gone. Also mentioned was the fact that some minor peddlers with whom we personally had never dealt were spilling. That was clear from the way bigger people tumbled into Federal quiz sessions like rows of dominoes. Those questioned were told rather than asked about their dealings, then advised not to waste time on denials since the law only wanted the maker. Our important client was the only one who knew the manufacturers, and he did not expect to be pulled in for a talk.

I received information eventually that the investigation seemed to be running out of steam and we could return. Our living apartment should be safe, because it was a recent acquisition and unknown. It had long been our policy, at my insistence, that nobody connected with business ever knew where we lived. The first thing to greet Lanning back at the apartment was his notice to report for induction. Confident that he knew what to tell the army doctor, Lanning set off for the induction centre on another dreary Monday morning. Several hours later he returned, with an ashen look of despair. One glance told me he'd been accepted into the army, also that something even worse might have happened. He uttered something about the F.B.I. being after him, and then it transpired that he'd escaped from the place after failing to be rejected. Lanning wouldn't listen to my suggestion of giving himself up and working for a psychiatric discharge.

Lanning knew somebody unlikely ever to be questioned, who had a four-F (unfit for military service) card he could borrow. Using this, he could obtain a driver's licence under the new name, give up wildcatting or anything else where arrest was likely, and live fairly free of the haunting fear of five years in jail. There'd be no attempt by the Selective Service to catch up with him through his home address, because Lanning's original registration had been under an assumed name.

Then came another letter that was to have much bearing on Lanning's future: from the little home-town girl he played with during his month away, informing him she was pregnant. It seemed that in the course of the affair this good Catholic girl had declared her undying love, then dropped her pants. She refused to take any precaution, and like a big dumb kid Lanning had tumbled into the trap. While he bemoaned his luck, I berated him for being so stupid as to have a bareback ride with somebody who obviously wanted to get married. My suggestion was to offer payment for an abortion, which the girl would refuse, and then bargain upwards. Not wanting to lose someone with whom I could work, I advised that he could escape marriage by paying for the support of his offspring.

New quarters seemed advisable to get us farther away from the centre of Los Angeles, where we were too well known. Much searching and a little bribery got us an apartment in a respectable court type of development in Pasadena. Neither our big buyer nor the owner of the safe house, where we kept the equipment when not in use, knew the suburb to which we moved.

Our final two hundred thousand gallons of gas was printed in

94

Pasadena, for immediate delivery. Seated in my Dodge with the parcel of tickets at his feet, our man was in a mood to talk of things to come. As we knew, he pointed out, war's end was close, and gas rationing would finish all of a sudden. For political reasons its death had to be quick and the order just delivered would probably be the last, but there was something else that could be good for a long time.

Sugar was going to be rationed for quite a while, and the man had done enough checking to learn that there was a lively market for this commodity among bakers and candy manufacturers. To phase us into sugar production the buyer placed a small order, with the promise of bigger ones if things went as he hoped.

In the following month a lot happened, beginning with the end of the war. Lanning's girlfriend wrote back for about the third time that she'd consider neither abortion nor adoption, and had to see him urgently. Our sugar tickets were completed to the great satisfaction of the customer, and I used some of my ill-gotten gains to buy an airplane. In the final days of gas rationing the bottom dropped all the way out of the market. Without waiting for the official announcement, we bundled up our remaining tickets and plates, for disposal down a stormwater drain. Then Lanning departed for the east to do something about his personal difficulty.

With my own airplane, I started the process of renewing my long-expired licence. First there was a flight with an instructor, revealing that I'd gone stale. Then there was the medical, by a designated examiner who didn't think four-F people in the draft should be flying airplanes. Only when I'd been found fit in all respects did the question arise, and my admission caused the doctor to blow up. It did my nerves no good when the doctor said he was tempted to report the whole situation to the Selective Service. As if expecting anything but the truth, he asked just what was so seriously wrong that I couldn't serve in the army. This was treading on sensitive ground, because in the doctor's present mood an admission of psychiatric unfitness would get me scrubbed from flying; the best I could come up with was that no reason had been given for my rejection. He immediately assumed that I was concealing some deficiency, or had put something over the army. In a voice reeking with distaste for me, the doctor said he couldn't pass me as perfectly fit and would give me only a limited clearance. This was good enough for my kind of flying, so I made myself scarce before the unfriendly physician could change his mind.

After some brush-up instruction I was able to practise such things as cross-country navigation in my Piper Cub. It was inevitable that the airplane would also be used in pursuit of other pleasures. Various women accompanied me on flights, often going back to the apartment afterwards. Where I lived was still a secret kept from all others. Making the most of Lanning's absence, I nearly got us evicted. With tight security no longer so critical, I ceased playing the part of a staid young business man. So many women were seen emerging from the apartment after breakfast that soon I was in trouble with the manager and his conservative wife. Those folk from somewhere in the Bible belt wanted me to move, and I refused on the grounds that what visitors I had were my own business. I could afford to be cavalier in my attitude toward these clean-living people, since all sugar pressings were made away from the place. Each time our big man came up with an order for one or two hundred tons, our equipment was picked up from the safe house, and the printing job done in a motel.

When Lanning returned he had more to worry about than the uncomfortable situation I had created in regard to our apartment. His determined little Catholic girlfriend would hear no talk of adoption or any other reasonable solution, it seemed, and being the stronger of the pair she won out on the main point; the new Mrs Lanning would come to California when accommodation could be arranged.

When the sugar business blew up, it was as unexpected as a thunderstorm on a clear day, and came with the speed of lightning. Late in the afternoon our buyer took delivery of a big package, then rushed off, saying he had someone waiting. Less than an hour later Lanning and I heard over the car radio that a man had been arrested in a bakery, in the act of handing over a huge number of counterfeit sugar tickets. It seemed that the man who had been so careful for so long had finally become careless.

Walking into a trap laid by Office of Price Administration agents was out of character for our man, so we decided to check up before making a move. Expecting the fellow's wife to say something terrible had happened, I was relieved when he

96

answered the phone. He already knew the story, and was arranging bail and a lawyer for his best salesman. Beyond saying that the man caught was solid and not likely to talk, there was little he could tell, but his advice was to get rid of all evidence. Our equipment was in the safe house, where it could stay until I'd taken care of a few other things.

Lanning folded up that evening, all the way. With his highly pregnant wife looking daggers at me for leading her husband into some mysterious trouble, they threw their things into Lanning's car and departed for the east. Despite his panic, Lanning gave me the phone number of where they'd be staying. Doubting my ex-partner's ability to stand up to questioning, I hoped he'd remain safely out of the way.

Until I decided that it wouldn't be a smart move, I seriously considered a flight similar to Lanning's. My name was already known, so I'd be a wanted fugitive unless I could stay and mend a few fences. There was no proof that I'd done anything, unless people who'd bought gas tickets could be persuaded to talk. An afternoon was spent informing certain key dealers that I'd been out of the black market for a long time, and would admit to nothing if quizzed. Early in the evening while it was still twilight, I drove from downtown Los Angeles toward the Arroyo Seco freeway, and Pasadena. There I'd do a final check on the apartment, to make certain that no trace of past activity remained. This was when I became aware of being followed.

An underpowered Willys with only the driver hardly seemed the sort of vehicle the government would use for shadowing suspects, but that car duplicated each of my turns through Los Angeles's touristy little Chinatown. The Willys held about five lengths behind as we went uphill on the freeway toward the big tunnel, and seemed to be struggling to maintain its position. So far, I'd done nothing to indicate awareness of being followed, but now there was a decision to be made. Either I could deliberately shake my tail, or do it in a way that appeared unintentional. Pointedly getting rid of the shadow could lead to arrest before I was ready, so I prepared to attempt something else.

Heading into the tunnel, no longer going uphill, I began gradually to crack on speed. Downhill on the far side I had a reading of fifty, really sixty with my oversize rear wheels, and the Willys was keeping up. If what I had in mind worked, the agent would only be able to report that I was a fast driver and his heap hadn't been up to the job. I could only hope that the car didn't have a souped-up engine. For the remaining downhill run the Willys held position, but then the freeway started its long climb toward Pasadena. Driving safely, I eased on another five miles an hour, and the distance between the two cars increased. Careful not to give myself away, I held to my new speed while the Willys slipped farther behind. When a sweeping curve put it out of sight, I went still faster.

Leaving the apartment next morning, I had a tail within two blocks. This time it was a powerful red Chrysler, instead of a little Willys, and in my rear-view mirror its pair of occupants looked like very determined law. More worrying than their presence was how they discovered where I lived. I was certain I'd never been tailed to the apartment, but with Lanning's behaviour over his wife problem anything could have happened. He might have led them to the safe house, placing it on a list of suspect premises—to be raided when they were ready to strike. If they already knew what that house contained, I'd be behind bars now and not playing this cat-and-mouse game.

These thoughts occupied me through several blocks of the sort of driving I was sure wouldn't let my pursuers realize I knew they were there. The equipment couldn't be removed from the safe house for permanent disposal before evening. Meanwhile I'd somehow have to spend the whole day tricking the detectives into thinking that I'd lead them eventually to the printing plant. When the time came I'd have to shake the Chrysler in some yet-to-be-figured-out way and then, as the finale to that very fast move, head for the safe house and disappear with the stuff before any raiding party might hit.

Embarking on the first of many errands to fill that endless day, I parked near a downtown Pasadena building containing a lot of doctors' offices. From an upstairs window overlooking both cars I watched the start and finish of a stupid action. A beefy fellow stepped out of the Chrysler, walked up to my car, peered inside and then unsuccessfully tried the locked door and boot handles. His partner remained seated in the law car, rather than take up a suitable position to observe my possible return in time to alert the inquisitive one. Just because they'd done one silly thing, didn't mean they would be easy to shake when the time came—or

98

wouldn't quickly pounce if they thought I was giving them the run-around.

From a doctor's office it seemed natural to go to a drugstore, and kill more time. Then I led the Chrysler toward Rosemead airport, where I kept my Piper Cub. Before getting there, I realized that my car needed greasing and an oil change—and for once welcomed the rush of trade that always comes when a lone attendant is on the job. Talking to friends at the airport, to create a new dimension in the agents' minds, saw me well past the middle of the day. Then it was time for a much delayed and lengthy lunch, during which I wondered if the government men sitting outside in their car had anything to eat. In sight of the detectives I used a phone near the café door, so now they could hope I was setting up an important meeting. Driving down toward the centre of Los Angeles from far southwards, the time approached for my attempt at losing the law—and I began to dread the consequences of failure.

One unsuccessful try would mean arrest, because I'd stand no chance of escape in a street chase. My Dodge with its oversize rear wheels would wind up to terrific speed on a long stretch, but with its lengthy body and heavy butane tank it could never match the Chrysler in a close contest. The government car would run rings around mine, I thought during a long run up busy Figuroa Street, so whatever I did had better be good.

Suddenly I realized that something about the way the Chrysler was driven might provide my opportunity. When I drove fast, it shot up close behind, as if its driver feared being cut off by a traffic light. Slowing down caused the enemy to drop back quickly, to the point of an overreaction. Every time I slowed down to look at one of the many used-car places along Figuroa Street, the Chrysler braked much harder, at least doubling the distance between us.

With approaching dusk most other cars including mine had their parking lights on, though the Chrysler driver hadn't yet followed suit. These were perfect conditions for my brake lights to show up well.

Still driving along Figuroa Street, I was approaching the Pico intersection, where possibly something could be done. After earlier slow-downs I held to the speed for which the Figuroa Street traffic lights were set. If I continued at my present rate, both cars would cross Pico on the green. Being familiar with the timing of these lights, I hoped to sucker the Chrysler into an impossible position at the busy intersection. With about twenty seconds of green remaining at Pico, and my car a good hundred feet short of the crossing, I hit the brakes slightly. That shunted the Chrysler close to the kerb at a slow-down rate better than mine. Using enough brake to keep my tail lights bright, I rolled half the remaining distance to the crossing. Keeping well into the kerb, as though I might be about to pick up someone, my Dodge rolled even closer to the traffic lights. Seven or eight lengths back, the Chrysler crept at my pace, and then it was time to forget those agents and watch what I was doing.

Easing into low, I moved my left foot onto the brake pedal, to keep the stop lights showing. Now I could only hope that my guess was correct, and there'd be another three or four seconds before the Pico light changed to red.

A car-length short of the crosswalk I applied all available power as the Figuroa Street light turned red again. The overlap period had elapsed by the time I reached the middle of the intersection, and my rear-view mirror reflected a pair of suddenly blazing headlights from the Chrysler's position.

In typical Los Angeles fashion the waiting drivers on Pico were on their way as soon as the lights turned green. Some blasted angrily at the Dodge temporarily blocking their take-off path, and anything coming up behind me couldn't have got through without a crunch. Building up speed, I checked the mirror to make sure the Chrysler hadn't found a way through, but there was only solid cross-traffic on Pico. After being led on all day those agents would be furious enough to force any possible break, so in a tyre-squealing turn I left Figuroa and took to the side streets.

Free of government agents, I made fast time to the safe house north of Sunset Boulevard. All equipment was loaded into the car, and the startled man and his wife were told that if anyone wanted to know anything, Lanning and I were only acquaintances—and then I was on my way out of Los Angeles.

At Bakersfield I pulled in for refuelling and a much delayed dinner. In the privacy of the café parking lot a heavy car-jack was roped to the press-case to give it extra weight: then I was back on the road headed north. Some miles before Fresno there was a

100

river crossing, so I stopped long enough to toss over some boxes of ink and paper. Headlights bearing down sent me scuttling back to the car, to drive on with the incriminating press-case still aboard.

Passing Fresno, I continued on toward San Francisco, stopping on the bridge over the Sacramento River south of Stockton. Early in the morning with no traffic in sight, the case sailed over the rail, to make a resounding splash when it hit the water seconds later. With that gone, I felt for the first time that the business of ticket counterfeiting was really a thing of the past. All that remained was one man who could say I'd forged ration tickets, and stacks of hundred-dollar bills in a safe-deposit box. Approaching San Francisco in the pre-dawn darkness, I had a feeling of security that was to last just one week.

Our big man passed on some news from inside the Office of Price Administration. It seemed they were about to spring their trap on "a major ticket forger", when misfortune struck. For a whole day two agents trailed the suspect without his waking up, and as he was leading them to where the tickets were printed, they were caught at a changing traffic light, when some fool woman driver cut in front of their car and propped.

Apart from that interesting little tale something made it advisable for me to establish my presence in San Francisco. When bad luck caused the agents in the Chrysler to lose me, they went to Pasadena, to see if I turned up there later in the evening. Until next day my place was watched, and then the agents decided that I was too busy printing more tickets to bother coming home. To show that I'd been in San Francisco rather than working a hidden press in Los Angeles, I did a couple of bank transactions that could later be verified.

Arriving back in Pasadena about 4 a.m. after a straight-through drive, I went to bed undisturbed. I got up about lunchtime, drove into Los Angeles without any sign of a tail, and spent the afternoon and evening visiting friends rather than business acquaintances. That night I parked in my usual place outside the apartment complex, and in the morning was awakened by a loud knock on the door. I was ready to open the door, when there was a ring of the bell followed by more knocking. Two of the three men I faced were from the red Chrysler, but the stranger appeared to be in charge. Announcing that they were Federal officers, he informed me that I knew why they were here, then asked if they could come in and look around. While two agents searched my apartment without showing a warrant, the one who spoke first told me they knew all about the fake gas and sugar tickets, so I might as well make things easier on myself by co-operating. Remembering the benzedrine tablets I sometimes used for all-night drives, and how they seemed to sharpen my wits, I reached for the bottle. With a casual remark that it was time for me to take my pills, I swallowed two, then dropped the bottle into an already searched pocket.

An agent went out to search my car while the head man, who'd long since changed his tactics, asked questions in a friendly manner. My fears that something might be planted in the car were allayed when the man returned to report that it was clean. I was then told it was time to go downtown.

My bennies were working well when we started down the freeway towards Los Angeles, in a car less conspicuous than the red Chrysler. Downtown turned out to be an office in a second-rate city building. After I was comfortably seated, the man in charge kicked things off with the simple statement that they were my friends. Then came some expansive talk about how interested all of them were in helping me. Feeling the effect of benzedrine, I thought it nice to have such good friends, even if they had seemed a trifle unsociable when they searched my place. From "helping" me, the talk switched to how the agents were going to "help me to help myself". I wondered if my new friends would still like me when they realized that counterfeit tickets were not among my conversational pieces.

To get their files in order, an amiable voice remarked, there were a few small details to be discussed. Since they were trivial matters at first, I saw our friendship lasting a while. Among names mentioned was Lanning's, and as with the others there was no point in denying that I knew him well. With good fellowship so well established, it seemed quite natural to accept the chief's suggestion that now might be a good time to go and gather the press and plates. Though I tried to sound free of rancour, my reply that I didn't know the whereabouts of such items introduced the first jarring note. No longer so friendly, they mentioned years in prison just because I wasn't being helpful, and how they'd put in a good word with the judge if I'd clear up this small matter.

On and on the session went, with my questioners alternating between friendliness and hostility. Reverting back to names, they settled on Lanning and demanded to know where he'd gone. For the first time the word "liar" was used, as a result of my knowing so little about the movements of a man with whom I'd had such a lengthy association. Despite anything I could say, they homed in on the idea that Lanning was the distributor, while my role was that of the maker. Suddenly trying flattery, the head man said that I had to be the one who made the tickets, because I was the only one out of the whole lot with sufficient intelligence.

During a friendly spell one of the agents went out and fetched me some coffee, which I drank with two more pills. The head man wanted to know what in hell were those things, and was I supposed to take them. Examination of the label on the bottle satisfied him. Benzedrine streaming through my system gave me the feeling of having this situation under control, up to the moment I was locked in a cell. Before that unfriendly gesture was made, I was convinced that the agents would have to release me through lack of evidence. There was plenty of innuendo, but no mention of a provable act of illegal nature. All they could do was to hint at something vague that could put me away for years, if I didn't hurry up and do the right thing.

Much time was spent discussing my movements after I'd slipped the red Chrysler. To show that they knew more than I thought, they detailed my every move on that day. After hearing about my week in San Francisco on personal business, one of the agents asked if I was aware that on two separate occasions I'd been followed. My claim of no knowledge wasn't believed by the two men I'd slipped, but for reasons of their own they said nothing. Where I erred was when the head man said that, according to reports, I was a fast driver. This led to discussion of the time I "hadn't been aware" of being tailed by the Willys. The chief said that an agent using his own car hadn't been able to keep up with me, and without thinking I remarked that with such a heap he shouldn't have tried it on the Pasadena freeway. Before the head friend finished saying that he hadn't said anything about the freeway, all eyes were on me, and again I was called a liar.

Nothing I said would convince the Office of Price Administration men that somewhere in Los Angeles I did not have a hidden print shop. Feeling as I did, I was tempted to tell my questioners that all those tickets were the product of a suitcase press no longer in existence. Not giving in to that, I said something else a few minutes later to bring the tide of friendliness to an ebb almost as low as when I was finally jailed.

That was at the end of still another rehash of the red Chrysler day, and it led to talk of my airplane. They had checked on its ownership, and the chief wanted to know how I could afford such a luxury if I wasn't involved in this ticket racket. Flippantly, I replied that aircraft were sometimes owned by people who had not made counterfeit tickets.

Until the chief said to someone over his phone, "We'll take him down and book him now", I thought I would walk away from that office. My only walk was to the car that took me to the U.S. Commissioner's Court, where bail was set at a thousand dollars on a whole string of charges. Then I was led in handcuffs across the street to the Los Angeles County Jail.

One telephone call would be allowed, the booking officer told me. My attempt to reach the big man was a blank. When his number failed to answer, I started to dial somebody else, and was knocked half-way across the room by a southern hillbilly in Sheriff's Department uniform. Telling this officer that I hadn't been able to get my number only brought an offer to knock my teeth down my fucking throat if I didn't shut up.

Late that night in a tiny cell the benzedrine effect wore off, and I was able to take realistic stock of my situation. Since those ex-friends had gone this far without evidence, I decided, they must be under strong pressure to make a case. Possibly this was part of a softening-up process, and they'd visit me in a day or so to see if I was ready to help myself. Rather than be in a hurry to make bail, it might be an idea to stay in jail for a while and put on an act of being helpless. That could raise doubts in their minds, and they might withdraw the charges. If they didn't, I'd send for a bondsman.

Not until the second morning did the agents arrive with offers of help. All kinds of wonderful things were promised, if only I'd tell where the plant was located. Before storming empty-handed from the interrogation room, one of the men said he'd personally see to it that I got a long sentence. When three more days passed

104

without a return visit, I asked one of the more civilized screws to contact our big buyer's bondsman.

The only important factor to my lawyer was that I had not made a statement. Of no concern were such trivial matters as whether or not I'd made the tickets. The lawyer's guess was that the Office of Price Administration had no evidence, but was annoyed enough to charge me and hope to Christ they could dig up something later. If nothing turned up, the government would bargain downwards. They'd offer to let me plead guilty to one or two lesser charges, and in time the U.S. Attorney's office might be persuaded to drop the case entirely.

Next to be contacted was the big buyer, and after mutual condolences over my arrest and his loss of a business he told me what he'd learned from his Office of Price Administration source. They were convinced that I was the man, and Lanning only an assistant. We were to be taken together and played off one against the other, but that misfired when Lanning couldn't be found, and they hadn't the slightest notion where to start looking for him. Also those friendly agents considered me a smart bastard for smugly denying everything.

Very interesting was the way the agents decided just who were the makers. Early in their investigations they spotted us as frequent visitors to car dealers who were known as sellers of fake tickets. In cases where phony tickets could be traced, the trail led to somebody with whom Lanning and I were in contact. Nobody seemed to be above us and supplying other distributors, so we had to be the forgers. As Lanning was seen much more often at suspect premises, they figured that he did the legwork under my orders.

Appearance of sugar tickets handled by the same firm resparked an inquiry that had gone stale with the end of gas rationing. Lacking any better starting-point, the Office of Price Administration was rechecking suspect car dealers, when sheer luck dropped the sugar salesman into their laps. Someone in the bakery tipped off the authorities and they forced the owners to co-operate, but their prisoner couldn't be linked to the used-car men. The agents assumed that there must be some tie-in, and set up a watch on certain suspect premises. My appearance at several places on the day the Willys tried to tail me looked very suspicious. They believed that I was running around organizing massive sales of something.

Arresting me was more or less an act of desperation. They didn't expect to find anything in my place, but hoped that I could be talked into incriminating myself. What made the agents more furious than ever was the self-confident way in which I parried their questions. Not once did it occur to them to make the connection between the pills I took and my attitude.

Next to be contacted was Lanning, and apart from being surprised at my arrest he seemed to consider himself out of the whole thing. I told him bluntly that this was a Federal matter and the government wouldn't forget about questioning him simply because he was three thousand miles away. Nothing I said would persuade Lanning to vanish from the New York area, and finally I agreed that there was a good chance of his not being traced.

Months went by with no move to bring my case into court. Having assorted charges pending that could bring a hefty jail sentence if ever they could be proved, I began to see the error of my ways. I returned to honest employment as a news agent on the Southern Pacific Railway, this time working trains between Los Angeles and El Paso. This gave me plenty of free time between runs, for flying or other legitimate pursuits. Little future planning was possible with a sword hanging over my head, but, as the lawyer put it, time was my ally.

Finally an offer came from the U.S. Attorney's office, to let me plead guilty to one misdemeanour count, and for this the prosecution would make no request for a jail sentence. A month later when the government dropped in on me with a Grand Jury indictment, I realized I'd made one of the biggest mistakes in my life—in heeding my lawyer when he said he saw little point in my acquiring even a minor Federal record. Lanning had been found, and had talked. He was turning state's witness in exchange for a plea of guilty to one felony charge.

No longer willing to deal, the prosecution was all out for conviction and a heavy sentence. With little chance of winning my case on legal merit, the lawyer took steps to see that it never came to trial. These were in the shape of "arrangements" with somebody in the U.S. Attorney's office, and also a man in the Office of Price Administration. This reduced the situation to where they'd let me plead guilty to two misdemeanours, and not oppose probation. Since anything less than two charges might

106

imply that the prosecution had been got at, they insisted on this number as the strength of my cop-out.

With the prosecution "persuaded" to run cold, and a favourable recommendation from the probation office in exchange for my promise to be a good boy, everything should have been cut and dried. What my lawyer didn't reckon on, to my sorrow, was a young unpaid snot of an assistant prosecutor and a brand-new, but tough Federal judge.

That judge was a frosty-looking specimen. Though he seemed less than friendly during an earlier adjournment appearance, my legal adviser felt there was no cause for worry. He explained that when a settlement between prosecution and defence was reached, the judge had little choice but to go along. The prosecution's not objecting to probation, following a favourable report, was normally considered to be clear indication to the bench that there was an agreement.

The whole set-up was wrecked by the prosecutor, who subsequently said a few words too many. His Honour read the report and was clearly ready to hand me probation for having possessed counterfeit tickets. At that point my troubles seemed to be over, but then the prosecutor chose to remark that in some cases of this sort defendants had been sentenced to a year. The judge promptly gave me twelve months, to be followed by a probation of a further year. While my lawyer was trying to say something, the gavel banged down, signifying end of case.

Feelings I would have liked to express in court, before getting rapidly hustled out, were strongly put to my lawyer a few minutes later in the lock-up. What he told me, with which I had to agree despite my emotional state, was that the deal with the prosecution saved me five or more years. Being hit with twelve months was just plain bad luck, but with good behaviour it would cut down to eight or nine. The only bright spot was that the sentence would be served in a Federal institution with decent food and civilized treatment, rather than in a county jail. It did little for my feelings when the lawyer explained that any other judge would have recognized and honoured a deal already made, and would have treated the prosecutor's remark as window-dressing.

Coming to court with the promise of freedom, I had not put my affairs in order, and I was really concerned about the fate of my Piper Cub. Against my wishes I had to follow counsel's advice, and let him put it up for sale; there were rumours of a tax investigation, and it didn't seem advisable to own up to possession of an airplane.

While I lay in the County Jail waiting for transfer to a Federal institution, I heard that the government had made short work of Lanning. Their promises of a trip to California along with appearance before a sympathetic judge were forgotten. He ended up with a plea of guilty in the nearest Federal court. He was sentenced to a year and a day on his felony count. They apparently remained ignorant of his draft dodging, or he would have faced much longer separation from his family.

Early one morning two other Federal prisoners and I were handed over to a U.S. Marshal, bundled into a car, then told that we were going to faraway McNeil Island. Being on a misdemeanour charge, I was destined for the farm rather than McNeil Island Penitentiary, but due to late arrival my first night was spent inside the walls. Next morning I was out of the prison and onto the farm, to perform about an hour of agricultural labour for the government. Mexicans who'd jumped the border too many times, along with semiliterate whites who had incurred disfavour in the Federal courts, did the farming. After an hour of picking something or other out of the ground, I was called from the field by an officer to take me to the filtration plant where I was handed the choice job of keeping filled with powdered chemicals some tanks that metered the stuff, with a peculiar oscillating motion, into the island's water-supply.

When the first three or four weeks had gone, time began to pass more quickly. Nights were spent in dormitories, and in mine a noisy farting contest started up each evening after lights out. There were no rules for these competitions, though it was considered bad form for anyone to claim credit for a fart not his own.

Winter was fast approaching, which in the Puget Sound region could mean cold and nasty weather. I learned that the way out of the cold was to be admitted to the prison hospital. That was inside the penitentiary, called the "mainline", and in its steam-heated comfort one could observe the snow through the windows. I dredged up my old "psychiatric problems", with my sights set on the neuro-psychiatric ward, which wasn't crowded. Prisoners

108

with real psychosis were shipped off to Federal mental institutions, so only those who were slightly around the bend remained in the N.P. ward.

The young doctor from the mainline showed genuine interest in my case and saw that I was transferred straight away. Having a separate room for each inmate, with doors left permanently open, and a large dayroom, the N.P. ward was a big improvement on where I'd just been.

The dozen patients were divided roughly down the middle, into two groups who had little to do with each other. Those for whom the ward was intended were avoided like the plague by ones using it as a refuge, because they couldn't be trusted. No dead-set maniacs existed in the place, but with the unstable there was the danger they'd report certain clandestine activities.

In the confines of the ward it wasn't always easy to keep the weak-minded from learning the hiding-places of pruno jars working up to full alcoholic strength. It was important too that they learn nothing of the occasions when "happy pills" were acquired by attendants and passed around to the trustworthy. Because the N.P. ward was rarely searched by guards, it was ideal for concealing jugs of fruit, sugar and water while they fermented themselves into pruno. What wasn't drunk by attendants and selected patients was traded.

One day one of the prisoner-attendants who ran the place in the absence of medical staff, and who had helped me stay in the ward, got thrown out of his job in disgrace for browning a slightly simple kid. The boy on the receiving end was silly enough to grumble about getting a sore ass, without objecting to the cause. From all indications an unstable patient who'd been rebuffed by the attendant was the one to inform the head doctor. With no private place for his browning sessions, the attendant would summon his little playmate to an empty room after lights out. Closing the door might have looked suspicious to the guard who periodically checked the ward, and also prevented his approach being heard. It was left open, and patients strolling up and down the dayroom could get a dim view of the activity.

On his first attempt the chief medical officer caught them in the act. Accompanied by a guard who quietly unlocked the main door to the ward, the doctor sneaked up to the room where the anal intercourse was taking place. He let out an enraged bellow that brought all heads poking from the other rooms.

To a man of such high moral principles as the doctor, the sight of an attendant cornholing a patient was simply too much; he was beside himself with fury. Shouting to the kid to wash his ass and get back into his room, the doctor tore into the attendant. As the guard led the attendant out, the doctor told the unhappy hospital worker that his place was with the pigs on the farm—not looking after them, but with them.

While there was plenty of laughter over what had happened there was also apprehension, since it might well lead to a general tipping-out of patients who didn't need to be in the ward.

Around Christmas the chief doctor took an interest in my mental condition, but didn't seem inclined to take drastic action during the festive season. When next the subject was raised, there were a few weeks left to run, so I suggested that for the sake of my mental health I remain in the ward. The day of my release came in due course, and I was presented with the most appalling suit I'd ever seen, plus twenty dollars and a railroad ticket to Los Angeles.

Arriving in Los Angeles after two nights of sitting up in the train, I went to a hotel to clean up and rid myself of all traces of prison. The person most interested in my return was a probation officer, and failure to contact him quickly would have returned me to McNeil Island for that second year. Within hours of shedding my prison suit, I moved into the comfortable apartment of a woman with whom I'd just started to get thick before being put away.

From my lawyer I learned that irrespective of the wishes of the probation officer, it wouldn't be a good idea for me to hang around. While I was away, the tax men had shown great interest in the fact that I'd never filed a return. With a possible further jail sentence in the offing, my adviser suggested I get a new passport and take a very long trip—and that with some luck, in the meantime, my file might come off the active list. I decided I'd take his advice and applied for a passport and visa for Australia. Under a scheme whereby that country's government paid part of my fare, and arranged passage, I needed a police no-record certificate. This was provided by the Los Angeles Police Department, on a standard form stating that the bearer had not been convicted of a felony within the past five years. A registered letter informed me that a passage was booked on a Matson liner sailing from San Francisco in a month.

My girlfriend found I'd done some cheating in our relationship and threw me out, but finally promised to write. My probation officer expressed concern over my not making haste in finding employment, and warned me I had better have a job by next reporting time, or else. There was neither job nor report on my next due date. By then my probation papers had been tossed into the sea, and I was a week out of San Francisco bound for Sydney.

7

Problems with the President's hair   the
magnificence of the Multilith   the delights of
deep etch   a beginner produces the almost
perfect twenty-dollar bill, and moves on to
bigger things.

MAKING MONEY, MAKING MONEY

The first few months in Australia would have seemed dull had
they not followed my period of inactivity at McNeil Island. With
no need to work in the foreseeable future I spent my time on a
whole string of affairs, among them an older woman who ran a
bookmaking set-up. Since Australians were mad gamblers,
illegal bookmakers flourished, as independent operators. Though
the last thing in the world to interest me was gambling, I became
the woman's partner when she sold me a half-interest in her
betting shop. I was arrested twice for illegal betting as a result of
lightning raids by special-squad police, having elected to take the
pinches to avoid the by now more costly court appearances of my
friend. Our partnership was about a year old when she caught me
dead to rights in an affair with someone else, and after an
ungodly row bought back my half-interest, then sent me packing.

Free of commitments I set off on a year-long trip to Europe
with a side excursion to America. Besides looking up old friends, I
contacted my lawyer in Los Angeles, who told me I'd better
return to Australia for a while longer. I spent a few more weeks in
Europe, and then from London took a P & O liner to Sydney.

This time there was no mixing of business with pleasure.
Through an acquaintance I bought the unexpired portion of the
lease on a "residential", the Australian term for flophouse. There
was nothing to do but collect rents and occasionally hire someone
to clean. Life was very easy—and rather boring. So with eleven
months before my unrenewable lease would run out, I took up

112

flying again.

Since my American licence had long expired, I had to go through the tests, but without all the hours normally required. This time I intended to stick with it until I achieved commercial pilot rating. Already I had more than enough hours, but I was deficient in night and instrument experience. With good instruction I covered ten hours of take-off and landing by oil flares only and of flying under a hood and taking orders from an instructor. Finally there were written examinations on such subjects as navigation and meteorology and an actual flight test to be passed. Of the several government examiners of airmen I drew the man with the most awesome reputation for failing people.

Boarding the aircraft with me on the morning of my test was an ex-air-force pilot, who, even out of uniform, had a military air. Assuming I could fly, he brought the hood down over my head as soon as take-off was completed. My vision was now strictly confined to instruments, controls and cabin floor, and at no time did I see the countryside over which my test took place. I responded to clipped commands for climbing, descending and tight turns, setting different courses with due allowance for compass precession, stalls and recovery, getting out of a spin and, finally, a talk-down to almost where the runway began. The hood was lifted off and the examiner announced I'd passed.

Although I felt exuberant, I had to get the airplane onto the ground, and the thought occurred to me that it had better be smooth or I just might get unpassed. When we were safely on the ground and my Australian commercial licence was only a matter of paperwork, I felt good about being passed by the toughest examiner.

Before the flophouse lease expired, I was picking up occasional ferry flights, and charters to remote places in the bush. Then I met a woman younger than myself, and we seemed to get along unusually well. Somehow the situation led to a fairly rapid marriage. Had this looked like being a conventional marriage I would have run a mile, but the girl seemed to have a good understanding of my nature, and little desire to settle into dull domesticity. Getting married was more her idea than mine, but after we'd thoroughly explored each other's mental and physical capabilities I accepted it.

With some money left from the gas-ticket business, and a self-supporting wife, there was no pressing need for a job when my flophouse lease ran out, but, flying fairly regularly for one operator, I began to have definite ideas relating to aerial photography.

A few quiet jobs were done as a market test while flying other people's airplanes, and the results were encouraging beyond expectation. It had apparently not occurred to anyone that a pilot taking pictures and controlling the airplane at the same time could do a better job—and with lower overhead—than a passenger-photographer. All I needed now was sufficient capital to purchase an airplane and equipment. I figured I was resourceful enough to think of a way around that problem. My way of achieving such acquisitions was to be no more than the logical outcome of certain earlier conditioning.

The gas-ticket period had taught me how worthless paper became valuable through no more than contact with a printing plate, but I had to face the fact that there were broad gaps in my technical knowledge. My first decision was that to produce good money there would have to be some heavy research, for the poor product only succeeded in attracting early arrest. I promised myself that if I saw the task beyond my capabilities, I'd cut it cold and remain content with small flying jobs—for the time being. Knowledge that others had created excellent currency made me believe that I could finish up with my own aerial-photography business.

American currency was the logical choice for imitation because of its ready acceptance anywhere in the world. Working outside the United States appealed to me because, until I passed money in America, my activity could not be subject to the jurisdiction of a Federal Court.

To keep myself financial I'd fly as chief ferry pilot for an operator known as Honest John. I flew airplanes he'd bought, sold or traded for shares in his worthless companies from place to place as required. What Honest John didn't know was that at the same time I was doing some profitable aerial photography.

My domestic situation also lent itself to what I had in mind. I had a wife capable of accepting the idea that marriage should neither be a full-time occupation nor taken too seriously, and her tolerance also extended to my business life. She knew, and was amused, about the gas tickets and only hoped I wouldn't do

114

anything to land in jail.

With a darkroom already set up for my aerial work, there could be no better place for the job than home. The storage of larger amounts of light-sensitive material likely to be ruined by somebody opening the door was an excuse for fitting a lock. For added security I could rely on my wife's ability to be close mouthed. It would only be necessary to tell her that, because of tax, my work was not to be discussed with anyone.

Back in gas-rationing days I'd examined bills closely enough to realize that no direct reproduction process could produce a good result. The image on government paper could be photographed, and photo-engraving with minor colour separation would yield plates capable of printing bills superficially resembling the genuine. Magnification revealed that, even on a brand-new bill, no portion of the finely detailed work was really free from flaws; those breaks in lines and streaks of ink bridging clear spaces would show up in any plate directly made from a photo of a bill, and the limitations of the printing process would further degrade the result.

Another factor was that government money is intaglio printed. For that process the machines use cylinders with the matter to be printed etched into the surface, and surplus ink is removed by a doctor blade. The presses are massive things, not suitable for the quiet operation I planned. In letterpress, another non-planographic method, transfer is effected by raised image contacting ink and then paper, and while this was excellent for ration tickets, currency called for something more sophisticated. My knowledge of the remaining common printing process— offset lithography—was sketchy, but I felt it might serve my purpose. Knowing its mechanics and its ability to print well on uncoated papers, such as the kind used for money, I planned to use an offset machine. In offset, the movement of ink to paper is via a rubber-covered transfer cylinder, so the plate never touches the surface on which it prints. With resiliency to push ink into the hollows of bond-type paper, the rubber blanket on an offset cylinder is still firm enough not to distort an image during rotary transfer.

In appraising my chance of getting away with a counterfeit operation I gave thought to the agency of the United States Government entrusted with frustrating such ventures. All I'd read about the Secret Service indicated that its agents were specialized men, intellectually superior to ordinary cops and noted for their relentlessness. Aside from protecting the President, their job was to suppress counterfeiting, and Federal Courts supported them with heavy sentences. Prior to the formation of the Secret Service around Lincoln's time—according to the scanty literature—counterfeiting was a popular activity. An amazing percentage of the nation's note issue was fake, and the government thought the situation was getting out of hand.

If my information was correct, there was a period years before the Civil War when the stuff was sold openly, advertised in newspapers, and discounted by bankers on a sliding scale, depending on quality and condition. Unlike the Americans, the British at that time took a harsh view of counterfeiting. For a people so preoccupied with punishment that the French referred to their liking for it as "le vice anglaise", the sight of a coiner on the gallows could be enjoyed as much as the death-throes of a slum child caught stealing food. While America still regarded counterfeiting as misguided free enterprise, England modified its law to provide for long prison sentences. About the time Britain stopped sending convicts to the dreaded penal colonies of Australia, America began handing out short-term sentences, but only until the penalties crept up to and exceeded the English in number of years. It took improved communication between law-enforcement agencies, advanced government production techniques, and the introduction of the physically smaller bills, to make counterfeiting something of a lost art. In America it had in recent times sunk to an annual production of under a million dollars.

Unofficial currency might have become a dead issue, had not private enterprise begun marketing the most versatile of small offset machines. The government couldn't very well suppress their sale just because in the wrong hands they could print money. The Secret Service did try to keep a list of purchasers, but it was never possible for the government to keep track of them.

Even so, those successfully obtaining machines still faced problems before they could churn out money. They had to be capable of photographing a bill, producing properly separated negatives and making plates from these. Fortunately for them,

116

the new little presses were so good that, even with poorly made plates, they could turn out passable currency. However, less than competent forgers were usually rounded up quickly, the more proficient lasting longer; but there were never so many top-grade people that the nation's money was threatened with serious watering-down.

On first inspection a piece of paper money appears difficult to reproduce. Closer examination suggests that if the thing is viewed as the end-result of several individualized production steps, duplication might not be so impossible. Next comes evaluation of the manufacturing steps. Plates to transform paper into money I thought I could make, but there was something about the background other than minute silk threads that struck me. A little thinking and I realized that the intaglio process must be responsible for this rich effect.

Ultra-thin lightly pigmented ink remaining on the cylinder after passing the doctor blade would have to go onto the paper, giving it a dull glazed appearance; knowing this, I could lay down my background tint by a mechanized version of what was done with the old "forgery-proof" gas tickets. Also to be considered were the tiny coloured threads in money paper, which could be duplicated by fine irregular lines on litho plates, but I doubted they were worth the trouble. On so many genuine bills they were hard to find. Expert checking would reveal my bills as fake in any case, so the threads barely seemed worth striving for as far as the general public and lower levels of banking were concerned.

From recent reading I had learnt of advances in platemaking. Smooth aluminium plates had replaced the coarse-grained zinc, and these could accommodate infinitely finer detail. There was also an interesting way of putting an image onto the better metal. Deep etch, it was called, and the name suggested a plate capable of carrying enough ink to make money look rich, overcoming the characteristic flatness of offset. The technical book I was studying explained how an image slightly recessed into the plate could take a generous inking and transfer it to the blanket without distortion. Before again reading those pages, I saw this type of plate as a solution to many of the problems of printing currency. Photo techniques for making this exciting plate were different from those for a surface plate. Here a positive transparency rather

117

than a negative was needed and it had to be right reading through the back, as put down on a sensitized plate. Offset plates must read as the final result, because they print to reverse on the transfer cylinder and then normal again on the paper. To get my reversed transparency, viewed from the front, I'd have to print the original negative emulsion side up in the enlarger, which would give me a wrong-reading paper enlargement, suitable for artwork. From then on the sequence of steps would lead to a correct metal-image reading.

Rather than an enlargement convenient for minor artwork, I needed a blow-up big enough for complete reconstruction; besides getting rid of rubbish that appeared on even the best government bills, there was another reason for this approach. Printing processes other than intaglio cause some ink spread, so if any of the original fine work such as hairs on President Jackson's head were used my job could appear coarse compared with the standards of the Bureau of Printing and Engraving. My artwork should be a shade thinner than theirs, so that the final print on paper would look as if it had been done by that department. There'd also have to be minor structural changes, if offset was to rival intaglio. Lines representing tufts of hair on the portrait were too close together to remain sharply delineated after transfer by a rubber blanket. There was a way around that problem. Nobody would miss a few hairs which could only be counted under magnification. And if the slightly thinned foliage were correctly spaced it should print extremely well. Different dot formation in the shading, carefully executed barbering for the President, and some other changes should transform the government's intaglio into something ideal for deep-etch offset.

My enlargements would have to be really big if the finer artwork were to be done without eyestrain. Some calculation of workable proportions suggested a photographic banknote about five feet long.

To gauge the effectiveness of my artwork I could examine it from far enough away that in perspective would be equal to looking at a normal bill at normal distance. For ease of handling, my enlargements would have to be made as halves, with overlap. When they were trimmed and butted together on a board, the roughness of the join wouldn't be a problem, since the actual reconstruction would be carried out on overlay sheets of plastic

118

tracing material. Matter needed on the final plate would be painted or drawn, using the picture underneath as a guide, and when completed the sketches would get their backs painted white for necessary photographic contrast. Green numbers and seal would be left out of the main plate tracing, for later build-up on smaller overlays.

Using highly recommended Kodalith film, I experimentally shot a well-worn twenty, capturing all the fine detail. Though the bill was dirty, I got a negative like a stencil, simply by following the instructions that came with the film. My photographic equipment was adequate for aerial work, but I lacked a few items for making fake money. The five-by-four enlarger would make my enlargements, and it could be used as a copy camera for shooting the initial negatives of a genuine bill. Then my equipment would cut out, because I did not own a five-by-seven camera, suitable lens or firm tripod to support it while photographing the finished artwork.

Most important, though, was to get a clean, crisp U.S. twenty, so I went to a bank and told the teller that I needed one as a present for a friend going to America; he dug up a good one. The lovely clean twenty was taken home and flattened on the baseboard of my enlarger while it had its picture taken. The enlargement was printed, washed and dried while my wife was out of the house, and then art materials were bought. At this stage I thought I'd stick to a single denomination, and the twenty seemed big enough to be worth while, but not so large as to attract attention. Working on the tracing material was sheer joy, and since President Jackson's portrait seemed the hardest part, I tackled it first. I had a little trouble with his nose and eyes, and as his stern visage grew even more severe as I built his face up, I indulged in a few departures from government engraving to bring him back to normal. From twenty feet away Jackson had seemed to be glaring at me in disapproval, but my modifications softened him down, and when my work was done on that long-dead President's face, I moved to other work.

Line for line my reconstructions of the front and back of the twenty were completed, with great care not to spoil what I considered really good artwork; in fact, I was so pleased with the way my artistic skills were progressing that the temptation to upgrade the operation to fifties led me to the bank again, just in

119

case. All this was done without my wife suspecting the unusual activity taking place in the darkroom. While she worked in a government office I functioned at home, and when there was a flight to be done, everything was locked away.

Then I was forced to a full stop, until a camera and other supplies could be obtained. A used five-by-seven Linhof camera was bought, but the need for a large-size Kodalith film and other Kodak materials led to uncomfortable enquiries. Since that company likes to assist professional photographer customers, I was asked awkward questions by a salesman trying to be sure Kodalith was the right film for my job. Also he wanted my address, so Kodak's travelling representative could save me coming in for supplies. I told him I needed Kodalith to copy line drawings for a client, and rather than give him a vacant allotment address I said I was moving in a few days, and didn't yet know my new business address.

Leaving Kodak, I thought about difficulties in buying supplies for platemaking. Except for bare plates, which can be typed or drawn upon, my needs couldn't fail to suggest some pretty advanced plate production. To ask for those supplies I'd have to concoct a better story than the weak effort at Kodak, for surely those engaged in selling such items would know that any counterfeiter going into action would be in contact with them. In the end I could only decide that when I had a press and was ready, some sort of cover would come to mind.

Next I carried out photography of my finished artwork to the transparency stage. With the reconstructions carefully lit for even illumination I began the task of image composing on the camera's ground-glass back. When finally I had the exposure right, my negatives looked like stencils, cut by mechanical means rather than rays of light. Contact positive transparencies were made by sandwiching negatives and raw film between sheets of glass, then exposing them to light before development. White paper under front and back positives allowed each to be studied, and they looked startlingly like their respective portions of a twenty-dollar bill. Minor artwork plus further photography provided positives of seal and serial numbers, the latter broken down into two-digit segments so that at press time they could be transposed to give a large number of combinations.

Nothing further could be done now until a press was acquired.

120

Not even the plates could be made before I knew what machine I'd be using. Discreet discussion with a printing equipment dealer, using the talk that I needed a small offset machine for business forms, revealed that there were only two real possibilities. One of these, the Multilith, was considered better than its only important competitor, the Rota Print, which was not a bad press, though it did lack certain features. It seemed a good idea to check the lesser possibility first, because knowledge of the press I didn't intend to purchase should enable me to ask intelligent questions about the other.

Using my rehearsed cover, and adding that I was taking over a duplicating business hundreds of miles away, I was given red-carpet treatment in the Rota Print showroom. My impression of the press over which the salesman waxed eloquent was that it was little more than a glorified duplicator. I saw no advantage in its combined inking and damping system, and did not think it suitable for printing high-quality fake money. Its most striking feature was its design, which was modern; also it wasn't noisy.

Then it was time to inspect the Multilith, and I wasn't long in the presence of this beautiful machine before realizing that it was what I needed. Looking at it, I visualized money pouring out the delivery end, while sheets of paper were automatically fired down the feed board. I could soon see that all features mentioned in the literature were present. I was, however, concerned about the noise created by a motor-driven vacuum and blower pump, but I figured this could be smothered by a turned-up radio. Apart from that, the press seemed ideal and free from anything else likely to cause me nervous strain.

Now that I knew what to buy, I began checking sources for a used Multilith. A new press could have been bought through an account set up to pay by cheque, rather than suspiciously handing over cash, but there'd still be the problem of delivery. Paying outright for a press and carting it away in my own vehicle would be remembered long after my window-shopping was forgotten. I felt the anonymity of the used market would offer better security. No small dealer had a secondhand Multilith, and so I turned to the machinery columns in the papers. A couple of weeks went by without result, and then the day after returning from a long country flight I acquired a press.

The model number was 1227 rather than the latest 1250 I'd

gone into raptures over, but according to my reading that only meant it lacked streamlining to cover its machinery look. The name of a rubber company was given in the newspaper ad., and within minutes I was on my way. The press hadn't been sold, a fussy little accountant told me, and then I was handed on to a middle-aged woman in charge of the section where it was located. I believed her when she said the Multilith hadn't been used for a long time, though she neglected to mention that whoever last ran off a job failed to clean the ink system. Caked ink was all over the rollers and the rest of the machine was dirty, but it was in good mechanical condition. Cleaned and set up in my darkroom, the press might look old fashioned but it would do its work. With its belts, pulleys and two motors showing, it seemed more appropriate for a press room than an office, though for myself I saw an advantage in its open spindly construction.

While the woman prattled on as though the sale of the years-old press meant something to her personally, I looked at the machine and realized how easily it could be taken apart. The modern 1250 would have had to be brought into my place in one piece, with help and probably half the neighbourhood looking on, but this could be sneaked into the house in sections. With the press came a lot of old plates and some cans of ink, so I could have cleaned the rollers and done a test on the spot. Instead, I was content to try out the mechanical and electric functions; the first of two switches set the cylinders rolling, started the tapes down the feed board and worked everything but the suck and blow pipes on the paper elevator. Just for a moment I thought how quietly this press would run in my darkroom, before realizing there was another switch to hit. Even in that big office the air pump sounded like something that should be run only in a factory. Quickly shutting it off, I wondered if the pump could possibly be partially silenced by packing with grease.

Purchase of the press involved the woman's rushing to get the accountant, my going to the bank for cash after turning down his offer to accept a cheque, asking for and receiving permission to disassemble the machine on the office floor and, finally, the assistance of two factory men in carrying the parts to a panel van hired during the short time I was away. To explain partially the sight of a man in a business suit and white shirt dissecting a printing-press on an office floor, with tools borrowed from the workshop, I explained to the accountant and interested spectators that mechanical and electric components were going to different places for overhaul.

Late that night all pieces of the Multilith were resting on my darkroom floor, after being in the panel van until the neighbourhood was in darkness.

Concealment of a printing-press would have been too much even for my wife, so with a few reservations I told her the truth. The machine was for making money, I explained, by publishing pornography. For legal as well as tax reasons, I continued, not a word of this must be mentioned even to close friends. She accepted that.

For two days the pieces of my Multilith lay untouched because of a trip into the country to bring one of Honest John's airplanes back to Sydney. Then I carefully studied the maintenance manual that came with the press. This contained complete operating instructions, also helpful hints on treatment for plates when they misbehaved.

Half a day's cleaning, oiling and assembling had the press ready for a dry run. While the cylinders were turning slowly, I walked around the machine to familiarize myself with the various controls. I started the pump, and promptly switched it off; in my darkroom it sounded like something to bring the neighbours running, so it was taken apart, packed with heavy grease, wrapped in an old blanket and then started again while the radio was playing. Though it still made a fair noise in that small room, only a faint hum could be heard from the backyard.

A full-scale printing test was undertaken, using one of the rubber company's business-form plates and paper brought home by my wife. The process of learning to operate the Multilith, I soon discovered, was a matter of not over-controlling the machine and of letting it do its own work. At first I darted from end to end making sure the feeder was picking up properly and the plate wasn't scumming—generally not trusting things to work unwatched. By the time I accepted the fact that most functions could be monitored from the control position, the balance between ink and moisture was established, and sharp prints were rolling off the press. After that session I felt competent at the controls of my Multilith, and quite able to print office forms, but for meaningful work I now had to obtain some

123

platemaking materials.

For all my dread of chasing down those items the problem simply solved itself. As a Multilith owner I went to the dealer's supply department with a carefully concocted story about having bought a printing business so far away that no representative would call. The man waiting on me picked my accent as quickly as I recognized his, then told me what part of America he was from and my tale was forgotten. His story came first, ending with his wish to return to California if he could stop drinking long enough to save the fare. More talk followed, I promised him a flight over Sydney, then said I'd bought a used Multilith. By the look on his face he seemed to think Multiliths weren't for such as me, so I used the pornography story that went over so well with my wife. He was sympathetic when I added that there wasn't enough money in flying, and I had to do something like this. That scotched the possible suggestion that my plates be made by professionals, and I talked about being a photographer and capable of doing the job with the right materials. Mention of deep-etch plates resulted in a phone call to a friend in a firm selling those highly specialized materials. When I met the fellow, I let him in on the pornography secret, and he presented me with *Platemaking by the Howter Deep Etch Method*. This, the solutions he sold me and the acquisition of grainless aluminium plates marked the end of a major problem. A whirler for coating plates evenly with light-sensitive emulsion was needed, but I envisaged a hand-drill turning a flat piece of wood with clamps at either end for this purpose; warm air for drying the emulsion onto the plates could come from the kitchen stove when my wife wasn't around.

From the day I bought my Howter supplies I couldn't go wrong. My first plate failed through using five minutes of direct sunlight exposure, sending Jackson's hair down the sink with the unwanted material. Two minutes seemed a more likely pro- position, and within an hour my plate was on the cylinder, paper was stacked in the feeder, and I was doing a final check of the controls.

In a state of great excitement I started the motor for the printing head, contacted damping roller to plate cylinder, let it turn a few times and then lowered the forme rollers. Only the image was inked, so I knew the plate wasn't scumming. Starting the second motor, to activate the noisy pump, sent a procession of sheets down the moving tapes on the feed board. Barely able to control myself, I let a few trial sheets go through, before snatching a sample from the delivery tray.

Though printed on cheap white paper that could never resemble currency, everything was there and sharp beyond my wildest expectations. A similar test using black instead of the correct green was run on a quickly made back plate, giving the same gratifying result. Inks of much better quality than those inherited from the rubber company were hurriedly sought from my friend at the Multilith place. Some heavily pigmented black gave so startling a result that it seemed to have physical impact. Green for the back was difficult to mix to the exact shade used by the government, so it took a couple of hours to get this to the point of looking right.

Next day I made an extra set of plates, so there'd be spares in case of deterioration. Making plates for a counterfeit operation is generally thought of as extremely difficult, though it is really quite simple once preliminary preparations are done. In less than an hour bare metal can be transformed into a high-quality printing plate.

A clean blank plate is wetted; I did it clamped onto my hand-drill whirler. When excess water has been spun off, some emulsion is poured onto the centre, after which the plate should be whirled, in a laundry tub or similar place where drops of yellowish emulsion turning to deep brown cannot be spattered onto walls and curtains. In the drying stage, when the still spinning plate is held vertically near a gas burner, a few stubborn drops may detach themselves and make for the ceiling; they should be cleaned off while wet, before they become unsightly stains that are most difficult to explain.

The dried plate is now light sensitive, though it can safely be handled for a few minutes in room illumination. It should be fairly quickly contacted to the transparency and printed by action of strong light on the bichromated emulsion. Doing things the primitive way, I used thick glass and clamps rather than the recommended vacuum printing frame. After film and plate are brought together, correctly timed exposure to light renders all emulsion not screened by opaque parts of the overlaying positive impervious to the dissolving action of the developer. After exposure, the plate does not show evidence that much has taken

125

place. There is a faint money image that can be accepted with equanimity only after enough plates have been made to realize its unimportance.

Development, the next step, should be carried out with celerity, first laying the plate on a flat surface and then swabbing solution all around the image area with a piece of cotton. A couple of minutes of that and the developer is squeegeed away, but the plate still does not appear as if anything very exciting has occurred. Bare metal can be seen in the bigger solids, but there isn't enough contrast for anything to show up really well. Now is the time to apply mordant, rather than yield to temptation and start a fresh plate. Mordant is etching solution, and as it eats into metal not protected by light-hardened emulsion a lot of tiny bubbles appear; the little bubbles that form where mordant is munching metal must be constantly swabbed away, so fresh solution can reach the surface. After a couple of minutes as much as possible of the mordant should be wiped off. A little cleaning job comes next, and failure to do it properly guarantees a plate not worth putting on the press. Water is fatal to the emulsion (now called the stencil) protecting the non-printing portions. Using water-free alcohol and plenty of swabs, every last trace of developer and mordant must be removed. If any is left, parts of the image may later "walk off" during the press run.

Magnification will now show that something important has taken place. Bare, clean and slightly etched-down metal can be seen at all parts of the plate that are to become ink-receptive, but because the soon-to-be-unwanted stencil still provides little contrast, what is revealed falls somewhat short of thrilling.

The next step destroys temporarily any idea that the plate could print money, or anything else. Black lacquer base, stuff with strong affinity for newly etched aluminium, is rubbed all over the image area; since its solvent dries quickly, all of importance soon looks damaged beyond repair. If the book didn't explicitly state the necessity for such a procedure, one would be tempted to believe that all was lost. About as much Johnson's Baby Powder as would be applied to a baby can now be gently rubbed over the plate; mild heat will help to absorb residual solvent from the lacquer base. Then comes the moment of truth: the removal of the stencil.

Removing the stencil is the operation which shows up failure in earlier procedures, and also the time to think back about whatever could have gone wrong if such is the case. If the plate is a disaster, the stencil will take parts of the image—even the whole of it—with it. Wetting and scrubbing with a brush is the only way to get rid of a stencil. For a minute or so the plate seems to be a total loss, with unwanted matter sticking like glue. Then the stencil begins to break up, but it takes a lot more water and brushing before it is all gone, to reveal in sharp detail the money image so carefully printed down. Rather than just admiring the newly made plate it is very important to protect it against oxidation. The freshly bared non-image metal can oxidize, and if this happens it will pick up ink on the press, causing splotchy prints. Protective gum must be applied to the plate, and left there until it is ready for work on the machine's cylinder.

My first successful plates saw much service, before being phased into actual money production. All paper testing was carried out with the front-of-the-note plate, while the back plate was used for colour experiments with different inks. Matching inks to various possible papers produced interesting results, some of them appalling. A few papers that looked good absorbed ink like a blotter, with fine detail going unsharp. Coating with clear or slightly pigmented ink vehicle tended to prevent penetration, but such papers were generally bad in other respects. So much paper was used in tests that the disposal of incriminating sheets became a problem, but a little incinerator made from a large can punched full of small holes, with a lid to prevent money-image fragments drifting on the wind, proved adequate. I had only to toss the can onto a heap of burning newspapers, and eventually flush the remaining ash down the lavatory.

Finally I reached the stage where seal and number plates were completed, the press was adjusted for optimum results, and the only thing delaying a full-scale printing operation was lack of a really suitable paper. The space-variation numbering system was fully tested and capable of extension beyond what would ever be needed, and now I was preoccupied with buying, trying and burning the product of different paper manufacturers. To qualify, a paper had to be the right thickness, have sufficient strength for the finished bill not to break in two when snapped, have no watermark and a feel at least approaching that of money.

When I located a paper that seemed pretty close to these

requirements, I bought a couple of reams. Printing sequence was to be background tint both sides either end, laying the groundwork for two bills from each quarto-size sheet. Green seals with letters at the beginning and end of still blank number spaces came next; numbering would involve repeated trips of paper through press, with segment positions periodically altered by lay-gauge adjustment and frequent plate changes. Back and front main plates would at last change the paper into currency, though the surrounds would still need to be guillotined. Some yet-to-be-worked out method to impart a used look to my suspiciously new bills would have to be found.

Top speed on my Multilith was six thousand impressions an hour, but at that rate it sounded like a steam engine. Anybody passing the house, I was certain, would know that something highly unusual was going on. Three thousand prints per hour turned out to be the best rate for making a lot of money without turning me into a nervous wreck. Before a long run I did the ink and plate changing to bring to completion a few dozen bills. Fresh from the press they looked like money straight from a bank. Crushed, folded and dirtied, they looked ready for a spending spree, if that sort of short-term action was what I had in mind. A final test was folding one of my bills down the middle and butting it against a genuine one in about the same condition. The fake half looked so much like a continuation of the good that only magnification showed anything. It revealed that my ink did not rise slightly above the paper as it did on government money; offset couldn't print like intaglio, but my bills weren't intended for people with pocket microscopes. What mattered was that my image intensity rivalled the official product, all detail was sharp and clear, and Jackson's government eye was no stronger than the one on the private side of his face. These bills could have been changed anywhere, but I didn't want a single one to circulate before I was ready to release a torrent.

Production was scheduled to fit in with my wife's movements, so I could at least open the darkroom door when she came home from work. Stopping the press involved more than just hitting two switches, so I allowed an hour for the operation. During that hour all rollers had to be cleaned, plate in use protected against oxidation and my hands washed free from stains. My wife wasn't inquisitive, though she did occasionally ask when pornographic production would commence.

Still working for a living, I had, at short notice, to lock up everything and go away for a couple of weeks. It was June 1956 and there were floods in the country about five hundred miles from Sydney, and this to Honest John meant money. Anything capable of getting in and out of small places commanded good charter rates, so I was sent west with an airplane. When the call to duty came, I had more than a hundred thousand dollars printed.

I gave a lot of thought between flights to the future of my money operation. Away from the printing-press I seemed able to think more objectively.

What started as an attempt to make and pass enough money to set myself up in aerial photography now seemed to have greater potential. I had succeeded beyond expectation in making good plates, and flying in the wide-open Australian outback I couldn't help seeing the whole thing in a broader context. Work on the fifties would go ahead when I returned to Sydney, with not a bill of either denomination floated anywhere until I had at least a million dollars. An attempt to get better paper would be made, because I wasn't really satisfied with the present one. And methods of circulation more efficient than single-bill flotation would have to be evolved. Wholesaling to others who'd do the passing seemed the only—and the safest—way ever to get anything like a million dollars onto the market. If unable to contact the right people, I could still float thousands on my own in different parts of the world. Though having a spare million would be reassuring.

A couple of people came to mind when I decided that it might be too big for me to handle on my own. One was an ex-British-Army officer I met on the ship from San Francisco, who'd do almost anything for money. He had spent time in the Middle East and, after getting to know me, talked of deals pulled off there. The other man was an aviation executive I knew very well, and for every honest dollar he acquired he gained at least ten by other means. He told me about some of his deals, and I'd heard he could be trusted. Some of his connections were in Hong Kong, where my money might be moved, and he had ways of getting things in and out of Australia without attracting attention.

The flood finally receded and I returned to home to begin

artwork on my fifties. After what I had learnt from the reconstruction of the twenties, the larger denomination went without major hitch.

Less than three weeks after starting to build up my tracings, the first test-run of fifties was coming off the press. There was some trouble with the portrait of Grant, but, unlike Jackson, this took less than an hour to correct. In following too closely the structure of the original, I achieved what should have been a good likeness of the ex-general. But viewed from an appropriate distance the gentleman seemed, unfortunately, to need a trim. A different broken-line formation, with some of the government's little dots left out, made Grant look the way he did on a genuine fifty.

A paper hunt taking in almost every wholesaler in Sydney was next on the order of priorities I set while flying in the bush, and this time I found something so outstanding that my already printed hundred thousand was immediately relegated to the status of second-class currency. In the time I was away, some chemical interaction had taken place between ink and paper in the money, giving it a slightly unhealthy tinge, but I felt sure the new paper did not have this weakness.

The following week I persuaded my wife to visit relatives for a few days, and in her absence quickly printed more than three hundred thousand dollars in the new fifties. Production continued at a slower rate after her return, but my fortunes soon built up to where I thought I'd better do something about contacts.

My first attempt at opening lines of distribution was a call on the aviation man, but he was in Melbourne for a couple of days. The ex-British-Army officer was very interested, and after examining a few specimens said he'd give serious thought to taking a bundle into the Middle East.

When I eventually contacted the aviation executive, my approach was different, because he was my biggest hope. Without explanation I showed him a bundle of fifties and asked if he could see anything wrong with them. To him such a question could only mean the money was counterfeit, so his main interest was whether the stuff was a good imitation. Deciding that the fifties looked real, he became businesslike.

Who printed the money wasn't so important as whether any had been circulated; and if it hadn't, what sort of price could be

130

arranged?

My insistence that none had been floated led to questions I could only answer by telling the whole story. I explained that I was only interested in sales outside the country, and he agreed that, apart from the risk, Australia wasn't big enough to absorb a worthwhile amount. He said he'd be willing to put some money into the proposition, and gave me five hundred pounds for promising him first crack at the East. His best eastern contact was a Hong Kong business man who made frequent trips to Sydney, and if nothing developed from that Chinese gentleman, he'd do something about it himself.

That my friend had talked to someone was obvious when he unexpectedly turned up at the house. He wanted to know if I'd make Australian ten-pound notes, and if so whether they'd be the same quality as my American money. I said I'd be technically capable, but not too keen because of my indefensible legal position if caught. My new associate said they were not for flotation in Australia, and if any drifted back there'd be no trace to source. It seemed the Hong Kong contact had a situation where one hundred thousand pounds could be dumped in one hit. For a while that amount would repose in the vault of a "financial institution", and there'd be a stink when it was discovered, but not much else. Having been switched for good currency of yet another country by an insider, the paperwork would lead to a dead-end. Apart from the injured institution, only the Australian Government would be upset about the forgery of its money.

A thousand-pound cash advance made me forget horror stories of Australian jails, and there didn't seem to be much risk in this. If I never saw another penny, I'd be a well-paid labourer. There'd be a second thousand when I could show a main-plate proof, to be followed by a similar payment on completion. At the conclusion of the Hong Kong switch I'd get half my friend's cut, which I realized would be whatever he chose to quote.

Allowing for possible feelings of generosity at settlement time, the man said his end mightn't be more than twenty or thirty thousand pounds. All that was pie in the sky, but the three thousand was real and I was ready to roll—and later listen to the woeful tale of what would go wrong in Hong Kong. Dealings in American money were to remain in abeyance until this was

131

concluded.

As an example of currency design the Australian ten-pound note was not impressive. Reconstruction involved colour separation photography to capture design patterns underlying the main plates. Still, there was much garbage on the big blow-ups that would be eliminated by common sense from my plastic tracings.

For security the Australian Government relied heavily on a watermark portrait of the Queen. Since I had no way of watermarking anyone's picture into my paper, it would have to be printed in such a way that it wouldn't look like printing. Since watermarks are seen by transmitted rather than reflected light, I was inevitably drawn to the conclusion that I should use a printing ink in the same tone as the paper. Right- and wrong-reading plates of the Queen's head were made for printing on either side of the paper, in ink vehicle with just a touch of pigment, with both impressions weak enough not to materialize against the background tint; when held up to light, their combined effect on opacity made the image highly visible.

When the Australian notes were finished, the man financing them wasn't ready to take delivery and spoke of a three- or four-week delay at the Hong Kong end. I used that time for intensive production of American money, and finished up with over two million dollars.

Still waiting for something to happen with the Hong Kong shipment, I began looking for a satisfactory way of ageing my U.S. bills. The Australian money was to go out as new, so it was no problem, but I needed a way of making American bills look as though they'd absorbed oily substances from much handling. Tests with light oil suggested that I was on the right track, though it caused the image to look lifeless. Then I had the idea that something oily, but soluble in water, might do the trick. Watered-down glycerine came to mind, and when the proportions were worked out my bills had the right toning. Complete treatment included crushing and crumpling bills immersed in the solution, so that after drying they looked like very well-used currency.

My first large batch of bills, about fifty thousand dollars, were processed in a laundry tub with a bucketful of the mixture. With bare hands I kneaded, crushed, bundled and squeezed the bills as if washing a great bunch of dirty socks. Only when my fingers and wrist muscles ached from the unaccustomed labour was the dripping mess lifted from the tub. Spread out to dry on newspapers the stuff looked like a genuine fortune—and then I was ready to put through another heap. I began to think that there must be an easier way to do this, and soon realized that it could be done in my wife's plunger-type washing-machine. Twisting and pounding at the mixture of money and solution the washing-machine slowly beat my bills into the wanted condition. Every little while I had to switch off and move the currency by hand, to keep the action of the suction cups even. Final touch was to put the cash in small handfuls through the wringer, which battered the bills more than ever and speeded their drying.

After the ageing job was completed, I was not idle for long. Following a flurry of conferences with the aviation executive things happened fast. The Hong Kong order was cancelled, since the man planning to do the switch was no longer available. I could burn or do what I wished with the Australian money, and the aviation man would recoup his investment in its manufacture from my American funds. Twenty-five thousand dollars in twenties would cover it, my friend said, and he just happened to have a safe outlet for such an amount in India. Money sent there would not jeopardize future operations, he explained, because it would be hoarded and not come to light for years.

More important, and for which a donation of fake money would be acceptable, the man had a safe way to get me and a big bundle of bills out of the country. I'd go in an airplane being ferried to West Africa, leaving the flight at Karachi, and the money would travel separately. From Karachi I'd fly by airline to Rome, picking up the currency at a city airways office. Leaving the country in this way neither I nor my papers would come under scrutiny, so there'd be no problem of trying to obtain a tax clearance. Details of how the package of money was to leave Australia cannot be revealed. There was, and possibly still is, a very safe way of moving fair-sized parcels in and out of the country.

Though anxious to get out and start circulating my money, I didn't expect to go so soon. The airplane was leaving early the following week and it was too good an opportunity to miss, so in a snap decision I told my friend I'd be on board. The only matters

133

remaining to be settled were such minor items as how he'd get further funds should the need arise. This had to be rather vague, based on my somehow keeping in contact, because I could not use the ex-British-Army officer. From the start I had told the aviation executive that he was the only one being allowed in on this, so I couldn't change my story.

All this left me with just four days to close down the manufacturing operation, get rid of the evidence and make certain other arrangements.

Back at the darkroom I was faced with what seemed, in the time, an impossible task. And it had to be done without my wife's knowledge. Everything was expendable, but with my demanding deadline it seemed best that press, plates and other hard-to-get-rid-of items should be boxed and stored under a different name. They could be disposed of quietly at some future time. I would also have to resolve what should be done with the money over and above that which was going to Rome.

All artwork was torn up and crumpled before being burned. Films and offcuts further fuelled the huge fire I soon had going, and there was little thought about what the neighbours might think or how I'd explain the mess to my wife when she came home. Anxious as I was to get rid of unwanted material, I wasn't quite prepared to risk burning currency on an open fire. Disposal of the Australian currency, for which I had no use, was not possible with my little incinerator. As the fire consumed more armfuls of stuff that could be embarrassing, I decided that the ten-pound note could accompany other funds into storage.

Before the ashes were cool, I left to purchase an assortment of lockable strong cases. Returning with these, I was confronted by my wife, who wanted an explanation as to why the backyard was covered in ashes, and most of her plants ruined. The boxes and my hurried manner were also of great interest, so with all this to explain I didn't even make the attempt. To top it all, she didn't yet know I was going overseas. In the midst of a mild tirade about burned plants I brought talk to a halt by saying that I'd be off to Europe in a few days. This drew her attention away from immediate goings-on, but brought its own pile of questions. She finally accepted the fact that all this was in furtherance of some highly confidential business—but I had to promise to have no more fires.

That evening I saw the ex-officer and completed arrangements for his profitable part of the venture. Being under the thumb of his clinging wife, his interest in a money-passing expedition rarely ventured beyond the talk stage. He still wanted to profit in any safe way possible, so I was giving him the lucrative job of custodian and forwarder of funds. I could not have handed this plum to the aviation executive, because he would have creamed too much off the top. Though the army man might be tempted, I had known him for a long time and felt that of the two he could be better trusted. Before leaving the ex-officer's place I agreed that he'd conceal a large box of money, and forward funds to me on request. It would be up to me to suggest safe methods, if and when the time came.

On my way home, to hear anything further my wife might have to add, I realized that the ex-British-Army officer must have lost some of his nerve. He was older and loaded with family responsibility, and his talk of past deals was more nostalgia than desire to participate actively in anything new. For what he'd do he would be well paid. Not wanting anyone less than wholehearted in the flotation, I was glad I hadn't attempted to rekindle his earlier enthusiasm.

Something that worried me slightly was the man's son, a teenager big in size but not in intellect. While I couldn't suggest to my friend that I had reservations about the boy's mental ability, I did say last thing before leaving that the money should be concealed where it couldn't be discovered by others in the family. He made a promise to bury it under the house.

A whole day passed dismantling and packing the equipment, and storing it in a warehouse under an untraceable name. As long as the bill was paid, the machinery plus a million dollars and the Australian currency would be safe. Not to go into storage was the second million and, owing to lack of strongbox space, the first-run twenties printed on bad paper.

Next day, with time running short, I bought two more lock-up boxes, one that held three-quarters of a million comfortably, and something smaller for the "worthless" twenties. The little box could also go under the ex-officer's house, without a key, so he wouldn't make a mistake and forward me the wrong money.

Late at night I delivered two steel boxes to my friend's house, then after a long drive through Sydney handed the aviation executive a package for shipment to Rome. At first I planned to send half a million in fifties, but decided that a quarter might be easier to handle physically when I reached Europe. Just in case nothing was waiting on arrival, I stuck twenty thousand in my pocket.

All the running around increased my wife's curiosity, but there were no unpleasant confrontations. Not too many women would have accepted my evasiveness in the way she did, on no more than an assurance I'd tell her all in time.

As promised, I left Australia without showing a paper. The old DC3 being ferried to Africa, to finish its long life as part of an emerging nation's airline, carried only two passengers out of Sydney. Neither crew nor the other free rider knew any more about me than that I was an unemployed pilot getting a lift. At Darwin, our final Australian port, I got a fright when the airplane was delayed two days. The Indonesians were being difficult about clearance to fly through their country, and in the time spent waiting I was certain it would occur to some official to check papers. Fortunately nobody asked about such things at Darwin airport.

Suddenly the flight was free to proceed. My apprehension must have been apparent, because after take-off, with the aircraft on course for Timor, the captain asked if I now felt better. I readily admitted I did and explained that I'd been anxious about the possibility of the tax people putting me through the wringer.

8

European adventures   Parisian
widow   Spanish gangsters   passing fifties hard
and easy   to England to buy a plane   to New
York and family again   a taste of
chocolate   Terry tags along   St Louis ruse.

STRANGERS ON A TRAIN

We spent two days in Singapore and I was tempted to launch a fifty or two there, but I decided that the first appearance of my money should be in Europe or America. From Karachi I took a fast connection to Rome, where my parcel was waiting. Rome also was tempting, but already I'd decided that first flotation should be in a country such as Spain, where two rates of exchange existed and money cashed illegally would bypass the banking system. After some thought I decided to take my bundle of bills to Paris, leave half at the American Express, put most of the remainder in similar safe deposit in London, then go to Spain with a few thousand. Rail seemed safer than air with so much cash planted in my luggage; crossing the border with a trainload of passengers was much less risky than fronting up at an airport customs counter.

With little fear I boarded the Rome–Paris express, to cross the French border thinking about something far removed from money. At Genoa a woman accompanied by two barely teenage girls came into the compartment I'd had to myself since Rome, and my only thought was that the more people around, the better, when customs officials boarded. While the train climbed the mountains out of Genoa, my eyes caught those of the woman every time I looked her way. Without knowing if communication was possible, I thought she had a lot of appeal. She was tall, strongly built and around forty-five, so if the kids were hers she had them late. She made the first attempt at conversation, in

137

French, which switched to fair English when she realized I couldn't cope. When the girls were asleep I learned that they *were* her daughters; she was a widow, they lived in Paris and had been to the Italian Riviera—and this friendship could continue after we got off the train next morning. We turned out the compartment lights and adjourned to the corridor.

Before we reached Turin, our tongues were in each other's mouths, and she told me I was the first man to do that since her husband, a French Railways official, died four years earlier. By the time we were approaching the French border at Modane, we nearly came in each other's hands in the dark corridor. I found myself preoccupied with the woman's need for a man rather than the fake money in my luggage.

Pulling out of Modane, it was agreed that I'd stay at her place for my few days in Paris. It didn't make sense for a woman like this to go without loving all that time and then tumble in so quickly, but I just had to go along; such passion and copious vaginal creaming suggested that there couldn't be a catch. My promise to kiss her everywhere brought such a hard squeeze on my penis that I had to tense myself against being milked on the spot.

While the train raced across France, she told me a story that seemed incredible. She came from a good French family—high cheekbones and cultured speech—and was a practising rather than a devout Catholic. Her marriage had been sexually satisfying, but since her husband's death she'd been celibate. Being French and practical, she realized that remarriage was acceptable only if she found a good lover sufficiently well off to compensate for the pension she'd lose; and so far no such man had appeared.

Prevented by conscience from seeking solutions to her sexual needs, she suffered increasing frustration. Celibate spiritual advisers gave moral support, but she found the denial of nature difficult. They persuaded her to believe that extra-marital sex couldn't be contemplated, to the point where the agonies of denial affected her health. A Paris doctor, for impersonal reasons, tried to overcome Church teachings. Failing to achieve success, he referred her to a psychiatrist in Lausanne. Somehow the Swiss doctor rooted out those deep-seated convictions, and convinced her that she had to lead a normal life. She was intelligent enough to respond after a few sessions and, freshly liberated, went to the Italian Riviera with the kids.

We organized my Paris stay: I'd go home with her and stay for breakfast, lunch and dinner; I'd then depart, to return quietly after the girls had gone to bed. I was also to make a point of taking my luggage to a hotel at any time after breakfast. After the way we played all night, I was more than happy to let the woman manage my Paris stopover. Printing all that money had been hard work, I thought with testicles sore from caressing, so I gave myself three days away from business concerns.

Nothing the woman had said earlier prepared me for where she lived, and there'd been no mention of a maid. Instead of the cramped Paris quarters I had expected, I was taken to a big apartment a mile or so from the Eiffel Tower. Later that morning half my money went into a box at the American Express, and our next separation was the act put on for the kids. On my return that night, instead of taking me straight to bed, the woman said I must first be given a bath. In a tub full of warm water it turned out that it was a bath I was to be given rather than permitted to take. Working on regions that could be smelly, the woman held my balls out of the way while she moved soapy fingers around and slightly into my rectum. When her fancy had been indulged, and I was clinically clean, I was dried with special assistance in critical areas. We soon went on to other pleasures. Putting my mouth where only my hand had been before, I reassured myself that my friend's glands were unusually active. Losing control fairly quickly, I came in the woman's mouth, and she pushed her snatch even harder into my face. When I could have pulled my head away and relaxed she was on the verge of coming, so I couldn't let her down. In a series of motions that made it difficult for my tongue to stay in place the woman came, but by then I wasn't so anxious to pull my face away. As her contractions died down, she let my half-limp penis slip out of her mouth.

Three more nights were spent with my friend, and though I had to leave before the maid arrived, or before the kids got up, I saw the girls at mealtimes. They enjoyed making me use what little French I knew, laughing at anything I said. Just how their mother explained me to them I never did learn. Leaving Paris, I told the woman I'd be in Europe for a few weeks, and would see her again before going to America.

As soon as I was alone and travelling again, my mind was forced back to my nerve-jangling mission. Passing through English customs at Dover, I struck a situation that could have turned ugly. A seemingly indifferent customs officer saw a badly planted bundle of fifties in the bag I was asked to open, and no longer remained so casual. Sight of the money transfixed him, and rushing through my mind were thoughts of explaining away more than a hundred thousand dollars. Not only was I certain of a thorough search, but a check to see if it was real. While I was furiously thinking of my denials, the customs inspector calmly remarked that it would be safer to carry travellers cheques. I promised to bank it when I reached London.

In London I was tempted to forget Spain and head for the United States. Then I remembered earlier thoughts about how bad luck or judgement could dump me in the lap of the Secret Service without even bail money or the price of a lawyer. Spain would at least provide the cost of those essentials in real money, and as a concession to my lack of experience I'd hit a couple of lesser cities. I chose to start in Seville and Granada.

Two days later I was in Seville, vainly looking for a reason why this was neither the time nor place for passing my very first fake fifty-dollar bill. Common sense told me to start spending like a well-heeled American tourist, but I still wanted to put it off for another day. Sanity prevailed, though with judgement not the best I approached the man behind the desk in a big hotel rather than someone of less stature. Changing my fifty would be no problem, the man informed me, reading off the legal rate from a paper. I then realized what he was planning and informed him that I knew the right price. He increased his offer and we both profited. My first fifty was launched and accepted as genuine— but I made a mistake in not being brave enough to change more.

My next mistake was buying something too expensive in a jewellery store as a pretext for changing my fifty. This time I bargained for a good rate, but on the basis of throwing away my purchase and changing my pesetas into hard money I could only make twenty dollars. Then came another hotel and I was bold enough to change two fifties. These deals were better than shops because nothing had to be bought, making the loss on each bill no more than twenty-five or thirty per cent. Bargaining for a good rate seemed to have the psychological effect of drawing a victim's attention from my bills to his profit.

I soon learned that around hotels, airline offices and travel agencies there lurked people anxious to buy foreign money with pesetas, but, unfortunately, Seville had only a limited number of such places. I worked more shops and, becoming selective, bought cheap items that would get my fifties changed rather than wasted. In time, my purchases became burdensome, so I started losing things down toilets, into rubbish bins, or wherever else they wouldn't attract attention.

By the middle of the afternoon my nerve weakened and I had an overpowering urge to get out of Seville. When I felt compelled to look over my shoulder, I told myself it was time to go. In less than an hour I was on a train for Granada, where next day I'd make a similar operation before getting out of Spain.

An individual I met on the train changed all that. My impression of the two men and a woman sharing the compartment was that they were racket people with no desire to keep it secret. The woman was flashy as any whorehouse madam, while one of the men seemed a nonentity who took his cues when to talk or shut up from the others. Leader of this trio was a man who seemed impelled to look and act like a gangster, and his concept of that image obviously came from old movies. Both he and the woman believed in letting people know that they were successful. So many diamonds adorned the woman's fingers that I thought she might own a string of whorehouses; the man had a diamond in his tie and also a couple of big ones on his fingers. Befitting his role of lesser light, the other fellow wore a black shirt with his cheap pinstripe suit, and no visible jewellery.

As a foreigner I came under friendly scrutiny, and a little way out of Seville the one who looked most like a gangster tried out his English. When my nationality was established, after I'd been given a drink of some vile-tasting stuff, the first question was whether I'd been to Chicago. The man with the diamonds was the only one who spoke English and so translated to the others. No other place in America was of interest, and when it turned out that I'd actually been to Chicago this was immediately conveyed to the others in excited Spanish. Having been to the focal point of his dreams, I was stamped as one of the man's own kind. His sizing-up led to the conclusion that I was stationed at one of the United States Air Force bases. But as a man who'd been to

Chicago it stood to the Spaniard's reason that there must be things in which I was prepared to deal. Nothing appealed more than American money, so with only enough bargaining to make it look good I let a rate be set that was very much his way. Following agreement on a price half-way between legal and black, it was time to talk about where and when a deal could be done. The fellow showed that he was an operator by not expecting me to be in a position to deal on the spot. He wanted to set up something worth while, and his pleasure was expressed to the woman, who became all smiles. Noticing her diamonds more closely gave me an idea of how big a deal might be worked. Having been asked how much American money I could round up within a day of reaching Granada, I was casting about for a figure. Four thousand dollars plus a few extra fifties was all the fake money I had short of Paris or London, but I didn't know whether such an amount should be mentioned. From the show of diamonds I thought that thousands rather than high hundreds might be appropriate. A stab at two thousand dollars brought enthusiastic response, along with questions about how speedily the money could be tapped. So excited was the fellow over the amount mentioned that I thought he might safely stand another two thousand dollars' worth of excitement. Finally, I suggested four thousand could be got from the base next day, and more a week later.

As the train slowed for Granada, I timed our meeting for late next afternoon—hoping that the banks would be closed by then. I knew I could be set up for a take-down, though my promise of future transactions was of some assurance. As a precaution my fifteen hundred dollars' worth of loot from Seville would not be on me, so it seemed I could only lose fake money; for a four-thousand hit, this seemed a worthwhile chance to take. As their guest I was taken by taxi to a hotel, seen safely registered and left on my own after reaffirming my promise to meet the man there at four next afternoon. My few excess fifties were cautiously released around the bigger hotels in the morning.

I bought a sleeper ticket on the night express for Paris, and left my suitcase containing all not needed for the deal at the station.

Minutes ahead of time the man showed up in the hotel lobby, accompanied by his follower—but without the woman. In the privacy of my room, with both Spaniards looking on, I counted

142

out my four thousand, watched nervously while a couple were examined, received bundles of pesetas I didn't check for authenticity, and the deal was over. Without the loquacity of the previous day my visitors left, after giving me the phone number to ring when I arrived with more money.

I reckoned five minutes would see those two gone from the area—and I promptly left the hotel. With four hours to kill, I spent the time in cafés, reflecting that the Spanish gangster should get clear of the deal without losing—I hoped. Possibly he wouldn't harbour ill feelings toward somebody from Chicago who got the better of him, but I didn't want to be around to find out. Only when the train began to move out of Granada station did I feel that the deal was sealed.

My pesetas were changed for American money in Paris and I spent two nights with my woman friend, before going back to London. From my stash there I picked up thirty thousand for a quick run through the U.S.—and also bought an airplane. Though I'd long intended purchasing an aircraft, doing it right then was spur of the moment. An airplane was not needed yet and later I mightn't be free to use it, but for my personal satisfaction I wanted to do the flight from England to Australia by light aircraft. Having two days to put in before boarding the *Queen Mary* at Southampton for New York, I thought of my plan and checked with an aircraft broker. In his list was a Percival Proctor for four hundred and fifty pounds, and I was interested for more reasons than low price. Cost was a consideration on a twelve-thousand-mile flight in a single-engine aircraft because it could easily be lost. But there were other factors. The airplane had suffered a slight prang, was in a workshop undergoing repair, and would be up to British Certificate of Airworthiness standard in a couple of months. Time of delivery suited me because I'd be floating fake money—for better or worse—at least that long. Despite its tendency to veer off the runway unless one quickly used differential braking on landing, the cause of the present damage to the aircraft, I liked flying the Proctor. The broker was reputable, so I accepted his guarantee rather than make an inspection trip to Newcastle upon Tyne.

What I was getting, sight unseen, was an ex-World-War-Two Proctor Mark 4, with a Gypsy Queen engine and without radio or modern navigation aids. Not the lightest of aircraft, the

143

Proctor is a low-wing four-seat tail-wheel type, of mostly plywood construction. It has room in the cabin for an auxiliary tank, which extends its range to seven or eight hundred miles. Lack of radio was not a worry, because I was used to airplanes without such devices, and I liked flight free from control. Although my chances would, I realized, be better in a modern airplane, I was willing to be a bit unreasonable about wanting to do an Australia flight this way. The risk element could be lightly dismissed, because in handling counterfeit money I was taking far greater chances.

I crossed to America by ship on the assumption, as before, that getting counterfeit money past customs might be safer as one of a thousand passengers from a big liner. There'd been stories in the papers about American Customs drug vigilance, and I felt that an airport could be a trap. In the five days it took the *Queen Mary* to cross the Atlantic, there was time to think about the U.S. operation, and decide on visiting my family.

It had been nearly ten years since I'd seen them, time for much to have been forgotten, so it seemed best to make the visit before anything should go amiss. I'd tell them that I'd done all right as a pilot in Australia, and was able to afford the trip. As for passing the money, I'd play it by feel, and work to no predictable pattern. If, by any chance, the Secret Service seemed on the trail, I could change number groupings from place to place and hit fresh cities with fresh bills. Though it would limit working hours I'd only pass money after the banks were closed; then nobody could check if suspicious, and it would give me time to vanish before business deposits were made.

I decided that I'd stay in America for two months, leave my passport on arrival in a safe place so that if I were caught and managed to make bail I'd have a way out of the country, and that was about all the planning I intended to do.

Guilt feelings were a problem I wouldn't contemplate. I thought my money was good enough to penetrate the banking system beyond the teller—so that the individual customer would be unaffected. The banks would be the losers, and I couldn't care less about them. Some flourishing businesses might get hurt a bit, but I had no intention of taking small shopkeepers who'd be damaged by loss of a few dollars. I decided to restrict my changing of fifties to businesses where activity was high enough

144

for this denomination not to attract attention; this would at least represent an approach to crime without victim.

While the *Queen Mary* was making her slow run up New York harbour, I concealed bills in shoes and pockets. Customs presented no problem, and after checking my luggage at Grand Central I proceeded to contact my family. I phoned New York University and was put through to Professor Baudin. My brother was still the only one with whom easy communication was possible, so I hoped things would go smoothly. We had barely exchanged greetings when he asked if I was in any kind of trouble. In a voice full of innocence I informed him that I was in no difficulty whatsoever and would like to see him.

We met in a Greenwich Village café. Our talk soon turned into a question and answer session, my brother becoming very suspicious of how I was financing an airplane for a flight to Australia; he certainly did not believe I'd done it on the proceeds of flying and aerial photography. He expressed the hope that I wouldn't embarrass the family, and, praying it would never happen, I proclaimed with a straight face that all my activities were justified.

Then followed several days with my family, so unmarred by incident that I genuinely regretted that the visit was not at a time when I wasn't involved in something. Until I realized how foreign my life was to theirs, I was sorry I'd not at least become one of them to the extent of learning a profession. But academic life seemed to me narrow and insular; so ingrained was the concept of universities as sole repositories of all worthwhile knowledge that they were surprised I held a commercial pilot's licence without having attended one.

Two days later I was in Minneapolis, clear of family and ready for work. This city was chosen because I felt that doing a series of places within a few hundred miles' radius of Chicago could make the authorities think the operation was based there. My plan was to establish a regional concept by intensively working an area, then confusing the issue by suddenly switching to a different part of the country. For the time being I'd use public transport in its lowest form, Greyhound rather than airline, and therefore less likely to be sought at terminals.

The first place that attracted me was a jewellery store—dollar-a-week establishment rather than a good place. There were plenty of customers, so nobody would waste time over my purchase. The nine dollars ninety-five watch I chose was selected as carefully as any genuine buyer would pick that sort of junk, but I had to insist on a cheap one for work and not on something good on painless payments. A time-wasting act, later to be discarded, was pulling out a couple of single dollars before looking annoyed at having to change my fifty. Only reading the denomination of my bill, the clerk put it in a cash drawer, handed me my change and moved on to another customer.

The next fifty got landed into a drugstore in exchange for a fountain pen and a number of smaller bills, and the paper I tested it on was not left behind. Around the corner was another jewellery store, so I acquired my second junky watch. This one was fast, because the salesman didn't try to talk me into opening a credit account.

Between touches I remembered four days starving in the Minneapolis jail for walking down the street when I was a hobo, and was glad I picked this town for a good going-over. Another jewellery clerk pulled me into a lengthy discussion of better things, and I resolved not to let this happen again. That salesman could later give a description of somebody who passed a fifty on him; there was also the time factor. Though this was a Saturday afternoon with plenty of shopping hours and no banks open, I still shouldn't waste valuable minutes on slow deals.

An unwanted watch was left in a bus-station men's room, and another, after acquiring half a dozen fountain pens from drugstores in the meantime, was given to a bum. A block from my last hit the fellow stopped me for consultation about his financial state, and doubt about the source of his next meal. He was given a handful of silver, before I thought of this as an opportunity to rid myself of another watch.

Handing one to the startled bum, I said that if he had a watch he'd know when it was time for his next meal or drink. So pleased was he with this gift that, on impulse, I gave him a fountain pen, with the remark that he could use it to write home for money. So the bum or his bar friends wouldn't think my gifts were throwaways from a cheque artist, I said I'd won them in a crap game.

By dinner time I'd abandoned in toilets or slipped into trash cans what seemed enough merchandise to stock a small store.

146

Takings were nearly two thousand in good money, and though I still had confidence my nerves were beginning to feel the strain. A good meal brought me change from another fifty, but by then most businesses were closed. Half an hour of a drugstore-only operation finished off Minneapolis; I collected my luggage from the airport and went by taxi to the nextdoor city of St Paul's bus station.

There was time to kill before the Chicago bus left, so I walked around St Paul looking for touches. A clothing store open for late trade sold me a replacement for the slightly grubby shirt I was wearing, and drugstores supplied me with watches, pens and packets of rubbers—dumped before I cleared out of town.

After the bus was out of St Paul I decided to get off at Milwaukee early in the morning, work such businesses as might be open on Sunday, and still arrive at Chicago in time for a night's rest. Chicago would remain untouched this time as I intended hitting other mid-western towns first, diverting possible investigation to such secondary places. I could do Chicago as a mopping-up operation.

As the bus bored through the darkness, I wondered how long it would be before anybody in Minneapolis or St Paul knew what had been done. Those bills could go through the banks undetected and it might even be safe to work a place to saturation, though I wouldn't put that notion to the test. What I could hope for was that many of my bills might go through the system to destruction as worn-out currency, without being spotted. They were on durable paper, and with normal handling would get tattered rather than come apart. Nothing could make me believe that each bill of the tons of worn currency burned in government furnaces would be checked. Fresh money would replace what was destroyed, but they'd need an army of people to check serial numbers and weed out fakes. As long as currency didn't scream falseness, a fair percentage had to slip through.

Banks might detect some of my bills, but anything I'd float could only be a drop in the ocean the way those places handled money, so their people wouldn't waste much time seeking it out. Warnings might be sent to business houses, but apart from number series, which changed from region to region, such notices could only alert merchants to beware of fifties that appeared genuine.

On the more positive side I had a lot going for me, netting such good money in one day. A hundred such days would make me independent for life—provided I didn't get caught. I would be able to go into my photography business as planned, without worry of being undercapitalized. I thought that maybe I was not being ambitious enough, that I should be going for all or nothing rather than merely chasing a few peanuts. I'd already run greater risks flying over mountains and driving on wet roads. If my nerves could last the distance, I could see real wealth being within my grasp. My nerves, however, would be the crucial element and for a further fifty miles I vividly pictured a series of situations, each leading to capture: the energetic store clerk making a grab for me because catching a criminal would be the high spot of his life; the Secret Service crashing into my hotel room, mentioning my offer of a pay-off to a Federal judge; a mob of citizens holding me down on the pavement while distant sirens wailed towards me; the more subtle business of the quiet request for me to "wait a while" in the manager's office while the store made "a few enquiries"; the humiliating march past a mob of staring customers. I consoled myself by remembering that the Secret Service would be more interested in who had the plates than in who was passing the notes. They'd do a scientific study of my bills to determine where the materials might have been obtained. That could only lead to a blank, because not one thing in my U.S. currency was of American origin. Getting to the source rather than catching a replaceable passer could require slow investigation, giving me time to get slightly wealthy before dropping out of business.

Just as success might be big or small, there could be degrees of failure. Anything could happen, from bailable arrest to lengthy imprisonment. If I managed to collect enough before trouble struck, it might be possible to pay off. By putting my passport in a New York safe-deposit box, and opening a bank account there to which I could remit funds, I was at least avoiding a situation where arrest would automatically be the end. The very worst to come out of this might be death in the form of a long sentence I wouldn't try to serve, but I'd taken equal risks flying doubtful airplanes in bad weather. Keeping in mind that something probably could be done if I hit bad luck seemed a comforting approach—if my nerves were able to last the distance.

What I didn't like, and thought of remedying, was the simple fact that this operation only had one passer. I remembered the woman I knew in Los Angeles when I was on parole, who was clever at cashing bum cheques. While thinking that this could be right up her alley, I recalled the mistake on my part that terminated a pleasant affair. Terry—her nickname—took it badly at the time, but she did, as promised, write to me in Australia. Her first letter hadn't exactly been steaming with passion, but there was some suggestion that the gates weren't closed. We kept in touch and planned a get-together next time I was in California, though in the context of my present activity I hadn't given her much thought. Suddenly I saw tremendous possibilities for the future of my exercise if she could be recruited. Many more bills could be passed, with mounting profits—even after allowing for the partner's share—and there'd also be the safety factor of working as a twosome, especially with a woman. From what I knew of her cheque dealings, Terry was so good at disguises and fake accents that she could have the Secret Service running in circles searching for a team of women passing fake money. She could mimic and pass off the accents of three or four nationalities, and if not dealing with people from those countries, could convincingly be anything from Southern hillbilly to cultured New Englander.

Long ago Terry told me about her methods, and they were so good she had never seen the inside of a police station. She wasn't a criminal type, never mixed with rough people, was intelligent, had the speech and manner to get by in the best of company. Terry's downfall—or whatever led to her becoming a proficient fountain-pen bandit—lay partly in her background and the rest in a job she held for some years. Coming from a family with money and social position she had been used to living well, and that lasted through her formative years. Then her father was cleaned out in a business deal, one in which he had no legal comeback, so Terry had to drop out of college. Her choice was limited to whatever job she could find or marrying some boring slob and going into the babymaking business. She chose the former. She eventually landed in the accounts section of a company big enough to handle a fair amount of money, mostly cheques, but not so large as to have an efficient book-keeping system.

149

Terry might have worked there until she landed a husband, but since her parents fought like cat and dog, marriage wasn't in her scheme of things. She liked men, but didn't delude herself that many would last a lifetime without wearing thin. Terry would remain with a man while romantic interest ran close to its peak, then drop him at the onset of disillusionment. Instead of hanging on to the bitter end, she would get out before, in her own words, the usual obnoxious masculine habits of drinking too much and farting in bed transformed her feelings into something resembling the bare tolerance most married women have of their husbands.

Terry's third boyfriend worked in a bank in Los Angeles, and it wasn't long before they discovered that their financial concepts were compatible with their emotional ones. They concocted a scheme whereby Terry took a few cheques each week out of incoming receipts, and handed them to her boyfriend; he cashed them and she cooked the books. The arrangement lasted through several audits, before the bookwork became confused. On the eve of the next audit, with the chief accountant claiming he'd get to the bottom of certain discrepancies, Terry remembered a faraway and very sick relative who required an immediate visit. The boyfriend, safely in the clear if there was no talking, extracted a promise that Terry would forget she knew him.

For the first time Terry thought about the possibility of jail. Frightened and upset over the boyfriend's brush-off, she got into her car and drove all night to reach San Francisco by morning. An office job without sidelines did not provide adequately for her tastes, and when she reached the stage of owing money to every establishment that would give her credit, and of her wages being garnisheed, she decided it was time to disappear. She swiped some cheques before leaving and cashed them on her way out of town. Floating those cheques had been so easy that Terry thought about it all the way up the coast to Seattle, and kept it in mind for her next job—under an assumed name. But she was very soon caught with her hand in the cash drawer, and escorted to the door with only her wages to that day—and almost flat broke. However, she went along and opened a cheque account, and left Seattle with a whole book of cheques. She went up and down the coast cashing them, but the first ones were pitifully small. Learning to make the most of her medium-height appearance, striking when she wanted it to be, she found that if the

150

circumstances warranted it was just as easy to write cheques for decent amounts. Through connections Terry was able to ascertain that no warrant was out for her arrest, and that the firm from which she took the cheques her boyfriend cashed had not complained.

Terry was hooked on cheques, and thought no more about getting a job. From then on her concern was to perfect her technique before perhaps one day landing in front of a judge. She was to survive those early, dangerous days without feeling the heavy hand of the law upon her. She made it fairly safe by a sense of knowing when it was time to give it a rest, and of how far she could safely push her victims. Terry believed that a lot of people didn't complain of her bouncing cheques because she kept amounts down to what her judgement suggested would not be hurtful losses. She knew she couldn't operate for ever without trouble, and made a point of saving some of her profits. Her long-range plan was to live on her investments when finally she was forced to sheath her fountain pen.

Before getting off the bus in Milwaukee, I decided to try to contact Terry by phone from Chicago. Milwaukee got more fifties than seemed right for a Sunday.

Next morning in Chicago all takings were remitted by bank draft to my phony-name "bail and defence" account in New York. The evening before I tried to phone Terry, to learn from a trusted relative that she was on a short trip and would be back in Los Angeles at the end of the week. Knowing the relative well, I identified myself and left a message for Terry about bringing her a "new fountain pen".

Some fast moving on my part, after transferring funds, got me onto a flight for Omaha, and I was in the business district of that city before bank closing-time. My flexible plan was to do some work in a couple of places, then contact Terry from Chicago about the time she'd arrive back in Los Angeles. Omaha was worked a little differently, so I wouldn't establish a pattern of buying only pocketable items. Some were purchased, though after buying a briefcase worth keeping, I spread my patronage to establishments handling bulkier merchandise.

Carrying a good briefcase seemed to have a psychological effect on me as well as others; it made me feel like a solid business or professional man in a position to order rather than ask for

151

what I wanted. I stuffed it with shirts, socks, books and all sorts of things, but when it was full I had a disposal problem. Those articles could scarcely be dumped in lavatories, and my solution resulted in changing another fifty for a cheap suitcase; in the bus-station washroom all purchases were emptied into that before it was left in a locker.

Money spent in Omaha was the same number series used in other places, including the fifty lost on the purchase of a ten-dollar watch. Rather than waste time changing two or three bills, it was good value to lose one getting out of a jewellery store full of "unrepeatable bargains". So persistent was the salesman that besides my "lifetime-guarantee" watch I walked out with a sixty-dollar credit note in lieu of cash change. Watch and note went down a sewer grating.

After other businesses closed for the day it was time for drugstores. One druggist went into fits of laughter on hearing that my girlfriend had left her douchebag behind in a motel, and urgently needed a replacement. Still laughing, he wrapped the thing up and took my fifty. Light conversation, I was finding, drew attention away from the size of my bills, and also eased my nerves. What to say was a matter of sizing up the individual concerned.

Before boarding a late bus for Kansas City, I put the last of my purchases into the suitcase, then shipped it—prepaid and to be called for—to New Orleans, where one day it would be opened as an unclaimed shipment, no doubt to become a puzzle to someone for a while. Early in the morning, while the bus rolled through some obscure part of Kansas or Missouri, I was suddenly awakened, to the horrible knowledge that I was probably trapped without hope of getting away. The bus was stopped, there were red lights outside, and a huge cop who looked like highway patrol followed by a smaller one were climbing aboard. As the lights came on, the big cop opened a slit in his broad leathery face to tell the driver that he'd like to have a look at the passengers. Hand close to holster, the smaller cop stood near the driver while the big one started a slow walk down the aisle. Not a doubt did I have that the hulking bull would stop at my seat and say something like "You just come along with me, boy." My thoughts raced like an express train, chance of bluffing it out— nil; hope of convincing him I was the wrong man—none; risk of violence if I put up objection—plenty, because he looked the kind who'd enjoy handing out a pistol-whipping in front of the other passengers. I'd simply have to go quietly and contact a lawyer. My seat was two-thirds of the way back and the big officer took his time coming down the aisle. Making bail was my only hope, and I was thankful for the New York bank account. Everything on me good or bad would be lost, and not available for my defence. I'd have to do everything the man said, or find out the hard way what the law in this part of the country thought of crooks who cheated honest people with fake money.

Then the cop was within three rows of where I sat desperately trying not to show fear. With arrest seconds away I wondered how this could be happening. Nobody in Omaha even looked suspiciously at my money, and there wasn't a way for one of those fifties to have landed in a bank so soon. Nothing made sense and I couldn't see how they had caught on so quickly, let alone knew that I'd be on this bus. Then the law was at the point where his bulk should halt before ordering me out of my seat, but he wasn't stopping. That cop wasn't interested in me, I had to keep telling myself, and he didn't want to play games by grabbing me from behind. Looking on with mild curiosity would get me by, while deliberate lack of interest might appear suspicious. Again those heavy footsteps went past my seat and I was frozen motionless by fear. Before getting off the bus, the officer's voice drawled out to the driver, "Some young feller tried to hold up a gas station, shot the attendant and hurt him pretty bad."

Between the highway barricade and Kansas City I got no more sleep. The fear I felt while that cop walked down the bus aisle was a terrible belly-cramping sensation. In the grip of it I'd have gladly quit counterfeiting right in the middle of this operation, but the crisis was over. No permanent nerve damage was done and I could continue working—as I did with flying after a situation where I would have willingly sworn off for ever while still in the air. I could only accept the fact that probably there'd be more frights, but everything might come out all right in the end. What had to be hoped was that if I took a fall it would come when my finances were in shape for heavy bribery, high bail, or a good lawyer.

Having most of the day in Kansas City before bank closing

time, I evolved a more efficient way of working the town. Using the bus station and its lockers as a base, I would radiate outwards like spokes of a wheel, but do the actual work on the inwards trip. That way I'd arrive at the bus station heavily loaded, dump my purchases and catch a taxi to the far end of another tangent. So there'd be no wasted work time, I spent hours walking around noting places to hit, and routes to be followed. After lunch and buying a sleeper ticket on a night train for Chicago, I was ready for business.

Working in from the outer edges of the business district, I took in places selling electrical, automotive and even small plumbing items. Anything not taking up too much briefcase space served as an excuse for changing a fifty, while towards the centre of town my buying reverted to city merchandise. Last purchase before each return to the bus station was a cheap suitcase; those not wanted for later shipment of goods were abandoned in lockers.

When a clerk was gone too long getting change, I realized that there was a serious weakness in my system. Sooner or later somebody needing change from a back room might see a Secret Service warning, or for some other reason think wrong thoughts, and there'd be an incident. I decided that when someone even started out of sight with one of my fifties, I should be ready to call him back instantly and pay with a suddenly discovered smaller bill. Though that would mean throwing away an occasional purchase made with good money, it would be very cheap insurance.

Only when the Chicago train was well out of Kansas City did I find out just how well I'd scored. So busy was I during working hours that I had made no attempt to keep track of wealth accumulation, but in my Pullman berth, with fast-moving train wheels drowning the sound of riffling paper, I got a pleasant surprise. My high-efficiency system produced half as much again as from Omaha in about the same working time. With nearly two thousand dollars gained from Kansas City, there could be another solid remittance to my New York account.

Before settling into a near northside hotel I decided to use the time until I contacted Terry working over some outlying parts of Chicago. This fitted into my regional concept as well as going farther afield, but better mobility was needed. Within a few miles' radius of downtown Chicago were a number of almost

154

citylike business districts, some so close together that I would be able to drive from one to another during working hours without wasting much shopping time.

For good cash a used-car place sold me an eight-year-old Buick. A story about trading the car in quickly if the right horse won caused the dealer to hand me the papers and not put through a proper registration. My receipt was in a name supplied for the purpose, and I was ready for work, using transport that was reliable—and inconspicuous. Most important, the car was not traceable if someone got my number or I had to abandon the heap. Without any kind of driving licence it was important to remember that this wasn't Australia—and be sure to drive on the right side of the road.

My first use of the car was in a business district far down on the south side of Chicago, where I had a bright idea for getting rid of unwanted parcels. Parked in a side street out of sight of the main one being worked, I left the windows open and a number of attractive parcels on the front seat. Returning with a fresh load only to find the earlier ones intact was a disappointment. It appeared that, of all places, Chicago could not even provide a sneak thief when and where one was needed. Then I realized that I'd done one of the most stupid things of all time, for if the cops had caught some bum stealing from my car, they'd need a complainant—and my kind of shopping would be a bit difficult to explain away.

My plan for working suburban drugstores that night went down the drain when I met a woman in a downtown café. Nothing was glamorous about this pick-up, but the woman was friendly and I was ripe for something. She was long in the tooth, slightly lacking in personality, said she wasn't married and had a rock-bottom job in an office. After talking a fair while we left the café, to head for my hotel.

Recovering from the shock of seeing hair on her breasts, I forgot myself to the extent of asking if she'd ever been with a woman who strapped on a dildo, and she became annoyed. There was nothing queer about her, she insisted after I apologized, but she was on hormone treatment and it had magnified her hair problem. Because the woman was embarrassed about what she had below, I had to turn off the light. When I said that there wasn't much I hadn't seen, she let me

155

switch on the bedside lamp, revealing a bush so mighty I wouldn't have believed it possible; I thought of running a finger through the fur to find out if it concealed some rudimentary male organ. Settled into the bed I learned that there was nothing wrong with the woman's female tendencies, and treatment she was undergoing bore no relation to frigidity. The mop hid no more than a box with lips so big that I thought she might have a slightly prolapsed uterus, and a well-working sphincter muscle. When she asked if my ideas of love-making were advanced, I lied slightly saying I wasn't a muffdiver the first time out.

For all her lack of personality and hairiness this woman wasn't difficult to like. She wanted nothing from me and was so anxious to please that I formed the impression she was desperately lonely, and getting little out of life besides brief encounters such as this one. She asked if I'd be in town the following night and I said I would; I suddenly had the idea of letting her benefit from my next bout of shopping. After promising to take her to dinner next evening I told my hairy friend that I could get her some clothes from the people with whom I'd come to confer in Chicago. She was so grateful, without even knowing if this was a line, that I decided to make our second meeting memorable, and probably kiss her where she'd like it best.

By closing time the next day I had a good collection of feminine items. To make the stuff look like trade samples rather than loot, some work had to be done before handing over. No fear did I have of the woman talking in the wrong quarters, but there was the risk that shop wrappings might tempt her to take some clothes back for exchange. After dinner my friend was brought to the room, and when she saw all the things spread out on the bed she stared in disbelief. Her first words were expressions of amazement that people would give away such items, but I told her my connections were top-level people used to dealing big. The two suitcases, I explained, were hers too, acquired from a very important baggage man I'd conferred with that day.

We got into bed earlier than the night before, and this time I forgot about the fur. She only had to wonder whether I was "advanced" long enough for us to start kissing each other's genitals. Probably she realized that my restraint the previous night had been caused by something other than inhibition, because whatever the fur was laced with eliminated the slight fish

156

smell. Since I expected to be in touch with Terry in the morning, we arranged that I'd contact her next time I was in town.

Terry got my message from her relative, and was waiting when I put a call through to Los Angeles. So friendly was she that it was difficult to realize that we had ever disagreed about anything. We arranged to meet next day at Los Angeles airport. I felt in a good mood as I set about winding down my Chicago operation. Car disposal was settled on the way to my first suburb, after a dealer agreed on a price and said he'd be there when I returned at the end of the afternoon. Driving on to my last hours of work, I intended to leave more than just the car with the dealer, but had second thoughts about that. What made me decide against presenting all those parcels to the man buying my car was the inborn loquaciousness of his breed. He'd have to boast to his friends about getting for nothing what was probably the by-product of some major cheque cashing; if there was publicity about counterfeit money, someone not benefiting from my largesse might talk.

Toward the end of the afternoon I began to worry about getting rid of the merchandise that was piling up in the car; even the glove-box was full of small items I stuck there. It was finally that hour when the more worthwhile shops were closing, and further pursuit of business would be based on greed and not need. From my last hit in a far north-western suburb there were fifteen miles of city driving to the dealer's place, and I wanted an empty car on arrival. The easiest way seemed to be to toss things out as I drove, so I did just that. Using back streets, I let fly a few parcels every time I was in a deserted block. Small and big stuff went out the window by the handful, although I tried to make my drops far enough apart for no two lots to be found by the same people. When a taxi dropped me at the hotel, after the empty Buick was left with the dealer, I felt my connections with Chicago were severed.

Anxious for a new experience before leaving town, I decided to find out why sophisticated men patronized expensive callgirls. Paying one with fake money appealed to me as a mischievous touch, compensating for old times when I couldn't afford whores. Asking a ferret-faced bellboy to get me the best resulted in the prompt appearance of a pleasantly spoken, rather attractive young woman, quite unlike the usual run of whore. After the two

157

previous nights I was not motivated by need, but the girl exuded sex and I began to feel anticipation. Conversational niceties came before anything so crass as putting a price on her wares, so when the subject was raised it was in the form of two hundred dollars needed to pay some imaginary bill. Payment was four fifties peeled from a thick roll, with two extras following a casual remark that money was no object as long as I enjoyed myself.

When I expressed interest in something more imaginative than ordinary intercourse, the girl's eyes lit up, as if she could really enjoy her work. Saying that many clients had special tastes, she plucked devices from an oversize bag, commenting on each as she did so. The little whips were for beating certain people on the ass, she said in a way to imply awareness that I wouldn't require such stimulation. Next came an electric vibrator with a lot of rubber attachments, also a box of creamy chocolates. A big rubber prick, she explained, was for men who were a bit queer, but on me she'd use a small one. The chocolates would play their role when the time came; meanwhile I was to get a very special massage.

Before I could say whether I wanted any kind of dildo, the girl had one vibrating madly around my rectum, then leant down to take my penis in her mouth. Still not consulting me, she poked two chocolates into her snatch, but I had no intention of going down on her with or without sweetening. When she smeared the dildo with vaseline and worked it up inside me I was still fairly certain about not wanting to slurp the chocolate out. Some gentle movement of the rubber thing made me think I might kiss her box without opening my mouth too wide.

Then she hit the switch, and forgetting earlier reservations I wanted to suck on that snatch for all I was worth. Knowing I was ready, the girl got on top and lowered her pelvis toward my face. My tool went back into her mouth, and with the vibrator going full speed in my rear we started to suck each other. Gobs of vaginal-flavoured creamy stuff came out so fast I could barely swallow quickly enough to make room for the next succulent mouthful. This couldn't last long, though after I blew my load into the woman's mouth the sensation of excitement remained. Unlike anything I'd ever experienced, I had no desire to pull my face out into fresh air. Each with our organ in the other's mouth we relaxed, and I could still taste a seepage of chocolate from the soft folds. After several minutes in that position we separated, and

158

as the dildo was withdrawn it uncorked the most mighty fart; I apologized and the girl laughed.

Much of the evening I'd paid for remained, so the hooker and I talked after she'd promised to bring me around again later. I began to have feelings of guilt about paying her with fake money. During a lull I suggested she take a close look at her fifties, because I'd won them at a gambling joint that was known occasionally to pay off with counterfeit. No fault did the woman find; I suggested that either she could keep those plus another half dozen I'd throw in or take the original price in smaller denominations. She jumped at the higher offer, and as a concession to caution said she'd keep them until her next trip out of town.

Going through the departure gate at Chicago airport next morning, I had a slight attack of the horrors. This was where any reckoning over my work in the city could easily happen, but I didn't dare look round to see if any plainclothes men were headed my way. Carried along with the crowd and trying not to appear nervous, I proceeded up the boarding ramp. My only concern then was that the A.T.C. would safely vector the airplane out of the heavy Chicago terminal area traffic.

During the long flight much thought was given to how I'd put my proposition to Terry. No conclusions could be reached, though I felt that however it got laid on the line, my cheque-passing friend would declare herself in on the deal.

Terry was waiting inside the gate at Los Angeles. All the way into town we talked about ourselves and what we had been doing, but mentioned neither counterfeit money nor my marriage in Australia. Terry had completed a couple of university courses, cashed a lot of bum cheques and worked in a public relations office, been an associate producer and director of several movies and, finally, had floated still more paper.

The movies were a joint venture and were just starting to do well when the District Attorney's office took an unhealthy interest in the subject. Terry was the mainstay of their production division, and scripted and directed several twenty-minute movies. The outfit made good profits hiring the films to certain exhibitors, but there were problems. A choice movie fell into the hands of an official more powerful than the police on the studio payroll, and the business became difficult to manage. They used good whores and pimps in their productions, their equipment was first class, and each film had enough story to lift it above complete crudity. Allowing for Terry's exaggeration, the films sounded like art rather than straight pornography—though the guardians of public morals didn't see them this way. The studio was raided, some equipment lost, people were arrested, but not Terry and her co-producers; enough warning came from the paid-off cops for the principals to get away, but it finished the movie business.

It was settled on the drive from the airport that I'd stay with Terry. In the privacy of her apartment I took an envelope containing a hundred of my fifties from an inside coat pocket and spread them loosely around our feet. She stared silently at the money, before asking in a voice strained with excitement whether it was real. That seemed the response of someone lost for words rather than a question calling for an answer, so I said nothing. Then the thought struck Terry that the money actually could be counterfeit, and she picked up one of the bills. Still bewildered she looked at one side, then the other. The desired impact had been achieved, so I told her the bills were "genuine" counterfeits and that I had printed them. Studying a handful, she said that she didn't think fake money could look so real. I put on a straight face and maintained that the important thing was that realness must be in the eyes of the beholder. Looking acquisitive, she eagerly asked just where she came into this. I explained that the money was entirely of my own manufacture, I had sole world-wide distribution, and the deal was still cool—because I'd floated only a few thousand dollars. She would travel with me, and unless she could think up something better, she would pass the bills, one at a time, for a half-share of the profit from them, with a worthwhile increase if she worked diligently.

Terry became full of suggestions, saw herself working places that would be awkward for a man, and was mentally spending fifties at five thousand dollars a day before I brought her closer to earth. I explained the need for caution and suggested that two thousand was a good day's take for one operator. She accepted this. We also discussed risks and penalties. She knew that handling counterfeit money was a Federal offence, but that appeared to be no deterrent. Her ties could be cut with a few phone calls, and the only man in her life, a lawyer, would be

160

phased out. I suggested he might be worth keeping on tap, but she said he was the overbred English type of American, whose idea of being a lawyer was to handle only dignified affairs such as property transfer.

Our varied travel prospects meant that Terry would soon need a passport. Long before the evening was over, our plans for the immediate future were completed. Terry already had a copy of her birth certificate, so next day she'd apply for a passport, to be picked up in New York. While that was being done I'd buy a good car for our trip across country, to be dumped for what it would bring on arrival in New York; as good as Terry's car was, it was traceable and therefore out. I reminded her of times she padded herself to look pregnant on cheque-cashing sprees and suggested this as a safe way of transporting large sums into America. She felt a big-money pregnancy could make her look a medical curiosity; with little bills perhaps, I said, but a fortune in fifties padded to round the rough edges shouldn't appear any more odd than a seven-month swelling. This was when I told about there being about two million dollars in Australia, a bundle in Paris and another in London.

Our first hit would be a big one, at St Louis on the following Saturday. That would allow time for a pleasant drive two-thirds of the way to the East Coast. After St Louis we'd work Cincinnati, Columbus, Cleveland and finally Buffalo—if funds remained. Those cities would be late-afternoon stands, but with two at work they should net a fair amount of money. Further U.S. operations could be planned after we'd been to Europe.

So much was discussed that when we got to bed I expected to be faced with an embarrassing anticlimax. Vibrator treatment in Chicago along with what happened the two nights before were things I wanted to forget while in bed with Terry, and I did at least to the point of saving face. Before going to sleep I thought of my foolishness all that time ago about me and someone not even worth a sniff where Terry took a crap. Besides being attractive she also, then, had an emotional depth I had not realized. As with so many women of her intelligence and temperament Terry had improved with age, and though she'd never seemed emotionally or physically limited she was now radiantly mature. Though as before she remained a passionate woman, there was a hard-to-define change for the better. Lying

161

beside Terry, I thought that for the foreseeable future we'd have an exciting time together.

Early on Monday morning, well before the rush-hour traffic started, Terry and I were passing through the endless suburbs of Los Angeles, toward our first stop at the desert town of Indio. Catching the full blast of heat off the desert, we wished we'd left the evening before and driven all night to reach the Arizona mountains by daylight. Old experience driving wildcat buses taught me to make night departures eastbound out of Los Angeles, but that was then and meantime memories had faded. We were stuck with a daytime crossing in searing heat, so I could only keep speed down to where our tyres wouldn't overheat and count the slow hours until climb-out approaching Prescott in the high country.

Coming close to that town, long after a brief stop at an air-cooled café in Blythe, the pair of us began to come alive. This was to be a rest-stop and Terry had something to say about eating arrangements; it seemed that although her appearance had been different on a previous visit to Prescott, Terry would feel more at ease if we ate at some out-of-the way spot rather than stopping in the main business centre.

On such a long trip there was little to do but talk, so as an exercise in semantics we spent time justifying our different ways of milking the system. Past Ash Fork, Arizona, and speeding east on Route 66, Terry rationalized about how she bounced cheques only on business men who could afford an occasional loss in their chase for profit. Her conscience was not troubled about re-routing to herself a little of the vast amount of money in circulation, while the moderate deficit was an inexpensive lesson in caution to the people involved. Town after town we passed had previously felt the sting of Terry's pen, and it wasn't until east of Tulsa that she was willing to show her face in public.

Like herself I wasn't out to harm anybody with my bills, I explained, nor did I seek vengeance against society because of fancied wrongs; all I wanted to do was to bite the system for enough to establish myself. Unlike most business men I wasn't engaging in sneaky little practices to cut costs in manufacture; my bills were made of the best materials obtainable—much better than the rubbish available in exchange for them—and they'd probably last almost as long as genuine currency. Having all that durability and quality built into them, I raved on, they could remain undetected right through to final destruction and still look real as they were shovelled into the treasury furnace. I finally suggested that my product wasn't watering down the country's note issue, but restoring the balance of genuine loss of money burned, buried and forgotten. This wasn't, Terry suggested, exactly a public service.

Before leaving Los Angeles we thoroughly discussed the use of bail bondsmen if one or the other was caught. Bail was the first thing needed in case of trouble, and a bondsman could be our means of establishing quick contact. If one or the other failed to keep an appointment, the one waiting would contact the appointed bondsman. Even if the police were treating the matter as an incommunicado arrest, an alerted bondsman could usually get results, and a lawyer quickly brought in by him would prevent in-depth questioning. It would be total disaster if we were both caught, but short of making prior arrangement with a bondsman this was a risk we'd have to accept. When operating, we'd arrange for frequent meetings, with fifteen minutes' leeway before emergency action; also neither of us would carry anything relating to the car or its location.

Thursday evening had us into St Louis in time to set up headquarters at a motel, and next morning Terry and I looked over the field of operation. We spent the rest of the day compiling work lists for each, so when the banks closed at noon next day there'd be no waste of shopping time. With notes on places to hit or miss completed, we both memorized the name of the bail bondsman with the biggest advertisement. Procedure would be hourly meetings at whatever parking lot we used, moving the car elsewhere half-way through the afternoon. That move would make our repeated trips to the car loaded with merchandise less obvious to parking attendants. During scheduled meetings we'd compare notes or analyse suspicion encountered; in any danger situation the threatened partner would return immediately to the car, to drive straight out of town as soon as the other showed up.

Promptly at noon on Saturday Terry and I left the parking lot and parted quickly at a busy intersection. On my return to the car there was nothing to indicate that Terry had been back with a load. As fast as my briefcase was emptied I was off for more, but next trip back there was clear evidence of Terry's work. On the back seat was a huge shopping bag, loaded with little packages. Looking at that bag, I had the deflating feeling that Terry, in her first attempt, was running ahead of me.

Terry was in the car with her third load when I arrived for the meeting where we were to move to another parking place. As I went toward our new location, supercautious not to break any traffic rule, she remarked that tension was showing in my driving. Though admitting that this was also a strain for her, she said she got a thrill out of it as she did with other dangerous things. She was intrigued with the notion of taking stores down with something that looked like money instead of long-winded tales followed by cheques. Though this was easy, Terry realized that if anything went wrong it could be sudden and nasty.

We saved drugstores for evenings when other worthwhile businesses were closed. On impulse I dropped my drugstore purchases into street corner mail boxes in preference to making trips back to the car. Working on a hit and walk basis, I finished the evening with a feather-light briefcase and a pocket full of money. Terry didn't think much of my using letter boxes for unaddressed merchandise and, rather than dump her drugstore contributions, bought an oversize bag with her first fifty and filled it with cosmetics.

How good St Louis was to us didn't become clear until we counted eight thousand dollars. Fighting the temptation to leave our huge collection of merchandise in the room and head down the highway with our profit, we prepared it for proper disposal. Since the motel people could give our car number and description after finding a room full of loot, we left nothing behind but our own used and discarded things. Everything to be wasted after getting us good money for bad went into suitcases for dispatch at Indianapolis.

We hit the road as planned. As we headed from the bridge over the Mississippi into the darkness of the flat Illinois farmlands, Terry talked about passing her first bills and her feelings now that she'd experienced involvement. During her early hits she'd been nervous to the point of talking too much, but by now she'd got the feel of the thing. Going into a city and working furiously to offload fake money followed by a fast late-night departure appealed strongly to her sense and love of adventure. She pointed out the advantages of being a woman in this business, because of

164

instinctive trust by others and the chance of convincingly acting confused and flustered in a tight situation. My only answer was that in a nasty showdown I would have the doubtful advantage of being able to push people aside and run.

The nearest Terry came to an incident was in women's shop, and she handled it the best possible way. The clerk headed for the back room after finding his register five dollars short of the change required, but she stopped him cold. Terry suddenly remembered that she wanted to buy something else, which just happened to cost a little more than the shortage.

At Indianapolis late next morning there was a brief stop at a bus station while I shipped our unwanted merchandise to Seattle, then we were back on the road. One of the ways to Cincinnati passed through the small university town of Oxford, so I asked Terry if she would like to see where my early years were spent. She was willing, so a couple of hours later we drove along streets I hadn't seen since I was a boy. Passing McGuffey School, I pointed it out as the place where attempts had been made to educate me. Explaining my privileged status, I told about the school being connected with Miami University and not accepting Negroes or Southern white trash; also about my father being on the university faculty. And how, irrespective of this, I had finally been banished for letting loud bean-farts in class; I had imagined that old-maid teachers would find such distasteful matters as noisy emissions of bowel gas impossible to discuss with what I thought of as the fossilized fool of a principal. I told her, too, of how I started on that kick by impulsively letting a really long and loud one with my ass cocked in position to make it reverberate against the wooden seat, causing the class to roar for some time—while the teacher's expression never changed.

Our Cincinnati operation, a week-day stop, was a scaled-down operation compared to St Louis. So after selecting our friendly local bondsman, we did a quick survey and got down to work. After dinner I bought a present for Terry in one of the town's drugstores. The assistant had been amused at my properly worded request for a vaginal syringe, which inspired a sudden impulse to have it gift-wrapped. Before giving me change from my fifty, the man carefully wrapped and decorated it with enough ribbon to make it look an expensive present. As we drove off into the night, Terry showed her appreciation of my nice

165

thought by tossing the thing out of the window into the darkness outside Cincinnati.

At Columbus we remitted to our banks all profits except for the few hundred dollars it might take to interest a bondsman or lawyer. After doing the usual, we were on the road again, this time bound for Cleveland, where, besides running out of money, we varied our working method. If there had been any official awareness of our fake money, it would be along the lines of either a man or a woman working a definite type of shop—we thought—so we switched roles. Terry hit my kind of store for the sort of thing I normally bought, while I took women's shops for feminine items. Quickly Terry learned that the best approach was to buy something for her "husband", rather than some boyfriend. A ten-dollar present could remain at that level without sales talk, when it was made clear that it was only for a spouse, while mention of a boyfriend usually brought suggestions that wouldn't leave much change from a fifty; all Terry had to do was to say cheap and husband in one breath to assure a quick transaction. We used this method through two meetings, and switched back to normal for our final excursion; with only a few fifties left it was time to select good things for our trip to Europe.

In a motel near Buffalo Terry looked over what I had bought for my "wife", and said the shop people saw me coming. Much of the stuff was dead stock that could only be offloaded on someone such as me, or got rid of in a clearance sale. We packed it all into cheap suitcases for shipment from Buffalo next morning.

On the way to New York, I told Terry that her work was top-notch and, in a lot of ways, better than mine. Now seemed a good time to mention the idea of putting over several really profitable deals in Europe; it was clear we worked well as a team, so I outlined briefly a few suggestions regarding diamond dealers and money-changers.

We would pose as typical American tourists—the kind that business people could smoothly take down—and would turn their interest to our advantage. At other times we'd be worldly, but that would be for special situations.

Our prospects seemed good. We reached New York, dumped the car on the first dealer, collected Terry's passport, picked up a supply of genuine fifties for a very special purpose and, without going near my family, were that night on a flight for London.

166

9

A Leica for life   on the Riviera   in and out of
Italy   Berlin bungle   a French Connection
diamonds galore   a phantom pregnancy
a real bargain at eight thousand dollars.

TRANS EUROPE EXCESS

After a couple of days in London Terry was ready to hit a few glamour centres, but I suggested bigger things should wait until we built up new reserves in Spain. A direct flight from London landed us at Madrid, where, in the guise of American tourists not willing to break the laws of police-infested Spain, we rejected a money-changer's approach. Somebody at the hotel also wanted to do a deal, but having shown our passports we had to disdain illegal transactions. We were, however, less scrupulous in the lobby of a big hotel some distance away. Here the money-changer found us more concerned with value than respect for local law, so what began as a fifty-dollar transaction became complex. Not wanting to completely destroy the man's hope that we were new to the country, I pushed him only two-thirds of the way to the illegal rate. My reluctance to change more than four fifties was Terry's cue to come in with the strident American wife role, wanting spending money of her own. Acting the appropriate marital part, I looked annoyed and said that after Paris she could spend her own money for once. From her bag there and then came a roll as big as mine, and four fifties went into the changer's eager hand, and as if to spite me she slipped off two more. Then I suddenly remembered a need for additional funds, and changed a further two. We told the man we'd be back when in need of more.

That deal was the first of an afternoon and evening of doing money-changers, and it was one of the biggest. Only one unofficial currency broker subjected our bills to scrutiny, but they passed muster. There seemed to be a feel in most situations that suggested an appropriate amount to change, and Terry and I knew when to stop without even exchanging glances. We avoided transactions out of character with our pose as tourists and ones where outside finance would have had to be mustered by momentarily tapped-out changers. Although we made good touches around major hotels or airline offices, Madrid was big, and friendly little deals for one or two hundred in less imposing places abounded.

Our agreed-on story in case of trouble was that the funds we carried represented gambling winnings, and to support it our rolls were well seeded with genuine fifties, in toward the middle where they couldn't accidentally be changed. We left at the hotel only enough to retread the rolls when they got dangerously thin, while everything else was in a case at the railway station.

Since we couldn't do justice to so huge a city in one day, and our money wouldn't land in the banking system, Madrid became a two-day stand. Not wanting to overdo it with the money-changers, we devoted our second day to some heavy shopping. Rather than a U.S.-type operation, changing one bill at a time, we hit jewellery stores for worthwhile amounts of quality items. As the indulgent husband of scatterbrained Terry I let her make selections worth upwards of a thousand dollars in a number of stores. In each place I called a halt just before finalizing the deal by apparently exercising a measure of control over my wife. While the jewellers looked as if they could murder me for killing a sale they'd just been drooling over, I told Terry that she should look in a few other places before buying. A sop thrown in each shop was that they should set aside Terry's selection, because it looked better than things we'd seen elsewhere. Doing it this way meant fast action when it came time to buy, which turned out to be just before the train left for Barcelona.

We looked over our loot in the train, and decided not to do it that way again. Buying retail got us a lot of very nice things that would have to be heavily discounted, and we'd shown our faces just a bit too much. Individual bills for throw-away items, we decided, would have netted nearly as much profit in the same time.

We met Barcelona's money-changers in the usual tourist areas,

168

and like those in Madrid they went down the drain for similar amounts. Again there was a two-day stand, the first day devoted exclusively to kerbside brokers. The second was simple American-style shopping, the only difference being that Terry and I stayed together. The only place we varied our fast hustle shopping was in a well-stocked camera store, but it wasn't premeditated. Seeing a collection of the latest Leica equipment, I decided that possibly there could be one exception to the rule against keeping things bought with fake money. Justifying such a breach was the fact that we were getting the illegal rate. Our bills should finish up in the hands of some broker, along with genuine currency from many sources, and not be traceable to where it was spent. Not being so interested in photography, Terry was content to buy a Nikon with only the normal lens. Nothing less than a Leica plus three lenses was good enough for me, and I'd have taken more but for the portability problem. There was no way I could predict its ultimate fate. With two thousand dollars remaining from the bundle brought from London, we considered a third day in Barcelona. While discussing this, our thoughts somehow drifted to Spanish jails and what they might be like. That night Terry and I were on a train for Paris.

Besides other superb goods, France had a reputation for producing some of the world's best fake money—for export only. French banknotes carry a nasty warning about life imprisonment for counterfeiting, and neither Terry nor I wanted to test the country's attitude toward even the lesser offence of passing the stuff. As an operational base we needed a European country where we'd remain clean. France was the logical choice.

Our Spanish money was changed for nearly fifteen thousand genuine U.S. dollars, which accompanied the Madrid jewellery into safe deposit at the American Express. Then I thought of a kind of deal that might be set up in France, without drifting too far from our policy of cleanliness. Involved in the country's Algerian troubles were dissident groups that could possibly use our money at a favourable discount, and I thought of somebody through whom I might make contact. There was a journalist I had known in California before he amounted to much, and who would never pass up an opportunity to make a fast dollar. Since then he had risen to be European correspondent for a number of U.S. publications, probably remaining as bent as ever. My last contact with him had been in Paris, when he'd told me about some peculiar goings-on in France. A call to the American Embassy press section provided an office number to check, and from that source I learned that my acquaintance was in America, and was returning to Paris in two weeks.

Terry and I decided to treat ourselves to four work-free days on the French Riviera. Being genuine rather than counterfeit tourists, we did the sights and lay on the beaches. Our only concession to work was to talk about the futility of trying to take down places such as the Monte Carlo casino. For the first time since Los Angeles we were together where we needed neither to work nor to travel. This was conducive to passionate love-making, so in an urge one night to do something different I urinated in Terry. This is supposed to be difficult with a good erection, though I'd done it many times and found that usually it gave the woman, as well as myself, great pleasure. Only by ceasing all motion and thinking about something quite remote, such as a stream of flowing water, could I manage; it can be messy to clean up afterwards and should only be done with a woman sophisticated enough to be receptive, but it does provide an unusual sensation and tends to delay orgasm. Taking my mouth away from Terry's snatch, I told her to lie flat on her back. After some conventional strokes to replace sucked-out lubrication I stopped deep inside. She waited for what might happen. Following my instruction not to move, Terry lay quite still until she felt the first warm gush way up inside her.

Feeling the volume of what I spurted before excitement cut off my flow, Terry was worked up to the point of digging her nails into my back. Putting that thrill out of mind I let go a bigger amount, still way in and not moving, but only a few drops leaked around the base of my shaft to run down between her legs. When I backed a little way out to make room for more, the leakage increased. Terry moved a hand under her leg and pinched together the rear part of her box in an effort to stem the outward flow. When Terry could no longer refrain from moving, I went forward in a frenzied plunge. Something had to go as I bored in like a piston going upstroke in a cylinder, and it went in great warm gushes between my tool and the walls of her vagina. It erupted with an almost burning sensation all over the thighs of both of us, drenching Terry's hand which still pinched to hold the

170

stuff inside. Terry came before I could bring forth any more of what remained in her vagina. What I did was like a douche removing all lubrication so subsequent action was painful, and pleasurable. Both of us got a masochistic delight from the rough friction of skin against skin without anything to make it slide easily, and Terry gave no thought to how sore her box might be later. The bed was in such a state when at last we finished that we could only look with dismay, and wonder how to avoid trouble with the hotel people. It stank, and neither of us could believe that anyone seeing it wouldn't figure out what happened. Then Terry got the bright idea of accidentally spilling a bottle of red wine on the damaged area, before calling room service. Wine-smell dominated all else, and for a large tip the maid was happy to restore the bed to its original state.

Most of Terry's soreness was gone when our holiday ended and we moved on to Italy. As foreign-exchange transactions were free from control in that country, and anything could get into the banks, we avoided money-changers like the plague. A day was spent running up and down hills doing over the shops in Genoa, part of the next day giving Portofino a little dusting, and then we were on a train for Rome. The Eternal City was big enough for two days, with parcels dumped all over the place, and on the way to Naples there were a few remaining to be tossed out the train window. From southern Italy Terry and I doubled back non-stop through Rome and on to Milan. The northern metropolis was our last stand in Italy, before a fast train took us safely through the mountains to Switzerland.

Money is sacred to the Swiss, so we had no intention of testing official feelings toward imitations. Activity in that beautiful country consisted of changing our Italian takings, setting up banking arrangements and sightseeing in the sterile city of Zurich. When it was time to board the Orient Express for Paris we left Switzerland quite uncontaminated by fake money.

Contact with my journalist friend was made the second day in Paris. He thought the call was social, until in a Montparnasse café I showed him a genuine and a fake fifty. Knowing my past in Los Angeles, he caught the drift of things almost before I could ask whether he could see anything wrong with either bill. No more preliminaries were needed, so I explained the goods and the market I was after. Though I told him otherwise, he thought my

171

fifties might have been some of the counterfeits printed by the Hitler government during the war. This was settled by directing the man's attention to the series notations on my bills, which indicated that they were produced long after Hitler was history. Only then was he ready to believe that this issue of money was entirely my own production, that it hadn't been heated up by overuse, and that I could supply large amounts in never-before-circulated number series.

The upshot was that he could contact a few people involved in North Africa. His cut would be a quarter of the price we received and he'd try for sales of around a hundred thousand dollars at twenty per cent of face value. I would have to handle actual sales if any, because he didn't want to get involved beyond carrying and showing a few samples. I didn't mention Terry's existence.

In a stroke of imagination befitting his breed, the journalist suggested directing suspicion over my money to the Communists. Investigative noses could be directed toward the Red East, he thought, by dumping a fair amount in West Berlin. American law-enforcement officials liked to see sinister Red influences in anything worse than parking in a bus stop, so an appearance of my money in that city surrounded by Communist territory might encourage them to think along these lines; that would make a neat tie-up with currency of the same manufacture already floated in other places. Since it would take a few days for him to make his contacts, the journalist suggested that I go straight to West Berlin. Terry thought that working it might be an exciting experience, so that night we were on another train.

West Berlin was uninspiring and the people looked the sort that wouldn't be easily bribed if things went wrong. Away from Paris and into this grim city neither Terry nor I really felt like working. Methedrine pills along with plenty of black coffee quickly put a new complexion on things. From a state of feeding each other's despair we both became exuberant, full of confidence and anxious to outdo ourselves taking down the West Berlin business people.

The arrangement was that Terry and I would meet every two hours at the railway station and check our purchases there rather than dump them, because honest, suspicious Germans might be tempted to hand things over to the police. To avoid overlapping, we'd use the Kurfürstendamm as a rough dividing line. Since

172

Germans could be expected to act on cold logic and without excitement over a sale, we'd be deliberate in our shopping. All day we kept meeting at the station for hurried discussions over black coffee and pills, not even taking time for lunch. We intended to stop for nothing before we boarded the train in the early evening for the run-back through the Communist corridor into West Germany.

Terry and I had just separated after walking away from the station together when I emerged from a shop to find her waiting on the sidewalk looking terrified. Knowing that something was dreadfully wrong, I looked around to see if anyone appeared to be after her. None of the moving masses seemed to show interest, but we were outside a store I'd just taken, so our meeting had to appear casual rather than born of the rising panic conveyed in Terry's eyes. As I resisted an impulse to drag her into a run, Terry spoke of her fear that the police would be after her and begged that we leave Berlin immediately.

Hurrying through back streets toward the station, she breathlessly explained how a man in a photo store had led her into a trap. Her purchase of an exposure meter went smoothly until the English-speaking manager started a conversation which at first indicated no suspicion on his part, but ultimately denied her any chance to retreat. He'd previously elicited the information that after leaving his shop she intended going to a nearby hairdresser. With obvious ulterior motive he offered to hold the bill until she came back. Banks were closed and verification was impossible, but he seemed hell-bent on preventing her from paying with other money and leaving. As Terry recounted it approaching the doubtful safety of the railway station, the business man wouldn't risk trouble by grabbing her, but demands for return of her fifty might have forced his hand. Without giving Terry a chance to say anything, he pointedly said he'd hold on to the bill until she came back. Terry had little option but to smile and agree that this would be all right. Her final attempt to salvage the situation by paying with German money was thwarted when with a hard-eyed look the shop man placed the fifty in a cash drawer. Trying not to show fear, Terry said she'd return in half an hour. Since we had parted only minutes before, she knew roughly where I'd be working—and looked in one store after another until she spotted me.

173

Getting closer to the station and, she hoped, a way out of town, Terry told of suppressing an insane urge to snatch her bill and run. We thought of the possibility that the bill might have passed inspection, and Terry's failure to return would be an admission of something or other, but neither of us had quite enough confidence in our money to go back and find out. The one thing we were sure of was that we had to assume the worst. That West Berliner was not the kind to pocket our fifty and call it profit, so there was every chance that the police had already been called. We considered rushing to Tempelhof airport and trying to board the first flight, but if seats were hard to get we'd be stuck in the one place the cops could check quickly.

The crowded station seemed like a sanctuary after our walk through the streets. Terry unchecked her case, went to the women's room and changed her appearance as much as possible. Nothing could be done about my looks, so I just had to hope that in the hour and a half before the train for the West left the police wouldn't get a description from other shopkeepers who'd taken fifties.

Terry returned looking a changed person, but possibly not different enough to fool that zealot store manager. We talked about getting rid of evidence. The fifties we'd both carried had already been flushed down the station toilets, but then there was the fat roll of fifties still in my suitcase. While every piece of evidence remaining in our possession was as close as the baggage room, there were vast numbers of fake fifties floating around West Berlin and no shortage of shop people able to identify us. We eventually agreed that we'd wait until we boarded the train, and that if that went without incident it would be wise to get rid of the bills.

Between cups of coffee and mixing with the crowd we worked out what to do going through the gate when the train was ready. Since Terry was probably identifiable, we decided that she'd go through first, carrying nothing incriminating. With the case containing the evidence I'd hold back a distance. If she were taken, I'd melt into the crowd and slip out carrying enough good German money to hire a lawyer. Otherwise, I would follow as a separate passenger; to play safe, we wouldn't even know each other until the train was rolling out of town.

The train for the West finally pulled up at the platform. People

174

surged through the gate, and Terry and I had to decide whether to be early on board, or leave our run to the last. All along we thought the cops would try for a gate arrest and not risk scaring us out by searching the station, so just then our nerves were in bad shape. At least three men standing near the gate could have been detectives, but Terry bravely walked past. From my vantage point I couldn't see her get as much as a second look.

Then it was time for my run. Carrying a case that seemed to weigh a ton, I headed straight for one of the ugly cars on that German train. With a slamming of doors, a blowing of whistles and a hefty jolt from the engine, the express was on its way out toward the Communist corridor. When most of the lights of West Berlin had flashed by, I removed the roll of fifties from my case and walked back to the car I'd seen Terry board. In the train corridor we were able to discuss things calmly for the first time since that terror-filled meeting outside the shop. Before very much could be said, I lowered a window and sent our roll of synthetic Western wealth sailing out into the darkness, where it would probably be found by some lucky group of Communist track-workers.

Terry and I talked about the future, as well as holding a post mortem on what might have led to the trouble. The future, as well as we could see it, was that in time this operation would become a thorn in the side of quite a few different authorities. Our job would be to see this coming and be out of business before any real crackdown, while trying not to panic before building up to a good score. The Secret Service wouldn't overlook what was going on outside the U.S. with American money, but it might take time to seek co-operation from other governments and stage a first-class manhunt. We concluded that such time as remained should be put to more sensible use than venturing into places with limited escape possibilities—such as West Berlin. For the immediate future we'd separate before the Communist checkout at Marienborn, remain apart through the change of trains at Hannover and get together again on the way to Frankfurt. Normal operations would be resumed at Paris, where we could replenish our totally depleted funds.

On past events we could merely speculate, and examine the possibilities. Only one hypothesis fitted the known facts. The store appeared to be one of a chain under the same management, since nearly every detail matched a couple of places I hit—and we had not operated in each other's territory. As an executive, the man possibly moved from store to store and could have seen Terry making a similar purchase in another branch. What probably saved our hides was that he wouldn't dare detain a customer without being absolutely certain of his grounds.

Our Paris journalist had made two contacts, but the best bet of the two was interested only in an exclusive deal. These people could play rough, I was told, so that was the way it was to be. The group operated in Marseille, but their Paris representative would meet me for discussion of price, delivery and amount. That evening, after I had picked up fresh bills from the American Express, I was handed over to the Paris man. Having done his part, my friend left me in a café, with the job of convincing a very shrewd Frenchman that I wasn't a petty hawker selling something that could be acquired from other sources. My answer was that if he had access to bank listings of counterfeits, he'd find that I was offering an unknown issue. When I offered the knowledgeable Frenchman enough technical details to convince him that I was the maker, he was prepared to accept me. When he had surreptitiously examined further samples, I guaranteed that anything delivered would be of the same quality.

Price was next, and I was told that my figure of twenty per cent was unrealistic. Half that seemed reasonable to the man, but after I extolled the many virtues of my product he agreed to split the difference. The amount he wanted was a hundred thousand dollars, and I had to admit that in the virgin series I could supply only eighty thousand for immediate delivery. More could be brought from London, I explained, but really large sums would have to be flown in from Australia. Talk about money in such widely spaced places seemed to impress him. It was settled that they'd take my eighty thousand, the deal would take place in Marseille next morning, and I was to be on the night train out of Paris. On arrival I was to call a number I had been given, and from then on to follow instructions.

Only at Marseille would anybody learn that I was not working alone. Terry travelled south on the same train, apparently not knowing me and carrying the money. At Marseille she headed for a hotel on the Canebière, where she was to get a room if possible, or otherwise wait for my phone-call in the lobby. This precaution had limited value, but at least I wouldn't be a sitting duck. If these people wanted to be persuasive, Terry and I agreed, we'd let them have the money and chalk it up to experience.

A phone-call told me where to stand outside Marseille station, and ten minutes later I was picked up by two men in a Citroen. One look at the silent driver's broad shoulders and thick neck made me decide that if he was the persuader of this outfit, I'd let our funds go down the gazoo without a word of protest. The fellow beside me in the back seat was friendly, spoke fair English, and, unlike his bodyguard or driver, seemed highly intelligent. He suggested to me a very capable ex-Foreign-Legion officer, and a man not to be crossed by anyone who couldn't travel fast and far. In a quiet side street the car stopped. I handed over a few samples for inspection, and as if talking from a position of strength said that if everything was all right, we could pick up the eighty thousand within minutes. Instead of a gun in the side to help me see reason, the Frenchman said only that I seemed to know what I was doing.

After inspecting the notes through a magnifying glass, he opened a large envelope to reveal a considerable amount of French currency. If the rest of my bills were the same as those shown, the man said, everything would be fine. It sounded very much as though anybody showing these people good stuff and subsequently trying to palm off rubbish would finish up sorry and battered. Without fear I asked to be taken to a phone.

Staying right on top of the situation, the man escorted me to a phone and listened while I spoke to Terry. Bonehead drove where he was told without opening his mouth, to where Terry waited on the sidewalk in front of the hotel. Exchange of envelope for package took place through the window, and I only had time to tell Terry I'd see her later; the Frenchman added a polite "Bonjour". We moved off and, with me still in the car, they weren't running any risk in letting their uncounted money go out the window for a not-yet-checked package. In a street far up the hills behind Marseille the car stopped again, and Terry's package was opened. Inspection and counting amounted to a spot-check, with bills pulled out at random for examination and one counted bundle measured against others for thickness. They concluded there'd been no misrepresentation and, give or take a thousand, it was all there. As if "Muscle" was relieved with the outcome, he sailed the Citroen down those winding roads to the centre of Marseille just as though traffic cops didn't exist. I was dropped off near where Terry was waiting and was told there'd probably be further dealings, through Paris. Terry felt anxious when I had not been allowed out of the car, but in the privacy of her room she had counted the probably genuine French money and decided that I'd be in custody only long enough for our stuff to be checked.

A conveniently scheduled flight put us back into Paris in time for me to catch the journalist at his office, and pay him his cut. His surprise at seeing me so soon suggested doubts about getting paid at all, so I explained that in this business I could not afford enemies. We arranged that I'd keep in touch, in case there were further orders from Marseille. Then Terry and I quietly vanished from Paris.

In a city that can't be named because of its location in a country without statute of limitations, Terry and I took four diamond merchants. Much thought went into our plan, which was based on the fact that many dealers just below big wholesale level had no scruples over transactions violating the customs laws of other countries. For this operation Terry and I were airline crew—a hostess and steward—and we'd make no secret of our diamond smuggling into New York. We'd be in the market for quality diamonds of half to one carat in preference to flawed little twenty-pointers usually bought for brides expecting babies. We would first make purchases with genuine fifties during banking hours. Then a delayed flight would cause us to do business outside banking hours. But this would still be a dry run with good money to reveal which dealers, if any, baulked. By a process of elimination the others would be ripened for bigger things.

We next needed to know enough about diamonds not to get touched on good-money buys, at least not beyond the break-even point in America or Australia. Our crash course in stone-valuing came from the retail end of the trade. Posing as a magazine writer doing an article on diamonds, Terry received tremendous assistance. Jewellers were so flattered at being selected for an interview that they told her about prices at different levels, what to look for in roughly assessing the value of a stone and other interesting facets. Terry took notes of all she was told, cross-

178

checking to make sure that there were no wild discrepancies. My contribution was to lead a couple of jewellers into conversation, pump them and remember what I was told.

Because of the way we planned to finish this operation, Terry and I made all of our approaches together. For a variety of reasons, ranging from hunch to suspicion that certain individuals were law-and-order types, different dealers were eliminated. Four were chosen after passing our unscientific tests, and, to cover socializing among them, each was told we would also make regular purchases from others. Our excuse for spreading the trade was that we didn't want any particular dealer to know of too big a shipment, and so be tempted by the U.S. Customs reward.

Terry and I bought from all four dealers on the same morning, each transaction being worth around twelve hundred dollars. Two merchants wouldn't deal until they'd taken our fifties to a nearby bank; another phoned to find the rate of exchange, and one put our money in a drawer before handing over his tiny parcel. Three days later we repeated our visits, this time grumbling because the airline shortened our stopover in New York. Larger purchases were made during bank hours, and only one dealer took his fifties around for verification or exchange.

The final orgy of buying, with counterfeit money, was four days later. There were serious flight schedule problems, and, already a day late because of "technical difficulties", Terry and I had to do our buying late in the afternoon. All this was carefully explained to our suppliers, along with the information that our New York people had been briefed to expect their merchandise off the "special flight" we were forced to take out that night. Rather than quibble when our selections passed the four-thousand-dollar mark, the three less bank-minded dealers were happy to accept payment in the "usual" fifties. Our story for always using fifties was the U.S. tax authorities asked banks to report people making big withdrawals in higher denomination bills.

Our cautious man was tackled last, when false payment had already netted us more than fifteen thousand dollars' worth of diamonds. He suggested the sale might wait until next trip. I agreed that it certainly could, but he might find us doing all future buying from other sources rather than find ourselves light

179

on the odd occasion when there was an airline emergency. The dealer saw reason and ensured the continuation of a profitable business relationship. Like our easy merchants, he supplied us with his home phone number, so that he could be kept posted on schedule changes or other unusual situations. My "special flight" was as a passenger to Paris, carrying all of our diamonds. A change of assignment left Terry in town overnight, to start her "Atlantic run" after she had made four important phone calls. She decided not to risk the city's well-policed airport for departure, but to make a speedy exit by fast train to a northern destination, and there connect with an indirect flight to Paris.

Saving the worst until last, Terry phoned our difficult dealer long before he'd be leaving home for work, and gave him, straight between the eyes, the shattering news that his payment for the latest lot of diamonds had been made with counterfeit money. Before he could go berserk, Terry told the fellow how lucky he was that she found out about the fake money so quickly, because this meant he wouldn't lose anything. Fearful that he might panic, she hastily said that the whole thing was due to a misunderstanding and his diamonds would be promptly returned—but meanwhile he mustn't bank the money.

Terry first told him she had been pulled off her run at the last minute, while the steward went on to New York with the stones. Meeting someone from another flight, she learned that the New York people had recently loaded other crews with fake money. She didn't think we'd been caught until examination of her remaining bills showed up two with the same number. Fortunately for all of us, Terry told the man, she had found out in time to cable her partner in New York. Instead of delivering the stones he'd return them next trip, and normal business would be resumed as soon as new contacts could be established. She promised to call back after phoning the steward, with confirmation that the diamonds would be brought back safely. Speeding out of town Terry wondered how the fellow would react when he learned that because of some "dreadful slip-up" in New York the stones had been delivered.

Terry's next round of calls was made from Paris. While I listened, she told each dealer about phoning me in New York, only to learn that I'd called my contact and delivered the merchandise before getting the cable. Before the screams from the other end could sizzle the line, Terry said that we were in this in a big enough way to stand any loss. Promises of three days before taking action were obtained on the strength of Terry's assurance that we'd redeem part of the money for bankable currency within that time. Those calls marked the end of the deal. Both of us felt that after their cooling-down period those hard-headed business men would consider their duty to the law less important than their lost money.

Before boarding a train for Brussels I called my journalist friend, and learned that no fresh order had come from Marseille. We hit Brussels hard with straight shopping, and further up the line there was another diamond deal. Unlike the one just completed, this was not elaborate, though a number of establishments were touched. It consisted of one round of small good-money buys in a lot of places, then doubling up on the amounts next day with our own product and going through like a vacuum-cleaner. Most of the dealers came in beautifully, and with a few minutes to spare at the station I again phoned the journalist.

Money was now wanted at Marseille, and on a night train headed toward Cologne Terry and I discussed the situation. Standing in the corridor, because there were no empty compartments, we concluded that our funds in Europe were down to just enough for three or four good shopping days. The dark country speeding past put us in a planning mood. If we were to do another Marseille deal, or anything else worth while, somebody would have to go to Australia. My arrangement with the custodian of funds in Sydney was all right way back when I thought small, but now little parcels sent through the mail would not suffice.

Terry's well-practised pregnancy act appeared to be the quickest and safest way of bringing finance from Australia in sufficient quantity to see us through Europe—and an American wind-up operation we were contemplating. She should enter, as well as exit, pregnant, and look as though it shouldn't have happened, by displaying prominently around her neck a little metal cross often worn by girls unlikely to encounter such disasters. She could acquire her swelling during a stopover in Hong Kong, where she would spend a couple of days to acquire a

181

suitable "arrangement"—and clothes. My man in Sydney would meet her at the airport, take her to his house and substitute money for padding. He'd undoubtedly try to get into her pants, I told Terry, but he was pretty harmless.

Our idea was for Terry to arrange a morning arrival at Sydney and be on an outbound flight that same evening. Any official comments on her quick departure could be answered by pointing to her belly and claiming the visit was over a family matter. Return would be non-stop to Athens—which we chose because we had never operated there—and if anything went wrong there should be every chance of paying off the officials. I could help by offloading part of Terry's pregnancy, thus easing the airport people's fears that she might be in danger of giving birth on the spot.

Back in Paris we learned that the Marseille Frenchman would accept seven or eight days' delay only for the new hundred thousand.

That evening I saw Terry off on her long flight. I phoned the Sydney man about which bundles of bills she was to be given. Terry hoped to bring out at least a quarter of a million dollars, but would take on as much of a load as seemed safe. She was hardly off the ground before I began to feel lonely. Next day I was due to fly to Tangier for a check on the money market in that wheeling and dealing city, but meanwhile the thought of a night alone in Paris was more than I could bear. The woman I met on the Rome-to-Paris train was pleasantly surprised when I turned up at her place, and there was the inevitable bath before we could get down to other pleasures. . . .

Most impressive was Tangier's vast assortment of banks, ranging from solid institutions down to store fronts that at best looked fly-by-night. This spectacle fitted in with all I'd heard about Tangier being a centre for dubious financial dealing and tax dodges. I went to the North African city with the idea that if there was any place in the world where some section of the banking fraternity could be approached with fake money it should be Tangier. Those shady-looking little banks made me pretty confident of a wholesale deal, but until Terry returned from Australia with funds I was only a salesman with samples.

Crooked as these financial establishments probably were, I couldn't just walk in off the street. I needed some local individual

182

who for a cut would serve as a lead into one or two bankers, and here I could take a risk. Tangier did not have the feel of a place where jail would be the result of bad judgement in whom I approached; the possibility of payment for a dignified departure seemed much more likely.

Much happened during my three days in Tangier, beginning with an affair at the hotel and ending with a hundred-thousand-dollar order from a banker. The affair was with a not-too-young French woman who came to Tangier for her holidays because it was cheap, and my banker contact was made through a tourist guide using the hotel as his headquarters. The guide was a sharp little individual with a well-developed ability to size people up. There seemed little risk in laying things on the line with a man whose profession was getting anything for anybody at a profit. I opened up by telling the guide that I had a proposition involving bigger money than he'd ever make hustling tourists. He knew several bankers who could be approached, so I told him to try the best one first and his cut would be a quarter.

That discussion took place at night, and next morning the guide forgot about his tourists while he led me through the streets of Tangier to a small bank. Downhill from the European part of town, and in an upstairs office, two men awaited our arrival. Without preconceived notions of how shady bankers should appear I was ready for anything, though the heavily bearded eastern Mediterranean type who was obviously number one of the pair did make quite an impression. All I could think, looking at portions of the broad face not covered by hair, was that here was a man whose life-blood was money. But my attention was soon diverted to a thick book containing pictures and de-scriptions of counterfeit bills, against which my fifty was checked before serious discussion began.

Not finding anything on my fifties in his publication, the banker asked whether I'd passed money in Tangier, or offered it wholesale to anybody else. I assured him that not one bill had been passed in the city, or shown to anyone besides the guide. The bank man said he hoped this was true, because there existed in Tangier an international organization that made the passing of fake money very risky. There had been such a lively trade in forgeries in the past, the man explained, that the governments of several countries had set up their own special force.

183

Next came close questioning about the origin of the fakes, amounts circulated, places worked, number series available, and finally just who in hell made the stuff. Sticking close to the truth, because anything else could be dangerous, I told all. Very important to the bank man was that currency wasn't being dumped around the world in quantities big enough to devalue the product, and draw heat. Somehow I had to establish just who controlled the flow. The only way of doing that was to air much technical knowledge, which I did.

Since I'd given the right answers, and my bills weren't in the book, the bearded fellow was finally prepared to accept the fifties as clean. Then came the bargaining. The banker said he'd only be able to use my money by sending it to other countries. My opening figure of twenty per cent was knocked to ten so fast that I didn't quite realize how it was done. At the lower figure I was given a firm order for a hundred thousand, and had to admit that at the moment I could only deliver twelve. My explanation about an associate arriving in Europe from Australia in a few days with additional currency was accepted. As a separate transaction my twelve thousand was taken for ten per cent in French money, the anxious guide given his quarter and promised his cut from the big sale direct from the banker.

My final night in Tangier was spent in the French woman's room, and then there was a flight back to Paris, where I remained long enough to have two baths, before picking up Terry's cable giving flight number and arrival time at Athens.

Entering the arrivals section of Athens airport Terry looked genuinely pregnant, even to the slightly vapid expression. In the taxi to town she said she'd managed to cram four hundred thousand into her belly pack, and the flight from Sydney had been an agony she wouldn't care to repeat. As predicted, my custodian of funds had tried hard for a quick lay. Before leaving his house, Terry practised walking with the arrangement, so she wouldn't prance lightly through the airport in a manner suggesting that what rested on her belly didn't weigh much.

Terry thought she looked about eight months gone, but to me it was more like ten or eleven. At the hotel Terry's pregnancy was reduced to more comfortable proportions by the amount I could safely carry. Rested from her trip, a not so grossly pregnant Terry accompanied me on a flight to Zurich, where we caught a train for easy entrance into France. At Paris she came down to normal size in the Gare de l'Est women's room.

Our Marseille order had first priority, and since it was unlikely to end in a hijack I flew down by myself. This time it was a street meeting with the hundred thousand in my briefcase, and the same two men in the Citroen took me to a quiet spot where the exchange took place.

Back in Paris, the journalist took his percentage, then Terry and I boarded a night flight for Tangier. Using a different hotel in case the French woman was still in town, I left Terry behind while I carried my briefcase downhill to the bank. What I brought was examined and counted, payment made, and for some reason I mentioned the existence in Australia of the unused twenties.

As far as I was concerned those bills were dead stock, but there were three samples in my billfold. Revealing their existence to a banker who paid such low rates made little sense in view of the trouble involved in getting out a worthwhile amount. Terry could hardly be expected to leave Australia with another bun in the oven, but already I had spoken—and started something.

The banker wanted the same size order as his fifties, at eight per cent less the quarter he'd hold out for the guide. Hoping to kill the deal, I said it wouldn't be safe to send my courier back to Sydney so soon. After learning that I had a custodian of funds in Australia, he said that any amount of bills could be sent in an ordinary package. Tangier was a free port, and he knew the right people. Not wanting to spend a week of our fast-running-out safe time waiting in Tangier for a not-too-profitable parcel, I tried my best to talk down the idea.

The bank man, however, had other thoughts, starting with my Sydney contact packaging the hundred thousand in twenties, and labelling it photographic goods to be opened in total darkness. After explaining that the parcel could be air expressed to a Tangier address, the banker said that I wouldn't have to stay in town waiting for payment. Talking about trust, and how he was a man of his word, the fellow with the beard suggested phoning Australia to send the money on its way. On arrival he'd remit payment by bank draft to anywhere in the world I cared to nominate. All I could lose was the cost of a call and some unwanted twenties, so I gave the name of a New York bank. I said I'd make my call from Paris that night.

From another hotel on a different continent I arranged dispatch of a parcel to North Africa, and then our European operation was phased out. Full shutdown involved more than just stopping all money deals, and boarding an outbound flight. There was much wealth accumulated during our stay, and it had to be placed where it wouldn't become subject to inter-government wrangling in the event of future difficulty. Most satisfying to both was a division of spoils. All jewellery, diamonds and good money were collected from safe deposit, and in our hotel room Terry and I took plenty of time working out a split that seemed fair to each. Then there was a trip to Switzerland for banking of funds into separate accounts, before Terry had a two-hundred-thousand-dollar pregnancy to London.

Diamonds and jewellery for disposal on the New York market were to cross the Atlantic on Terry's belly, along with a hundred thousand dollars for a final U.S. clean-up. During a planning session we decided to kick off in Mexico City before hitting within America, since the detection of our money there could cause still further confusion. The bundle remaining in London would go into my airplane prior to departure for the Far East and Australia, for use in a Singapore-based operation. Some could be used in ports of call between London and Singapore, and authorities would hardly connect fake money with an old airplane passing through.

Much as she loved adventure, Terry didn't want to accompany me on the long flight east, especially after I had warned her of the perils and hardships likely to be encountered. The general plan was that after we worked off our money in America we'd separate. Terry would remain in California while I returned to England for the start of my flight. From some point approaching Singapore I'd cable her, and she'd cross the Pacific to meet me in that city. We'd then work a few places and consider the operation finished.

Before leaving London with Terry I learned that my airplane wouldn't be ready until I returned. In case heat had been generated in a few places, we intended to travel to America via Dublin to Montreal and then by train to New York.

While Terry made herself pregnant in the hotel room we talked about our European caper, and how it might have been

186

improved in the light of later knowledge. We first admitted to slight feelings of depression that could not altogether be dispelled by thoughts of what lay ahead. With no more sudden and fast trips in and out of such varied cities some excitement had gone out of our lives. Irrespective of what happened in the future, Europe could never again be the same for either of us.

Despite our taking desperate chances, luck had been with us all the way. But as far as the Continent was concerned we were quitting while we were on top. The wholesale deals had been pretty safe, but not so the other transactions. Taking the diamond merchants was dangerous because we had overexposed ourselves to smart business men who could intelligently help the police. And going into West Berlin on the journalist's advice had been insanity; everything about the place, including ways out, was wrong.

On the shopping front, however, we hadn't pushed our luck too far, and to us our pose as American tourists couldn't be faulted. Our most costly mistake had been in not working Spain longer; we could have taken a lot more from the money-changers before moving on to the rest of the exercise. On the positive side of our European tour was the fact that both Terry and I made a lot of money, and we wouldn't have to worry for a long time.

Terry's pregnancy boarding the airplane at Dublin looked like a trifling misfortune compared to the gross peasant-like one she had coming from Australia. Montreal involved no more than going through formalities, and when the New York train stopped at the U.S. border there was barely an inspection.

Two busy days were spent in midtown New York getting rid of diamonds and jewellery. Not dealing with the stuff as if it might be hot, we managed to fetch pretty good prices in the various jewellers' exchanges. The one mistake in New York was made by me, and it had nothing to do with business.

When the valuables were all gone, Terry and I banked the proceeds, put all but twenty thousand dollars of our money into a safe-deposit box and bought tickets for a late-night flight to Mexico City.

On the flight to Mexico City Terry and I decided to attempt a retail drop of twenty thousand dollars, possibly with pre-arranged legal protection. Wholesaling was out, because we hadn't even brought enough into New York to make that worth while, but both of us thought of the Mexican capital as a place where anything including law could be bought easily. The idea was to arrange our legal contact first, then shop the city at least partially free from fear.

Leaving Terry to go sightseeing, I spent our arrival morning negotiating with a lawyer. A well-connected American put me on to a legal adviser supposedly able to fix anything, following a tale about a friend who expected early arrest over some cheques. I made it very clear that I wanted a fixer rather than just a good courtroom fighter.

The lawyer saw right through what I thought was a good story, and asked if I'd yet passed any counterfeit money. My little lie about spending some fifties only to discover afterwards that they were fake had seemed a good way of sounding the man out. Still thinking I was putting something over, I expressed the fear of arrest because of that unfortunate occurrence. This was the point where the lawyer put a stop to further insults to his intelligence. From then on the lawyer and I understood each other, and a look of money came to his eyes. What followed was a battle of wits, after it was established that a deal could be made with the police if either I or my woman partner were caught. My figure of ten thousand dollars as the amount to be passed wasn't believed, so I had to admit that if all went well there could be a little more. To strengthen my bargaining position, and discourage the lawyer from having his police pals take us for the lot, I made promises of bigger things in the future. If our planned three-day spending spree came off without trouble, I said, we'd come back later with a team of people and really flood the city.

Two thousand dollars in advance was the amount agreed upon, after the lawyer examined some of our bills to make sure they were good enough not to cause massive complaints from the public. For that payment either of us would be out within hours if caught, and we were advised to carry a hundred dollars each in good money for the arresting officers. Whatever it cost to square higher police would come out of the two thousand, and each of us was to carry one of the lawyer's cards. In the remote event of communication failure between police and attorney we were to contact the latter after each day's work, otherwise he'd check the stations to find out where we were held. Two thousand seemed cheap insurance for floating twenty thousand less losses

188

on purchases, and when I talked it over with Terry she agreed that we were probably quite safe in trusting such a straightforward crooked lawyer.

Terry and I checked into one of Mexico City's bigger hotels, which provided good safe-deposit facilities for our takings as well as a place to stay. In a more out-of-the-way establishment we took a room for storing purchases and excess fake money. Instead of abandoning vast amounts of merchandise around town we'd hop taxis to the second hotel when overloaded, and simply leave the room full of things when we were finished with Mexico City.

We worked the city fast and furiously for three days, and our biggest concession to caution was to try to avoid hitting places on the heels of each other. Calls to the lawyer were made as scheduled in any of the shops. About a thousand dollars remained unspent at the end of the Saturday afternoon that should have seen the wind-up of our operation, and our counsellor suggested keeping out of trouble because he would be away until Monday morning. That was when we should have quit.

Instead of accepting discretion as the better part of valour, we had to go on and make Mexico City a full twenty-thousand touch. So many shops had been hit that we needed an untapped source of revenue, and found it in the bars and nightclubs that seemed to be just about everywhere around town. Since neither would stay on our feet long if we had to sample the wares of such establishments, we limited our activity to buying bottles of liquor for consumption elsewhere. Distance separated these drinking joints, bottles were heavy to carry and couldn't be inconspicuously dumped, so we hired a car and driver for our night tour of the city. Always leaving the car at least a block from our hits, Terry and I worked together, soon collecting enough bottles to make an alcoholic's mouth water. Using our mobility to spread the business around, we intended to keep at it until the last fifty was gone, and finally present our very obliging driver with all the wet goods. Departure from Mexico City was to be on a Sunday-morning northbound flight, or so at least Terry and I thought until later in the evening.

Not many fifties were left when from the moving car I spotted still another place to hit. This one was a fairly big nightclub, but from the outside there appeared no reason why it shouldn't be good for a bill. In a bar off the main room where a noisy orchestra played I made my pitch, and at first everything seemed normal. Terry stood beside me as I passed over my fifty for a bottle of Scotch, but instead of handing over change and purchase the fellow behind the bar said something to a couple of men in dinner-suits before disappearing through a doorway. As time passed with no reappearance of man or money, while those men obviously watched us, Terry and I began to exchange worried glances. Our first whispered words were that we'd probably not be allowed to get near the door, and we might need our lawyer first thing Monday morning.

The barman came back accompanied by a big man in another of those dinner-suits, and our fifty was in the hands of neither. Straight to where Terry and I stood came the man in the suit, to say in a voice loaded with meaning that we'd have to wait for our change. Putting down a sick feeling, I replied that this would be all right, looked to see how Terry was taking it, then eyed off the distance to the street door.

Terry looked tense and ready for anything when the man walked to where the others stood. Quiet talk was possible because of loud music from the other room, but the only sensible thing I could come up with at first was that we'd have to get out of the place. That eased my tension slightly, so I said we could stick around long enough to appear unworried, then Terry might say out loud that she was going back to the car for something. If she made it up the street to where we left the car, without being followed, she could wait there until either I turned up or the police arrived. Should anybody tail her, she should try to catch a taxi to the centre of town, then a second one to our hotel, and if I didn't get there contact the lawyer on Monday.

Terry suggested having our driver bring the car to the front of the place, but this I rejected. A car outside the door might be a lifesaver, I quietly told Terry, but I'd rather take my chances running than trust our driver not to prop if someone shouted the Spanish equivalent of stop.

Acting unconcerned we started toward the door; I held back to make clear that I had no intention of leaving with Terry. Neither of us looked toward those three dinner-suited men, though from the corner of my eye I could see that we were being closely watched. Making even more clear my intention of staying, I let the distance between us increase as Terry got close to the exit;

then with a wave of her hand she was gone. Turning to walk farther back from the door, I sensed a relaxing of muscles under those suits.

Another minute of waiting slowly passed, and not being able to stand much more I was ready for a fighting try at escape. My chance of getting through the door looked about even if we all took off at the same time. A surprise move might give me an advantage, but I wanted something better. Terry might panic if she saw me disappear into the darkness with a mob in close pursuit; also in a town like Mexico City there could be real danger of knife thrusts or other violence.

Bluff seemed the best way out, so I approached the man who told me to wait, said I had to tell my wife something and would be back. As he mentioned the change, I arrogantly turned my back and started for the door. My advantage in surprise got me to the doorway, before some words I couldn't understand were shouted. Speed rather than talk mattered at that instant, so I shot outside, turned in the direction opposite to the car and ran for all I was worth.

Pounding of feet and loud shouts came from somewhere behind, but I was too busy making for the nearest corner to look back. Running faster than ever I thought possible, I rounded the corner, to see a long block ahead with no place to duck for cover. Down the block I headed and soon I was aware of only the sound of my own feet, but there was too much danger of stumbling in the dark to risk turning my head. After another corner and a further half-block I slowed down to look back, saw nobody obviously after me, and then kept on running to still another street. More turns followed, and approaching the car from the opposite direction to where the chase started I saw the flashing light of a police car coming to a stop in front of the nightclub.

Our car still waited where we left it, luckily parked facing away from the scene of trouble. Terry saw me coming fifty feet away, and opened the back door so I could slide in beside her. The driver had his head turned to look out the rear window at a second police car joining the first, but he was willing to go forward in the direction of my pointing finger. As we were being driven out of the danger area, Terry said that she had seen the start of the chase and hoped I might go around back streets to approach the car from the only safe direction.

191

All we could conclude on the way into the centre of Mexico City was that this was a situation similar to the one in West Berlin. Somebody must have seen us pull the act in more than one place, and there could have been some telephoning before the final call to the police. As in Germany the trouble did not seem to start over appearance of the bill, but our act was so stereotyped that anyone seeing it twice would have to become suspicious. Further speculation was pointless, because there were such important matters as getting out of town. Though we paid our protection money, neither of us were prepared to trust that lawyer all the way when it came to the crunch.

Getting out of Mexico City was one of our fastest ever moves, and connections couldn't have been better had we planned this departure. At a busy intersection our driver received enough pesos to make this a memorable evening, and was then told to consider the bottles as a gift if we weren't back in an hour. Out of his sight we caught a taxi to our main hotel, forgetting the other place because it contained only merchandise. In record time our things were packed, good money collected from the hotel safe, and we were in another cab headed for the airport.

Terry and I did not want to find out how long it would take the unpaid Mexican police to seal off all exits. A flight for Paris was departing in an hour, but that seemed a long way to go just because we'd been frightened in a nightclub. American Airlines had something for Chicago via San Antonio in ten minutes with plenty of seats, so we bought two tickets for the Texas destination. Long before daylight a tired customs inspector at San Antonio airport cleared us and we went into the town. The ashes of our last four fifties continued on to Chicago in one of the airplane's toilets.

Trail was broken less than an hour later, when we boarded a Greyhound for Dallas. On a flight to New York Terry and I decided not to overreact, just because an ordinary evening of passing fake money had degenerated into something hectic. Instead we'd arm ourselves with a fresh supply of fifties, buy a car and hit the road to take in a few American cities.

At New York there was a pleasant surprise in the form of a six-thousand-dollar bank draft from Tangier. That plus our Mexican profits were banked before we bought a near-new Buick, in Newark because Terry and I felt that New York licence plates might be conspicuous.

Philadelphia was hit the same day we bought our car, after the banks were closed. That made a little dent in the twenty thousand taken from our New York safe-deposit box, and the merchandise bought stayed in the car boot while we went on to do Baltimore next afternoon. Because it might be like waving a red rag in front of a bull, Washington was left untouched. The Secret Service could have taken it as a personal affront, we felt, if we did over the city where they were headquartered—and where the Bureau of Printing and Engraving strove mightily to produce money others couldn't duplicate.

Pittsburgh's merchants were unlucky enough to get us on a Saturday, when we could devote more time to them. On a lonely mountain road offshoot all the stuff accumulated in our car since Philadelphia was dumped; then Terry and I were on our way to Buffalo.

Detroit was to be the last of the eastern cities before we returned to New York. There we'd pick up all the fifties in safe deposit, drive across to the West Coast and in untouched territory work off the lot. Instead of things going to plan we lost the Buick in Detroit, all of our clothes except what we wore, and seven thousand dollars in fake money. Only by the narrowest of margins did freedom fail to go the way of our possessions, and departure from Detroit was not the way we intended.

Just short of the point of no return, I saw that our car was staked out, and I didn't know whether they mightn't already have Terry. We were working separately, and this was my fourth trip back to the parking lot. Spotting the first detective before turning to carry my load in, I thought he might only be scrutinizing our out-of-state car, but walking past the gate I saw a vehicle in a far corner that had to be law. Acting like a pedestrian going past, I could only be certain that two or three people were in that unmarked car with its give-away antenna at the rear— and Terry could be one of them.

Seeing the detective through the wire fence saved me, but I had to know Terry's fate. After a building cut me from line of sight I realized that probably they didn't have her, because activity in the parking lot looked as if the stake-out was just being set up. That cop looking in our car was probably making sure he had the right one, and wouldn't be near it longer than necessary.

If Terry was already in custody, they'd be out of sight waiting for me, so apparently I was lucky enough to approach in time to get the warning. Into a sidewalk rubbish bin around the corner went my loaded briefcase. Not worrying about passers-by, I dumped my fifties into a café garbage can farther on, and now I had to intercept Terry before she walked into the trap. Two parallel streets led to the cross avenue where the parking lot was situated, and Terry had to come down one of these to dump her parcels. There was no way I could guess which street she'd use. Either could be watched from an out-of-sight position, but if she came along the other I couldn't stop her short of the parking-lot entrance.

If I rushed up the street I was watching to the next corner, Terry would have time to come down the parallel one unseen, and that was too much of a gamble. The only way both routes could be covered was for me to alternate back and forth between the two intersections at intervals of about a minute. Fortunately the distance from one to the other was shorter than the long block Terry would have to walk whichever street she used. To move between the vantage points I'd have to face the ordeal of passing the parking lot. Both sides of the avenue carried a fair amount of foot traffic and I could use the far one, but I'd still have to pass in sight of the detectives each time I made the change.

Sooner or later they'd notice me, I thought in desperation, and then came the idea that if I didn't look like a suspect for passing fake money there might be a chance. Wearing a business suit, I could fit some description the cops might have, but that could be changed. Off came my coat and tie inside the doorway of a small office building, while I hoped Terry wouldn't choose that moment to make her appearance. These were dropped on the floor after everything important had been jammed into the pockets of my pants. By the time I hit the street, almost running to set up a vigil, my sleeves were rolled up, my hair was in a mess, three buttons were ripped from my shirt, and I hoped to pass for a bum coming off a bad binge.

Too much time had been wasted transforming from business man to booze hound, so I had to check right away to see if Terry was headed down the other street. From the opposite side, half staggering to fit my appearance, I saw our nice expensive Buick standing there with nobody near by. They could hardly have

194

arrested Terry and got her out of sight in time to reset the trap, so I still had a chance.

Again I was out of sight from the dangerous part of the parking lot, but Terry was not to be seen coming down this other long block. Back to the other corner I went, along with a group of people going the same way. Overdoing the drunk act might get me picked up by a city cop, I thought, as I made still another trip.

Still there was no sign of Terry, and turning back to check the other street again I saw something to send real rather than faked weakness to my legs. The two men turning into the parking lot in an inconspicuous car could only be more law, but they looked like bright Federal agents rather than Detroit city police. Their car went past the office to the rear of the lot, so the attendant must have been told to keep out of the way while a pinch was being made.

Wondering how many trips the same bum could make without attracting attention caused me to think of using vehicle traffic for a cover. Timing my runs to get through shielded by a slow bus or truck, I managed several more trips. Then far up the block somebody came into sight who could only be Terry.

The untidy figure with messy hair and half-open shirt made no impression on Terry, until I spoke. In a voice reminding me of West Berlin, and almost dropping her load, she asked what was wrong. I said the law was after us and we'd have to get out of sight right away. Terry seemed to think that I'd physically broken away, so leading her into a building similar to the one where I left my coat and tie I told her what had happened.

A door on the way to temporary safety at the rear of the building was marked "Attorney at Law", but from the shabby surrounds I thought he'd be a lawyer for traffic tickets rather than the kind we might need. In a fast and excited conference we decided that Terry should change her appearance, and then we'd get out of the neighbourhood quickly.

Coming out of a ladies room carrying nothing but her handbag, Terry looked the sort who'd pick up a drunk like me in a low-class bar. Her hair was worse than mine, her expensive lightweight coat was gone, her dress was pulled and twisted, and from the appearance of her face she could have been drinking for a week. Looking like people who'd been ordered out by a caretaker, we stood near a stairwell window, while I told of my belated suspicion of having been followed from a jewellery store. There was little time to waste on such discussion now, and talking about getting to someplace where we could plan our next move, I noticed that the window afforded a partial view of the parking lot. Out there in plain sight was our Buick, and a little way off one of the official cars containing three men crouched down so they wouldn't be seen by anyone approaching on foot. Not lingering to study the grim sight of what the authorities had set up for us, Terry and I hurried out of the building and up to the main street.

Feeling safer in the late-afternoon crowds we flowed with the tide for a dozen blocks. Then a dim bar seemed a good haven, so in a booth at the rear with a couple of unwanted drinks we began to talk. Before discussing how to get out of town we tried to assess the full extent of damage and danger caused by capture of our car and contents. Most important was that nothing in the Buick might give a clue to our identities. After much mind-searching both of us were pretty certain that we'd not become careless on that score. Usable fingerprints could be found, if the attendant hadn't smudged the best of them when he parked the car. They'd take time to match with my Federal record, and I might get away with denying connection with the car at the relevant time. Terry would have to get caught for hers to mean anything, because she'd never been printed.

Not too well concealed in a suitcase was a stack of fake fifties totalling around five thousand dollars. When the cops grew tired of waiting and forced a door, they'd know they had the right car, and only needed the owners. Personal possessions would indicate a man and woman team, if they hadn't already learned that from our victims. That was as far as Terry and I could go in sizing up the car situation.

Because we remitted after each city, the only good money lost was a lot of unbanked silver. Had we left good paper in the car during our dumping trips, as we did in some cities, our financial condition would have befitted our appearance and narrowed the avenues of escape. Bulging in Terry's bag after flushing her fifties down the toilet in that building was a lot of very good money. Added to what I had, it amounted to nearly three thousand dollars.

Getting out of town fast was even more of a consideration when

196

we realized that already a search could be under way. By now those stake-out cops would almost have to know that we weren't coming back. Besides getting descriptions of how we looked at the time from the parking-lot attendant, they would have been told how we frequently turned up at the car to dump purchases. Our failure to come back after a reasonable time, which had already long passed, would be a dead give-away that somehow we'd become alerted.

Before Terry left me in the bar to go out and buy a jacket and shirt, so I'd look half civilized, we discussed ways of getting out of Detroit. Too much was at stake to take anything for granted, so we'd have to assume that Federal and local police were already doing their best to bottle us up in the city. Air, bus or train had to be ruled out, because even this early those means of exit could be covered. Also we couldn't place much reliance on change of appearance, because real professionals would be involved in this hunt. Then the simplest of all solutions occurred to us, and Terry rushed off to get my things.

When she returned, I changed in the bar toilet and headed out to see about buying a car. This time we wanted something self-respecting passers of fake money wouldn't be caught dead in, so I hunted up a "working man's friend" type of dealer. Of all the heaps in his yard the one that looked most likely to stand up to a night's driving was a small pick-up truck, so I bought it for three hundred dollars in twenties. As the truck's radio didn't work, and we'd need to keep up with the news, I purchased a portable on the way back to the bar to collect Terry.

Driving south toward Toledo we monitored the news broadcasts, but there was no mention of counterfeit activity. While fiddling with the radio, I told Terry about missing the trap by seconds, the likely-to-be-discovered way I'd dumped counter-feit money, coat and briefcase, and my struggle to cover both approaches to the parking lot.

Then we went on to a searching discussion of just what had gone wrong. Terry's logic almost eliminated the possibility of warning notices, because as she reminded me we were using new series money. From a closer examination of what slightly alarmed me in a jewellery store, some interesting factors began to emerge. Achieving total recall, I now made the full connection between a customer of that store and an earlier hit.

When I handed over my fifty, a man down the counter appeared to take mild interest, before resuming conversation with the clerk waiting on him. On its own this meant little, but that customer's clerk intercepted mine as he was getting change and they held a brief discussion. Following this talk, the man serving me seemed to take more than usual interest in my appearance. That buy was my last one before a third dumping trip back to the parking lot. With overconfidence born of too much of this kind of work, I dismissed the affair as nerves, after a cursory check to see if I was being trailed.

Now it seemed fairly clear that, as buyers will do, the other customer had gone to more than one store to make his selection. Becoming curious at seeing the same individual make similar purchases with a fifty-dollar bill in two different places, he obviously communicated his suspicions to the clerk. Frightened of the consequences of false accusation and wanting to play safe, someone from that store had almost certainly followed me to the car and then made a report. Quick checking by the police while I went on oblivious to danger would turn up the fact that a lot of fifties had been changed by someone of my description. Stake-out of the car would be the inevitable result. That was the only way Terry and I could put it all together and make the pieces fit.

Toledo was passed on a southward heading, with a stop only long enough for Terry to rush into a junky shop and buy a few things. Since her dress was a wreck after what she did to it, Terry put on a cheap one in the store, and when she came back to the truck her appearance was more in character with the way she travelled.

Beyond thinking that we'd re-outfit in New York and buy another car for a drive to the West Coast, we didn't try in those first hours out of Detroit to make many plans. When Detroit went out of radio range without anything on the news, Terry and I discussed how to wind up the U.S. operation. The country was more or less finished for shopping, but there was a possibility of wholesaling on the West Coast our sixty thousand still in New York. Pittsburgh news came on long after our Buick should have been torn apart, again without mention of fake money. Hundreds of safe miles away from the scene of terror, I decided that some of my old Los Angeles used-car contacts could be let in on the deal.

Approaching Harrisburg, we thought of getting rid of our last link with Detroit, so the truck was to be abandoned. Rather than leave it on the street for the cops to find and trace, I paid a month's storage in a parking lot. The Detroit papers we bought in New York carried no story, so the whole thing had to be put out of mind as something we'd never understand. We could only speculate on whether all of those cops were local, and after opening our car had split the contents and kept quiet.

With new clothes and another good car we arrived in Los Angeles a week later. Terry's old friend at the bank agreed that fake money could be useful for covering temporary shortages, provided the stuff was never allowed to slip into circulation. After finding that our money wasn't on any regional hot lists, he gave Terry twelve hundred for ten thousand dollars.

Checking my car dealers was slow because in the time I'd been away changes had taken place. Some had gone bankrupt and were trading under different names, a couple of the best were in jail for fraud and others had since left for parts unknown.

No single dealer was strong enough to take all of our stock, but I did track down several who'd take five or ten thousand. Orders were taken on the strength of samples shown, with no deliveries to be made until all or most of the bundle was sold. Because these men could be linked to me from the old gas-ticket days, I didn't want them floating money while I was still selling in town.

One dealer I wanted to see had moved to San Diego, and after hearing that he had a solid business I drove down. Walking into his office behind rows of good cars, I seemed to be interrupting a meeting where everybody had to fill in papers. After greetings were exchanged in the privacy of an inner office the dealer said that I'd picked the one day of the month when his salesmen had to write out their parole reports. More important than the salesmen reporting to their parole officers, the man asked in his strong Southern accent to just what did he owe the honour of my call.

When the bargaining was over and further lying on either side would have been pointless, I had an order for twenty thousand at fifteen per cent. To get that amount I had to be reasonably truthful about business done in Los Angeles, and give assurances that nobody would be on the streets with the stuff ahead of him. The fellow's plan was to have a couple of friends look after the car lot, while he took his crew of parolees to Los Angeles and supervised their activity.

After the deliveries were handled, Terry and I made the almost fatal mistake of going to San Francisco to dispose personally of ten thousand remaining dollars. One terror-filled period of three hours in a city across the bay from San Francisco left Terry and me in a state of near shock, barely relieved by the trouble coming to an end short of total disaster. A minor incidental was that it cost us the profits of several places. None of this would have occurred had we stuck to our resolution about further shop work after Detroit.

Probably we became careless because this was the final phase of our American operation. My plan was to fly to London in a couple of days, while Terry would depart much later to meet me in Singapore. What took place was the inevitable outcome of our decision to work that little bit extra, when we should have stopped. So dulled were our senses by the sudden impact that neither of us realized how lucky we were that it was two city detectives who made the arrest and not the Secret Service.

We were in San Francisco and thought it a good idea to cross the bay to work off the last few bills we had. The place can never be mentioned because cops have long memories, and might "find" something incriminating if ever one of us passed through again; since the town had a small detective force, any detail that could identify officers or pinpoint exact location must be deliberately vague. Probably the biggest mistake we ever made was tackling a community not large enough for our kind of business.

Only five hundred dollars remained unspent when, with no warning or chance to dump the evidence, Terry and I were bundled into a police car. The town had few stores where small items could be bought, so we had returned to our car half-way through our shopping to leave parcels and intending, as a precaution, to move to another kerbside parking space. Terry was already in her seat when I got into the car. There was nothing to suggest our activity had aroused suspicion.

Just as we moved from the kerb, a car materialized from nowhere to cut us off. So perfectly timed was the manoeuvre that we barely realized we were caught, until two men leapt from the car and manned a door each of our car. Neither of us had time to say a word before we were ordered out with hands up. When I'd

200

been frisked for a gun, it was sneeringly remarked that we should have stayed in San Francisco and not tried to work this town; this gave me some slight hope of their being local cops.

One of the detectives locked our car and pocketed the keys. We were then pushed into their vehicle and told—not asked—what we'd been doing. When the older and tougher cop accused us of passing counterfeit money, I didn't even bother with denials. I was so disgusted at falling into this trap that I was unable to act in a normally defensive manner. I thought in terms of bail and run in preference to argument in a hopeless situation. Terry's position was better, if only that her bail would be lower, but it was of utmost importance that we did or said nothing to antagonize these detectives.

With enough evidence on us and people who could identify us, this was not a time to stand up for our rights. When I freely admitted passing fake money, the initial hostility of both officers seemed to vanish. Since I was playing for a cash settlement instead of bail, all efforts were made to establish friendly relations. One of the policemen said he thought we were only cashing cheques when they started watching us; this meant they couldn't possibly be Federal, and my hopes of doing business began to rise. Making no move to drive off, the cops began to ask questions. Who we were and where we came from were easy to answer untruthfully, because there wasn't much pressure. Growing bold, I asked if there were notices out, or whether we'd been caught by sheer bad luck. It had been our own carelessness and they hadn't checked for outstanding notices.

My hope of coming to terms rose when the older detective repeated earlier suspicions that we had been floating cheques. Each cop had gone into different stores expecting to learn that paper had been hung, but instead had discovered that we were buying goods with fifty-dollar bills. When he remarked that the store people hadn't been told their fifties were probably fake, I began to see ourselves walking away from this for a price. In the way cops have of talking to each other for the benefit of a suspect, one suggested they could take us to the station and call the Secret Service.

There was no move to get the car started; this seemed to mean that now was the time, so I put it pretty straight on the line. With bare reference to what this would cost for bail and lawyers, I reasoned that things might be simpler if we just paid our legal expenses directly, and then headed out of town. Neither detective was outraged in the way that I'd heard some are when offered a bribe, nor did they act insulted before softening down to ask how much. The officer doing most of the talking said he doubted whether we had enough to make it worth their while. Looking at the ashen expression on Terry's face, I asked what it would take, which brought some rather close questions about just how many places we had worked. My explanation that we were new at the game resulted in a sharp order to cut the crap; we'd been observed working, and were obviously professionals.

Starting with an offer of two thousand for each officer, we entered into a round of haggling that didn't stop short of double that figure. Freedom would have been beyond purchase, but for the fact that we had not remitted our San Francisco takings. As it was, we had difficulty convincing the officers that we had no more—apart from a little expense money. The older cop remarked that eight thousand for getting out of doing ten years was a real bargain, and on that point neither Terry nor I could argue. From a suitcase came our legal fees, and one of the cops quipped that they didn't want our fake fifties, because in a few days the police station would probably be full of them; even in the cause of crime prevention they wouldn't take our fake money. Their concession to that was to suggest that we would be a long way off before floating any more.

It came as crushing news that we would have to be arrested, and for a moment Terry looked like a nun who'd just been told she was pregnant. The reason made sense; several people had seen the incident and a few others in stores were aware of police interest in our doings. Without complainants there was no need to start a big case, but if merchants screamed later it would look better if there had been some sort of arrest. Petty theft was to be the charge—with a cheap watch as evidence—and the woman involved would not be caught. They'd be out looking for evidence of bigger things when I made bail. To make it look straight, Terry was to wait an hour before getting me out, which would cost most of the genuine currency we had been allowed to keep.

At the station my pockets were emptied, I was booked under the name on a temporary driver's licence, then locked up.

202

Thoughts about stung shopkeepers turning up and events getting beyond the control of the detectives made my hour in jail seem like ten. Finally the turnkey unlocked my cell door, the desk officer advised me to play it straight, and Terry and I were on our way.

Making fast but legal time through the suburbs east of Oakland, we were keyed to a high pitch and could only talk furiously about what had just happened. Both agreed that as of now America was finished, that we'd been fools to shop after Detroit, and that the car should be dumped as soon as we returned to Los Angeles. There was some danger of those paid-off cops putting our number on the air, we thought, if there was a loud rumble from local business men.

Splitting the car proceeds ended all dealing in America. Compared with Europe, Terry and I felt that our closing-down tour of the U.S. had fallen short of unqualified success. Neither of us experienced any of the regret we had felt on shutting down on the other side of the Atlantic. From Detroit onwards it had turned nasty and terrifying and now we were glad it was over. Losing the Buick and all our things was no great tragedy, but it damaged our nerves. Pushing our luck in going to San Francisco could only be attributed to some temporary madness. Now it was all over and I was ready and willing to leave. Terry and I would meet in Singapore with renewed hope, but the near-escapes in Mexico City, Detroit and the unmentionable northern California town were experiences we'd not forget for a long time. That night Terry saw me off on a flight to London.

10 Off and aloft   Athenian cold shoulder   tummy-ache over Turkey   on the mat in Baghdad monsoon passage   final humiliation off Singapore.

FLIGHT EAST

Three days after leaving Terry I was in London getting ready for my flight to Australia, with two passengers standing by. One was David Graham, a young teacher from Washington I had met in a New York ticket office, and the other fellow, Barry Hill, was someone he had later met in London. I hadn't thought of company for the flight until I started talking to David, telling him about the airplane and my plans. His interest was aroused and he asked if he could come along. To him the trip represented adventure, and I thought the flight might be more pleasant with company.

All I knew of Graham was that he'd recently finished university after taking a couple of years off, that he was from a good family with State Department connections, and though intelligent was unworldly. The thought of what the fellow or his family would think of flying with a pilot who was a counterfeiter was perversely appealing, but there was also the practical consideration that Graham would lend an air of respectability to the exercise. Mention of such stopovers as Baghdad, Calcutta, Bangkok and Singapore excited him, so I quickly advised him to consider the discomfort, the element of risk, and the fact that he'd be permitted to kick in a couple hundred dollars for fuel. He wasn't to be discouraged, so, hoping he'd be able to overcome the effect of his protected upbringing, I told Graham he'd be welcome aboard.

Then came all the paperwork. Since the airplane was on the British register, their Air Ministry was stuck with the job of providing assistance in getting clearances to transit countries en route. They were not very enthusiastic about an American hitting them with the problems, but became cordial when I said I lived in Australia. One of their experts worked out a route covering the twelve thousand miles to Sydney. Across Europe and southern Asia, down the Malay Peninsula to Singapore, along the Indonesian islands to the Timor Sea and over to Australia—the planner worked it out in detail.

By then the Air Ministry was treating the flight seriously, and to sustain that attitude I informed them that my crew would include a navigator; unknown to him, Graham was appointed to that post, with the reservation that he'd function solely as custodian of charts since his navigation would probably be about boy-scout level. Mention of a navigator brought further respect from those English old-school-tie types, and I wondered how they'd take it if they suspected that the captain of a British aircraft receiving their help planned to load up with counterfeit money and dispose of it along the line. All sorts of upper-class English expressions were imaginable, and while savouring this I was brought back to reality with the advice that parts of my route might not be available because of Arab antipathy toward Britain, but it was thought there'd be some way of getting me through.

Graham was informed of his elevation to navigator status, and went with me to Newcastle upon Tyne to collect the aircraft. He had, as expected, no concept of map-reading. But more important to me was his lack of fear. His crew appointment pleased him, even when I explained that he couldn't safely be entrusted with any navigating. The papers would list him as "navigator" to simplify matters, I explained after we landed at London's Croydon airport, but he would only have to keep the charts in order and hand them to me as required.

I was certain Graham would be an ideal foil for activities not related to flying the airplane. His open "All American Boy" manner would give our flight something which I couldn't contribute, with officials in different places taking a less jaundiced view of the operation. My "overgrown college boy seeing the world" could be kept out of the way by explanations that I was seeking pleasures he wouldn't understand, and if anything went wrong he'd only be embarrassed, rather than in real trouble.

205

Clearances became a nightmare, with not too much choice beyond an almost impossible route through the Middle East. This was through eastern Turkey to the Tigris River, along that to Baghdad and on to the head of the Persian Gulf. With the long-range tank I'd install, distances would be manageable, but the Air Ministry advised against the route because of extremely high mountains before reaching the Iraqi desert. They finally advised me to fly to Athens and check with the British air attaché there for onward clearance. Pakistan, India, Burma and Thailand would be advised to expect our flight, with Indonesian clearance being arranged at Singapore.

The only tank I could locate suitable for cabin installation was a thirty-gallon lightweight copper thing intended for hot-water systems. Though it would be safe enough, I was told by an engineer at Croydon, it didn't meet Air Ministry specifications. He advised me to carry it as cargo to Rome and have it connected there, because the Italians weren't so fussy.

Then Graham met our second passenger. Barry Hill was a young New Zealander who'd been working in London and was on his way to Australia to get married. He was such an unassuming type that I couldn't understand his considering this flight. Telling him what he was in for failed to put him off, so after making his fuel contribution he was signed on as flight steward. His duties on board would consist of passing refreshments forward to the pilot and navigator. The reason I asked them for fuel money was to substantiate my poverty pose.

My crew members had little in common. Hill would be absorbed with what awaited him in Australia, so I guessed he would be interested only in the flight and the sights. But things could be different with Graham. As an innocent away from home for the first time he was sure to be touristy, while having an eye for other pleasures. He had told me of his affair with an older woman in London, and his upbringing showed in his reluctance to let me meet her, or even admit the ten-year age difference. When I told him that older ones were usually best, he said he'd not like his family or friends to know what he had done. He asked about opportunities on the way, so I told him there'd be plenty if he happened to enjoy medical treatment. All my crew knew about me was that I owned the old Proctor and wanted to get it to Australia. Running this as an economy flight suited them and I

206

wanted to be inconspicuous while floating fake money, so we agreed to stay at cheap hotels.

After collecting maps for the flight I had one final job to do, and for this I went alone to Croydon airport. In the gloom of the hangar my briefcase, containing the hundred thousand from the safe-deposit box, was tossed into the cabin while I did an inspection of the airplane. When nobody was looking, I slipped into the pilot's seat and attacked the door linings with a screwdriver. Watching for anyone coming close, I quickly removed a lot of little screws to release the lining and allow access to the spaces behind the outside skins of the two cabin doors. Bundles of fifties were crammed into those spaces while I kept a nervous lookout, and when all my money was hidden I replaced the linings. To slip out a few bills for use in ports of call, I'd need only to remove a few screws. After my packing was done, I looked at the red emergency levers above both exits, and wondered what would happen if during some flight situation I was forced to jettison the doors. Before leaving I checked the raft and life jackets for correct stowage, and also made certain that our unconnected long-range tank was safely secured.

Looking back at the airplane, I was struck with the thought that it didn't have the appearance of something that should be setting out on a twelve-thousand-mile flight. As a Second World War construction it had never been intended for such flights, and all the years that had passed were beginning to show. Seeing that airplane alongside modern aircraft it didn't seem reasonable that I should be able to fly it half-way around the world. With some foreboding I thought that expecting this outmoded airplane to fly over mountains, desert, tropical jungle and open sea to Australia might be hoping for a lot. But then, looking at it differently, I realized that I was only trying to accomplish a series of little flights which would all add up to a big one. I'd done little flights in airplanes more primitive than this, so if I didn't push too hard we'd probably get there.

We assembled next morning at my hotel near Euston Station with minimal luggage, and took a taxi to Croydon. Formalities for leaving England were completed, but because we had no radio our Paris clearance was to the outlying field at Toussous le Noble. With a fair load it took a lot of runway to get off, and at minimum height we turned to a heading for the English Channel at Dover. Over the water a thick haze limited our visibility, so keeping on a compass course for the French coast I assured my nervous crew that there were no problems. Actually there was one: a coating of oil on the windscreen that became more noticeable in clear air over France. No great amount was blowing back, but dust particles picked up in the Channel haze were further restricting forward visibility. Crew fears were allayed by my shouted statement that old engines had a tendency to leak oil, but it would be checked at Paris, and in the meantime it was easier to navigate by side reference than strain my eyes looking ahead.

Paris came into sight on time, and before heading for the airport I entertained the crew with two illegally low circuits around the Eiffel Tower. On final approach into Toussous I was dragging it fairly low when there was a sudden shout from Graham. Pulling the nose up, I looked out his side in time to see the small figure of a man disappearing under our starboard wing. Easing off on the power, I continued our landing and, after rolling to a stop, informed Graham that we'd been safely clear and that his shouting at such a critical time was most disconcerting.

My hope for only an overnight stop at Paris was thwarted by Graham, abetted by an official. During the French formalities I said we'd leave next morning, but Graham wanted to stay longer, and the official sided with him by saying such a short stop in Paris was unthinkable. Agreeing to two nights, I arranged for an engineer to check our oil leak. Having somewhere to go where I'd be sure of a needed bath, I saw little of the others in Paris. A letter from Terry was at the American Express and still, it appeared, there'd been no publicity about fake money. Terry looked forward to our meeting in Singapore, so I gave an optimistic estimate of three weeks en route, and suggested that she think of leaving Los Angeles when she heard we'd passed through Calcutta. I also told her which ports I'd check for mail and promised progress reports.

Since neither of the crew was in a fit state for an early start, we didn't get to the airport until fairly late. The engineer's report on our oil leak was that it couldn't be located without taking a lot of things off, and if our rate of consumption didn't increase between Paris and Rome we'd probably make it to Australia. Prior to

208

take-off, both Graham and Hill had things to say about missing our Cannes night stop, so I told them that if they'd cooled it in Paris this wouldn't have happened. To reach Rome next evening, I continued, we'd have to refuel the aircraft on arrival at Lyon—then sleep in the airport waiting-room to get a first daylight departure.

Lyon lay beneath in a pall of industrial haze. After a good French meal at a café near the airport we bedded down in the waiting-room. The same café provided sandwiches and filled our Thermos flasks with coffee, so the flight steward was able to serve breakfast at first light after we climbed onto a heading down the Rhône toward Marseille. After leaving the river and crossing some mountains, a new heading put us over the Mediterranean past Toulon, where the remaining refreshments were passed forward with the Cannes–Nice complex showing on the horizon. With our flaps down we lined up for final approach. The air flowing through both open windows was blistering hot.

We were in the middle of a heatwave, and facing two hours on the ground while various things were done Graham and Hill hiked off to a nearby beach. Instead of telling them they should have their heads read for venturing into the hot sun, I stressed the importance of being back on time.

The airplane was ready to go, I'd finished lunch, and it was half an hour before my crew appeared, with excuses about Graham meeting a girl on the beach. Short-tempered from the heat I told this overgrown boy that eventually he might grow up. Minutes later we were cruising in cooler air along the Riviera, toward Genoa.

Estimated time to Rome was just under four hours, with all but the last few miles coastal. After the French Riviera we'd come around to a more southerly heading, passing seaward of Genoa, and then follow the Italian coast to the point of turning inland across some hills to Rome. Again owing to lack of radio we'd have to use a secondary field, this time Rome's Urbe airport. That suited me because in Rome I didn't want to show my face more than necessary, and according to the Croydon engineers Urbe had workshop facilities for installing our long-range tank. I could stay at the airport watching the work during daylight hours.

After Genoa, I made good a promise to let Graham fly the airplane. He'd been told the basics, so with his hands and feet on the dual controls he followed my movements through a few gentle turns. Once he relaxed his death-grip on the stick, and realized it was best held like the bow of a violin, his flying improved. For about twenty miles he kept the aircraft more or less on course, before tiring and asking me to take over.

Flying down the coast, with Livorno airport on the port wingtip, I noticed something boring down the runway, without realizing that *we'd* caused sudden activity. Streaking in a climbing turn toward a position behind us, the military airplane was behaving strangely. Overtaking on our seaward side, after an anxious moment, it passed so close that even its U.S. Air Force markings were sharp and clear. Cutting ahead of us, the military aircraft began letting down and was rolling along the runway before we lost sight of the field. All this was rather startling to Graham and Hill, so I explained that the Air Force had apparently decided to buzz us after spotting us on radar and failing to get radio response on the route frequencies.

On the short inland run to Rome we hit dust, so our approach had to be made with an almost opaque windscreen. Before turning onto final approach, a short runway with a frightening railway embankment at the far end was visible from the side, to disappear from sight while I put down full flap and used the hangars as a guide for a short field landing.

Four days passed while we were illegally installing and flight testing our long-range tank, and trying to find the source of the oil leak. The Italian engineer advised me to fly on, unless it got worse. He and I had become friendly while the crew did the sights of Rome, so on the last night he invited us to dinner at what he called a "real" Italian eating-place. Using the excuse of having to fly next day, I drank a lot less of the red wine the others hit so heavily, so it wasn't until late next morning that my crew were in any fit state for departure. This mattered little because there'd only be a short flight out of Rome to our final night stop in Italy, at Bari.

Athens direct would have been more convenient, but even with our long-range tank that would have been pushing luck. Brindisi, south of Bari, would have shortened the long flight to Athens, but it was not available without a radio. Rome–Athens in a day, dealing with two sets of Italian officials, would have been a neat trick, but impossible.

210

In the same heatwave as at Cannes we took off from Rome, following a tense run toward the railway embankment before the superheated air finally lifted us clear. Crossing Rome, I delayed our climb to give the crew a close look at the place they'd enjoyed so much, while their captain tried to remain out of sight. Near the Volturno River I made a course change, to cross the Apennines on a heading for the Adriatic coast. Over Italy's backbone there was severe turbulence, and I was too busy flying the airplane to take much notice of the navigator and flight steward—other than to hope they didn't make some disgusting mess. Both were pretty green by the time the coastal plain came in sight, but though the air was still rough they had apparently hung onto the contents of their stomachs.

Bari from the air looked interesting. There were quite a number of ships lying in the harbour, and passing over on a backtracking circuit I noticed that some of the freighters were big. The thought occurred that Bari might be a place to unload some fake money; there'd be lots of seamen around, and plenty of business in the bars and whorehouses. On the final turn I thought of getting rid of Graham and Hill for the evening, and then was too busy with the airplane to think about it any more. In my briefcase there were a couple thousand dollars for just such a contingency.

An old hotel reminiscent of North Africa with its black and white tiles, slow overhead fans and open cage elevator provided a big room with three beds and a balcony. During dinner Graham again mentioned his family's close connection with the American chargé d'affaires at Athens. This had been talked about before, but now he went into detail, saying that we'd all be on the receiving end of some hospitality. The wife of that official was a lifelong friend of Graham's mother, and they also knew the man fairly well. My guess was that Graham might finish up as a house guest, and that the remainder of the crew would be lucky to score a lunch. Graham's anticipation was a pleasure to observe, while mine was restricted to something in the more immediate future.

By the time we finished dinner, much awaited darkness set in and I separated from the others, with some excuse about "chasing something down".

Cafés and bars full of half-drunk seamen were easily taken on exchange deals, in which I let myself be clipped on the rate.

Whorehouses were different—a bit like going into a butcher's shop without wanting to buy any meat, but needing desperately to change a fifty-dollar bill. One madam mistook my deference for the concealment of a different kind of appetite. When I told her I'd just got laid, she didn't believe me. When I said I didn't want to catch anything, she resented the remark. In a raucous whorehouse voice, loud enough for all to hear, the woman chided me for not telling her that what I really wanted was a boy. If it was boys I wanted, boys I could have. I quit that place in a hurry and moved on to easier touches.

Urging my crew to an early start for our flight to Athens, we were at the airport before any bank could open. Flight planning for Athens brought fresh warnings of a peril mentioned by the Air Ministry in London—to avoid Albania. The Italians were saying our aircraft would be shot down without warning if we strayed off course into that country's airspace. In perfect Air Traffic Control English, we were warned to give Albania a wide berth, since its pilots could be hazy about location. With all tanks full we were heavy, and used a lot of runway before the controls stiffened enough to lift off. Keeping well clear of risky areas, we left the Italian coast for the Greek island of Corfu, where Graham was called upon to do his duty as navigator by handing me a chart. A changed heading brought us to the mainland of Greece, over barren country before a long boring run up the Gulf of Corinth to the canal at its head.

On this leg the smoking ban enforced by a tank full of fuel in the cabin was felt by both pilot and navigator. Hill could take or leave smoking, the same as I suspected he might be able with something else. Relief from boredom came in frequent recourse to the flight steward's coffee bottles and pissing in screwtop containers, until the Corinth Canal was below and we could look forward to arrival at Athens. Not hitting any dust during the long run, our windscreen remained clean enough for us to sight Athens many miles ahead on the horizon.

Such was Graham's confidence in the American chargé d'affaires that he insisted on making contact even before we located a hotel. From a café off Constitution Square he phoned the United States Embassy, learned that the chargé was out of town, but was put through to his wife, who invited us all to stay at the official residence. A car was on its way to pick us up. So unlikely did all this seem that I asked if the woman knew there were three in the crew, and the circumstances of our presence in Athens.

I felt the arrangement was bound to come unstuck when the lady's better half returned to town next morning and saw three "strangers" in the place. Certainly, for me, staying at the official residence of a chargé d' affaires would be a novel experience, and at the opposite end of the pole to the last United States Government dwelling in which I had been a guest. Graham with his background and Hill with his pleasant manner might pass diplomatic muster, but I doubted my success in such circles. Young people did adventurous things such as turning up in old airplanes looking the worse for wear, but to a chargé d'affaires I'd almost have to appear as a dubious character leading these boys astray.

Approaching a junior-size mansion overlooking Athens, I thought it might be possible to ask for U.S. as well as British assistance in getting through the Middle East. We were met by the chargé's wife, and while she was making a fuss over Graham I wished she wasn't married. Dinner was on a patio looking over the lights of Athens, and it was settled that we must be guests for the duration of the stopover. She called me captain, since Graham had kicked it off that way, and in the prevailing air of hospitality I promised her a flight over the city.

When the chargé arrived home next morning, our visit came to a sudden end. We were out on the patio, there were sounds inside and the chargé's wife excused herself. As her absence grew ominously long, there were meaningful glances between Graham and the rest of us, and then a displeased man strode purposefully into view. Trailing him was the woman who'd just been so bright and full of life, looking as if she'd just experienced something unpleasant. Greetings with a note of rebuke were extended to Graham by the chargé, while Hill and I received bare nods. Looking from me back to Graham, the chargé seemed to be silently telling him that he should know better than to bring such people into the home of an important government official. I would see the funny side of this later, I thought, but for the moment I thought of the embarrassment to Graham's family and to him.

The chargé's wife looked uncomfortable during the process of

213

easing us out, and by the time she had mentally mustered some unexpected State Department people to stay, she'd almost convinced herself that such was the case. Graham promised to keep in touch while in Athens, and then with the chargé we were driven back to town. I explained our Middle East problem to the chargé, who was more friendly with us safely out of his house and willing to see if the embassy could help. When I added that the aircraft was on the British register, he became businesslike and directed me to their officials.

Though the British air attaché wished our troubles had not landed in his lap, he gave all possible assistance. Cables went off to various places; we checked at his office day after day, and one route after another was closed as replies came in. After nearly a week there remained one last resort. Through Turkey and down to Baghdad involved no flight stages beyond our range—if we could get across the mountains east of Ankara. So I asked the attaché to apply to the Turkish capital for clearance.

Day seven brought a reply, and when the man said we'd have to apply through London, meaning weeks of delay, I said the Turks could stick their clearance up their asses because we'd be off in the morning. The attaché, a gentleman to the last, pleaded with me not to embarrass his government. Before leaving his office I gave a half-hearted promise not to do anything rash, a promise I naturally had no intention of keeping.

In the week already spent in Athens nothing was accomplished, not even the floating of some fake money, but the chargé and his wife did score a flight over the city. Graham and I were picked up by the embassy car, and at the airport the chargé studied our Proctor with the look of a man who'd like to stay on the ground. His attractive wife was enthusiastic, so all he could do was to climb in and hope for the best. Having failed to seat his wife beside me, I felt somewhat piqued as we circled Athens. I couldn't help thinking of what would happen if we were to come down and the contents of the doors were scattered all over the place. Returning my passengers to Athens' big international airport, I thought we might be invited to dinner, but we simply received the finality of a lift back to town.

That evening I informed Graham and Hill that we'd depart uncleared for Istanbul in the morning. They appeared to worry, so I explained it would be more of an official nuisance than anything terrible. Our flight plan with Athens Air Traffic Control wouldn't relate to diplomatic clearance, and we should be handled as a normal operation into Istanbul airport. I'd pass it off as a misunderstanding when the Turks caught on and, as captain, would do the lying. In this situation our lack of radio was an advantage, I continued, because we'd be airborne when the other end woke up and there'd be no way of ordering us to return to Athens. The Turks would most likely allow us through, after suitable apologies. Then we'd need clearance through Iraq— and that wouldn't be a place to try any stunts; so we'd just have to make the best of all available official channels.

As I'd promised not to take off without seeing him, it seemed distrustful for the British attaché to phone me at the airport while I was filing my flight plan. If the man really wanted to stop us, he could have phoned the airport officials rather than the briefing officer to ask for me. This seemed a way of covering himself, though I had again to promise not to do anything hasty. The next step was to get airborne quickly, as already the delay would land us at Istanbul long after clearance officials had gone for the day. Only a good tail wind could get us into Istanbul before dark.

Finally we were at the beginning of the runway, waiting for the flashing green take-off signal—and at that stage any light from the tower would have looked green. Without needing to go colour blind, we were rolling before the green light stopped blinking.

Toward the end of the Aegean Sea crossing, abeam a fair-sized island with the Turkish coast just visible, our engine suddenly quit. So unexpected was the power-loss that I was barely aware of startled shouts from Graham and Hill. Before attempting anything else I moved the fuel selector to a main tank, and when we'd lost about five hundred feet gliding toward the island the engine came back to life. At the roar of power the thing that had my stomach in painful knots relaxed its grip. Climbing to cruising height again, I explained that our long-range tank had run out ahead of time, and that either we'd been given short measure at Athens or our consumption had shot up. The cabin tank had no gauge, but the two wing tanks had and would get us safely to Istanbul if all went well.

Much of our track to Istanbul was through corridors between restricted areas marked on the chart, ending in a long run down the Marmora Sea. Without the resources for pinpoint accuracy, navigation along the Marmora had to be by compass, time and map, taking care not to stray. An hour before Istanbul the air began to get hazy, and visibility was soon very limited. The shoreline disappeared completely, so from our last known position I estimated the time we should arrive at a point over the sea abeam Istanbul airport. As the sun set astern, the haze thickened, and all that could be seen was black water below. Assuring the others that we weren't lost just because we couldn't see anything, and our fuel supply was adequate, I held closely to our heading. Full darkness came ten minutes before we were due to turn shorewards, with nothing in sight beyond the red and green glow of our navigation lights.

When the time came I turned toward land, and traces of light soon appeared in the murk. Next came a complex of lights that *had* to be Istanbul airport, so I blinked our landing-lights and was answered by a flashing green signal. More flashes following the appearance of twin rows of runway lights indicated clearance to continue our landing; I put down full flaps after turning onto final approach. Lining up between the lights rushing toward us, we got our wheels onto the runway, but before we rolled to a stop an airplane that looked the biggest thing I'd ever seen was almost on top of us.

Something made me glance up and back through the plexiglass in time to see two widely separated, blazing white landing-lights heading straight for us. Pushing the throttle to full power I applied left rudder and braked, in a desperate attempt to get clear of the runway. About the same time as we bounced off the concrete into darkness, still gathering speed, the other airplane shot past with a deafening roar of powerful engines at full blast. Clearing the portion of runway we'd just left by a margin of no more than twenty feet, the aircraft sounded as though its pilot had slammed on all available power to clear us, and even then it had sunk closer to the ground before climbing to safety.

We were still bouncing into the blackness much too fast when I realized we were clear, chopped power and brought the airplane to a stop. In my blind panic to get clear of the runway I had forgotten our landing-light, and taken a chance on taxiing into a ditch or whatever. Moving back to the runway I talked to the crew about the slip-up in the tower, then became emotional and

216

shouted abuse at those goddam stupid Turks who cleared the airplane to land on top of us.

It didn't require much imagination to give a graphic description of what would have happened to those aboard the aircraft, as well as ourselves, had the pilot been unable to abort his landing. Leaving aside thoughts of fifty-dollar bills from our doors floating amidst the horror, I continued to give vent to my feelings about Turkish air traffic controllers. Since ours was a small and ill-equipped aircraft and the other was a big four-engine thing, I thought the crew might think I was in the wrong. With the terminal approaching, I told Graham and Hill that one controller had clearly given us the green signal at about the same time as another fuckwit gave radio clearance to the large airplane. I explained about the other aircraft being in landing configuration and how, if it had sunk to the ground after clearing us, it would have neither risen again nor stopped before the end of the runway. I skipped details of how that class of aircraft with flaps and wheels down—trimmed for landing—would be difficult to control on such a late balked approach.

In front of the terminal there was great excitement, and from the expressions on some faces we weren't popular. First to talk was a very excited Frenchman, accusing me of nearly causing the crash of his line's Super Constellation. For a horrible moment I thought I might be unable to prove my contention of being cleared to land. If those Turks in the tower denied clearing me, I'd be in the position of a pilot showing criminal disregard for air safety. Feeling defenceless, I told the Air France man I'd been cleared by light signal because my aircraft had no radio, and before the hostile Frenchman could say much a Turk turned up to explain that a tower error had caused the near-miss. So grateful was I toward the Air Traffic Control official, I almost thanked him before realizing that was the least he could do.

In the midst of the excitement we discovered that not only had the tower people cleared two airplanes to land at the same time, but they had failed to pick up their error, leaving it to the alertness of the Air France station manager to prevent a disaster. He had been in front of the terminal, watching for the arrival of his company's airplane, when he saw the navigation lights of something small letting down toward the runway. Then to his horror he saw the Super Constellation lights emerge from the murk, also on final approach; he ran instantly to a phone directly connected to the tower and told them to send the Constellation back into the air.

Inside the terminal I was reminded of the fact that we'd arrived without diplomatic clearance. It was mentioned as something that could be fixed up by contacting Ankara next day, and not connected with air traffic problems. Our flight was legal as far as Air Traffic Control was concerned; details had been received from Athens, we were within our E.T.A. and had followed correct landing procedure after getting tower clearance. Since a major incident had occurred, I was told that there would be an investigation, and I should be at the airport in the morning to make a statement.

Istanbul, after mainland Europe, looked like a place where progress had long ago ceased, and it was difficult to get accommodation. A hotel finally referred us to the Y.M.C.A., on a hill near the Blue Mosque, and here we found beds in a huge flophouse-style room. Most of the Y's inhabitants appeared to be young Americans or Englishmen hitch-hiking to or from places where the grass grew tall, and could be smoked without hindrance from local authorities.

Istanbul was the scene of Graham's first visit to a whorehouse, and nearly his last after some days later developing soreness in the genital region. He had met a local university student in town while I was making my statement at the airport. The fellow was a Jordanian named Hassim, came from a family with money, attended Istanbul's American University, was almost old enough to be classed a professional student, planned a trip to New York the following year for further study of something or other, and was primarily interested in politics and sex. Politics meant the Palestinian Arab problem, but since he couldn't do much about that he concentrated on the other thing. I met Hassim in a café with the crew and reported that we'd be clear to fly through Turkey in a day or two.

It was in London that I first noticed a tendency for Graham's nostrils to flare in situations suggesting sex, and while Hassim talked about whores the reaction became apparent. Graham's nostrils flared like a horse, and Hill remained politely bored. Graham finally asked if Hassim would take him to a cathouse, and then turned to me as if my permission might be required. He

218

had let himself in for what I hoped would seem a few well-chosen words of advice. As captain of this flight, I began seriously. It was up to me to discourage anything that could lead to clap or syphilis, and a visit to an Istanbul whorehouse was an unacceptable risk. The suggestion of medical care in remote places came in for a mention, but the nostrils still flared. Under pressure from both Graham and Hassim I gave in, on condition it was only a blow job; this term offended Graham, so I agreed he could have the kind of intercourse he wanted, provided he used a rubber.

Hassim led us to where both sides of the street were lined with whorehouses. Crowds of Turks milling about window-shopping, with occasional ones and twos succumbing to the calls of rough-looking hookers, did not cause Graham's nostrils to retract.

Most of the Turks looked as though they could afford no more than to stand around watching their more fortunate fellows. Used to this meat market, Hassim made his selection and walked through a doorway. A hefty woman with bare breasts hanging nearly to her navel attracted him, and Graham was left to make his own choice. As we passed more doorways, each containing a couple of almost naked whores, I expected Graham to admit that this was not for him. Nothing in his background suggested that he could dive into a set-up like this, though the nostrils remained distended.

A whore young by the standards of the street caught Graham's eye, moved her body in copulatory motion, and Hill and I were left standing on the sidewalk. With his earlier start Hassim soon re-joined us, and then much too quickly Graham came back with a sheepish expression on his face. Hill wouldn't have picked it, but Hassim and I knew something was wrong; the contemptuous action of the whore in the doorway provided graphic con-firmation. The woman remarked in broken English about his being an old man, and further humiliated her unsuccessful customer by holding a finger rigidly in the air before letting it droop toward the ground. Hill joined in the laughter over Graham's failure, and my suggestion to take himself in hand further upset him, so Hassim stepped in. Looking concerned for Graham's welfare, he advised solving the problem immediately, before there were psychological consequences. I got into a pseudo-serious discussion with Hassim about long-term difficulties that might ensue if something weren't done quickly, and all the time we talked as if Graham weren't there; then I almost spoilt it by telling him the thing would have to be licked. Hassim suggested we look for another girl.

Graham spotted one slimmer and younger than most and walked through a doorway, after pointedly requesting the rest of us not to hang around in front of the place. Taking Graham's request literally, Hassim removed himself from the sidewalk by disappearing into another whorehouse. This time Graham was inside long enough to have succeeded, though when Hassim returned and brightly asked if he'd licked the thing our earlier levity returned. Graham yielded no actual details and requested us to show a diminished interest in his sex life.

Clearance to transit Turkey meant another trip to the airport, and this time I slipped a couple of thousand dollars from under one of the airplane's door linings. Leaving the crew to imagine what they liked about my secretive amusements, I left them again to spend an evening as a seaman. In the port area I carried out an operation similar to the one at Bari. Since Turkey had an arbitrarily low legal rate of exchange my bills weren't likely to get into the banking system, and if a few did, the evidence would point to some unknown ship.

When we left Istanbul for Ankara, where we'd try for clearance through Iraq, the airport officials insisted that because I was American I'd have to pay our landing fee with U.S. currency. Small American bills, not the kind from the airplane doors, took care of that, leaving intact my couple thousand dollars' worth of doubtful-value Turkish lira.

Take-off was back over the Marmora Sea, with perfect conditions for the short leg to the Turkish capital. From overhead, Ankara looked like a place I didn't want to be in, and approaching its outlying airport I noticed that most of the aircraft on the ground bore United States Air Force markings. When we were nearly finished with landing formalities, two American sergeants who'd been looking at our airplane started a conversation. When they learned the nature of our flight, one suggested that it might be possible for us to use Air Force facilities. Disappearing for a few minutes, while a Turkish official filled out still another paper, the sergeant returned with news that his C.O. had given permission for our airplane to be brought onto the American base.

From then on the men of the Ankara Air Force Base couldn't do enough for us. They insisted on doing any maintenance we required, down to replacing parts if possible, and told us to use the non-commissioned officers' club in Ankara for our meals. Hotel accommodation was the only thing we'd have to arrange, after apologies for having no place to put us. We were also invited to use their bus service for travel between the airport and town. With the two sergeants we went into Ankara, had dinner at the club and settled into a hotel.

Since Ankara was also short on hotels we had to share a large single, only to learn early next morning that our room directly faced a Muslim place of worship. An hour of walking through heat and dust had been enough for all to see that the old Turkish village section had little to show besides poverty, while the new planned city had as much atmosphere as a penitentiary with widely separated cell blocks. A muezzin calling the faithful to early prayer from the nearby minaret gave us a good start for our first day in Turkey's capital. From then on, everything seemed to go wrong.

First disaster was a critical delay in getting clearance through Iraq; then when that looked like straightening itself out, Graham's pecker got sore, and when we were finally free to go I got sick. By then we'd encountered such frustration that with my judgement badly impaired we took off anyway.

We called initially at the British Embassy, where the air attaché said that he'd already heard about us chaps from Athens. He quickly explained that British relations with Iraq weren't the best because of the recently burned embassy at Baghdad, so we should try dealing with the Iraqis directly rather than through his office. Talking as if he'd decided that perhaps we weren't such bad fellows after all, the attaché said we might emphasize the fact that the aircraft was commanded by an American. As an afterthought he added that local Iraqi officialdom was in a state of flux and embassy personnel was constantly changing. What the Englishman said about Iraqis was an understatement, and it took nine days plus two attachés to get us cleared; all details right down to why we wanted to fly to Australia had to be forwarded to Baghdad twice, because the first attaché screwed up his paperwork before leaving the job.

On our sixth morning Graham told me, with shamed expression and nostrils not flaring, that he had to see a doctor. Without considering other possibilities, I asked just what had happened in that Istanbul whorehouse, and whether he had in fact used a rubber. Pressed for the truth, Graham said he had used one but it had come off, so far up the girl that she had to fish it out with her fingers. I berated him for not saying something at the time so that prophylactic treatment could have been sought. As with so many things in Ankara, Graham's sore and dripping penis became a matter for the United States Air Force. Graham told a sergeant he might have strained it, but the fellow laconically said it sounded like clap. Arrangements were made for an Air Force doctor to look at the tool. Graham insisted on going alone to the clinic, to return later with a tale of suffering a strain. Not wanting to embarrass him further, I resisted asking if he had a particular strain of gonorrhoea.

After Graham's second visit to the clinic I quietly pumped him for details. Evidently a tough military doctor, with none of the bedside manner that accompanies a big bill, got Graham to admit that he had screwed a Turkish whore. The doctor said he was sorry Graham was a civilian, because he'd like to order him confined to barracks. Telling Graham it would serve him right if his dick dropped off, the doctor gave our navigator the best possible treatment, together with some fatherly advice never to do such a damned fool thing again.

Waiting for our clearance for onward flight we had little to do but talk—mainly about Australia. To get away from any notion that the whole country was advanced, I began with an explanation of the still strong Irish Catholic morality; although that Church controlled only a third of the population, it held sway in many moral situations. Drunkenness, gambling or kicking people's faces in for fun were acceptable, but the law managed to be restrictive in areas below the belt. These values together with old English ones and widespread latent homosexuality resulted in a set-up where the sexes were widely divided. What Graham would notice, I continued, was the way males of limited intelligence compulsively assert their manliness; big boys who'd be chasing girls in other places get their kicks playing manly games in front of them, and afterwards skulk off in the company of males. Parents brag about how clean-minded their

222

oafish sons are, instead of suspecting there might be something wrong with them. Australian manliness is accepted as best exemplified in being slopped-up on beer whenever possible, and spending most free time with male mates. In a country with a high rate of frigidity and lesbianism the system works, and there is reasonable accommodation between the sexes.

All I told Graham about Australia was likely to make him drop off before we reached the place, and there'd been no mention yet of mild distrust toward Americans. Leaving that out, I described Sydney, and how its being a large international city made the place less typically Australian.

After this discussion some of the Air Force men tried unsuccessfully to find the cause of our oil leak. Lacking replacement gaskets, they decided that it might be best to leave well enough alone. Then came our clearance through Iraq, valid for three days only unless we wanted to reapply and await another response from Baghdad. One of the days was already wasted because it was too late for departure. What I hoped for was to reach Baghdad in a day, or the northern Iraq town of Mosul, and that would mean a dawn take-off.

First stop out of Ankara would be Elâzig in eastern Turkey, and there we'd take on all possible fuel for what could be a direct flight to Baghdad. Reaching that city non-stop from Elâzig would depend on how easily we could cross some high mountains heavily loaded. With daylight departure and no en-route delays we hoped to arrive at Baghdad by evening, even with an added fuel stop at Mosul. To make our dawn departure we had to clear the Ankara formalities in the evening, and sleep in the Air Base canteen. After a final dinner at the N.C.O. club, with a number of the men we'd come to know, we were driven to the base in an Air Force car.

For a take-off as soon as there was enough light I put in our flight plan when we arrived at the airport. During the walk in the dark from the civil block to the military side a pain in my stomach suddenly got worse. Earlier it had been like a belch that couldn't bubble its way out, but now it felt expanded to proportions too monstrous ever to find an exit. Re-joining Graham and Hill among the canteen tables and chairs, I was more than ever aware of intense pain running right through my mid section. Hoping to belch or vomit it away, I contorted into all sorts of positions—

223

even poking a finger down my throat without result. All that came up was a lot of snot and I was getting worried, because this was not like any food poisoning or gastric disturbance I'd ever known.

I stretched out on a settee and, aside from alarming the crew, my half-asleep groaning attracted one of the Air Force men. Shining a flashlight on me, the airman asked what was wrong, and I could only describe my feelings. While I still hoped to manage our early-morning take-off, Graham and Hill went into a conference with the airman. Upshot of that talk was the ordering of a car to take me to the military hospital in town. Around midnight I was taken into the dispensary, while Graham and Hill waited outside, and an orderly commenced his examination. Eliminating the more likely things one by one, he finally suggested that either I wait until morning to see a doctor or take a chance on some pills. Since the pain had eased from something the orderly gave me to drink, I settled for pills—and a drive back to the airport.

Nobody slept that night and there was even talk about staying in Ankara until I felt better. Fear of more complications with the Iraqis overruled my common sense; the pills were working, so I told the crew we'd depart as planned. Between pills and coffee for breakfast I felt capable of facing the day but would have preferred it without flight. Then the sky began to lighten in the east and it was time to walk out to the aircraft. The crew still looked concerned, so I assured them that everything would probably be all right once we'd got off the ground. In the cold, flat light of dawn the deserted airport seemed unreal, and I wondered if it would have been better to have waited for at least a day.

Of all the people we met at the base, the only one to see us off was the man who had sent me to the hospital. The next sign of life was a green light from the tower, when we were lined up at the far end of the runway. Take-off into the cool morning air was quick, but before very long we were climbing hard just to clear the rising terrain. Above the nine-thousand-foot level, with our engine straining and the ground only a little way down, my pains returned worse than ever. Nowhere in sight would do for a landing we would walk away from, I realized with a feeling of panic, and even making it back to Ankara seemed doubtful.

During a momentary easing of the pain I decided that since we'd made it this far, we might as well try to get to Elâzig. The crew didn't notice my distress, since I tried not to show it—they were lethargic after a sleepless night.

Then the boulder-strewn valley we were flying over began to narrow, the ground rising faster than we could climb. Our altimeter showed more than ten thousand feet above sea level and ahead was a ridge we wouldn't clear. Now, along with increased pain, came dizzy spells. The boulders grew big and seemed to pass under us faster; all I could think of was to put on more power, rather than turn, before it was too late. Escaping the nearby rock was of less concern than the way I felt, until I suddenly remembered the ridge and how important it was to pass over it.

Not until I reefed the airplane around in an almost-too-late turn did Graham and Hill realize that something was seriously wrong. I was aware of the ridge showing up closer through our oily windscreen, but its failure to sink below hadn't registered. Had the others known enough about flying to see that we were on a collision heading, they might have shouted a warning. With a sense of horror overriding all else, I suddenly realized what was happening, slammed on every last bit of power and started a ninety-degree turn to head us parallel with the ridge—if we didn't smash into the ground first. Frightened to make a really steep turn at our low air speed, which would stall the airplane onto the ground, I could hold only a moderate angle of bank and hope we weren't going to hit.

Far-away and disjointed shouting didn't altogether relate to the urgency of having to complete my turn. More important was that we were swinging through ninety degrees without hitting, and the hard ground was slowly falling away. The near-miss shocked me out of dizziness and pain and left a feeling of great concern, along with thoughts of what in hell I'd tell the crew. Our escape couldn't pass as part of normal flight, even to people who'd never been off the ground, so I gave an explanation before panic developed.

Safely in the clear, I said a downdraught had caught the aircraft, forcing us to turn for more height. There'd been no real danger, I lied, and then truthfully admitted to not feeling well. Coming around for a second try high enough to scrape over, I

225

assured them that we'd reach Elâzig.

Then it was time to forget crew or my insides, because that ridge was not the last of our problems. Ahead lay some tricky navigation to thread us through mountains we couldn't possibly climb over, so I had to do some map-reading that wouldn't allow for mistakes. First step was to identify a couple of the higher peaks, pinpoint them on the chart, and then steer the initial heading of a many-legged track that should lead us to lower country. The way my mid section felt caused me to twist around trying to find a comfortable position, but the mountains were looming too quickly to allow attention to matters not connected with flying.

When a very high peak was abeam to starboard, we turned toward what appeared as a solid wall, but which, according to the map, should have opened up to reveal a narrow pass. About the time I was beginning to wonder if our map was accurate, the opening appeared as an almost bottomless gorge where sides rose high on either side of the airplane. What lay below was almost hidden in gloom, and after a turn to follow the base of a peak the floor began rising toward our flight path at a startling rate. Application of full power set us on a climb equal to that of the rock-strewn gorge bottom, though we were still in a turn and unable to see far ahead. On either side the walls were beginning to pinch in uncomfortably close, before a final sweeping curve put daylight straight in front at our level.

A short breathing spell was long enough for the pain to make its presence felt again, and then came further concentrated map-study for the next leg. There were still mountains around, except for a twisting path to lower ground, but all that laborious climbing was over. Instead of struggling for height we now had severe turbulence, and again I had periods of dizziness.

More pain-killers gave me added confidence as I set our final course. On reduced power we followed the ground down to where the air coming through our open windows was hot and my pain pills no longer worked. When Elâzig was in sight I had an urge to vomit but couldn't, and there was still the landing to be done. Calling to Graham and Hill that this might be a rough one, I was able to forget my feelings long enough to line up for final approach and put us onto the runway without a bounce.

Climbing out of the airplane, I felt good enough to make my

way into the airport manager's office, where it hit again. In no time I doubled up in my chair and the airport manager said he'd get a doctor, before leading me down the hall to a dispensary containing two beds. Finally the doctor arrived, a short man with a huge moustache and crumpled white suit, and the airport manager tried without success to clear the room of a crowd of curious Turks. Since the doctor spoke no English, the airport manager had to translate my symptoms. Much poking and probing resulted in a massive shot in the rear of what I was told was morphine. The stab of the big old-fashioned hypodermic brought grunts and groans from the assembled Turks, as if each felt the needle going into his own ass. When they'd seen enough, the airport manager sent everybody, including Graham and Hill, out of the room and soon I was dead to the world.

Coming to, I wasn't even sure it was the same day, but the pain was gone. Learning from the crew that I'd only been out for a couple of hours, I told them my trouble seemed to be over, and there'd still be time to refuel for a flight at least to Mosul. The airport manager said it would be desirable if we could get out, because foreign aircraft were only allowed to stay overnight in cases of extreme emergency at places without customs facilities.

Normally fuel would have to be brought from town, the official said, but the officer commanding a light-aircraft observation squadron based at the field had offered to fill us up with the compliments of the Turkish Army. Within minutes I filed a flight plan, collected the crew and we were taxiing toward the military hangar. While his men filled the tanks, the officer talked about our flight, then wished us luck.

Boring down the runway on take-off, we blew a tyre. At the worst moment, with our tail up just short of lift-off speed, there was a violent pull to port. The blowout wasn't heard because of engine noise, but I knew our trouble right away and had difficulty controlling the airplane. Without wasting time I had to decide whether it might be safest to force a take-off, and worry about landing when we'd used most of our fuel, or try to bring the airplane to a stop. In seconds I decided that we couldn't get into the air, so the problem became one of stopping in one piece. Switching off the ignition and closing the fuel selector seemed risky, because bursts of power would be necessary to keep the rudder effective down to a low speed if we weren't to make

227

matters worse by leaving the runway. Brake on the good wheel, plus power bursts on full right rudder, prevented our slewing out of control at high speed, and finally when we had slowed down enough to do no harm I let the airplane ground-loop three-quarters of the way around.

Barely had we come to a stop, when a crowd of Turks came running across the field. The Turkish Army arrived with equipment, our cut-to-pieces tyre and tube were replaced from spares carried in the cabin and again we were ready for departure.

My shot of morphine was still working as we headed toward a fresh range of mountains, appearing as a high escarpment in the distance. Coming closer in a hard climb, the aircraft was caught in vicious downdraughts, forcing us to circle endlessly to reach crossing height. This wasted fuel that would have got us to Baghdad minutes ahead of darkness, so when we eventually crossed over at more than ten thousand feet I could only plan on reaching our alternate field at Mosul. Then the morphine wore off, and there was some pain but no dizziness.

Hours of mountains, gradually diminishing in height, brought us to a final little ridge and then the flat emptiness of the Iraqi desert stretching to the horizon. Coming down the thin black line of the Tigris River twenty minutes later, with Mosul in close sight, we were inspected by a pair of fighters. As they dropped off on descent after zipping by at high speed, a green flare shot up from the airport, giving us clearance to land.

From the moment of touchdown we were under military control, beginning with armed troops surrounding us on the runway. The officer who inspected the cabin ordered us to follow a jeep to the hangar area, and then everything down to hotel accommodation was arranged by the Iraqi Army. Our only escape from direct supervision was when the officer who drove us to the hotel said we could walk around town for a couple of hours—before curfew.

My only food since Ankara, some buttermilk sort of substance, put an end to the remnants of pain. Like most unpleasant situations I put it right out of my mind, after hoping it wasn't an ulcer or worse. In the morning we were picked up by an army vehicle, and every detail of departure, down to lining up on the runway, was under military scrutiny.

228

Take-off for Baghdad was with minimal fuel. Our speed was slow to build up in the hot desert air. Instead of heading down a runway, we seemed to be rushing toward a wide lake of water; the mirage appeared to engulf the runway from close ahead, but receded as a feature that could never quite be reached. So oppressive was the heat even at six thousand feet that Graham had to jam dirty shirts and used maps under the perspex to block the burning rays of the sun.

Baghdad was an agony from the moment we touched down, with the ground temperature at 125 degrees and more military control. Everything was inspected, past and future ports of call queried, and three hours later we were informed we could leave for Kuwait next morning. Civil police controlled our town arrangements, again taking us to a pre-arranged hotel and giving the curfew warning. The only laxity was that in the morning we were free to make our way to the airport by taxi.

Before we were allowed to leave a troubled Iraq, I was warned that under no circumstances were we to touch down at Basra. On a heading for the Gulf west of Basra we had to bore through desert duststorms much too high to climb over. Our windscreen became a dull brown thing admitting faint light, and when occasionally the desert could be seen through swirls of dust it appeared as a sea of rolling sand dunes without trace of vegetation. Looking down made me think of forced landings and death by dehydration, and hope to hell our filters wouldn't clog before we could reach the Gulf. A flickering oil-temperature light constantly reminded me of heat as time passed and more desert was put behind, but like most terrifying phenomena, the desert came to an end, the Gulf showing up through the side windows.

With the coast came clear air, but this could do nothing for our caked windscreen, and the Kuwait landing had to be entirely by side reference. Final approach involved twisting to one side and then to the other to make sure I kept the runway directly in front of our desert-dusted windscreen. Close enough to be certain where the runway was, I only had to keep the airplane straight and wait for the side markers to come up.

At Kuwait, those concerned with air traffic were surprised to see us and anxious for some reasonable explanation of our arrival. The English Chief Controller, in a very proper voice, wanted to know why I hadn't informed them of our arrival by radio on

229

approach. There must be some excuse I could offer, he said, for ignoring their repeated calls after sighting our aircraft. While we were on the subject of my aeronautical shortcomings, it might also be interesting to hear any comments I'd like to make about our arrival in Kuwait without filing a flight plan at the point of departure. My accent, when I began to talk, brought a look of understanding to the man's face, as if it suddenly became clear why the flight of an English registered airplane was conducted in such an un-British manner. Apologetically I explained that our aircraft had no radio and a flight plan had been filed at Baghdad.

Mention of Baghdad amazed the controller, suggesting that nothing should arrive from there; I handed him my copy of the flight plan. He was friendly, so I stressed the obvious fact that the Iraqis should have forwarded details. When I said we were out of England bound for Australia, the official expressed surprise that in this day and age an airplane lacking communication equipment and at least one radio navigation aid would attempt such a flight. I wondered what his comments would have been had he known just what was in our airplane. Then he told of the mild flap when we were first sighted, along with further confusion when the aircraft came close enough for our British markings to be seen. Other than something not even known to have been trapped in the Iraqi revolution, they could think of no reason for a rather old-fashioned British aircraft to be coming from that direction, not answering radio calls. There were some choice remarks about the Iraqis before we went on to complete formalities for entering Kuwait.

In Kuwait's heat we decided that being clear of trouble areas we'd make all possible speed to Karachi, our next major port. After I had worked out distances and anticipated delays at each stop, the best way appeared to be to go only to Bahrain next day. With dawn departure from there we should complete two long route segments in one day, to bring us to the Pakistani town of Jiwani. Since that could be a place for formality delay, we'd make it our second night-stop out of Kuwait, leaving only a medium-long leg into Karachi.

With no town visits planned until Karachi, we loaded the airplane with enough tinned food to see us through. Since navigation to Pakistan from the Gulf was straightforward, Graham would be expected to assist our flight steward in food

230

preparation. And as there happened to be a British Army base next to the field at Bahrain, we arranged our next day's dinner in their mess, preparing only a pre-daylight breakfast after a night in the passenger lounge. Then came a mostly over-water flight of nearly five hours to the tiny port of Sharjah.

Remote as Sharjah was, its airport had a dining-room. Presided over by a couple of elderly Indians who probably remained because there was nowhere to go, the dining-room looked as if it had survived since the era when twin-engine biplanes on the England–India run used it as a feeding stop for passengers. Enough tables and overhead fans remained to accommodate a load of passengers of the period when hostesses and meals on board were the ways of the distant future.

In the dry desert air all except the two Indians remained in a good state of preservation, and the walls were still adorned with posters advertising airlines that had long ceased to exist. Apart from a little desert dust, those old Indians seemed to be struggling to run the dining-room as if hoping against reason for a return to better times—when perhaps a biplane might arrive with a dozen passengers to be fed all at once.

Departing Sharjah, we crossed the Oman peninsula, leaving the heat of the Gulf behind for the cooler air of the Arabian Sea.

A long offshore run put us into Jiwani at the end of daylight. Accommodation here was better than at Bahrain; the A.T.C. people lived on the field and let us use a spare bedroom. Not a flight a month landed at Jiwani, so the airport was little more than an emergency facility, also used for training air traffic controllers. They worked, by radio, aircraft in and outbound from Karachi. So remote was the place that for them our arrival meant a welcome break in the monotony, and a rare chance to have letters airlifted out. For this small favour we were given dinner and breakfast, Pakistani-style. There were no passport or customs inspections because nobody existed to carry them out; all formalities would be done at Karachi.

Our flight to Karachi was only a matter of following the coastline, and well within our E.T.A. we were on top of that ugly, sprawling city. Overshadowing all around it in the distance was the giant hangar built in the early thirties for a dirigible service that never came into being, and toward that we steered to find the International Airport. Karachi was to be a much needed

231

two-day rest stop. I resolved to resume the role of seaman for a night, and since I needed a couple of thousand dollars from the door lining, I sent Graham and Hill ahead to start formalities.

Two letters from Terry were at the United States Consulate, the second one a rushed note containing something slightly alarming. Terry had heard part of a radio news story about counterfeit money, and thought fifties were mentioned but wasn't sure; by the next newscast the item had been displaced and a check of the local papers revealed nothing. She feared that one of the car dealers had been caught, possibly spilling to save himself; if necessary, she'd send cables to Karachi, Calcutta and Bangkok in the hope of reaching me quickly. I figured it would take time to trace the action to the other side of the world, so I changed my two thousand in the same way as at the other seaports, and by lunchtime the third day we were on our way to India.

Allowance was made for delay inherent in departing from major cities, and four hours plus was my estimated flying time to Ahmadabad, a night stop. Our plan was to make the best possible time across India, before another good rest stop at Calcutta. From Ahmadabad we'd go to Allahabad with an in-between fuel stop, and, if conditions were right, from there direct to Calcutta.

Clear of Karachi, there was a long coastal run to India, via the Rann of Kutch. Leaving the sea behind until the far side of Calcutta, where the Bay of Bengal crossing would begin, we were over low hills and the first green vegetation since Europe. Along with some swampy tropical overgrowth came the start of India's vast railway network, and a confusing situation. My experience of railways marked on charts justified the old pilots' expression "iron compass", but starting across India it wasn't working that way; the first line was where it should be, but from then on they weren't to be trusted. Junctions that shouldn't exist turned up and lines headed off in wrong directions; and as these were polished, they indicated heavy use. So many old-fashioned steam trains smoked along supposedly non-existent tracks that I had to forget railways as a navigation aid and rely on the airplane's compass. Ahead of some solid cumulus build-ups closing in on Ahmadabad we landed minutes before the airport came under a heavy tropical downpour.

Ahmadabad was big enough to have a good airport dining-room, and after dinner we would have gone into town had the deluge let up. The rains lasted until morning, and we spent a miserable night in an insect-infested waiting-room.

We took off at dawn for Bhopal, down a wet runway and into most marginal weather. Leading toward Bhopal was a pretty reliable railway, though it wasn't of much use because of thunderstorms we had to dodge. The place was finally located and, like Ahmadabad, had officials who wasted plenty of time before we were allowed to refuel and depart for the four-hour flight to Allahabad.

Twenty minutes after lift-off any thought of making a direct track over the lengthy range of mountains separating us from Allahabad and the Ganges River was abandoned. Ahead were cumulus masses billowing thousands of feet above any height we could reach, and this was only the start of the monsoonal weather we'd encountered since Ahmadabad. All we could do was let navigation go to hell and twist our way between those towering columns to avoid flying into one, since their forces were obviously greater than those of the airplane.

For at least three hours we never knew our exact position, but I kept rough notes of headings and times. I could only aim to pick up the Ganges somewhere to starboard of track and follow the river to our destination, rather than expect to hit Allahabad on the nose. Reaching the place in a straight-on approach was possible only because late breaks in the cloud cover, where the mountains settled down to hills, allowed me to relate a couple of off-track towns to the chart and to take up a correct heading. Prior to that we were treated to some awesome fireworks in the gloomy canyons between cumulus columns, when lightning lit their interiors with an unreal and weird glow from way above to far below our cruising level. While that went on, the mountains were hidden by lower cloud; I eased the fears of my crew by promising we'd soon be out of all this.

With lower country came rain squalls of solid grey from ground to cloud. There was plenty of room to steer around them, so I didn't have to fly through and risk damage from large hailstones. Allahabad airport was hidden under a mass of grey during our approach along a river intersecting the Ganges beyond, so we circled until it drifted away with the wind. Between that and the next squall coming up the Ganges we saw

233

Allahabad on the far side, and I decided to snatch a quick landing on the water-covered runway.

In a brief interval without rain the airplane was refuelled, pushed into a hangar, and our accommodation problem settled. A conversation between Graham and Hill and two Indian Airways trainee pilots resulted in our being given a room in a building they occupied. We all had dinner in a nearby Indian café, eating food that could be risky the night before flying in an airplane lacking toilet facilities. Graham's internal schedule went wrong that night, so his morning farts came many hours early— and had more to them than the noise of which he was so proud. These releases smelled suspiciously like substance, and were too much for the solitary overhead fan. That slow-turning antique might have coped with a couple, but the things came in an endless flow—to settle into stratified layers in the room. At Hill's and my insistence Graham's bed was moved over to the window.

Aside from the navigator's wind routine running off the rails at Allahabad, our schedule for crossing India was upset by monsoon weather next morning. Sheets of rain came almost unbroken, Allahabad airport was closed to both in and outbound traffic, and the forecast was that we might get away after midday. That meant no direct run to Calcutta, and Air Traffic Control advice was that we try for the town of Gaya, with a chance of getting out of there on the following day. The only way of reaching Gaya appeared to be tracking down the middle of the Ganges past Benares, and hoping the weather would let us go overland where the river swung north. After some hills a railway should lead us into a valley, and Gaya.

Between squalls we took off, throwing up great sprays of water, and set course down the Ganges. A thousand feet was the best height we could manage, before cloud bottoms began pushing us closer to the water. Pressed toward the river in steps to six hundred feet, we could still see the shores, except for numerous patches blotted out by curtains of dark and ugly grey. Because of squalls we couldn't always hold to the river, and detours inland to get around big ones became necessary.

As we approached Benares, a very long line of squalls stretched across the river, blocking the city from view. Short of heading way off to where there might be hills, there was no choice but penetration, so holding midstream we bored straight into the

234

mess. Slamming into that downpour was almost like hitting something solid—as far as noise was concerned. I'd throttled back slightly and we were flying at reduced speed, with nothing but dense grey in front, when the roar of our engine was dramatically silenced by heavy water crashing against the airplane at a hundred knots. Thoughts of structural damage flashed through my mind. We had entered this stuff about four hundred feet above the river, so there was little margin for error that close. We were barely able to see our wingtips, let alone anything ahead or below, so it was necessary to fly on instruments to hold height and to stay on course.

Exit from the squall was as sudden as entry, and the relative silence caused me to check that the engine was still giving normal power. Ahead of us the Ganges was broad and clear, with the city of Benares off our port side. More important than Benares, however, was some suddenly noticed damage. Streaks of bright red along our wings' leading edges gave me a start, until I realized that it was only undercoating showing where paint had been chipped off in the squall. The others failed to notice the red scars on our nice silvery finish, so I didn't say anything; I wondered if there might have been hail mixed with the rain. The cabin's cracks and crevices shipped only enough water to make things a bit sloppy. More was to come.

Leaving the Ganges, we found the cloud base was higher and were able to follow the railway for a while. Close to the hills there were a couple of possibilities for crossing without losing visual contact or flying into a dead-end. Well into the hilly region, through a windscreen still clean from its dusting before Benares, I saw a brown object appearing as a large speck—then rapidly growing to a frightening size. It struck me that had it been any ordinary bird it would have shot by or banged into the airplane by now, but the thing grew still bigger and kept coming toward us.

Before I could even contemplate evasive action, the object was gigantic and seemed to be veering from nearly dead ahead to our port wingtip. Closing distance narrowed to where speed robbed the thing of detail, and suddenly it was gone. We waited for the sickening thud of impact—and there was none. When the hideous brown mass had safely gone, I realized how lucky we were to have maintained a course which was obviously slightly off collision; any evasive panic action of mine might easily have brought it straight through our windscreen. Badly shaken by the experience I told the crew that we had passed a very large eagle, and that I could only hope to Christ we'd never hit one; any bird that big could hardly fail to bring the airplane down.

Cloud almost filled the valley where I hoped to find Gaya, though occasional holes revealed ground below. A railway carrying two steam trains led us to the yards, but the town was under a cover of white reaching dangerously close to the ground. Then a rift exposed part of Gaya. Referring to the chart, I turned onto a heading for the airport, with an estimated three minutes' flying time. In due course some buildings and part of a runway were seen by looking through a small cloud hole; it wasn't big enough to spiral down, and, lacking knowledge of high spots near the airport, I was afraid to risk a descent where the ground couldn't be seen.

Tracking back and forth over the nearly hidden airport, I finally found a hole that looked good for a steep-turning letdown. After a tight spiral toward the ground within the confines of that hole, we broke clear about three hundred feet above anything solid, in a fair position for a very short final approach. Trails of vapour swirled past while trim was set and flaps were lowered hurriedly, but the runway never went out of sight. At its far end a grey wall of water moved down, shortening the field as we approached. My last notch of flap plopped the airplane onto the ground while there was still enough runway visible, but there was no time to turn off and taxi toward the terminal. All we could do was to remain on the runway headed into wind with our engine running, and wait for the squall to pass. Soon all outside was black; our wings rocked in wind trying to blow us backwards against the brakes. I had a foolish feeling that the cabin would be crushed by the weight of water. And then it was all over.

Gaya was small enough for its Air Traffic Control people to be very friendly; they provided us with accommodation on the field and drove us to town for food. They told of fears for us when the E.T.A. had passed with neither sight nor sound. When first the airplane was heard but not seen overhead, they thought we were searching for the field. Our sound had become faint as I searched for the hole, and they thought we were flying into the distance, lost. Then we were heard again, with a change of pitch indicating

236

power reduction, and they concluded we were taking a desperate gamble on a blind letdown. Until I explained our descent through a hole not visible from their position, the Indians believed that sheer luck brought us to ground.

Transport to town was by ancient motor cycle and sidecar, with me in the best seat and the other two on the pillion and pointed sidecar nose; for Graham and Hill the ride was their first chance to see something of India besides airports. The Air Traffic Control man took us in and out of the depressing railroad centre of Gaya with only one drenching; having bought food, we had a good cook-up on return to the airport government bungalow. It was late morning before the cloud base lifted enough for us to escape from the valley.

Our flight to Calcutta began with a certain amount of fear, and ended with paint ripped from the leading edges. More eagles were sighted and missed. We flew through a range of mountains by following a river with low cloud cover, which made it like a railway tunnel; approaching a junction with another river, where we had to be sure to take the correct branch, the cloud began pushing us down toward the water.

Unable to look at my chart with the canyon sides so close, I relied on memory of earlier study, while flying low to keep visual contact. Just before exit there was a narrowing of the walls as the river curved right around a peak, and while it seemed a tight fit toward the end we were soon in the clear with all of the land ahead below our height.

Though we hadn't been forced to share the limited air space of that tunnel with eagles, they were around again now that we'd emerged and several passed on either side; an oil film on the windscreen made it less than perfect for eagle spotting. With the land falling away and cloud in stratified layers, it wasn't too long before we were on top of a sea of white without a break anywhere in sight. For a good hour we flew along seeing nothing of what lay below, on a compass heading for Calcutta based on our last known position. Then came a rift allowing us to slip underneath, and soon we were over a railway pointing in the right direction and seemingly in the right place. Held to less than a thousand feet by cloud, we followed the railway through towns far more numerous than the map would have us believe existed. There was still no real deterioration in the weather, just light streaks of rain

237

trailing down at quite a few points.

Next, the railway was leading us past a mile-long string of steel mills and towns, not shown on the chart and still a fair way from Calcutta. From gazing at all this I was shortly brought to the reality of whether we'd get through what almost seemed the home stretch: large segments of horizon were turning to a shade of bluish black, and clear portions between seemed to be getting smaller. Somewhere in that murk should be a junction where our railway met a line from the north, bringing Calcutta within less than forty minutes' range. By the time the lines came together and the airplane was switched to the right set of rails we were down to five hundred feet and beginning to scrape the noisy edges of rain squalls.

The chart indicated only one main line to Calcutta, but soon an equally important-looking pair of tracks angled off in roughly the general direction. The extra would either be a bypass or for freight trains headed for some outlying yard, I decided. So in weather getting worse by the minute we stuck to the original. This one would angle in closer to the Hooghly River on its approach, so if visual contact was lost we could divert cross-country and hope to pick up that pathway.

Following the line as it disappeared into dense blackness, I told the others that what was about to happen would be noisy, but probably not dangerous. Within seconds it was as dark as if an early twilight had overtaken us. The railway was all but lost to sight—and the sound was deafening. Water was coming into the cabin from more places than it had over the Ganges, which made me think we could be sustaining damage. Hoping to reduce impact force I cut speed by fifteen knots, and wondered if water was getting under the door linings to soak my counterfeit money. Drainage worried us, because we were taking so much water that if it didn't find a way out, the airplane would become heavy and hard to manage. It never happened. Forced to fly often at levels as low as two hundred feet, we seemed in very real danger of striking any low hill in the vicinity, so I abandoned the idea of seeking lighter spots and got back over the railway. No farther ahead could I plan than to stick with those tracks to the centre of Calcutta, and at that point decide how to reach Dum Dum airport.

Eventually the line was leading us through what must have

238

been an endless string of towns, because there were always buildings alongside the tracks. There were brief periods when the rain wasn't so solid, and during one of those lulls I noticed that any leading edge paint left after Benares was all gone now. Trackside buildings grew bigger, forward visibility improved to half a mile or more, I was able to climb to four hundred feet and we were definitely over Calcutta's outer reaches. As if the huge city was important enough to be spared the lashing, the entire centre suddenly revealed itself. From a couple of miles off, on climb to a thousand feet, we were able to see all the major buildings and crowded streets. Using the Howrah Bridge over the Hooghly as a starting-point, I set a compass heading for the airport; a few good localized squalls had to be gone around before Dum Dum came into sight and we could enter the circuit for a landing.

We spent three days in a Calcutta Salvation Army hostel—on the advice of the airport fuel agent. Thinking the man might be judging us by our appearance, I said we could afford something better, so like a true Christian he sprang to the defence of that worthy organization. After saying that Calcutta had little in the way of good hotels, he told us the Sally Hostel was one of the best places for Europeans. My mention of staying at the Y years before brought the reply that it still existed, but was for Indians rather than foreigners and wasn't too clean.

The hostel was primarily for missionaries, but a call from the fuel official confirmed we could get in, subject to approval of the major in command. To pass inspection we cleaned up before going into town. For an officer in charge of such a large establishment the English female major didn't seem very military. Neither did she appear to be militantly religious. Unlike some of the guests, who obviously had religion with a vengeance, the major was a warm and friendly woman, but that did not prevent her telling us the rules of the house: no drink to be brought into the place, no getting liquored up outside, no smoking in the dining-room, and no immoral behaviour. She explained that some of the missionaries were not broad-minded people, but the less than reverent way she spoke of some of those spreaders of the word made me think she cared for them as little as we would.

The major gave us a big room with three beds in a part of the building far removed from the faithful, and showed similar foresight in the dining-room arrangement, with transit air crew, tourists and such occupying tables on a balcony where there was a breeze and a view. Those whose lives were lit by inner conviction were relegated to the gloomy interior, where hot fetid air was stirred by overhead fans. The kindly woman advised against eating away from the hostel, since Calcutta was rife with dysentery.

News from Terry was that she was standing by ready to go—and that there was no news. It didn't seem a good idea for Terry to show her face in Singapore before my arrival, and so I cabled her to await departure instructions from Bangkok. Because Graham saw fit to ignore the major's advice about outside food, we had to spend an extra day in Calcutta. It also caused a twenty-four-hour postponement of certain financial transactions I planned for the eve of our departure from India. The job did get done, with bills that might have got wet in a sweaty seaman's pocket rather than inside the door of an airplane flying through monsoons.

On the day of our departure for Burma things went wrong, and caused an emergency landing, after dark, at Akyab. Normally I would not have considered take-off that day, but after my monetary activities the night before I felt committed to a policy of flight. When we arrived at the airport, it was closed for departures; the meteorological office offered slight hope for the afternoon, but when the weather finally improved, there was barely time to reach Akyab in daylight—even if all went perfectly.

Approaching the Bay of Bengal, we lost time going around major squalls, and with the swampy Sundarbans of the Ganges Delta still in sight I was resigned to landing at Akyab in poor light; those slimy mud flats stretched all along the coast of East Pakistan (now Bangladesh). Ahead were cumulus build-ups rising to great heights; these violent masses caused further course changes, and I considered putting down at Chittagong, despite advice from Calcutta not to land there unless absolutely necessary.

Running along the East Pakistan coast after finally crossing the top of the Bay of Bengal we came abeam Chittagong, and I would, had there been less red tape, have landed. Weather ahead didn't look too bad, so I fell into the trap of thinking we might reach Akyab about the time the street lights were coming on.

Half an hour past Chittagong the airplane was miles out to sea, practically surrounded by a fresh lot of storms. These disturbances, some black right down to water level, were blocking our return to Chittagong and forcing us still farther from the coast. We twisted our way finally to land and were in sight long enough for me to establish our position, before again being pushed out to sea. More than an hour of intermittent sightings followed; the weather changed from cumulus to lower cloud loaded with rain squalls, darkness came and all that could be seen from a thousand feet were occasional whitecaps on the black sea. Eventually we arrived at a position over the Bay of Bengal which I estimated to be ten or twelve miles west of Akyab. We noisily scraped a few unseen squalls while I flew partially on instruments searching eastwards for some sign of light. A new fear was that Calcutta hadn't forwarded our flight plan.

Graham and Hill were more than just a little nervous, despite my assurances. Then, in the far distance, there appeared some blurred lights. On the chance that Akyab Tower was manned, and had a line of sight out to sea and was looking for us, I briefly switched on our powerful landing-light. We were at that point established on our run toward shore, and soon a brilliant green rocket flare shot high into the distant murk. Slowly falling to the right of the main cluster of lights, the flare still burned after I answered with a second blink of our landing-light. In the darkness of the cabin I could sense the relief.

Half-way in, when the tower people possibly thought we'd been cut off by shifting cloud, they sent up another rocket. This was blurred by rain crossing our track. Our landing-light again lit the propeller like a great metallic disc as I let Akyab Tower know that we were fully visual and fast approaching the coast. Even after taking the light into account, Akyab's runway lighting seemed unusually blurry, and close down on either side of where we were about to put our wheels I saw open-flame oil-flares. When we touched there was a high-pitched whine, dropping in tone as we slowed down, and after stopping I saw that between the flaming oil-pots Akyab's runway consisted of no more than lengths of steel grating laid end to end on bare ground.

After a jeep had led us to the terminal, the Burmese at Akyab

241

treated us as welcome visitors. Our lateness and the bad weather over the Bay of Bengal had caused much worry before the airplane's landing-light was spotted out to sea. Long before the sighting, when there was still a trace of daylight and we were past our E.T.A., a Burmese airliner was asked to check a few remote places where we might have landed. When that aircraft failed to locate us, it was thought we might be tracking out to sea rather than risk flying coastal. Calcutta advised that we were without radio, so no futile calls were made; the flares were lit before dark in the hope that we'd find our way into Akyab somehow. When we still failed to turn up, there were fears of our being down at sea, though a tower watch had been maintained for any light that might appear in the distance.

One of the friendly Burmese explained that the flares would have been left burning and a lookout maintained until well past the time our fuel would have run out. For a place to stay we were taken to another of the bungalows maintained in these parts of the East for visiting officials. The airport people used the English colonial term "rest house", and during the drive to its location in town we were told that the caretaker would arrange dinner and breakfast.

Cloud and rain in the morning made it pointless for the jeep to collect us before midday, so we killed time on the rest-house veranda observing passing traffic. Looking worse off but as easygoing as I remembered them from years before were great numbers of Burmese. Unchanged since the end of British rule was the country's vast dog population and they appeared as well off as ever. Unlike the miserable hounds of India, Burma's dogs gave the impression of enjoying a lasting relationship with the people—based on a one-way traffic in food.

After our difficulty in getting to Akyab from Calcutta it was a relief to find that our flight to Rangoon involved little more than pointing the airplane in the right direction. With only a few rain squalls and some cloud we followed the coast to a point below Akyab, then turned inland on a direct heading for Rangoon. First the Irrawaddy River came into sight, and next we were over the top of Rangoon passing the high gilt-painted or gold-plated pagoda across the railroad tracks from the business district; a final heading took us to the airport.

Had I not promised the crew two days in Rangoon, I'd have

242

been content to leave within an hour. To them the city only needed an Eastern atmosphere, which it had, and should not be as dirty as Calcutta, which it wasn't, to be worth seeing. Graham and Hill spent much time wandering around the present shabby and rather depressing version of what had long ago been a pleasant city, and in which I had once enjoyed an affair and negotiated a number of loans. Not wanting to cast gloom on their pleasures, I simply said I'd seen it before and would rest until it was time to leave. Nothing about the place or its economy could tempt me into becoming a seaman on the final night.

Out of Rangoon we had good weather. We flew out over the swampy region of the Irrawaddy Delta, and made our way down the coast for the early part of the run. We then turned inland to jungle and mountain—a vast, never ending, timeless green hell. Dense overgrowth covered mountains and valleys, so no ground could be seen and nothing could be related to our chart. There were no great heights to overcome in crossing to the flat part of Thailand, but of the thousands of miles we'd travelled since England this region seemed one of the worst for a forced landing; it was without trail or indication of ever having been penetrated, and an airplane going down would have been lost for ever.

With a feeling of relief that the hill country was behind us we sighted a distant coastline marking the start of the South China Sea, and then dodged a little weather until Bangkok lay straight ahead. From overhead, it looked like any other East Asian city, except for the canals jammed with Chinese-style boats. It wasn't until we were in the airport terminal that the difference became clear. We were now in the real Far East, where the people were altogether different. This did not go amiss with our navigator, who, while I dealt with formalities, was looking hungrily at pretty Thai girls; for the first time since seeing the doctor at Ankara his nostrils flared. On the long drive into town we passed a big sign advertising a massage parlour, which Graham studied as if all memory of Istanbul had faded. As definitely as I had resolved to play seaman on our final night, Graham was determined to get laid in Bangkok. I withheld my usual disease warning until he took a more positive step than putting his nose to the wind.

At the consulate there was a letter from Terry. I replied with a cryptic cable instructing her to depart immediately for Singapore and check into the Adelphi Hotel. After dinner Graham announced his intention of going out alone, and I, in turn, offered him some carefully chosen words of advice. I told him, too, about things not always being what they seemed in Bangkok, and how he might let himself in for a shock if he made a bar or street pick-up. I explained that a lot of Thai men passed themselves off as women, and unless he felt like running his hand up a leg or two before making a deal, it would be wise to patronize a reputable whorehouse.

My financial activity was carried out on the final evening, after informing the crew that we'd make a crack-of-dawn take-off. The reason for going so early, and leaving our hotel before daylight, was my wish to make the two legs into Singapore in one day. First stop would be Songkhla, in the far south of Thailand, where we'd be delayed only for the time it took to fill all our tanks for the long jump to Singapore. Since formalities did not always go smoothly at flight departures, I wanted to avail myself of all possible daylight.

Bangkok's pre-dawn darkness was quite still as our taxi headed out toward the airport, except for a strange tinkling. Few signs of life were to be seen, but from all quarters in the dark came sounds like people busily ringing cowbells. The explanation for the mysterious ringing at such an hour was that it was done by Buddhist monks, and was probably the time they set out on their begging rounds.

In the dull early light Bangkok looked almost dead from the air, but it passed quickly as we headed toward the southern shore. Weather was perfect all the way down the Thai coast and there were no navigation problems. All I had to do was to pick the right place for turning landward toward Songkhla. Though that out-of-the-way town had only a small airport, it was in radio contact with Bangkok, and we were expected.

Among those at the terminal was a self-important airport manager, who took over with a show of authority. Endless paperwork was given first priority, then there was a long wait for the fuel tanker (during which time we had lunch from supplies in the airplane), and finally the officious little man sprang the best time-killer of all. When everything seemed set for the long flight to Singapore, the manager said he'd have to phone the chief of police to come out from town to clear our departure. Had the fool made this call when we arrived, events a few hours later would have taken a different turn.

In the time it took for the police chief to drive his old car to the airport, and check every piece of paper, I saw our chance of crossing the Malay Peninsula, to use the shorter west-coast route, diminishing by the minute. Weather was building up inland and I still hoped we might get across at a narrow point to the south, but that policeman could not be persuaded to hurry things. Despite Songkhla's obsessive attention to detail it would later emerge that the most important and basic procedure of all was overlooked. . . .

After a long run to get off the ground in hot air, our initial heading was to a spot marked Kota Bharu. We flew to and past the place where I had hoped for a short cut overland, and it seemed we were committed to the long run down the east coast. All was fairly clear on our side of the peninsula, but a few miles in from the coast the cloud was right down to the hills and worsening. Two hours out of Songkhla, beyond where tracking inland would have saved us much time, I switched from the long-range to one of the wing tanks.

Fifteen minutes ahead of the time it should have been empty, the port wing tank ran dry and our engine quit. After flying this far from London with me, the crew were growing accustomed to sudden silences, and there was no panic during my quick change to the other wing tank. We had now been more than three and a half hours in the air, running behind time because of headwinds, and I was thinking of putting down at Mersing for the night in my reluctance to displease the Singapore airport officials by an after-dark arrival without a radio. Mersing, with an adjacent airport shown on the chart, was about sixty miles short of Singapore; at our present rate we could estimate arrival overhead close to final daylight.

My reaction to the tank running out was to review our fuel condition and try to decide if our consumption had increased or if we'd been given short measure at Songkhla. The wing tanks had appeared full when the caps went on, though I might have been careless in the heat and not checked closely enough. Visual inspection of our long-range tank was not possible owing to the filler-cap location. Splashing from a carelessly held hose could give the impression that it was full when it wasn't, so there was a frightening possibility of our not having the forty minutes' reserve that tank should contain. The only decision I could make was to switch immediately to the long-range tank and run it dry, leaving us with one nearly full gauge-equipped wing tank. At the very worst our fuel position would not become critical before Mersing, even without whatever the long-range tank should have contained. Graham and Hill were advised to expect another power loss, which came less than twenty minutes later, and I decided that we definitely were committed to a landing at Mersing.

Daylight was fast failing when we arrived over Mersing, and heading to where the airport was indicated I saw timbered country in its place. Foolishly I used up minutes and precious fuel searching for it, instead of cutting right then for a quick run to Singapore. When no usable piece of ground showed up anywhere, our only way out was to track in the rapidly settling tropical darkness toward the island, hoping our fuel would last the distance.

In the final traces of light some hills appeared ahead, as dead black under solid overcast. As we used extra power to get over the hills, I thought that with luck we might reach the closer military airport on Singapore Island. Our fuel-gauge pointer was well down into the bottom quarter, though it seemed early to mention my thoughts of a possible ditching. Graham and Hill were already quite aware of what had happened at Mersing, and somewhat on edge. Studying the chart by our cockpit light, I decided that we'd definitely reach a river coming from the north to empty into the Strait of Johore, so at least we'd escape the hopelessness of going down into the jungle in darkness. Compared to that form of sudden death, the prospect of open water below when our engine quit for the last time seemed almost as good as reaching an airport. So frighteningly low was the gauge now that I gave us little chance of even getting to Singapore's military field.

Ditching was not a thing I'd previously done, but I had some idea of what to expect, though darkness added a terrifying complication. Thinking about pulling it off in the dark gave me a sick feeling, as I wondered how in hell to judge height accurately to flare out and lose speed before final impact. I'd also have to fly the airplane straight and level, with no visible horizon, or a wing

246

might touch first and send us cartwheeling across the water as we broke up. Without thinking about what was in the doors I realized they'd have to be jettisoned on the way down, or we might get trapped in the cabin. Then there'd be the matter of preparing Graham and Hill for ditching. That, though, could wait until all hope was gone.

After the longest miles I had ever flown, the river was just visible below, and far ahead the overcast was beginning to glow. With a little fuel indication on the gauge I began to think that we might have a fair chance, but that reflected light on the cloud base indicating Singapore city was not coming up fast enough. Through intermittent rain some lights soon appeared that could only be on the closer eastern end of Singapore Island.

About five miles short of the military field I prepared Graham and Hill for ditching. The fuel pointer was now almost on zero. While I was instructing them to tighten their seat belts, and keep their arms in front of their foreheads until the airplane stopped, the lights ahead came noticeably closer. Not knowing whether to expect panic or anxious questions, I was amazed at the calm manner in which both accepted my terrifying instructions.

Singapore glared bigger and came so close that we only needed two or three minutes of power—though I might have to do a dead-stick landing. The engine, however, ran longer than that, and we arrived over the field with plenty of power; then for some unknown reason the man in the tower refused to turn on the runway lights. Crossing the Strait of Johore I picked out hangars by lights between them, but of the runway there was no sign. Furiously blinking our landing-light to indicate that we urgently needed to get down, I swung around in a turn directly over the airport. No rows of lights came on to reveal where in the void of darkness the runway lay. At fifteen hundred feet we circled the field with landing-light flashing continuously, and then an answer came from the tower.

The sole acknowledgement the tower saw fit to give us was a powerful searchlight beam, which swung in an arc before it stopped to point the direction of Singapore international airport. Cursing the fool in that tower for not having the sense to realize that we were in trouble, I pointed the airplane straight at the source of the beam and flashed as fast as I could move the switch. Fuel was at rock bottom and the engine ready to quit any second, but it wouldn't have been too late for a landing even if I had to sideslip from some awkward position. One little move of an idiot's hand would have switched on runway lights that the airport most certainly possessed. But all we were offered was more swinging and a useless pointing of the searchlight. Nothing was left but to turn from the hidden runway and fly out over the water on a heading for Singapore—and fly until our engine quit.

No questions of concern came from the crew, and beyond my saying that we'd ditch there was little talk. I had said earlier that ditching wasn't too dangerous, but I was thinking in terms of daylight when it would be possible to see what I was doing up to the moment of contact. Graham and Hill took me at my word, without referring to the factor of darkness. I had also neglected to mention that a fixed undercarriage aircraft would ditch badly and flip onto its back after hitting. With no one to give me confidence in my ability to set the airplane safely down on the water, I was worried and hoped against reason that it could be done successfully.

Although the gauge was on zero, I still hoped there might be enough fuel in the bottom of the tank to take us within gliding distance of Singapore airport. I was hanging on desperately for an outside chance when our engine quit. Without any spluttering the noise simply stopped, and we were on our way down.

A shout of alarm came from one of the crew, but I was too busy with other things to take much notice. Twelve hundred feet showed on the altimeter as I trimmed for glide, trying to estimate where in the darkness we'd hit the water. For a horrible moment I thought we'd never get out of this and that trying to fly the airplane was no longer important. Then my instinct for self-preservation took over. I realized there were procedures to follow and I'd have to do them correctly.

More than two hundred feet were lost positioning the airplane to run parallel and fairly close to the shore, where there were a number of lights. Unwittingly I eased the stick back while relieving my tensions in a repeat of ditching instructions. A frightening judder ran through the aircraft. Forgetting all but that warning of a stall and a likely spin straight down, I pushed the stick forward to get more speed. We were now going down fast, with the luminous pointer on the air-speed indicator shooting past the sixty-knot mark. Safely under control we went through the six-hundred-foot level, with the airplane awkward to fly against its windmilling propeller. Getting the feel of the aircraft in this condition brought us closer to the dark water surface, and more things had to be done quickly.

The landing-light had to be worked to attract attention on shore, our doors needed to be jettisoned soon, and to get more lift I'd have to lower the flaps. With no speed-killing level-off over an invisible surface—doing it too high would have resulted in a dropped wing—I could only fly the airplane with the flaps keeping it controllable at a few knots slower. The shore lights could serve near the end as reference for level-wing flight, so we'd take the impact with wheels and forward section and not be smashed to pieces. Two notches of flap gave the desired effect, then the red emergency handles were jerked.

Both doors flew off into the darkness with a loud cracking sound, and there was a violent rush of air through the cabin. Altimeter readings no longer had meaning, and all that mattered now was the angle of shore lights off to port. At eighty knots the airplane controlled well but was sinking fast, bringing those lights dreadfully close to our own level. Against instinct I had to resist temptation to start easing back on the stick.

When the lights were straight out the side, I remembered about protecting my face and forehead at the last instant. I was too late. All at once there was a roar like a fast train entering a tunnel, but many times louder. I felt myself pulled forward by a weight several times my own, and my head smashed into something that gave under the strain. A powerful restraint across my lap doubled me over, my head hurt, and water swirled into the cabin with tremendous force. There was a dead silence, unbroken even by the bubbling of air. When I opened my eyes to the stinging of sea water, all seemed black until I became aware of a faint greenish light. With a start I realized that we should get out as fast as possible. Pushing toward the door opening proved futile. I felt trapped in the water-filled cabin, and then realized that my seat belt was still fastened. Released, I seemed to be swimming longer than ever my breath could hold out—and without knowing which way was up. Finally, my head broke the surface, and all I could do was gulp great breaths. I turned round in the darkness and dimly saw the rear underside of the airplane poking out of the water at an angle.

Things happened quickly—a call across the fuselage to where Graham was hanging on, questions about Hill, Graham's disappearance underwater to emerge with Hill in tow; and finally talk about whether anyone was hurt. Nobody was— except for a scrape on Graham's leg and a gash on top of my head where it had penetrated the instrument panel. I learned later that Hill was a non-swimmer and would have drowned but for Graham. On the way down Hill quietly told Graham he couldn't swim, and then courageously lay back and awaited his fate in silence. I thanked Graham for handling the situation in a manner not to leave me with the loss of Hill on my conscience.

There was movement of lights on shore, about a third of a mile away, and before long a couple of launches were headed our way. Sharks were mentioned and instinctively I looked down, to see again the green glow indicating our cockpit light functioning under water. Fear of the light attracting anything was momentary, for we were soon pulled into the first launch to reach the scene.

Headed for shore after informing the Englishman commanding a crew of two Malays that all on our aircraft were accounted for, I realized that my wallet full of genuine money was gone and I only possessed a waterlogged passport. Closer to land I thought apprehensively of the doors full of fake money, which might have released their contents on impact or remained afloat for later recovery, and decided right there on my line of defence.

Till I was blue in the face I'd deny knowledge of carrying money—counterfeit or otherwise—and would insist that if any was there it had been planted by criminals in one country for recovery in another, and meanwhile act the poorest man in Singapore. My suitcase, containing photographic equipment and money collected en route, was not watertight, so from the upside-down cabin it could be presumed to have already sunk to the bottom of the strait. Those doors were heavy and strongly built, and I hoped they also were on the bottom.

According to a Royal Navy officer, we had crashed off Singapore Naval Base. They had pulled us out of the water, and from the moment of stepping ashore we were in their care. As we climbed from the launch a crowd gathered, and a pair of Singapore Fire Brigade engines arrived, sirens screaming. From the navy officer's house—where we were taken for liquid stimulant—an ambulance took us to the naval hospital. So efficient was the Royal Navy that a doctor—in a dinner suit, having been called from a party—and a medical team were waiting when the ambulance arrived at the casualty entrance. As soon as we'd been examined and treated—my head-bleeding stopped and various bandages applied—we were sedated and put to bed.

Before the sleeping stuff worked, I thought about Terry on her way to Singapore. Soon she'd learn how I had lost our funds, though on its own that was no tragedy, since there was plenty more in Australia. What mattered was that I might be questioned, and in no position to do anything for a long time—if ever. After deciding to deal with all that when Terry arrived, I thought about the airplane and its loss, but this seemed vague, unimportant. I was then aware of nothing, until a naval orderly woke me with a tray of breakfast.

11

Everything lost, everything to play for   Graham,
the clean-cut "All American" salesman   hullo
easy money   goodbye Terry   capital starvation
and other meaningful expressions   Miss Pepsi
Cola gets a refit and Australian Air Photos is
born.

SINGAPORE CAPER

After breakfast my hopelessly mixed-up thoughts were interrupted by the start of activity. First, someone reported that our
aircraft had been salvaged by a naval tug, and towed to the
slipway. Then an officer informed us that the Royal Navy had
been in touch with our consulates, and the New Zealand people
were sending a car for Hill; he was puzzled that a United States
official had said they were not concerned with survivors from the
crashed aircraft. This shocked Graham, so I beefed up earlier
criticism of State Department people by suggesting that most of
them were pricks. The naval officer promptly told us not to worry
because the Royal Navy wouldn't see us stuck. They'd take us to
the consulate by car, and if assistance were refused, we'd be
brought back to the Naval Base, to stay until something could be
arranged.

A couple of officers then questioned us on just what had
occurred the night before. They'd been in touch with civil
aviation people—who hadn't even known of our flight's existence
before the crash. The fact that Singapore Air Traffic Control did
not know we were on our way made it clear that the Thais had
not forwarded details, and helped to explain why someone in the
military airport tower had not given us runway lighting. Many
questions were asked about the searchlight episode, followed by
much talk between the officers, which led to a polite suggestion
that making an issue of the matter would only embarrass another

military service without benefit to anyone. The damage was already done, one of the officers explained, and there'd be an investigation. In the meantime it would be appreciated if I'd not mention the incident to the press or others. Thinking about the doors of the aircraft and how little I wanted anything looked into, I promised not to make an issue of the fact that some fool wouldn't give me runway lighting.

Later came a confrontation with reporters and photographers from the Singapore newspapers. They were waiting outside the hospital when we left on our way to see what remained of the aircraft. Forgotten was the fact that, quite apart from the unknown fate of those jettisoned doors, my face still shouldn't appear anywhere. I even suggested to a smiling Chinese photographer that he'd do better if he removed the lens cap from his camera. Looking embarrassed, he pulled the cap off and snapped, while we answered questions about the crash and our flight from England.

The sight of the airplane on its back where it had been dragged up the slipway made me wonder how anyone had survived. With the cabin roof crushed in at least a foot, and the instrument panel deeply dented at no more cost than a cut to my head, it seemed impossible that we had all escaped without serious injury. Worthless as the airplane had been, the sight of it lying dead on its back was depressing. The good money that went down with it—and the other kind hidden in the doors—didn't matter very much while I stood on the slipway having a last look at the aircraft that had seen us safely out of so many seemingly hopeless situations. With plenty put away, I couldn't get too upset over a suitcase containing the price of a modern airplane lying at the bottom of the Strait of Johore.

What hurt at the moment was the loss of the old Proctor, despite its oil leaks and other faults. Before turning away, I tried to shake my mood by rationalizing that what I'd given for the airplane represented about half a day's trading, but it didn't work. Only when I made up my mind to obtain another airplane in Singapore, and continue the flight to Australia, did my feelings of deep depression begin to disperse. Walking from the wreckage, I told Graham—Hill had already been whisked off by the New Zealand consulate—of my intention. If he still felt like flying with me, he'd be welcome to continue as my navigator.

At the United States Consulate I forgot my resolve not to make an issue of anything. Accompanied by a Royal Navy petty officer, Graham and I walked into the place, to be practically ordered out by some officious bastard. Seeing us in the clothes we'd worn through the crash, the man shouted that it was no use coming here because the consulate was unable to assist. Going into a white-hot fury, I loudly informed him that I wasn't interested in his comments, but would like to speak to somebody important. Graham and the navy man stood in silence while the official informed us that the consulate already knew about me. I could only imagine that the doors had been found, or that they'd received news of me from somewhere. From sudden fright I switched back to fury, after learning the sum total of the consulate's knowledge from sneering remarks about my having knocked around the China coast years before. What this snot knew could only have come, I decided, from old records hastily checked. These probably showed that long ago I'd made a run through the East making loan applications, and had been careless about repayment.

I now felt bold enough to insist that once again I'd like to speak to someone who wasn't so obviously a junior employee. The thought occurred to me that if I hadn't lost my airplane, I could have arrogantly told this ass that I'd appreciate being addressed as captain rather than just by my surname. Our Royal Navy escort seemed astounded by such goings on in a consulate, as did Graham. While the insulted official was fetching someone to handle what was apparently too much for him, my navigator pleaded with me to calm down. In the midst of my telling Graham that I hadn't started yet, the man returned with someone who looked more important.

Without even being asked, this fellow said that the consulate could not extend financial help. Not liking him any more than the first man, I said that the Royal Navy was generously providing assistance. Officers of that organization, I went on, had been of the opinion that in situations such as ours the consulate could be expected to offer aid. Sensing that neither liked my reference to the Royal Navy, I said that one of its officers had been told that the consulate had no interest in our predicament. Finding that hard to believe he had sent us in with return transport, just in case the information was correct. The discussion

254

suddenly ended when I told the older man that I didn't appreciate being insulted by one of his pipsqueaks on arrival.

On our way back to the base Graham forgot his conditioned loyalty long enough to remark that the U.S. officials didn't seem a very friendly lot. He questioned whether their animosity might be toward me rather than our situation. Admitting that my name could be on a list for reasons not worth discussing, I maintained that as distressed Americans we were entitled to consular assistance. In language shocking to Graham, and amusing to the British Navy man, I went on to express my exact opinion of those minor diplomatic assholes.

Very quickly the story of what had happened was all over the base. Since I, as owner of the airplane, was supposed to have lost all I possessed, the British were appalled by such treatment; they unquestioningly provided their shipwrecked or air-crashed nationals with all possible assistance. I could only agree that the Americans weren't much help, hope nothing so embarrassing as an airplane door turned up, and go along with my situation of being stranded without funds. The only actual cash between us was the small amount in Graham's possession, but we soon looked respectable in clothes generously provided by various navy men.

The Singapore evening papers featured our story and pictures prominently on their front pages. Their account was reasonably factual, incorporating much information drawn from us by a friendly Australian reporter and including a reference to doors jettisoned on the way down. Hurriedly I read on, to feel my tensions ease with no further mention of doors. My overwhelming fear was that, to tidy up their paperwork, the officials might want to gather all parts of our airplane, and might even appeal to the public to hand in anything they found.

A collection was taken up for us that night in the petty officers canteen, and for once I actually felt guilty about accepting money. Since I was supposed to be without funds anywhere in the world, there was no choice but to accept, and to express my thanks. Next morning the officer-in-charge of the diving school sent his men to the bottom in an attempt to find our lost luggage, but it was a hopeless task. The area around our point of impact— far from where the doors would have landed—was searched. The divers reported thick mud swirling up in clouds and that there was no chance of sighting anything.

Then the Royal Navy took us into Singapore to a good boarding-house for Europeans run by a British organization known as Toc-H (this letter combination originally represented the telegraphic call sign of a Belgian rest house for First World War troops). The Toc-H management heard of our situation through military channels, and offered us a month's free board.

As soon as we were settled in, I checked the Adelphi Hotel, but Terry had not arrived. There was a cable confirming her departure from Los Angeles and mentioning a couple of days' stopover in Hong Kong, before Singapore and business. Going into the quiet Adelphi, I was glad I'd decided on that place, and not the Raffles. At the time of giving instructions I'd thought it best not to use the one hotel in Singapore known to every tourist, or anybody who'd read Somerset Maugham. Now that there was publicity, and worry about doors, I was more than ever relieved not to have to walk through the lobby of such a famous establishment and ask for Terry. Later that evening Graham and I saw Hill for the last time, before he boarded a safe and luxurious Qantas flight for the final third of his flight to Sydney.

Graham seemed willing to stay with me long enough to find out if there really was anything to my talk about another airplane and the continuation of our flight to Australia. He obviously suspected something phony about my tale of being broke, but wouldn't ask questions. Perhaps Graham could play a part in what was taking root, though rather than mention anything to make him think that more than the instrument panel was damaged when my head flew into it I decided to keep quiet for a while.

Wondering if the crash might have impaired my thought processes, I gave the idea great consideration. Each time I thought about the tremendous publicity generated by our arrival in Singapore, the idea came on stronger. Coverage like that meant the end of anything to do with fake money, because I'd no longer be invisible, but for what I now had in mind it could mean the difference between success and failure. Where this brainwave seemed ideal, apart from the profit factor, was that it would tally with denials I'd have to make if those doors were discovered.

Several things occurred that strengthened my resolve, and I fully realized what a tremendous asset Graham would be if he could be recruited. A spate of offers of financial assistance came

256

over the phone, and I took careful note of all names and addresses. Next came a call from the friendly Australian reporter, offering to plant, within reason, any story helpful to our future plans.

Finally, somebody wanted to sell me an airplane on a low deposit. As a clean-cut "All American Boy" Graham could fit perfectly into what I planned, though with his honest nature he'd have to be handled carefully. At first, I would assure him that there would definitely be another airplane. Then I'd feed him minimal information while he was being phased into the operation. This would have to be done in such a way that he'd be well committed before he suspected that my principles were less lofty than his own. Graham had more or less "grown up" since leaving London, and had had a few corners knocked off during our rough trip. He'd taken the sore pecker well for somebody of his background, and dangerous flight hadn't appeared to worry him too much. Above all, his conduct during and after our crash made me realize that he had a lot of potential.

Returning to the Toc-H from a run into town, I was told that an inspector from the Singapore Police had called to see me, and that he'd be back later. Graham was present, but the inspector only asked him when I might return. That sounded ominous. Trying to act unconcerned while imagining all sorts of possibilities, I could only sweat it out until summoned to the Toc-H office by a Chinese houseboy. I felt reassured by the sight of only one Malay officer, but I soon wondered whether his briefcase contained salvaged currency. The policeman asked casual questions about the crash; I began to feel he was uninterested in the details and was really sizing me up step by step. I did my best not to show concern, but worked the angle of my financial position for all it was worth. Round One was over, and the inspector turned to what I hoped was the real purpose of his visit. Papers came from his briefcase, he spoke of an official report on the crash, and while taking it all down he learned enough of my life's history to make me feel uneasy. His last words were that my navigator and I should apply for permission to stay in Singapore for the time it might take to straighten out our affairs. As he left the Toc-H, I wondered if I'd ever see him again.

After explaining the police visit I talked to Graham about my plans for an aerial photography business in Australia, and how there might be a good position in it for him. On our flight out he'd mentioned the possibility of working in Sydney for a few months. After I talked some nonsense about certain feasibility studies that must first be carried out in Singapore, the subject was changed.

Next morning Graham accompanied me to the airport, for a look at the aircraft offered on a fly-away and pay-later-if-ever basis. It turned out to be barely worth the deposit. Near by, however, was a nice four-seater Auster, which, according to the man in charge of the Royal Aero Club hangar, belonged to a local Chinese business man and was for sale. When I explained to Graham that the high wing of the Auster would be good for aerial photography, he showed a stronger than usual interest in airplanes. He came with me to the office of the owner, when I agreed to buy if the price could be chopped to something less than the twelve thousand Singapore dollars asked. My promise to buy within a month, subject to inspection, brought a thousand-dollar cut and a look of utter wonderment from Graham.

Leaving the office where I'd expansively committed myself, I ignored Graham's questions and instead talked of the opportunities in aerial photography. I explained how money could be made by flying over a city and taking whatever looked profitable. People who'd be hard to toss for an order to take something would succumb when shown a good shot of their building, construction site or whatever. I told Graham that this was where I envisaged him fitting into the organization; part of my plan for recruiting Graham was to speak of an organization in discussing something so far non-existent. This sugar-coated way of presenting the idea of picture-hawking seemed to impress him. His honest appearance and forthright manner would, however, play an important part in certain work that must be done in Singapore before the other could take place; this aspect wasn't yet to be broached.

I explained that there weren't many competent operators in aerial photography. It usually involved a team of two—a photographer and a pilot—but this didn't always work well. Pilots seldom knew exactly what a photographer wanted, and it was difficult for them to position the aircraft as required. Rapid communication at the critical moment was made impossible by the extra noise of a wide-open side window, and there was little time in a fast-moving aircraft for final corrections that made the

258

difference between an ordinary shot and a good one.

The ideal situation was for the photographer to be the pilot; the airplane could be flown by side reference to what was being shot, corrections applied without shouting back and forth, and the picture taken in the instant before the opportunity had whipped past. The airplane remained manageable while the pilot was busy with a camera, because it hadn't time to react drastically. Slipping to give a side-on approach, or in a tight turn to shoot fairly straight down, the aircraft could be controlled by a knee grip on the stick while feet worked the rudder pedals. It was usually possible to get off three or four carefully aimed shots in this way—even in rough air—but by then the airplane was getting itself into a state where it needed a restraining hand.

The day after my airplane negotiation Terry reached Singapore, very worried by having read about our crash in a stale Hong Kong newspaper. Though there was no reference to fake money or injury, she was in a state of great anxiety during her hastily caught flight out of Hong Kong. Until we met she could only hope there was no more to the story, and assume that what was in the airplane had been well enough hidden not to be discovered. In the circumstances we agreed that further counterfeit activity would be too dangerous; though disappointed at forgoing the excitement of a fresh operation, Terry seemed almost glad in a way that it was all over. Although there was no place for her in it, I told her of my new scheme, and she suggested a few additions to the paperwork that would make the proposition more defensible. She was so amused by my audacity that she decided to stay in Singapore long enough to see if the operation would get off the ground. As a general precaution we agreed to meet only in her room at the Adelphi, and not risk being seen around town. Graham, who knew nothing of her existence, would continue to be kept in the dark.

Not wanting to worry me until convinced that I'd suffered no after-effects from the crash, Terry let me finish talking, then casually mentioned that the Secret Service was onto our fifties. Casually or otherwise, there was no way Terry could break that news without giving me the same feeling as when that airplane engine ran out of noise. I listened anxiously while she told of a visit to her bank connection. His bank had received a circular describing bills that could only be some of those we offloaded in the Los Angeles area. All the fellow could learn was that the Secret Service seemed to regard our fake money as something fairly local, and was conducting an investigation around southern California.

With our Far Eastern money flotation a dead issue, and Secret Service talk out of the way, Terry was ready to let me in on what else had gone on during my absence. Talking in circles, as if not knowing where to begin, she finally blurted out that she might be getting married. My reaction was to wonder why Terry was going on with this out-of-character rubbish, but she insisted that she was seriously contemplating such a step. Around the time of our Athens delay she had met a doctor who ran a lucrative practice in a better-off working-class part of Los Angeles. Aside from the fact that Terry's doctor friend made money about as fast as I could print it, he didn't particularly excite her. She hoped that in time she might come to love him. It seemed he'd been too busy to pick a wife and had little experience of the opposite sex. He took to Terry in a big way, but rather than try to get into her pants and then think about getting married, he approached things the other way. This was a novelty to her. To her probable future husband, Terry was a woman of sufficient means not to marry him for anything but himself. She thought there'd be little danger of anything coming up out of the past, but if something did, she would bow out with the best settlement her lawyer could get. She expected to be married in five or six months.

Graham was pressing for further developments in our plan, and obviously thinking of leaving Singapore if I didn't come up with something soon. The deal needed a field test, so I promised to have the answers quickly. I called at the office of one of the people who had offered financial assistance, and outlined my plan to buy locally and fly to Australia another airplane. The aircraft would be operated in an aerial photography business, and to finance the venture I was offering interest-bearing shares. It was clear that the fellow liked my idea and would buy within reason. Avoiding misrepresentation I admitted that this wasn't a gilt-edged offer, so it mightn't be advisable for any single investor to commit himself too heavily. At fifty Singapore dollars per share the man said he'd take four; that was probably twice what he'd have handed over for nothing, and well short of the kind of hit that could be classed as a swindle.

260

In working this out, I decided to strike a balance between genuine investment and a shot in the dark that might show no return but could do no real harm. For sums of one or two hundred there'd be no need for security. It was important that there be no overselling, since something solid might arouse official interest. Handled the way I intended, it shouldn't cause any complaints. Large amounts could be raised through small sales to a lot of people. Setting interest at the high rate of twenty-five per cent for three months seemed psychologically sound to Terry, who thought that sort of figure suggested sincerity on my part to repay. Promises of repayment with interest wouldn't constitute fraud until such time as I was long gone.

One way or another the police would soon know what was going on, though on our side was all that favourable publicity over the crash. Nobody was really getting robbed, and it seemed likely that in an easygoing town like Singapore little would be done about stopping the exercise. It was pretty much of a bare-faced bite, though it promised to be a good one.

When the first shareholder in our new organization offered to write his cheque on the spot, I had to explain that the certificates weren't yet printed. I folded the man's cheque and promised quick delivery of the paper; I asked for permission to use his name when approaching others, and besides giving that he wrote down a list of a dozen other officials in overseas company branch offices.

Half-way through the afternoon I'd collected over three thousand Singapore dollars, worth about a third that in U.S. dollars, and had several notebook pages of people still to be seen. Not a turndown did I get, nor were there many sales as small as a single fifty-dollar share—and still the certificates were non-existent. A share buyer referred me to a friend at the local Multilith agency, for a fast printing job. Suitable forms were produced—by the same make of machine that had turned out my fake money.

Design work on the certificates was easy because there wasn't any. All they contained was typed matter in capital letters, a specious screed at the top setting forth the terms of investment, a dotted line for separating into two halves, and blanks for signature and amount. On the bottom tearaway portion, which would become part of our organization's share register, there was lined space for recording details to impress the buyer. Since only

261

those within the organization would need to know the volume of sales, they were not numbered.

A touchy point came up when the English Multilith man asked how many certificates would be required. To suggest that a thousand might do the job nicely would almost be an admission that the operation was a swindle. In the closely knit European community, news such as that would travel faster than ever I could do the rounds of potential investors. Thinking of getting more printed in one of the Chinese places around town I suggested two hundred, and the Multilith man ran off three because some might get spoiled. No charge was made, and even before bringing Graham in I was delivering share certificates to our backers.

People had been phoning or talking to each other since my early calls, and so effective was the Singapore grapevine that I began arriving in offices as an expected visitor. Nobody refused to see me and, not to be outdone by their friends, new investors offered funds. If they didn't already know how many shares others had bought, I showed them a few carefully selected certificate butts, and always scored for amounts indicated or more. Only because their offices were in the same buildings as places to which I'd been referred did I make a few cold calls. With guesswork name-dropping, these also were successful. To stimulate the memory of anyone having less than total recall of the event, I carried a couple of newspaper front pages relating details of the plane crash.

During my first day in the field I saw more clearly the logic of Terry's suggestion of a good interest rate. I was dealing with men accustomed to things that read right on paper, and all this implied high likelihood of repayment. No investor would hold his breath awaiting financial return, though my businesslike system obviously meant the difference between smashing success and gathering in only a few dollars.

That evening Graham and I had the first of many serious talks about the future of our embryonic organization. I outlined the concept without saying I'd already pulled in money. Graham's expression implied that I shouldn't have kept him hanging around Singapore for anything so improbable, though his criticism wasn't quite that harsh. He thought that, honestly run or otherwise, such an effort would never produce the price of an

262

airplane. If the thing wasn't on the level, he wasn't interested. Letting Graham dangle before pronouncing the scheme honest and feasible, I asked him why he was so positive it wouldn't work. I cut him off in the middle of his argument and dramatically announced I'd been selling shares and had averaged well over a hundred dollars per investor. For further impact I opened my newly bought briefcase, to show proof in the form of more than four thousand dollars. Bundles of cheques and currency, along with certificate butts and pages of fresh prospects, were more convincing than anything I could say. Now seemed the moment to get Graham committed to the organization.

After what he'd seen, Graham's doubts trailed off to nothing. In a businesslike way I said that since the viability of the proposition was now established, we should discuss *his* position. He could be manager of sales, promotion and publicity, and his employment would begin immediately. Remuneration would be around thirty per cent of takings and would begin when we became operational in Australia. Though this might appear to give me the lion's share, I'd be up for all expenses. During the promotional phase of share selling his costs would be paid from current receipts; his present activities could be regarded as valuable training for the future. I emphasized the importance of teamwork.

Graham's sudden question about how and when payment was to be effected caught me slightly off guard. I referred him coolly to details of repayment in the text of our certificates, but I figured Graham was smart enough to realize that we'd probably be gone before payment came due. With that out of the way, I explained that certain tactics were purely stratagems, and would not imply lack of scruples or tarnish our corporate image.

Next day, after I'd spent the night with Terry relating all, Graham and I were in Raffles Place, at the centre of Singapore. His list contained only well-recommended people, but among them there could be a couple of duds, and I wondered if Graham's moral right at the start would survive anything short of instant success. Rather than work my own list and let Graham fend for himself, I decided to handle him like a hothouse plant until he'd made three or four sales. From the start he was successful, though there was a touchy moment when his second prospect was inclined not to buy and had to be talked into taking

263

one share. Graham handled that well, pushing for a sale instead of walking out with his tail between his legs. Already I felt that he had the makings of a salesman, but to be on the safe side I wet-nursed him through two more calls.

At our lunchtime sales meeting Graham reported a string of successes, along with a single turndown that wasn't traumatic. Reluctantly I talked about what Graham must do if questioned by a minion of the law. What worried me was the chance of some official telling him the promotion looked like a fraud, when I wasn't present to undo the damage. I assured him we were working within the law, and that if anybody questioned that fact he should be referred to me.

To make Graham feel right about going to the best nightclub he could find after his productive day's work, I told him that it was "justifiable expenditure of shareholders' money on executive morale"! Sooner or later he must realize that he'd been a prize sucker, but on the credit side for him was the fact that he'd finish up with a good position in an aviation organization. This was doubly assured after the way we raked in money during our first day as a team. Without querying whether it was a fair arrangement, Graham was handing over his takings, and reluctantly accepting a little bit for recreation. Because I liked Graham, my feelings about taking advantage of him were eased by the thought that he'd finish up doing something interesting in aerial photography.

Within a week Graham was averaging three shares to my two, and I saw to it that, wherever possible, Americans were placed on his list. So much was he like somebody or other from whatever college most of these people had attended that they just couldn't turn him down. His only failure came later when we'd broadened the scope of our operation, and he tried to make a shareholder of the American ambassador at Kuala Lumpur. The ambassador's polite refusal, using the excuse that his position didn't permit his participation in commercial ventures, did not dampen Graham's enthusiasm. British, Continentals, Chinese and even a few Indian business men listened to me and wrote their cheques, but it took Graham's open-faced honest manner to rope in the Americans.

Graham knew when we'd shot past the price of our airplane, and began to ask when the sales drive would come to an end. I reminded him that we would need photographic equipment to

264

carry out the work for paying off our shareholders. All the time there was friendly rivalry over who could sell the most shares. Even on his off-days Graham never lost, because I did the counting. Once we met by accident in a building opposite Collyer Quay, and Graham was upset because his being nearly out of certificates might cost him the day's competition. As if begging a favour, he actually asked me to let him have a few, and in the manner of a sportsman I obliged. Once again he came out winner for the day.

Terry left Singapore a few days later. Our parting wasn't so easy, because we both knew it would be a long time, if ever, before we saw each other again. For a while we relived the excitement of Europe and America, and tried to convince each other that some time we'd be doing it again. But things could never be as they were in the past: Terry and I were sufficiently in touch with reality to know that, despite what either might say in the present emotional situation, a repeat performance would only land us in prison. Our arrangements for meeting in the future were loose. Since we both felt a short and quick parting would be easier, Terry went to the airport alone.

Graham was with me when I completed the purchase of our airplane. The price had already been bargained down and there was no reason for the owner to take shares, but Graham actually talked him into taking five hundred dollars' worth. Being practical, the Chinese obviously considered his investment as additional discount. Graham didn't sense this and insisted on talking about repayment. Wishing he would shut up after making his point, and just fill out the certificate, I counted out ten and a half thousand dollars in local currency before receiving papers making me the owner of the aircraft.

Then came revalidation of its certificate of airworthiness. The Aero Club's chief engineer took care of that—the most costly item being a propeller replacement. The one on the aircraft wouldn't pass inspection, because the glue holding it together was suspect; others of that type had shed their metal leading edge sheaths in the air, after being in the tropics for a while. All this meant delay and more selling time while we cabled Australia: to one of the few factories still making wooden airscrews. We both continued selling shares, until our propeller arrived. A strong pep-talk had convinced Graham of the idea of raising additional funds for equipment; perhaps he'd need a Leica of his very own, a legitimate corporate expense for occasions when he'd be taking ground pictures for the firm.

I flew the airplane on a short run over the city for its test flight, and then decided on a trip of a few hundred miles. The Malayan capital of Kuala Lumpur, loaded with people to whom we'd been referred by Singapore backers, happened to be the length of flight I figured would be good for our aircraft. Before we could take off I had to seek out a Chinese printer to replenish our supply of certificates. Had Graham not seen my thick new bundle of five hundred he mightn't have chosen this time to question my honesty, but he saw and challenged. I repeated the importance, if we hoped to stay afloat, of our firm's finances being adequate. In my latest pep-talk the phrase "capital starvation", I found, had impact, as did business expressions (such as amortizing our obligations) used meaningfully or not.

Flying again after the crash seemed strange at first, and to make it even more so, I hadn't flown an Auster for a long time. My landing following the test flight was acceptable. Then, taking minimal luggage and plenty of certificates, Graham and I were off to Kuala Lumpur. Stepping out of the airplane after a couple of hours over the Malayan jungle, I told Graham with a straight face that it was his job to inform the press of our arrival. He took the remark seriously enough at least to pretend to look outraged. A week in Kuala Lumpur resulted in our skimming off a lot of cream, and we ended up collecting more than the cost of our already paid-for airplane. There were still a lot of people who hadn't yet been offered the opportunity to participate, along with some back referrals to further Singapore investors. With a dull weekend coming up, we flew back to Singapore.

Again the question was raised about when I'd admit that we'd collected enough. Realizing that despite my understatements we'd already pulled in a hefty bundle, Graham wouldn't take my crap about capital starvation. He accused me of intending to continue until we ran out of suckers. Rather sharply, I told him that this was a word I never again wanted to hear in connection with our enterprise. In the same firm voice I went on to say that repayment to every backer would be dealt with only when we were properly set up in business, and not before.

Graham, for the first time, put it to me straight that he felt my intentions must be less than honourable, but resignedly realized he was too far in to pull out. He said that his involvement had been against his better judgement, but his desire to believe in the proposition had apparently blinded him to the obvious.

I bounced back with ideas for major financial restructuring of the organization. Since small businesses often failed quickly, we might as well risk a good crash instead of a squeaky little grind to a halt. Whether we cracked up big or small, no single investor would lose any more. Also we could discount collective rage, because there was no way in which the backers could get together to demand legal revenge. My claim that our firm should have a second airplane—plus additional equipment—threw Graham into a state of internal conflict. His urge to get out of something that had gone too far just about had to be overpowered by my latest outrageous idea.

I decided it was time to boost the young man's morale and suggested that after a further week in Singapore we should take a break and go to Hong Kong. We'd go by airline and treat the excursion as a well-earned holiday. To an already cynical Graham this sounded like going farther afield for more share peddling, so I had to explain that while we might hold a few interviews the trip would really be for pleasure. With the help of a planted newspaper story about our acquiring the aircraft of a well-known Chinese tycoon, shares sold as well as ever in Singapore; the thing seemed to be swept along by its own momentum.

During what started as a routine sales call, I bought our second airplane. When I spoke to the executive of the big, international soft drink company, he said he'd been expecting me. I started on my set speech, but he held up his hand for me to stop. He said his company owned an airplane, which was written down to a very low figure; we could have it for that amount, and this would be a much better deal than any shares he might buy.

I'd seen an Auster covered with soft drink ads in the same hangar as mine, so I knew what he was talking about. Eight or nine thousand Singapore dollars would have been reasonable, but the airplane was on the books for three and a half. Also its log books were available, showing that both engine and airframe were in basically sound condition. Lacking were nice cabin fittings and a fifty-gallon long-range tank, like the one in the

Auster we already had; but that tank could be taken out and brought back to Singapore, if this aircraft was to be flown to Australia. It also had a suspect wooden propeller. To save red tape our present propeller could be unbolted at Sydney, brought back along with the tank and used for a second ferry flight.

Within half an hour I'd paid for the airplane with investors' cheques and had a receipt promising a refund in case of any major unknown fault. The airplane had been used for advertising Pepsi Cola in glowing neon under the wings before being stopped by the authorities—because crowds were jamming the streets staring at the display.

Only then did the Pepsi-Cola executive tell me that there could be a minor ruction with the Aero Club over my purchase. They'd been offered the aircraft months before at a price somewhat higher and had agreed to buy, but had done nothing about finalizing. With what seemed like an obvious lack of interest in the sale, the soft-drink man had decided not to bother contacting the club's chief again. The manager of the club blew off steam when he heard the news, but then cooled down—or so we thought until later.

At lunch I astounded Graham with the information that our organization had bought its second aircraft. We took the afternoon off, to go out to the airport and inspect our acquisition. Our first aircraft was equipped with an electric starter, which meant no hand-swinging of the propeller. It also had a six-channel radio—of no use on the flight to Sydney because its frequencies were wrong. These conveniences, along with a rug on the cabin floor, were non-existent in the new airplane, though the greatest difference was in appearance; it was painted to a colour scheme and design not necessarily appealing to all tastes. To me, the airplane looked cool for a hot place like Singapore. Graham wasn't too impressed with the gigantic bottle of Pepsi Cola on the fin; it had been frosted nicely, to make it look as if it had just come out of a refrigerator. The artist had repeated his work on the underside of each wing. Product identification in English and Chinese was stuck wherever there was space, and the only comment I could make to Graham was that our airplane did look unusual. On the cowl was the ship's name, Miss Pepsi Cola, as opposed to the unoriginal Spirit of Singapore in smaller letters on our other aircraft. Graham suggested that the Pepsi stuff might

268

be painted out, but the club manager suggested we leave the aircraft as it was.

Graham's troubled feelings surfaced again when we returned to town. He was concerned whether he'd go to Australia on the first or second flight. Explaining that I could manage the four-thousand-mile flight to Sydney without the help of a navigator, I emphasized the importance of his representation in Asia during my absence. Since I was the only pilot, Graham had to accept the fact that he was elected to stay behind and work with the investors. Aided by the Australian reporter my flight would get publicity and, I explained, generate a new crop of willing backers. With both of us absent, there wouldn't be any way of channelling these fresh funds into our firm.

Graham and I were each given a fine Rolex watch, the same week as we bought the cheap airplane. Graham tried to sell shares to an official of the company handling Rolex watches, and was made a counter-offer of a free watch for each if we'd pose for pictures with the aircraft, to be used in an advertisement. The airplane to be shown was definitely not the Pepsi Cola one, and we weren't getting watches of just ordinary Rolex high quality. Instead we'd receive special models designed for airline pilots and such, and according to the company's advertising campaign "Favoured by Men of Action". Our "Action", according to the man writing the copy, was flying long distances in light aircraft and relying on Rolex watches for accurate navigation. Had he been less given to flights of fancy he might have said that in future we'd rely on Rolex rather than my Omega that had somehow survived the crash. Besides getting my "navigator" and myself a good watch each, the ad. would suggest in print and picture that a solid firm backed our venture. While complimenting Graham, I said that this might allay investors' fears over our unduly prolonged sales drive. As "Men of Action", I said seriously, it would seem only natural that we'd do things in a big way.

In that eventful week Graham and I turned from being gentlemen flyers to aircraft brokers. An official letter from the Aero Club stated that, in view of our purchasing a second aircraft, the committee now considered us dealers. And as such, we'd no longer be permitted to use the club's dining-room, bar or other social facilities. Nothing was said about anything so profitable to the club as its hangar or workshop. A call to the manager confirmed that we were still *persona grata* in those important quarters. Up to then we'd been able to eat at the clubhouse, but as social unacceptables we would in future have to patronize the passenger terminal. This was like being told to use the tradesman's entrance. It brought forth strong opinions on club committees in general, and those small-minded bastards in particular. There was some discussion about whether serving on committees developed pettiness in people, or only brought out what was already there. A run through our share register showed that at least we hadn't taken down anybody on that committee. With more publicity in the pipeline it seemed late in the game for much damage by a smear campaign. We decided that the best thing might be to simply forget the incident.

Graham and I set off for Hong Kong, and Graham was so taken with the place that we were there two days before I could get any useful work out of him. On the flight from Singapore he deserted me, to sit with a young French woman. She left the airplane at Saigon to join her husband, leaving Graham dejected for the rest of the trip. The first night in Hong Kong he visited two whorehouses, because he got laid too early in the evening to last all night. Next day there were tourist sights for him to see, and only one call at a hookshop afterwards.

Then Graham was ready to become a "Man of Action", and for a start he went like a vacuum cleaner through a big office building. Since the ground in Hong Kong was not so well prepared by publicity, it wasn't possible to whip up community involvement, but we soon learned how to compensate. Speed was the need, and we wasted little time on talk. We went for maximum impact with newspaper clippings, quickly dropped two or three names that might impress, and didn't bother saving doubtful situations. If names of others could quickly be obtained we wrote them down, but Hong Kong was very different from Singapore; the best way to work was by fast hustle.

Inevitably, we ran out of certificates, and while that shortage was being rectified by a printer in Kowloon there arose the old problem. Like a ritual for whenever we ran out of paper, Graham brought up the silly subject of when this would end and how we'd repay. All of my tired old arguments were trotted out again, but this time they weren't enough. We already owned two airplanes along with a choice collection of the best photographic

270

equipment. To Graham's knowledge, we had sufficient cash in reserve to operate for at least two years without taking a dollar in revenue. Suddenly I thought of interest on unused capital as an item offering protection to our shareholders' funds. The ratio of capital to physical assets had not previously been discussed, so talking as if I'd learnt all about it at the Harvard School of Business Administration, I began to give forth. For book purposes we could value each airplane at twelve and a half thousand and our photo equipment at ten. Then we could take on a conservative debt load of five hundred per cent of assets, including present reserves, and be well protected against loss to either ourselves or our backers.

Anything short of that would be a disservice to our shareholders, I continued. They'd lack the protection of a firm financial foundation pulling in compound interest, so for a while longer we'd have to get in and fight for the survival of our organization. Graham refused to cop my piffle without argument, and mustered a few caustic remarks while we coasted into our second week of share-pushing in Hong Kong.

With our rapid turnover of prospects, takings began to drop toward the end of the week. We planned that Graham would go direct to Borneo by ship, while I flew back to Singapore to take the first of our airplanes to Australia. This meant that Graham wouldn't be in Singapore to witness the harrowing sight of my departure for Australia while he was forced to remain behind. With great care we worked out a plan for the most efficient utilization of Graham's time pending my return from Sydney to Singapore. On the Saturday night following our Friday closedown in Hong Kong, he was to sail for Borneo. There he'd work through whatever seemed worth while, returning to Singapore at around the time I'd be crossing the Timor Sea on the last leg to Australia.

Before our planning reached what Graham was to do after finishing Borneo and getting back to Singapore, I informed him that I'd decided on a name for our organization. The firm would be registered as Australian Air Photos, with headquarters in Sydney. Graham's position during my absence would be General Manager (all operations), Asia. While Graham accused me of giving that title to stimulate sales, it had put him in a good frame of mind for what remained to be done after Borneo.

First would come some fast work in Singapore, hitting while publicity over my departure was fresh in the public mind. Since the Rolex ad. would be in newspapers and magazines by then, our firm should have more standing than ever. On the strength of that alone, a lot of extra shares might be sold. Anything showing those watches along with us and the airplane must have selling impact, I explained, because it could imply that we had backing from the highest levels of the Rolex Company in Switzerland. This was too much for Graham, causing him to say emphatically that he wouldn't put that one over.

Since I'd have things to do in Sydney, I would not be able to catch the first airline flight back to Singapore. Giving little detail of what was to be done in Australia—besides registering our firm and setting up bank accounts—I told him I planned to be there at least two weeks. When Singapore was beyond sustaining his activities, he could turn to Kuala Lumpur, the pleasant city of Penang, and such lesser places as Ipoh. To avoid excessive money build-up, he was to remit to the firm through the local office of an Australian bank. I didn't mention that this would place our funds beyond the reach of authority, in case of trouble over the racket being worked too long. I promised that my return from Australia would see the wind-up of the entire share operation.

12

Missionary meal in Semarang   Timor Sea
jitters   Blackall balls-up   my little wooden
propeller and me   a close shave   Sydney
touchdown.

HEDGEHOPPING THROUGH
AUSTRALIA

On my return to Singapore all effort was concentrated on
preparation for the Australian flight. Work was proceeding on
our second airplane, but in a leisurely manner suggesting that the
club wasn't doing us any favours. From the manager I extracted
a promise that work would be completed on my return, except for
installing the already used long-range tank and the propeller for
the second trip.

The Indonesian Military Attaché told me I'd have to fly to
Jakarta direct and not make a planned fuel stop at Palembang.
With peculiar logic he also said I could land at Palembang after
Jakarta, though I'd already made it clear that this was a straight-
through flight to Australia. All my talk about an overloaded take-
off out of Singapore, with no desire or reason to double half-way
back, failed to make any impression. Safety meant nothing to the
man, so I was left with the worry of getting a very heavy airplane
off the ground.

On departure morning, with the press well represented as a
result of earlier information, I discovered that my rubber dinghy
was missing from the aircraft. Locating a replacement took so
long that the flight had to be postponed until the following day.
Publicity-wise, this improved the story. The evening papers
covered the delay of an "epic solo flight" due to a missing life-
raft; copies of this, along with the Rolex ad., were left for
Graham's use on his return to Singapore.

Next morning, in the presence of a single reporter, I prepared

273

to depart for Jakarta. With the cabin tank filled fifteen gallons past the red line, denoting maximum content relative to position aft of the centre of gravity, I dreaded this take-off. Making the airplane still heavier was all the photo stuff stowed forward. Getting a green flash from the tower I eased the throttle toward its limiting stop, hoping for the best. For the first third of the runway I wondered if the aircraft would ever reach lift-off speed, but around the half-way point things began to look encouraging. Then my new fixed-pitch wooden propeller seemed to get a better bite on the air. The airplane rolled faster as the end of the field approached, and a gentle back pressure lifted the wheels off. Then speed built up to where I could initiate a cautious climb. Since the aircraft wouldn't fly well with its excessive weight, my swing-around to get on track for Jakarta had to be gradual.

Over the downtown Singapore office buildings, occupied by a lot of people who helped pay for the airplane, their investment passed at barely five hundred feet. Approaching the Equator, and with nearly an hour's fuel burned off, I climbed past the two-thousand-foot level. Where the division between hemispheres crossed my track was calculated by running an imaginary line from below a point on the coast of Sumatra. When that was gone, there remained almost five hours of flying before I could expect to sight the island of Java.

Passing abeam of Palembang, I felt far removed from the drudgery of share-hawking, so my thoughts turned to the fake money that had kicked all this off. That operation seemed slightly remote, except for recurring fears that somehow something might point my way. Time was my strongest ally, each passing day making it less likely that I'd ever have to pay the price. Of more immediate interest was that in the few weeks since our crash I was set up to run a new business, with two good airplanes and plenty of equipment. Making it really satisfying was the small fortune in financial reserves held by the organization—meaning myself. What I'd stashed away from the counterfeiting operation probably wouldn't be needed for a very long time.

Flying over the hellish-green Sumatra jungle on a direct fuel-saving track rather than along the coast, I thought about the improbable relationship I had with Graham. Up to a point I understood his considering it all a big adventure, and blinding himself to the fact that our share-selling was shady. It seemed

274

incredible that he staked no claim—other than expenses—on what we were taking. Why somebody of Graham's intelligence would fail to see me as a murky individual was something I'd never understand. Possibly he equated me with other people he'd known around the same age-group who appeared worldly, but managed to be that way legitimately.

When Graham grew tired of working for me in Australia, I guessed he'd go back to his family. If the story went the rounds in those circles, his reputation would suffer little real damage. To those high-principled people he'd only be a victim of my unscrupulous ways, while to others with a broader view Graham would be a prize fool for handing me all the loot. Nobody in possession of the facts would think he'd deliberately done anything crooked. It was not for me to question the motivation of the goose helping me to lay such a fat golden egg.

The Java coast was coming up on the horizon, so it was time to put pleasant thoughts of Graham busily selling shares out of my mind and plan my approach to Jakarta airport, I learned on the ground that my clearance was only good to this point. It was up to the local military officials to decide when I could fly through the rest of Indonesia. Four days were spent running between different offices before my clearance turned up, though the time was not entirely wasted. I was referred to a hotel used by Americans from the Sumatra oilfields. They visited Singapore regularly and had read about our crash. I told the story in greater detail and sold shares, in no big deal, but I did use up my twenty or so certificates before handwriting half a dozen to accommodate additional investors.

Clearance came too late in the day for me to go to Denpasar on the island of Bali. Instead I headed for Semarang and was there taken in charge by an American missionary—and the only way I could repay his hospitality was by not offering him the opportunity to participate in my investment scheme. As a man interested in flying—as well as spiritual matters—he watched my landing from outside the terminal building. Picking my accent when I spoke to one of the airport people, the man of religion approached me. From that casual meeting came a Southern-accented offer to spend the night in the missionary's house, have dinner and breakfast, and then be driven back to the airport on the following morning. What the friendly fellow modestly referred to as his house turned out to be a very attractive structure in the middle of a grassy compound that included a girls school.

In such surroundings it was important to watch my conduct, but still I managed to make a slip. Introduction to the missionary's attractive wife went very well. As a gentleman pilot passing through I did all right, until the family sat down to dinner. Taking a slight forward movement of heads as a signal to grab a fork and start feeding my face, I prepared to stab something on my plate. I became aware of a slight coughing sound. Not reacting fast enough I allowed cutlery and crockery to clash noisily, while grace was being said. A signal of that nature couldn't be interrupted once it was under way, so there was to be no second chance. All I could do was to get the fork out of my hand quickly, and assume what I hoped would pass for an attitude of reverence. Until the early bedtime of these good people I was on edge lest the talk turn to religion, and bring from me an admission that I'd never been saved.

During the drive to the airport next morning I remarked that in a few weeks I'd be coming through Semarang in another airplane, accompanied by a navigator. The point was taken as intended, and I was given instructions for contacting the missionary on arrival.

Aside from morning cloud, the weather was good out of Semarang. To make sure my flight wasn't too simple, the Indonesian authorities at Jakarta had insisted that I keep well clear of the city of Surabaja. Bali showed up after passing the eastern end of Java, and then it wasn't far to Denpasar. Its airport was on a narrow spit of land, with the sea close to either end of a long runway. Bali was a night stop too, because the next leg was to be a long one. To reach the Timor airport of Kupang, my last stop before Australia, I estimated more than seven hours in the air. On take-off I'd be very heavily overloaded, making the safety margin of extra lift in early-morning air worth while. I came to the conclusion that Bali was touristy and overrated.

Starting down the runway in the cool morning air, I was not sorry I'd taken my time. Before the airplane built up useful speed I thought I'd have to return to the terminal, to offload some of the heavier photo stuff for onward shipment by airline. Then I got rolling, and with the runway's end frighteningly close was able to lift off in a slow climb toward the sea. As with leaving Singapore,

276

it took a long time to reach two thousand feet, and then there followed what seemed endless hours' flying past island after island in the Flores group. For more than six hours I sat in the same position, unable to light a cigarette because of the cabin tank; I was now at the point of turning from the islands for the final sixty-mile open-sea crossing to Timor.

Kupang's dirt-strip airport had only a miserable collection of buildings, all looking like war leftovers. On one was a weathered sign in English, reading "All pilots report here". From appearances not many would have reported in recent years, but to that building I went after parking the aircraft. For a place that would serve as an occasional jumping-off point for small airplanes bound for Australia, besides getting some local traffic, Kupang was well organized. Accommodation at the only hotel was arranged, a fuel truck was sent for, and I was driven into town in an ancient jeep.

Early in the morning the jeep brought me back to the airport, I was given a route forecast for Wyndham in Western Australia, then cleared to leave Indonesia. Estimating five hours to Wyndham, I wasn't too overloaded with fuel. Darwin would have been my destination, had I not been worried about all the expensive photographic equipment on board. Customs were likely to be strict at this main port of entry, while Wyndham was secondary and reputed to be easygoing.

I faced more than two hours over the Timor Sea, after climbing away from Kupang, and that would only bring me to a landfall, followed by a long stretch over one of the most barren parts of Australia before reaching anything resembling civilization. Few ships go around the northern part of Australia, but nearly an hour out of Kupang there appeared on the far horizon a smudge of smoke. That smudge, which slowly became a ship straight ahead on track, was a comforting sight over the lonely sea. With no land visible, I'd been passing my time watching engine gauges for the slightest sign of malfunction. Sight of that ship might have put me too much at ease. During the night at Kupang mosquitoes had buzzed interminably, and then I'd had a poor breakfast before preparation for take-off. Only when I relaxed into a comfortable position, after deciding that the engine would pull me to Australia, did I become aware of how tired I was. The last thing I remembered before falling asleep,

277

besides the monotonous drone of the engine, was gazing at the compass to see if I was still on course for my landfall at Cape Londonderry.

Dead silence was shattered by a loud roaring noise, and with a jerk I was suddenly wide-awake and frightened. It seemed an eternity before I could grasp the situation. Looking out the side window straight down to the sea, I was shocked into a realization that I was supposed to be flying an airplane. By instinct I whipped the aircraft out of its steep, spiralling descent, then brought the nose up to the horizon. All I had lost was something over five hundred feet, but I must have been out for a while. To get into that tight downward turn I had probably eased forward on the stick, while pushing my left foot onto the rudder pedal.

When the airplane was back to normal flight, I thought about what would have happened if I hadn't come to in time. Worse still would have been waking up in time to realize my predicament, but too late to effect a recovery. I figured it would happen again unless I found some way of keeping awake. Poking my head out the window helped, and so did some black coffee from the bottle filled at Bali; though it meant I'd have to piss in the bottle later, I drank all the coffee at once.

An estimated fifty minutes before Cape Londonderry I began to think about arrival at Wyndham. This was the point where my thought processes became somewhat disordered. Staying awake was no longer a problem, but now I was assailed with unreasonable fears—of authority and its representatives. What did I have in the airplane that might lead to trouble? Fake money was out because there was none of the kind, and smuggling wasn't involved since everything was out in the open. Something had still to be wrong to make me feel so apprehensive. Interpretation of customs rules would determine whether or not I had to pay a thousand or so in duty, but I was prepared for that. There still seemed to be something in the airplane that shouldn't be there.

Making a mental inventory of what was stowed in various places, I suddenly realized what it was. In my briefcase were large bundles of certificate butts, and in my present state of mind I felt those could cause trouble. Written on each was the name and business address of an investor, along with the amount subscribed. Any official totalling up a handful would have to see that a good swindle had taken place, and that some important people had been touched. I vizualized the whole situation running out of control to the point of Singapore being contacted. It became obvious that those butts would need to be out of the airplane before touchdown, and so the fate of our firm's share register was sealed.

Bundle after bundle of share butts went out of the window, to start their two-thousand-foot drop to the Timor Sea. When the last of the papers was gone I felt tremendously elated, as if nothing—not even the engine—could cause problems. I'd simply have to tell Graham it had to happen, and that the fresh lot of butts might have to suffer the same fate at about the same spot. All of our shareholders would then be on an equal footing. Getting a perverse kick out of this situation, I imagined arguing with an outraged partner that it wouldn't be honest for us to create preferred shareholders. I imagined that Graham, if I ever mentioned it to him, would not approve of the way I had tossed our register of investors into such a lonely sea as the Timor.

My devious thoughts kept me awake until Cape Londonderry came up in the distance; a slight course change corrected an error that would have brought me three or four miles abeam, instead of straight on. I was reasonably satisfied with my navigation for the Timor Sea crossing, and convinced that leaving my navigator behind to sell shares was a most satisfying way of doing things.

At Wyndham several people awaited my arrival, but I was confined to the aircraft until the port doctor sprayed the cabin. In a strong Australian accent an airport official told me that I was twenty minutes beyond my E.T.A., and that there'd been concern for my safety. Because Wyndham didn't average a foreign aircraft arrival a year, the local police sergeant was deputized to act as customs and immigration officer. This friendly cop was on the scene with papers to be filled in, and his inspection was only a formality. Accepting my word that none of the photo equipment would be sold, he cleared airplane, self and contents into Australia. Since Wyndham wasn't a full facilities point of entry, it was required that I proceed to Darwin, where I'd hand over a sealed envelope, containing the completed papers. This dogleg was unexpected, but the sergeant assured me that there'd be no further inspection.

At Darwin next afternoon I was cleared without a look at

279

airplane or contents. Then I refuelled and took off for the run down the middle of Australia. I only made the tiny settlement of Katherine before darkness fell. There I overslept badly and could fly no farther in daylight hours than Tennant Creek. Expecting another night in an Australian bush hotel, I was lucky enough to encounter a second gentleman of religious persuasion. He saw me land, recognized the aircraft's markings as foreign, and was interested because he was also a pilot. As at Semarang, conversation led to my being invited to spend the night with him. He had a parish running hundreds of miles into the bush, and a house in town where he lived by himself. His Auster airplane was in the process of being rebuilt because he'd flown it through some wires. Hearing of the cleric's experiences, I wondered if there mightn't be something in the idea of being looked after from above.

Early departure started the day I hoped would break the back of my long and dreary flight across Australia. Nearly five hours over boiling-hot country brought me to the dusty little Queensland town of Cloncurry. Cruising at two thousand, I had to navigate as if at sea, since nothing on the ground tallied with my chart. Giant kangaroos were the only signs of life, hopping like rabbits from under dried-out trees as the unfamiliar aircraft noise disturbed them.

Cloncurry was a lunch-and-fuel stop, and here I failed to make allowance for minor trouble with my gift watch from Singapore. At Kupang I was unable to move the hands to a new time zone; the watch still kept perfect time—for a zone left behind. I managed to depart Cloncurry for the long haul to the bigger town of Blackall, thinking there was an extra hour of daylight. I was careless, but Cloncurry Air Traffic Control should have picked up the error when they checked my flight plan. They didn't, and the result was a mighty disturbance for the town's residents. I chose Blackall for my night stop instead of somewhat closer Longreach, because it would mean an easier run next day. All would have gone as planned, had I not arrived over Blackall at night. Overflying Longreach in the belief that I had sufficient daylight for the final eighty miles or so to Blackall was a serious mistake.

After nine hours of flying in the glaring Australian sun, my judgement was bad. Not until Longreach was well behind, and

280

ground shadows were long, did I become aware of what I'd done. I made things worse by thinking I'd slip into Blackall with a trace of daylight remaining to see the runway. Overlooked entirely was the fact that this part of Australia lay close enough to the Equator for there to be little time between daylight and full darkness. Twenty minutes short of Blackall there was still plenty of light, but by the time I'd flown half the remaining distance I could see only vague outlines of ground detail. Five minutes later all was in darkness, except for a blaze of lights ahead indicating Blackall. Not knowing whether the airport would be lit up because I was expected, or if it was only a country field with nothing, I checked its position on the map. With the town coming up fast, I could see no lights of any kind in the indicated direction.

A wide circuit around Blackall failed to reveal lights in any quarter that could possibly be an airport. If I didn't take a chance on my fuel holding out and head back to Longreach, I was left with only one solution. Aiming at one end of the town's main street, I throttled back into a steep descent. Levelling off just high enough to be clear of any wires that might stretch from one side to the other, I slammed on full power. Making all possible noise, I flew down the middle of Blackall's best-lit street, pulled up sharply at the far end, swung round in a turn and dived back for a run the other way. By the second pass people were scuttling out of buildings. It was most important not to overdo my act and hit something. Another pull-up and turn started me on a third pass down the main street, and when this was completed, I climbed to a safe height in the darkness, to await results.

Since Australian country people are pretty resourceful, I felt quite safe circling around while they gathered their forces. Car lights converged from all over the place, and soon there was a great procession heading out of town. Like a long train the lights formed into a single line, the lead car speeding into black nothingness, those behind keeping pace. Still circling, I watched as the leading cars left the road and milled around in a wide-open space.

While others were still streaming out of town, early arrivals at the airport were lining up with headlights all beaming in the same direction. As I held over the field, gaps in the line of lights were filled by more cars; thoughtfully, the far end of the grass

281

runway was marked by a couple of red tail lights and not a single beam was pointed toward my approach path. With cars lighting every inch of the runway, I was able to land without problem.

Late arrivals were still coming onto the field after I rolled to a stop, and a mass of people surged toward the aircraft as soon as I cut the engine. Among them was the editor of the local paper, accompanied by Blackall's police sergeant, who, I learnt from the newspaper man, was responsible for the excellent job of marshalling all those cars in such a short time. Everybody seemed as happy as I felt about the successful end to the crisis, and no one appeared upset at having been dragged out to the airport by a pilot so careless as to arrive after dark.

To the police sergeant and those close enough to hear I expressed my appreciation, before answering questions from the newspaper man on how I happened to arrive after dark and the origin and destination of the flight; I also requested the mention of my thanks to the people of Blackall. The sergeant wrote down a few details for his records, and then the cars began to file down the road back to town.

At the hotel I was the object of momentary curiosity, but by morning the incident had been forgotten.

My next leg to Bourke brought me to within less than five hundred miles of Sydney, but with not enough time to complete the flight in daylight. Sydney Air Traffic Control would not have appreciated a night landing by an aircraft unable to communicate by radio, so to make for an easy run into Sydney next morning I decided to go to Narromine, where the airport was only five minutes' walk from the main street.

As I approached the mountain range separating inland from Sydney, the weather looked appropriate for completion of my flight, but when I reached the ridge the cloud cover to ground level didn't appear to allow any way through. Then I recalled the existence of a route for such situations. This was familiar territory, and a change of heading pointed the airplane toward a deep valley running to the other side in a roundabout way. This route would enable me to remain well below hilltop and cloud level. Going into the valley was like entering a huge cave with a grey roof, until it narrowed down after a few miles. With walls pinching in and ceiling close above, I spent a few anxious minutes wondering if I mightn't have made a mistake, for where I expected the tunnel to end, the walls seemed to be coming even closer to my wingtips.

I suddenly remembered that there was a big dam under construction, and that there could be wires strung from side to side. I climbed quickly to where I was almost penetrating the cloud base. Long after I expected, the walls broke away, and as if the aircraft were spewed out of the tunnel I found myself over the flat plain west of Sydney.

I then headed for the secondary airport of Bankstown, where my wife and a couple of friends were waiting behind the tarmac fence. Touchdown at Sydney seemed an anticlimax for a flight that had begun twelve thousand miles away in London. After all I'd been through, I felt that the end-of-the-line city of Sydney should be lit by brilliant sunshine, instead of the dismal low cloud and patchy rain that greeted me.

There was, however, a fat bank draft from Graham and a couple of letters to bring me up to date on his achievements in Borneo. The news coverage of my departure and the Rolex ad. had proved fruitful adjuncts to the operation in Singapore and Malaya, but he felt these areas were now just about done.

I wrote to Graham straight away and suggested he might like to take things easy and enjoy himself in Penang—for a holiday—until I returned. This was in no way to be taken as an instruction to do the town over. The day before I left Sydney for Singapore a letter arrived from Penang, complete with bank remittance advice!

There was also news from Terry, and some of it sounded ominous. Her marriage was going through as expected, but she'd learned something new from her bank connection. The U.S. Secret Service had picked up a man for passing fake fifties, and as far as Terry could ascertain he had worked for one of my car dealers, but had implicated no one. None of the dealers had met Terry, so she wasn't in any danger. My answer to Terry made little mention of trouble, because it seemed pointless to worry her when she was trying to make a clean break from the past. Whatever happened in Los Angeles, she'd no doubt tell me quickly enough.

Right now thoughts of fake money brought feelings of apprehension, so no contact was made with either of the two men in Sydney who knew of the business. For the time that I'd be in town, I didn't want to clutter my mind too much with that affair; they could be seen after I brought in the second airplane. What occupied me now was the aerial photography business: there was a lot to be done—and in a way not to attract attention.

Safely beyond the reach of potentially irate shareholders, I decided not to follow my original plan of forming a company. My overseas assets were well concealed, and those in Australia soon would be, so with luck no government department would ever locate them. The business could be registered as a one-man show, and its visible assets legally protected in safe hands. A company would be pointless and also exposed to official scrutiny. Operating on my own, with Graham as sales manager, I need not possess so much as an airplane. If Singapore or other authorities made representations to the Australians, there'd be nothing to grab but the contents of the "organization's" cheque account. It could be held at no more than I was willing to lose, while the bulk of capital would go into untraceable accounts.

An Australian regulation allowing only British subjects to own aircraft in commercial operation gave a perfect excuse for what I planned to do with the airplanes. These could be tempting targets, in the unlikely event of a few vindictive shareholders getting together and hiring a lawyer. Registered in my wife's name, the airplanes should be out of a court's reach. As a British subject she could put them on the Australian commercial register, with papers concocted to show that she'd used both aircraft as collateral for a loan; they'd be someone else's property if there was a blow-up, and the photographic equipment could evaporate. In the remote event of major trouble with my wife, she could be trusted in a matter of this sort; even though her pants mightn't always stay up when they should, she would play this straight. All I told her for the present was that there'd been a terrific deal in Singapore, but it wouldn't stand the full light of day. There were two airplanes that would need to be registered in her name, but details would have to wait until later.

Finally my affairs were in shape—the only vulnerable assets those not yet brought into Australia. The name Australian Air Photos was registered, and a modest bank account opened. Apart from collecting the long-range tank and the propeller, I was ready to take off for Singapore, to pick up Graham and the second airplane. To save paperwork both propeller and fifty-gallon tank went as personal baggage—to the slight consternation of the reservations people at Sydney airport. Difficulties about leaving Australia without a tax clearance were sidestepped by use of an airline ticket I'd bought before leaving Singapore.

Everything on my final day in Sydney took longer than planned, and it was early evening before the necessary parts had been taken from the airplane. My flight was due to depart in less than two hours and there was no time for getting to my wife's place, picking up my briefcase along with needed papers and changing my clothes. All I could do was to go as I was or cancel. I had little choice. My wife had long ago reached the point of asking no questions about anything I did, so when I phoned instructions to grab my briefcase and rush it to the airport she simply promised to be there. When she asked about clothes, I said I'd go in what I had on and buy new stuff at Singapore.

Enough paper and string were in the hangar to wrap the tank, but there was none for the propeller. Both items were bundled into a taxi, and off I rushed to Sydney's main airport. Walking through the passenger lounge wearing old clothes and carrying a wooden propeller and a paper-wrapped fuel tank, I looked enough out of place to attract a heap of stares. My wife, who had also not dressed for the occasion, carried the briefcase containing passport and ticket. Together we strode up to the check-in counter. By then my ticket was awaiting me, so there was no haughty suggestion of going to the freight office. It didn't add to my popularity when I asked that my luggage be handled with great care. One of the clerks lifted the propeller as if it were an item best not left under the gaze of other passengers and another grabbed the tank; both pieces of baggage were promptly taken out of sight.

The flight back by airline, landing only at Darwin and Jakarta, seemed unreal after the long journey down in the Auster. Meeting Graham, it felt strange to be back in working territory so quickly. Both of my baggage items were left at the Aero Club hangar, and the engineer promised to have our second airplane ready within the next few days. Before discussing anything else with Graham, I thanked him for working Penang. His cynical reply was that from the tone of my letter he felt as if he were under orders—and what's more he'd moved on to Ipoh after that.

Later, Graham handed over a good-sized bundle of cash and cheques, together with all the butts he'd accumulated since Hong Kong. I said nothing of the fate of the previous lot. Instead I listened to his experiences since going into Borneo, and had to admire the way he'd handled things. As a man without guile, Graham had done extremely well, for little more reward than my unstinted praise. We agreed that the whole thing was at long last finished, and repayment was envisaged as something that would eventually be looked into. As the time for deception seemed to be over, I admitted that the deal might have been slightly outside the law, but, provided there was some return, we wouldn't be seriously guilty.

Three days later I came close to being guilty of something serious—in the view of an inspector from the Commercial Crimes Branch of the Singapore police. Waiting for the engineer to install our long-range tank became boring, and caused a slight wavering in our resolve to sell no further shares. Anticipating a situation where we might feel like doing a little business, I gave an account of my Sydney flight to the Australian reporter. It was published. A couple of days of desultory selling just about cleaned up the strays, and all would have been uneventful had I not done business with a certain American. He came to us unsolicited and seemed more a simple rustic than a man of the world; his lack of common sense was little justification for what I did, but the five hundred U.S. dollars thrust into my hand was irresistible.

One of the Toc-H residents met the American in town and brought him back for dinner and steered him into what followed. Everybody in the house seemed to know what we'd been doing. In a city such as Singapore nothing of that nature could stay secret for long. Instead of regarding us as undesirables, these British and Europeans were amused by our activities and considered us a pair of characters. None had the slightest idea as to the magnitude of the deal. When the young Englishman introduced his new acquaintance to Graham and me, it appeared to be for no other reason than that we were present.

The American had been working on a Thai construction job in a non-professional capacity, and was on his way back to the States. To me the fellow was simply someone who'd strayed ten thousand miles too far from the cornfields, and was a crashing

286

talkative bore. I wished the Englishman would hurry up and take the fool away. Instead, he started to regale him with tales of our being aviation executives. Leading the moon-faced rustic to the slaughter like a sheep, the Britisher told our story. Clippings were shown and shares were mentioned. The sound of five hundred dollars was music to my ears, although for some reason the deal had an aura of trouble; during my writing of ten shares at fifty Singapore dollars each our buyer observed that I was making a mistake, because his five hundred was American money and worth three times that amount! Payment was by cheque on a California bank.

It was cashed next morning by a local institution accustomed to putting through our firm's paper. That afternoon I received a phone call from the American. He told me he'd changed his mind about investing, and I suggested that was his privilege; he said he'd stopped payment on his cheque. Before I could explain that I'd already cashed it, but would refund his money, the man drawled on to say he'd been in touch with the police. That word hit like an electric shock. When my nerves had settled down, I asked why he'd done that without contacting me first. All the sense I could extract from our prize chump was that his visit to the police had something to do with preventing a misunderstanding.

I became annoyed at that stupid slow voice repeating what he'd done, and I told him off in simple terms he'd be sure to understand. There was a click on the phone as he hung up, leaving me to worry. Somebody had obviously wised him up, but what really mattered was whether the cops would be interested. Though the police must have known what we'd been doing, this sale would seem of swindle proportions and not just a harmless nibble. The authorities might not press a fraud charge, but they could get at us in other ways—such as seizing our second airplane. Luckily the bulk of our funds, plus the most expensive aircraft and photographic equipment, were safely out of reach in Australia. Arrest seemed remote, because I was pretty certain the Singapore officials didn't like doing that to Europeans unless absolutely necessary. The worst that could happen, I decided while feeling like a fool for taking that American, was that we'd lose one airplane and whatever money could be located.

Graham looked sick when I told him. While I was assuring him that everything would be all right, there was a call from an inspector at the Commercial Crimes Branch, inviting me to his office within the hour. Telling Graham I was off to try to square things with the cops, I said it was decent of them to do it this way rather than subject me to the humiliation of being carted off in a police vehicle; I assured him I'd take full responsibility.

Often, on my walks through the city's business district, I had noticed a sign reading Commercial Crimes Branch on a small building. I was never able to pass that structure without feeling a slight quickening of my pulse. I had to learn to accept the presence of that ugly little building, but always felt that passing too close to the door might bring an invitation to drop in for a chat. And now, here I was, seated at the desk of an Indian police inspector. In front of him was the certificate I'd given the American. Had the inspector started with direct questions to which I could have given appropriate answers, the session might have been less of a strain. But my opponent was too intelligent for anything so simple. Instead of asking things that would have given me an insight into his way of thinking, the officer just told me he'd like to hear the whole story of this share-selling business. In this way I was placed in the position of having to be fairly truthful, because I couldn't be certain how much he already knew.

Half-way through my tale about community effort and the shares being sold in small parcels, the inspector cut in to say that he knew all about that, but what he wanted to know was why I had varied my procedure by trying to take the American for an amount much larger than a "donation". This was the first time donation had been mentioned, so it seemed that the policeman wasn't impressed by my little story of paying back. From explaining the general operation—which the cop seemed to regard as a harmless bite—I was now accountable for something he considered an attempted swindle.

So far, it was clear that the officer wasn't aware that I'd already cashed that sap's cheque. What I dreaded was the moment when I'd be asked to hand it over. The five hundred dollars I'd gladly have paid back, but it would have looked a lot better could I have produced the cheque! Thoughts of counterfeit money and airplane doors raced through my mind, and I felt like kicking myself for having cashed the fucking thing.

288

When the inspector said that the complainant had stopped payment, I did not enlighten him.

Hoping to steer the discussion onto safer ground, I said the man had sold himself and not been pressured. He countered that the buyer would have been entitled to believe the shares represented honest value. Whatever I tried to put over, this intelligent Indian was one jump ahead of me. Most likely he was saving the cheque until last, when my supply of lies would be exhausted. If I extricated myself from this, I thought, it would only be because the Indian wasn't harsh and vindictive. Suddenly and unexpectedly the officer indicated the end of the interview and suggested that Graham and I begin our flight to Australia as soon as possible. I thanked him for his consideration and promised to oblige. There was no mention of the cheque!

Back at the Toc-H I put Graham at ease by telling him that we weren't in trouble, but had merely been officially advised to make ourselves scarce. Such was his sensibility that the notion of being asked to leave town was appalling. I insisted that we had more important worries than this minor detail. After being asked by Graham if I'd refunded the money, I explained the delicate situation of my having cashed the cheque. Our problem, I went on, was that the inspector might still think about that cheque. Even worse, he could nose around and get some idea of how big an operation we really had pulled off.

This could stir a few hotheads among our backers, and it would take only one person applying for a court order to freeze our local assets. If this story went the rounds, people might get the wrong idea and think we were swindlers rather than fairly honest aviators. I told Graham that our salvation lay in rapid flight. I rang the engineer at the Aero Club and he promised to have our airplane ready for departure by lunchtime next day. We could then be safely out of harm's way in Jakarta before nightfall.

With this settled, Graham and I headed for the Raffles bar, to ease our tensions and celebrate the final close-down of the operation. Instead of a couple of drinks putting Graham in a mellow mood, he became somewhat reproachful. By then I was feeling the effects of what I'd had, so his accusations were countered by some not-too-well-chosen words. Without further thought I told of the firm's no longer having a complete register of shareholders. Despite his look of shocked amazement, I related the whole story of heaving the butts over the side into the Timor Sea. Suitably fortified by another drink, Graham went on to ask if I even knew how much we'd taken from all those people. My reply was that, offhand, I couldn't give a total, but we could quite truthfully say that our organization was adequately capitalized. To close the discussion, I suggested that Graham might see the humour of the whole act once I'd lifted our airplane off the runway tomorrow.

Next morning we had an uneasy three hours' wait at the airport, during which I half expected the police inspector to arrive on the scene to ask about the cheque. Finally the airplane was rolled out, test flown and, with all tanks filled, ready for a non-stop flight to Jakarta. Only the hangar crew watched us taxiing to the end of the runway. As we flew over Singapore, I shouted to ask Graham if he could see the funny side yet; his voice was lost in the engine noise.

Jakarta afforded the same four-day delay. At Semarang, where the missionary had invited me to make contact again, Graham was briefed about saying grace before starting to eat. This time the police routed us out of bed at about two in the morning—because there was a rule that transient foreigners could only stay in a hotel. The missionary, who'd never heard of the regulation, made his peace with the cops before we were driven to a dump in town. Once out of Semarang we were slowed by a strong headwind, which delayed arrival at Bali by more than half an hour. Bucking this wind was to add a lot to our flying time. By departure time next morning it was blowing straight and hard down the runway. Anticipating a low run to Kupang, I took on all possible fuel, making us heavily overloaded; the wind had the equivalent effect of greater length of runway, so the aircraft lifted off well before the end.

A position check an hour out of Denpasar showed that we were making a bare sixty knots, and our speed held close to that figure as one island after another was identified on my navigator's chart. Changes of altitude made little difference. With no more refreshment than dry bread and black coffee we flew for eight hours and forty minutes before touching down at Kupang.

In the same hotel where previously I'd had a bad night, Graham and I were both battling for sleep when, in the middle of it, I explained how this had affected me on the earlier trip.

Next morning over the Timor Sea, and this time wide-awake, I shouted predictable thoughts to Graham. At what seemed the appropriate moment I signalled to him. He opened a case and delivered all the latest certificate butts to their fate. Looking resigned to anything I might do, Graham watched as my hand, clutching the remainder of our firm's share register, poked itself out into the slipstream.

At Wyndham there were few questions about the airplane's contents. Darwin was an unscheduled night stop because of a slightly late arrival, and when our papers had been handed over and we'd refuelled, I just couldn't get the engine started. More than an hour of off-and-on propeller-swinging in the tropical heat produced no response beyond an occasional splutter. The engine, a type notoriously hard to start unless completely cooled down from its last run, was just being stubborn. The weakness would be solved with installation of a vibrator coil at Sydney, but at Darwin it delayed us until too late for departure.

With our schedule completely thrown apart, we left Tennant Creek in the afternoon, and put down at Camooweal near the end of daylight. After parking at the town's bush airport, a car containing a uniformed police officer stopped alongside. The cop's interest turned out to be in aviation; he was familiar with every airplane that normally came into that remote little town, and sighting a strange one in descent over the place was enough to bring him to the airport. At first, he stared in awe at the English and Chinese lettering and the pictures of Pepsi Cola bottles. The way in which he strolled over made it clear that there was nothing official involved, so talk flowed freely.

Within minutes Graham and I were invited to spend the night in the constable's house. The cop lived right at the back of the police station, so I wasn't too far removed from legal territory. It was a novel experience for me to be a house-guest of the law. My navigator took it more in his stride, and he and our police host got drunk that night. Since I had to fly next day, I went easy on the strong Australian beer.

Instead of going to Blackall, we made a night stop at Longreach. Fuel for a through-flight to Sydney was taken on at Bourke, but as on the previous trip shortage of daylight put us

291

onto the ground at Narromine. This time approach to Sydney was straight over the Blue Mountains in clear weather. My flight from London, started so long before, was finally ended.

13

Clap-cured Graham shuffles off   curtains for
Terry   bail, gentlemen, please   manna from
heaven   cyclothymic and all that.

UP AND DOWN

Within three months Australian Air Photos was a thriving concern. In his capacity of General Manager, Sales and Promotions, Graham enjoyed being part of the operation and threw himself into expanding the business. Aided by his Far Eastern sales training, he began persuading companies to become regular clients. Against my advice that it would be a waste of time, he started pursuing government departments, pulling in good orders from various branches of local, state and Federal government.

Aerial photography was a technical challenge, so I strove to produce the best possible work. Coming up with pictures pleasing to our clients gave me a lot of satisfaction, and brought referrals to some choice assignments. It was a new experience to stay in a place long enough to get the reaction from work I'd turned out, and rather pleasant. Being accustomed to the notion that anything I produced made onward travel highly advisable, it just didn't seem likely that this aerial activity in Sydney could go on for too long without a hitch. Motivated by conditioned reflexes I wasn't too scrupulous about keeping business records.

Competition was no problem because I was the only pilot-photographer in Sydney, or the whole of Australia—as far as I could learn. After our first photographs had generated interest, we were given many long-lasting assignments, such as progress shots on major construction projects. One of our best was that of

293

the building of the Sydney Opera House. Government officials, who for years had been associated with courts and jails in my life, were now just people providing business. To keep me from feeling too much like a fish out of water there were touches of illegality in our methods: taking pictures as well as flying the airplane placed me in constant violation of civil aviation rules. More serious— and eventually to cause a minor conflict with the tax people— was my lack of respect for paperwork demanded by non-customer branches of government.

Terry and I were still in touch, though she had married her doctor within months of returning to Los Angeles. With no further news about fake money the subject gradually dropped from her letters. Terry said she still missed the excitement of the past, and all she could do now was to think of those old thrills, and wish there was a way to relive them. Though I was flying and doing interesting work, I could understand exactly how she felt. Being comfortably established in a respectable business had its compensations, but I often had a yearning to toss it in and once again live dangerously.

Numerous letters from Far Eastern backers turned up, to remind me that I might have inadvertently neglected repayment on certain shares. Graham never heard of these; it seemed best not to upset him over matters that should be forgotten. A form of release was prepared for those investors unwilling to overlook the past; it stated that our firm was performing its intended function, but there simply wasn't sufficient income to pay our outstanding obligations in full. Along with thanks for reminding me of our indebtedness went the explanation that a number of records had gone astray on the flight to Australia and it had been difficult to keep in contact. On a detachable portion was space for the investor's signature, and a single sentence stated that on return of the signed butt we'd refund ten per cent—on the understanding that should our threatened bankruptcy fail to materialize further payments could be expected.

Nobody bothered to collect their refund. The firm's address for people I wasn't anxious to hear from was my wife's place and not where I lived; since the pair of us functioned better with a degree of separation, most of my nights were spent in the apartment I used as a work-place. I simply told her that letters from Asia were unimportant and referred only to money owed by the firm, and

294

she knew immediately what to do with them. Only after a couple of weeks without a letter did I realize what was happening, and then it was too late to undo the damage. As a result a lot of investors failed to get our offer, and there was little choice but to dismiss the entire Eastern operation. Since our firm's image already stank in those quarters, I wasn't too fussy about answering any further correspondence she subsequently passed on to me.

Australian Air Photos carried no suggestion of bad odour in Sydney. Our reputation for putting out first-class work provided entry into good circles, with the result that the unsavoury origins of the business receded even farther into the background. We were also socially accepted, and while this was normal for Graham I found it strange. For the first time my habit of putting smelly episodes out of mind once I was in the clear didn't work very well. Being a respected member of the community instead of expecting to disappear at any moment was pleasant if, at times, a bit boring. But for quite a few months I was still troubled by feelings of apprehension.

With Australian Air Photos so well known, there seemed a real possibility that the story of our capitalization might trickle down from the East. In the offices where we were so well received I could imagine all sorts of snubs if ever the real tale got around. When letters finally ceased coming, I decided that our organization had comfortably risen above its murky origins.

With the novelty of launching the business wearing off, Graham became homesick, and I was in constant fear of losing a good salesman. I eventually woke up to the fact that thoughts of home came on strongest during slumps in his sex life. In the firm's interest it became part of my job to ensure that this remained full and active, and little did Graham realize just how I schemed and pimped to keep him happily at work. He only had to mention Washington to start me on a frantic hunt for some available girl. Luckily for Australian Air Photos, the woman who finally brought Graham to grief was someone he met on his own: this particular dose of clap was acquired from an American woman he met in the office of one of our clients. It led to complications because during the incubation period he'd played around with a couple of other women, and now, in all conscience, he would have to warn them to seek medical attention. He figured that the easy way out would be to phone the pair, stay in Sydney only long enough for his two remaining shots of penicillin, then clear off to America. Putting the firm's welfare first, I had to prevent this at all costs. After much coaching, he made his calls—and Australian Air Photos weathered the crisis.

Several months later Graham told me that he'd booked his passage on a ship to America. By then Australian Air Photos was so strong that his departure posed no threat, though I still hated to see him go. He had become so much a part of the firm that the idea of operating without him just didn't seem right. He'd done such a good promotional job that all I'd need would be someone with sufficient intelligence to handle deliveries. I tried to persuade him to remain with the firm, but it was more than I could do, and when the big P & O liner slowly moved away I was at the pier to see Graham off.

I was tempted to put the counterfeit operation right out of my mind, but there were a few loose ends. I had still to settle with the custodian of funds, under whose house money had been planted and who'd loaded Terry and forwarded the parcel to Tangier. Then there was the belated thought that the locked box containing a million dollars, along with my hundred thousand Australian pounds, might be safer under that house than in the storage place. It seemed possible that some warehouse employee might get into the container, and then go on a disastrous spending spree. Once this notion entered my head, that money box couldn't come out of storage fast enough, though the other items could be left behind. This move put all the really incriminating material into the custody of a man who had so far proved extremely reliable.

Three years went by so quickly I hardly realized they'd gone. Apart from comparatively interesting work, the one highlight was a visit from Terry, on the world trip she'd promised herself after she'd been married long enough to justify such a holiday. This was something of a letdown, because there was nothing new we could plan together. Besides our mutual interest in a way of life that could no longer be, there was only sex, and without the other even that was not the same. Two weeks in Australia was all Terry could manage, and despite our talk to the contrary we both knew that it was all over—for ever.

After parting with Terry I again thought about my fortune in

296

fake money under the house. The counterfeiting job had long since served its purpose of lifting me a big step up in the pecking order. With the share deal as thick icing on the cake, fake money was a commodity no longer needed. Another two years would see me safely past the American statute of limitations. Having another shot seemed unlikely ever to be necessary, and could turn out to be a case of sending the jug to the well one time too many. I suddenly decided to burn the money, then relegate the whole thing to the status of an interesting memory. One reservation was that the aviation executive, who financed my Australian production, might still have a safe way of wholesaling a bundle in the East. The thought didn't come to fruition until I'd incinerated all but half a million dollars, in a steel can perforated with tiny holes.

Retrieving my good-quality money from under the ex-officer's house, I simply told him it was to be destroyed. I had left a container with less than perfect currency behind, which really should have been destroyed before I left Australia. The box was buried much deeper than the rest, and when he told me that digging it up would be a major job, I agreed to let it remain underground for the time being. It didn't worry me if at some distant date the currency was unearthed and treated as an historical curiosity.

As I settled even more into the routine of flying and picture-taking, communication with Terry became less frequent. She seemed to be adjusting pretty well to her new life, and so was I—after a fashion. I was tempted at times to do something with the half million unburned dollars in a box hidden in my darkroom, but realization that I mightn't be so lucky a second time was enough to keep that reserve hidden, perhaps for some special opportunity in the future.

A firm knock on my door early one morning telegraphed the message that it was more serious than a parking ticket I'd forgotten to pay. I opened the door, to face three men in plain clothes. In the manner of police who know they've got their man, the oldest of the three introduced himself as a detective sergeant. Full of confidence, he asked if they could enter. While they trooped in, my mind was on the box of counterfeit money. I had not the slightest doubt why they were there. The paralysing fear

I'd been prepared for years ago just didn't hit. In its place I experienced a fleeting hope that, legally, I might be safe. No time for further thought was left when the big detective mentioned the man who'd stored my money, and asked if I knew him.

What followed was routine. As I admitted to possessing certain fake American money, my mind filled with ideas. Somewhere I'd read that owing to a weakness in Australian law little could be done about the manufacture of foreign bills—provided none had been circulated within the country. Not a single fake bill had I ever floated in Australia, so with hope overtaking reason I thought the situation not too serious. Also, there was the time-expired United States statute of limitations. With half a million dollars and a raiding party in the house, this was no time for denials. After my first admission I said I'd like to consult a lawyer, which elicited a snapped response that there was plenty of time for me to see one after I'd made a voluntary statement.

My assumption that all was known proved wrong when I was asked how I came to be in possession of the money. After saying that the answer was really quite simple because I'd printed it, all three detectives looked amazed. Suddenly I was aware of just how much I'd admitted, though it didn't matter. There were even a few undestroyed printing-plates in the box I proceeded to drag out. Caught as I was, there wouldn't have been any point in putting the police to the bother of a search.

My self-preservation instinct clearly cried the wisdom of complete co-operation; from my knowledge of Australian law I knew the right to counsel was not a thing to be pushed. What I had to decide quickly was the sort of voluntary statement I'd make. Since any kind was admissible in court, I'd go for a willingly given one. Reluctance to co-operate, I'd been told by others in the past, could lead to an "unsigned record of interview" with suspects who, out of contrariness, refused to put their names to the literary efforts of the interviewing detectives. There seemed little to be gained by doing it the hard way.

Transfixed, the cops stared into the open box. Hands reached in to pull out bundles of money, and I watched hopefully to see if fistfuls of currency would disappear. Hungrily as those officers looked at all the wealth, no shrinkage took place in my presence. Yet with the passage of time, the pile of seized evidence did somehow seem to become smaller. Thinking that Sydney police might be reachable, I tried without success to proposition the sergeant. Closely examining some of my bills, the detective asked if this money might be profit from changing the other kind; I assured him that it was definitely counterfeit.

While I was considering raising bail from resources they'd never find, a horrifying discovery was made. In full view, after the box had been partly emptied, lay four of those old Australian notes that had been overlooked in the burning of the issue. I could only watch dumbly while they went through some films and plates, to find a few bearing Australian images; these had somehow also escaped burning in my long-ago orgy of destruction. As I reeled from the impact, there came another knock on the still-open door, but this was only the woman next door passing on a phone message; calling out to me that my wife's place was being raided by police, she suddenly saw I also had visitors, then beat a hasty retreat. After about an hour of looking around my place the cops were ready to take me into town. On the way to where my "voluntary statement" would be made, the equipment in storage was collected. Since nothing could harm me further, I had told the detectives where it was located.

Partly recovered from shock, I turned my mind to the question of bail. I also wondered if I'd be able to settle the matter in a reasonable way, or if I would have to slip out of the country before the case was heard. Unaware of the terrible gap in my knowledge of Australian law, I continued to be pleasant and co-operative, and since it seemed I wouldn't be allowed counsel until I did what the cops wanted, there was no alternative.

While playing along, I decided there'd be no need to offer much information on the international scope of the operation. I could also deny fraudulent intent in the manufacture of the ten-pound notes. Australia had converted to the decimal system since they were made, and not one of my old-style bills ever saw the light of day. Weak as it might sound, I would claim that they were made as a technical exercise. Nobody could prove otherwise.

Mentally I abused myself for not having checked the contents of that box. Now I'd have to play the part of an eccentric, capable of doing something like that just to see if it could be done.

Seated in an office inside the Sydney C.I.B. building, the detective sergeant began to take my statement. Carefully he took it all down in question-and-answer form, which worked to my advantage because a lot of sensitive points weren't covered too well. Slowly the history of my counterfeiting activity was put together, gaps in the officer's knowledge filled in where I felt they would do no harm. All this was carried out in such a friendly manner that when we reached dangerous ground, my answers were generally accepted as truthful. Flotation—legally referred to as "uttering"—often forms an important complementary charge to forgery. When this touchy matter was finally broached, it became clear that my policy of co-operation was paying off. The police appeared willing to accept my contention that I'd never passed money in Australia. In the hope of reasonable bail, I was desperately trying to keep the number and type of charges under some sort of control. Though the detective wasn't telling me too much, he did say that bills from under my ex-friend's house had got into circulation. And from scanty details I gathered that the man's not-too-bright son had found the buried box of rubbish, and, with a friend, had passed some of the second-rate stuff.

Then came the sensitive matter of my fake ten-pound notes. Here I was vulnerable, because if the cops wanted to play dirty they'd only have to say that some time back a few of the bills had been detected. Rather than threaten anything like that, the detective told me, after taking a phone-call, that according to the treasury no fakes of that issue had ever turned up. This meant that at least I wasn't faced with the serious charge of uttering Australian currency.

The police seemed to be labouring under the illusion that they were doing a great job for the United States Government. From their remarks they expected the Americans to have priority in dealing with me, because the United States would have the lion's share of the charges. Letting the Sydney detectives in on the secret that the Americans would do precisely nothing might have encouraged them to make more of what fell within their own jurisdiction; the little matter of the United States statute of limitations was not mentioned.

Finally, my statement was typed up, and I was told that after a night in the lock-up I'd appear in front of a magistrate. Low bail would probably be set, because the offence was so old—and I made the mistake of believing that. Before being taken to the

300

central police station I was allowed one phone-call, the detective ready to cut me off if I talked out of line. I used it to ask my wife to contact a good lawyer. My hope that there wouldn't be much press interest was dispelled on leaving the C.I.B. building. Waiting outside were several photographers, and on the drive to the station I saw newspaper placards spelling out in bold type the headline about an American arrested over a "million dollar counterfeit plot". That was the end of my intention of propagating the story to friends and business acquaintances that the whole thing was the result of some ancient misunderstanding. It was frightening in the context of settling the case quietly, or stalling on bail until I could wind up my business and do the disappearing act, since creating such a stir at the start seemed likely to mean really big trouble.

No matter how things went, my respectable way of life seemed almost certainly at an end. There mightn't even be much of a business to wind up after I was released on bail. There was concern, too, for my girlfriend; to make disaster complete, this hit when I'd formed what looked like being a permanent and faithful attachment. Coming from a good family, my woman friend accepted me as an odd ball in an exciting occupation. She thought aerial photography was glamorous and liked coming along on flights, but wondered why my life wasn't such an open book as that of others in her circle. Telling little because simple stories are easier to remember, I'd been fairly vague about my past. While she accepted it, others in her family tended to see something sinister in this. After seeing more placards I hoped my friend's grown daughter, who liked me and wouldn't take too harsh a view of this, would be present when the story hit home.

Following a sleepless night in a cell full of drunks, I learned another harsh reality of Australian law. This came from the pair of lawyers my wife contacted: one was a solicitor, who'd handle the case if I wanted to retain him, and his companion was a barrister, who would do the court work if the case went that far. What I found out before court opened was that the right to bail did not exist. According to both attorneys, after I calmed down enough to listen, bail could be granted or denied at the discretion of the magistrate. Making it worse was a one-shot form of appeal, consisting of a single approach to a high-court judge, who'd probably rubber-stamp the magistrate's ruling. Though I knew

Australia had no bill of rights, and just about anything could be used by the prosecution, it was an even worse shock than my arrest to find out that I might be denied bail; this could mean up to a year in jail before trial, without any chance to wind up my affairs or clear out of the country.

Without being permitted to see my wife, I was taken into the courtroom. Charges were read, and they all related to forgery, with no mention of uttering. My hopes rose as the solicitor made his bail application. The prosecution had no objection, provided the amount was substantial, so now I was certain that I'd be out within hours. From the bench far to the front of the room where sat the magistrate came the words "Bail refused". While I stared stupidly at my lawyers, expecting one or the other to jump up and object, the magistrate set a date for preliminary hearing about a month later, As a cop led me out toward the cells, one of the lawyers said he'd see me in a few minutes.

Wondering how final that bail refusal might be, I experienced an agony of waiting. Eventually the more open-faced and pleasant-mannered of the two lawyers appeared; he was the solicitor Irwin Ormsby, who would initially handle my case. The barrister with him earlier was one of Sydney's best, Ormsby said. He'd probably be brought into the case quickly, because it looked like blowing up to fair proportions. My big worry was bail, while Ormsby seemed more interested in such things as extradition to the United States and exactly how much I'd told the police.

Talking through the cell bars, I said I'd admitted everything that could be proved. Ormsby remarked that I should not have made a statement, and I told him why I had. His worry, as far as my future was concerned, was that I'd be handed over to the Americans. He seemed to think the Australian aspects mightn't be all that serious, but the United States authorities would definitely drag me back for a long sentence. Ormsby wouldn't believe me when I said the Americans would do no such thing on account of their statute of limitations. Paying little attention to my insistence upon America's lack of power in this situation, he talked about twenty or thirty years in a U.S. penitentiary. Still all I wanted to talk about was bail.

Finally Ormsby was half prepared to accept, subject to checking, the idea that my offences were legally dead in America.

302

Then he assured me that bail could be arranged some time before my case came to trial. If only Australian offences were involved, he thought the magistrate might reconsider his decision. No more could be done until he'd studied the charges, so he left after promising to see me next day in the remand section of the State penitentiary. Until I'd been transferred to that place, I wouldn't be allowed to see anyone—even my wife.

Since Australia has no county jails, prisoners awaiting trial go to the nearest penitentiary. For me it was the infamous Long Bay establishment, where I soon learned that the presumed innocent received worse treatment than those serving sentences. It is difficult not to regard prison guards generally as scum; those at the penitentiary seemed for the most part a pretty poor lot.

After a trip in a van driven by an officer whose contribution to the cause of punishment consisted of violent braking, the day's collection of prisoners was dumped inside the forbidding gate of the jail. Singling me out as the prisoner dubbed a "master forger" by the newspapers, a guard decided I rated special attention. This hideous specimen, with an oversize face in front of a skull suggesting limited cranial capacity, seemed to think I needed to learn who was boss. Through puffed lips the screw shouted for all to hear, "So you're the bastard who made all that money. The papers said you was smart. You don't look fucking smart to me." My failure to reply brought forth an enraged scream: "You answer when I talk. We know how to take care of cunts like you in this place." Another guard, this one with a face starting as a pointed chin before widening out to ears that appeared twice the normal distance apart, began to abuse another prisoner; this distracted fatface from me before I was forced to think up a safe answer.

When fatface had finished calling the roll, everybody was herded into a big room, ordered to empty their pockets onto the floor and strip naked. Trailing the guards searching clothes and belongings were a couple of time-serving prisoners, who openly looted for cigarettes. A short man with a broad, grinning face and no uniform walked around looking at the naked prisoners through thick glasses. The man beside me said quietly that this was Daisy, the male nurse; one of Daisy's functions was inspection of fresh prisoners for signs of infirmity, though his gaze did stray toward certain anatomical appendages.

303

In a tiny cell with two subnormal youths I spent my first night in the penitentiary. Next morning in a crowded exercise yard, where prisoners were allowed for about seven out of each twenty-four hours, I met several who'd lived through this dreary routine for periods approaching a year. While wondering how to exist this way for long on food little better than garbage, I was called out to one of the boxlike rooms where attorneys conferred with their clients.

This time I was confronted by three lawyers, the two I'd already met and a junior associate of Ormsby. While the big, burly, youthful mid-thirtyish solicitor was the brains of that combination, it was his older "junior" I inadvertently offended. All that seemed to interest the three was the long-range implication rather than my plea about bail. Extradition to America was no longer an issue because the law had been checked, and from the barrister there was talk about a technical defence against the Australian charges. Not wanting to be around to chance a trial, I constantly interrupted to ask about bail. Finally the "junior" lost patience and told me to stop worrying about a few months in jail, because I was facing fourteen years in any case. Uncontrollably I shouted, "Jesus motherfucking Christ", and my offence to the man's religious sensibility took precedence over the fourteen years he'd just predicted. The air was cleared when the barrister began asking questions, and writing down my answers.

Tall and lanky, with a shrewdly hard expression on his face, the barrister asked no more than necessary. His manner gave me some confidence. Already I'd dismissed the "junior" as being of little importance, while the barrister struck me as a seasoned veteran of the criminal courts. My impression was that he'd be an unemotional, impersonal, cold-blooded craftsman.

When finally we got round to bail, the boyish solicitor had what sounded like a good idea. No less than the chief magistrate had refused me bail, but Ormsby would apply for a special hearing on the one day of the week the man habitually was absent from court. A couple of years before there'd been a case in Melbourne where some people charged with making and uttering Australian ten-dollar bills, of poor quality, were allowed bail. They set a precedent, so Ormsby thought a different magistrate might give me favourable consideration.

304

In the week before my "special hearing" I was visited by my wife, also my girlfriend and her daughter. Most shocked of all was my girlfriend, because brushes with the law were completely foreign to her. Little could I tell her beyond what she'd read in the papers, except that everything would be all right eventually. Later I was to learn of the full impact of all this on my friend, and also of the strong moral support provided by her intelligent and lovely-natured daughter. My wife, who had her boyfriend living with her by then, accepted it as a bit of rotten luck; she offered to help in every way possible, at any time.

Going to court from the penitentiary involved more than just being transported to the place. Prisoners had little chance to appear at their best in front of the bench. They were rousted from their cells about six a.m. and given practically no breakfast; a cup of brown water passing for tea, plus a cold gristly bone known as a chop, was expected to sustain the accused through long hours leading to actual court appearance. For prisoners with somebody outside there was a way around this. The police at the courthouse allowed food to be brought in, so Ormsby advised my wife to be there with sandwiches and coffee while I was still in the holding cell.

After my first decent food for a week, I began to feel that this nightmare might really be over soon. Ormsby was talking to me through the bars when my name was called. Entering a different courtroom, my counsellor said that this was great: we'd be getting a good magistrate. My first indication that something had gone wrong was the sudden change in Ormsby's expression. I looked toward the front of the courtroom, to see the head and shoulders of the chief magistrate. A smile on his face seemed to say, "So you smarties thought you'd put one over me by getting a hearing on my day off." Ormsby could only whisper that somebody must have told him of our application, and being chief magistrate he'd been in a position to come in and snatch my case from the docket.

Giving forth his best, Ormsby pointed out every reason why I should be granted bail. Ours was a lost cause. A different prosecutor cited such things as Interpol and possible United States interest as reasons for bail denial. On our side, even my contracts to carry out aerial photography for the state failed to make any impression. Ormsby made very clear the lack of

American concern, to get one minor concession before bail was formally refused. He kept the door slightly ajar by persuading the magistrate to agree to reconsideration after the committal hearing, in another three weeks.

During my first nights in the tiny cell I sustained myself with thoughts of eventual bail—and a dash for freedom. After this latest blow my situation seemed hopeless. The weak promise Ormsby extracted from the magistrate faded to nothing in my thoughts, and it looked as if I'd be cut off from the world for the foreseeable future. In my darkest moments I even thought they'd lay it on extra heavy, just because a technicality put me beyond reach of American justice.

Bail would probably be refused when I again appeared in court, so it looked as if after all this time I'd come to the end of the line. There'd be little choice but to do what I'd planned years before, if hopelessly caught. No judge in Australia would be likely to view kindly that a strange foreign law protected me from prosecution in the country against which I'd really offended. Most probably I'd face a taste of British justice, to the tune of fifteen or twenty years.

What that would turn me into physically and mentally I had no intention of becoming. All that remained now, unless something unexpected happened, was to plan the easiest way of doing the necessary. Quite rationally, I could accept the probability of having to do it; while my life might finish up shorter than expected, it had been interesting and, at times, exciting. Lying awake in my cell, I thought it best to go out while those memories were fresh rather than hang around till nothing was left. Otherwise it would all slowly decay, and I would finally be released as a vegetable fit for little more than putting in my time in city parks and flophouses. With the money I'd put away, physical conditions mightn't be so bad, but I knew that, mentally, years of confinement would gnaw at me slowly. Everything considered, it seemed best to do the job now; it was like leaving a party while it was still a little bit good.

There'd be a few weeks of hoping something might be worked out, but meanwhile preparations would be made. With conditions as they were in that penitentiary attempted suicides were frequent, and successful ones not too far between. The latter were jokingly referred to by the screws as another one necking

306

himself. Those not making the grade received treatment that amounted to extra punishment. Of the limited possibilities, something chemical seemed better than one of the crude methods.

My first step would be an approach to the prison doctor. The yard was the source of most knowledge within the jail, and there I learned about the medical set-up. A clinic separate from the main part of the penitentiary served the remand section, and was usually presided over by the more friendly of a pair of doctors. When the wrong doctor, a German suspected by some prisoners of having served on the staff of a concentration camp, was in attendance, anybody reporting sick was likely to be abused. If the elderly English physician was on duty, according to the yard gossip, I'd get pills for any reasonable complaint.

After my second visit to the clinic, using nerves and sleeplessness as an excuse, I engaged the doctor in conversation. Speaking to me as an equal, after we'd talked enough for him to credit me with reasonable intelligence, the English physician maintained with some emotion that it was a disgrace to put me into an institution so vile as this. Knowing the age of my offence, he couldn't understand my not being granted bail; nor could he see any useful purpose in the authorities pursuing the matter, when I'd so obviously rehabilitated myself long ago. When I stressed my sleeping difficulty, the doctor said he could do something, though there were limitations imposed by the jail officials. Because of what he described as an unfortunate incident, when a prisoner saved enough pills for permanent sleep, the two nightly knockout capsules I requested would have to be taken in the presence of a guard.

The screw in charge of the block wasn't a bad fellow, so I was able to talk him into a cell change. Already I was learning that some of the guards were unfortunates who couldn't hold better jobs. Getting away from the two morons and into a cell with only one other prisoner was part of my plan for carrying out what I might have to do without attracting attention. The idea was to slip the two capsules under my tongue before taking a drink of water, hope the guard didn't hang around long enough for the damned things to melt, then spit them out unobserved by my cellmate. My new cell partner was a non-criminal type, tormented beyond his breaking-point by a nagging wife. He

307

faced anything up to ten years for attempted murder. We got along well, but I did underestimate the man's powers of observation.

Capsule collecting was easy, with a guard who never hung around longer than necessary. Sometimes the gelatin melted thin under my tongue, but not once did I taste the powder inside. The first night I saved both pills, hiding them in a matchbox, and the result was that next evening the officer had to wake me so I could take my medication. Being less than bright but good natured, his only comment was, why in hell did I need sleeping-pills when I had to be wakened to take them! For a fear-stricken moment I thought that, in a place so aware of pill-saving, the guard would put two and two together. Instead of searching for hidden capsules, he accepted my explanation about sometimes going off for a few minutes. After the almost sleepless night when I started my collection, I decided to allow myself the luxury of one each evening. With the kind of time I faced, some extra days to gather the required amount didn't matter. Escaping long nights thinking of what the future held in store, if I allowed things to go that far, seemed well worth a little more time in jail.

From other prisoners I learned a lot about the workings of the country's justice system. It seemed that the junior I offended with my language was probably close to the mark when he mentioned fourteen years. Unable to use the great Australian excuse of drunkenness for something so long drawn out as counterfeiting, I stood little chance of getting a break. Apart from murder or extreme violence, planned financial offences brought the heaviest penalties. As a general rule, brawn received better treatment in the courts than brain.

Though the screw was fooled by my "swallowing" act, the mouth-wiping after he'd gone didn't go unnoticed by my cell-mate. Late one night when we were talking about our troubles, he said suddenly, "I know you're going to knock yourself if you can't get out. Don't worry about me, because I'll never say any-thing." I replied that I didn't have much choice, though I'd wait until all hope was gone. The friendly fellow reckoned he'd find some way of doing the same thing, if he copped a heavy sentence; he expected to get two or three years, and was prepared to serve it. Following his advice, I made a tiny slit in my mattress, to hide the capsules in the stuffing; there they'd be unlikely to be discovered during a routine cell search, and I wouldn't be risking a beating-up and transfer to the observation section.

Even in the prison exercise yard there was social stratification, with inmates of similar intelligence sticking together. I was quite quickly drawn into a group of older men facing serious charges, and among them were three other commercial pilots. With nothing to do but talk about present cases or past experiences, and how not to repeat the mistakes that brought the professionals back into jail, the yard was a hotbed of antisocial discussion. One of the airmen was so besotted with some woman that he neglected to take to the air, after cashing a string of cheques. Another was a Frenchman called Pierre, who planted a bullet within two inches of his wife's box while firing at her boyfriend. My manufacture of currency captured Pierre's imagination. Despite his own troubles, he would laugh endlessly as I described various details of the operation. He was so amused to think of one man manipulating the controls of a small press, to churn out practically the same kind of money normally produced only by large government plants. Pierre remarked often that he could visualize the set-up, with me wearing a green eyeshade and the room lit by a bare overhead light; except for the eyeshade, he was close to the mark.

On one of the occasions when my case was up for discussion, Pierre suggested that if bail were allowed I must fly over the jail and drop some cigarettes. None of the pilots thought that putting them into that tiny yard would be easy, but they'd benefit prisoners somewhere. Above all, such a stunt would infuriate the screws. Little thinking I'd ever be in a position to carry out a cigarette-dropping or any other kind of flight, I made the promise.

Besides analysing each other's capers, and working out how they could be improved, there was much talk about different judges; discovering which ones were dangerous for particular offences was the big worry, and how to ensure that their lawyers channelled them into the right courts for sentencing. Prisoners on breaking charges were in absolute terror of one judge, who was notoriously unsympathetic toward burglars. According to a widely circulated story, the judge's house had been done over by a former client, who, besides removing valuables, had taken a crap in His Honour's bed. Since my crime was fairly unusual, it was generally agreed that whichever judge I fronted would be a

309

bad one.

One morning I was called out of the yard by a time-serving prisoner, who needed only to have a quiet word with the guard to get me through the gate. As a time-server working in the cell block, the man wanting to discuss some private matter with me had the run of the remand section. Pulling a prisoner out of the yard for a quiet talk in his private cell was one of his unofficial privileges. Away from all others the fellow handed me a cup of cocoa made with genuine milk, some food that was not jail issue and finally a packet of forbidden "outside" tobacco. While I enjoyed my feast after a famine, the man explained that this placed me under no obligation. Should I feel inclined to do him a certain favour, he'd continue to look after me with food and cigarettes for however long I might be in the remand section.

Anticipating what this intelligent prisoner wanted, I pointed out that manufacture of fake money was not a job for those without technical ability. As someone above the usual run of prisoner, serving the final months of a sentence for business fraud, the man realized that counterfeiting wasn't accomplished by some magic formula. The fellow had experience as a commercial artist, so, apart from my liking to eat and smoke, I felt any knowledge I imparted would not be wasted.

Through resentment at being treated like an animal, I felt justified in passing on what I knew. The hard-won years of "respectability" were gone, and if it was to cost some government heavily for the sake of my having a few comforts, so it must be.

Over a period of days the artist took notes on a method of making lithographic reproductions of line drawings or currency. His notes were so worded that, if found, they wouldn't prove anything. In an envelope addressed to someone outside, they'd leave the prison in the personal custody of a guard on the man's payroll. True to his promise, the fellow looked after me until I went to court and was no longer in the yard awaiting his call.

Twice a week my wife visited me, for the permissible twenty minutes. Keeping Ormsby on the job was one of the things she did for me, and once to save him some time she brought out some papers requiring my signature; he'd phoned the jail for permission for me to sign the papers, but the piglike officer with a crown on his sleeve snatched the papers before I could even look at them. When I argued that this had been arranged by my

310

lawyer, he just snarled, "I decide what you can sign", and walked away with them. Though my wife kicked up a fuss, they wouldn't let her talk to anybody of importance. Only when she'd contacted Ormsby, and he'd done some phoning, did a very sullen fatface let me sign the papers. After that my wife was treated insultingly each time she visited, and left to wait before the guards would call me from the yard.

Shortly before my arrival a bright young prisoner found a way of making the lives of some officers less pleasant. To the joy of those in the know, the fellow pulled off what was referred to as the brown toothpaste job. Cutting the butt-end off an empty tube, the enterprising villain shaped it back into the form of a hollow cylinder, then spooned a medium-soft turd out of the toilet, and fed it into the space he'd created. With the rear rolled up so it wouldn't backfire when squeezed, he washed his hands and was ready for business. Guards constantly put their keys into locks when they moved around, and the idea was that a surreptitiously applied squirt of crap would make the mechanism work more smoothly by providing lubrication. Also, the keys would pick up a little lubricant each time they were inserted by the screws. With the things continuously going from hand to lock to pocket and back again, officers in that part of the jail would discover that for some strange reason their hands as well as clothes were becoming smelly. A number of locks were treated with a crap injection via the toothpaste-tube nozzle, and enough to cause a fair stink must have rubbed off into different hands and pockets. No officer would give the prisoners the satisfaction of admitting they'd been fooled by the stunt. When the turd in the tube was used up, its owner threw the empty away before there could be an investigation or check of toothpaste colours.

A couple of days before my hearing Ormsby and the barrister visited the jail. Very pleased with himself was my barrister, because he'd found technicalities that should allow us to beat three-quarters of the charges. That meant little to me, since obviously I'd get the same sentence on what was left. When both lawyers agreed that this might happen, I suggested an insanity defence. Before they rubbished the idea, I suggested old American records might lay the groundwork of mental instability. Faced with fourteen years, I explained, I could bug out and probably put on a convincing act. I was told to forget it,

311

because this wasn't America and I'd only make my position worse.

Both knew how unstable defendants sometimes were admitted to better-type institutions, to be released after "miraculous" recoveries, but this was the time to learn that things didn't work that way in Australia. A defendant considered insane almost automatically got what could amount to a life sentence. Detention "until the Governor's pleasure is known" was the legal definition of the sentence I could expect if found to be of unsound mind, and it would be served in the penitentiary. Only raving lunatics were sent to a mental institution, with return to the penitentiary when they quietened down enough to be controlled by the screws. Manageable cases were kept in prison, with little hope of parole. Usually it was many years before the Governor decided that it was his pleasure to authorize their release.

Psychiatry could be useful, Ormsby thought, if I made bail and obtained a couple of reports for submission to a judge. Coming from eminent practitioners, of whom Ormsby knew a couple, these could define problems short of a psychotic condition and suggest that imprisonment must result in mental destruction.

When I was led into court all was in readiness, with stacks of counterfeit money on the bar table for everybody to see. Each time I glanced upwards toward His Worship, or more important when he looked down at me, there was that fortune in fake currency as a reminder of the enormity of my crime. With a sinking feeling I thought that its bulk would outweigh any consideration that I'd been "straight" for a long time since printing the stuff. My wife sat behind the rail, looking as sick as I felt at the sight of all that evidence.

During the first day the prosecutor called one witness after another, to tie up everything in a neat package. Since it could seem vexatious, and irritating to the magistrate, my counsel asked few questions. One in particular that could have caused an uproar in the court was not asked by my barrister. When the amount of money found at my place was mentioned, I wanted to shout that it was more than a hundred thousand dollars short; I failed to see how accusations of police dishonesty could damage my defence. Luckily, I only whispered my thoughts to the barrister, and he very smartly told me to shut up about it, or I'd

312

never be granted bail. During lunch recess he explained that the magistrate would have judged it the allegation of a smart defendant trying to shed guilt on the police.

Much later, after all the legal matters had been settled, two detectives were permitted to "resign" over the missing money. Stories circulated of my currency turning up in the wrong places, and the press reported that resignations had been accepted from certain officers.

During a lull in proceedings the barrister showed me a paragraph in a law book, saying that if I could understand this I'd see where we'd beat most of the charges. In the context of forgery the law defined a banknote as a form of currency issued by a bank or company engaged in the business of banking. According to that old Australian statute, I was guilty of no offence as far as the American money, making such an impressive display, was concerned. United States currency, issued by a Federal Reserve Bank, failed to meet the definition of bills issued by a company in the trade of banking. Before I could think about miracles in the low court, the barrister explained that though he'd cite the law he probably wouldn't get far at this stage. The magistrate could almost certainly be counted upon to dodge responsibility by remanding me to Quarter Sessions on all charges. Where the legal point might prove useful, he said, would be in persuading the magistrate to allow bail. If His Worship thought most of the charges would fail in a higher court, the rest of the matter could pale into insignificance. Four Australian banknotes with no evidence of uttering wouldn't look too significant when a big international case was threatening to fade into thin air.

An early witness was the man under whose house my box of worthless money had been buried. He'd certainly been promised immunity, in exchange for the well-rehearsed tale he proceeded to relate. Unable to look me in the face, he told of my having long ago left a locked box, contents unknown, "in his garage". Prompted by the prosecutor, he admitted that, out of curiosity, he'd cut the box open. Observing that it contained American money, he closed it, returned it to its resting-place, and that was the sum-total of his evidence. Minutes later it was to emerge that the man's fully grown slow-witted son, independently of his father, had later looked into the opened box. He too noticed that

313

it contained American money, and for no particular reason had removed several bills and shown them to a couple of friends. Father and son being such "innocent" types, it remained for the friends to do the dirty work; learning of all that money unguarded in a garage, they collected it early one morning and went on a spending spree. These witnesses concentrated solely on what was needed to nail the principal offender, and nothing more. When I asked the barrister if he was going to rip them apart, he advised it would be pointless at a hearing where the result was a foregone conclusion; it would only serve to annoy the prosecutor and foul up the bail application.

Next in line was a United States Secret Service agent, who got his free trip to Australia for confirming that my bills had not been produced by the American Government. It had already been made clear that my case was statute-barred in America, so the agent didn't go into that. Led by the prosecutor, he did say that my product was of very good quality and would definitely pass the lower levels of the banking system. Actually, the bulk of it had passed a hell of a lot farther than that. Answering a question, the Secret Service man made the startling revelation that only about thirty thousand dollars had been detected. While such a low recovery figure made me wonder about the efficiency of the Service, the answer to a follow-up question left no doubt. When asked if the Secret Service had any bills in its files similar to those on exhibit, the agent said it did not, since, after each year, all fakes that turned up were destroyed. He admitted to relying on his memory of my note issue. From lack of evidence to the contrary, it appeared that there'd been no analysis of materials used in making my money. Apparently the Americans were never aware that the currency had been produced in another country. To pronounce officially that my bills were fake, the agent said they'd been printed by a process not used by the United States Government. That I already well knew!

My counsel's turn at the witness consisted of initiating a friendly conversation, a complete break from the so far grim proceedings. Leading the agent into a discussion of Secret Service work, the barrister had magistrate, prosecutor and all others listening silently, while the man explained his organization's responsibility for protecting the President and suppressing counterfeiting. Making psychological capital out of this di-

314

gression from what had been heavy-going, my lawyer asked the agent if he'd ever personally guarded a President. No court official showed signs of wanting to get back to the case in hand. All listened with great interest, as the Secret Service man told of an occasion when he'd assisted in protecting President Johnson on one of his trips.

With the case stood over to the next morning, when further witnesses would be heard, my barrister made an impassioned plea for bail. If the door had been left open a crack on that other occasion, this time it showed a little daylight. The magistrate silenced my lawyer by saying he might give favourable consideration, after hearing evidence the following day. That night I took both sleeping capsules.

Before my sedation arrived, I heard on each hourly news broadcast a rehash of the day's events in court. Much was made of the Secret Service man flown out to testify, but no word of U.S. inability to prosecute. Most sensational were tales of stacks of fake money manufactured by an American aerial photographer.

At the end of day two bail was set, after a fresh submission by my barrister. There'd been a procession of uninteresting witnesses before the lawyer livened things up by describing my England-to-Australia flight, including crash and jettisoning of doors. Presenting an old newspaper account for His Worship's perusal, he said with much emotion that I'd not engaged in illegal activity since. Fortunately, there was no one to offer evidence of share dealings in the period following the crash. After the magistrate had read the old Singapore story, he remarked in quite a friendly manner that it seemed the court was lucky to have a defendant.

The witness I thought would kill my chance of bail headed the note-printing section of the Commonwealth Bank of Australia. He came across as though he'd like to put me out of circulation for all time. With little prompting the hostile expert described the Australian bills as "extremely dangerous notes". Prompted by the prosecutor, the witness maintained the notes were deceptive enough to pose a major threat to the nation's economy. Beating my lawyer to the punch, the prosecutor asked whether Australia's currency-production chief had seen similar counterfeit notes in circulation; the witness strove mightily to give an impression of hedging in saying that none had so far been brought

315

to his attention. I got the distinct impression that he resented the quality of my notes more than the fact they were fake. At a later proceeding the detective sergeant told a judge that the currency expert had remarked that some of my work was better than his men were capable of producing. Flattering as this was, I did not appreciate it at the particular time and place.

That note-printing chief's evidence represented the low point of day two, but time passed and the sting wore off. When some points favourable to me had been brought out, including a remark by the detective sergeant that my aerial photography was the best he'd ever seen, the magistrate was ready to listen to my barrister. Finally His Worship announced that under certain stringent conditions he'd allow bail. To me, that was the cancellation of a death sentence. Reading off the charges and setting a value on each, the magistrate reached a grand total of eighteen thousand dollars. This was one of the highest bails ever set in Australia, and as if that weren't enough, there were the stipulations that I was to report twice daily to a police station, so the chase would be prompt if I tried to slip away. My passport would have to be surrendered before release; since flying was part of my work, it would be permitted on the condition that I was not to enter the cockpit of an aircraft unless accompanied by another pilot.

Though an estimated half-day of the hearing remained, my lawyers wanted time to prepare their final submissions. The case was stood over for nearly a week. Then Ormsby and I talked about putting up bail, with the result that I remained in jail those extra days. Neither bondsman nor self-bail was legal in Australia, so I couldn't put up my own money. Where such a large amount was involved, it could be risky to do it through a dummy; anything fishy at this stage might have brought cancellation of the magistrate's bail order. It would be best for me to sit quietly until the hearing was resumed, Ormsby advised. At its conclusion the magistrate could probably be persuaded to lower the amount of bail.

The following week His Worship did exactly that, after rejecting all submissions by counsel on points of law. On every charge I was remanded to Quarter Sessions, but bail was lowered to ten thousand. The requirement to fly with another pilot was set aside. In the holding cell Ormsby said he'd be able to stall trial for at least a year, and a lot could happen in that time.

Bail was posted within days. Aided by the hidden capsules, my cellmate and I did easy time while arrangements were being made. Waiting to be called from the yard, I handed out the luxuries acquired from the commercial artist fellow who intended to make his own money. None of those on the receiving end had a hope in hell of getting bail, yet all wished me the best of luck. Before walking off to the front office with the screw, I reaffirmed my promise to fly over the jail on a cigarette-dropping run.

After a friendly talk in Ormsby's office about what it felt like to be back in the land of the living, he casually remarked that I needn't be in any great hurry to jump bail. Besides stalling the case for a long time, he'd be able to give me ample warning before it came to trial; also the twice-daily reports to the police could be eased by a later court order.

Away from jail surroundings I realized that Ormsby and I would get along well, because we seemed to understand one another. A half-hour professional consultation stretched into a two-hour talk session. Before it was over, Ormsby made it clear that he did not regard me as a criminal. Any time I was around town with time to spare I'd be welcome to drop in for a visit, as long as he wasn't tied up with a client. He'd accepted my invitation to come along on a flight within the next few days.

After I promised not to discuss the matter with the press or anyone else, Ormsby told me that a portion of the main exhibit had vanished from the courtroom. During lunch recess on the second day the courtroom had been left unguarded, and the first officials to return found a trail of my fake bills in the corridor leading away from the place. No check had been made to find out how much of the currency was missing. Ormsby stumbled onto the scene while a couple of police were gathering up what had been carelessly dropped, or left on the floor to appear that way, by someone departing in a hurry. Enough people witnessed this discovery to confirm that a theft had occurred. The matter was being kept quiet for the present, but if any bills were detected in circulation an unknown sneak thief and not the police would get the blame.

My reappearance in the offices of clients of Australian Air Photos brought many a look of puzzlement. After being

317

publicized as the "million-dollar forger", who'd escaped detection for years, my presence caused a variety of reactions. With men accustomed to thinking big, there were no problems; to them, I'd simply tried something and had the bad luck to be found out. Some small fry holding minor jobs wanted to act as self-appointed watchdogs for their bosses, and I had some difficulty getting through. But to the important people, all that mattered was that I could deliver the goods—and quite a few were intrigued by the way I'd printed my own money.

No customers were lost, and all wished me well in what I might face in the future. In a quarter where I expected to be *persona non grata*, I was welcomed back as though I'd been away sick. Departments of the same government that wanted to put me on trial might have been expected to refuse further dealings with Australian Air Photos, but that wasn't the case. Their concern was not with the past, but whether I would be able to continue taking pictures. The two most important departments, Public Works and State Planning, did a lot for my morale when I needed it.

Reporting to the police morning and evening was a damned nuisance, though a lot better than being in jail. After signing the station book one morning, and having my usual friendly chat with the sergeant, I headed for the airport to do my cigarette-dropping flight. I wondered how the cops would react to possible complaints from the penitentiary officials, but if anybody didn't like what was going to happen, I did have an excuse. A little truth-stretching would account for a series of tight turns right over the top of the large jail. From an unsuspecting government client I especially solicited an assignment to photograph some land within a stone's throw of my target. To get exactly the right angles I'd have to do a number of illegal low runs as well as my steep turns. As a nervous chain-smoker—especially when flying low in the rough air I'd certainly encounter over the jail—it would be necessary for me to have a good supply of loose cigarettes on the empty co-pilot's seat. These could accidentally bounce out the window as a result of a jolt!

Before boarding the aircraft I emptied the contents of twenty packets of cigarettes into a paperbag. My first low run over the jail, after locating the remand yard, was to let the prisoners know I'd arrived. So they'd be sure who it was, I made plenty of noise.

318

On approach I throttled back, pointed the nose in a dive toward the crowded little exercise yard and, when the airplane was really close, slammed on full power to pull upward into a steep climb. Only after turning for a second dive was I able to see the result of my first.

The usually lethargic lounging prisoners were all bunched in the middle, frantically waving their arms. One man, obviously Pierre, had his shirt off and was flapping it up and down. Following a third dive, I was ready to start cigarette-dropping. My performance stirred the screws too, though they weren't exactly waving their arms. In the circular courtyard, separated by bars from the exercise spaces, figures in hated blue uniforms were beginning to cluster. Fatface was visible, waddling out from his office. The guards stared up as if they didn't know what to do, and for an instant I had thoughts of a rifle-toting wall screw starting to shoot. This seemed remote, but one of that lot would possibly think of calling the Civil Aviation Authorities. They'd quickly identify the aircraft, because I was in the area on a flight plan; that would lead to a call on the radio, demanding some sort of explanation. Aside from screw action it seemed likely that air traffic controllers at Sydney Tower would notice my disappearance from their radar screen each time I went into a dive, but there were no calls.

Dropping cigarettes by the handful involved extremely low runs, and even from as far down as I dared fly the yard was a difficult target. Wind could only be estimated from distant smoke, so my drift calculations were crude. Everything going over the side had to land well within the penitentiary walls, and by weight of numbers a portion would have to land in the right yard. When the last of the cigarettes were gone, I decided that this scene should be recorded on film. A final dive livened up the scene again, and then there were some steep turns along with sideslips while I shot almost straight down with a telephoto lens. With those shots taken, I climbed back to the legal height and fulfilled the job for which I was being paid.

Back at the airport I expected an order to report to the briefing office, to give an explanation for my unseemly aerial behaviour. No such instruction came over the radio as I turned off the runway, nor was there any hint of official displeasure when I reported to the police that evening. I could only conclude that, not knowing how to deal with such an event, the unimaginative prison authorities did nothing.

Finally my case was called for mention in the Quarter Sessions and I had to appear, but it was stood over without any date for trial. While I was in that dreaded place, the judge eased my reporting requirement to once daily. Afterwards, Ormsby told me he'd learned from within the enemy camp that the prosecution were undecided on how my case should be conducted. One reason they weren't pressing for quick trial was uncertainty on the applicability of the law. Of more concern was the idea of an open court, which with technical evidence expected to be presented by the defence might turn the court into a classroom for counterfeiters. They were likely to request a closed court and the defence would object, so this would probably open avenues for further delay.

Ormsby had to act under the assumption that my case would run its full course; any acknowledgement of the possibility of my jumping bail, he explained, would place him under legal obligation to report it. Since there might be an outside chance of beating the case, he thought it would be worth calling in a second barrister. The man he had in mind was one of Australia's most highly qualified Queen's Counsels. A conference was set up and the Q.C. saw, as did the other barrister, where he could toss most of the charges.

Days later, after the new lawyer had consulted some obscure rulings, he reported that all but two could be beaten, but it would probably be necessary to go to the highest court in the land to accomplish this. Since appeal bail was practically unknown in Australia, I'd languish in jail for a long time.

The Q.C. advised against fighting the case in this way, because the years served in bad conditions, imposed as a deterrent to such appeals, could be dead time. The time I got on the unbeatable charges wouldn't begin until the legal processes were exhausted, and credit for time already served would be dependent on the charitable mood of the judge. Much better tactics, thought the Q.C., would be for him to put up a good fight in Quarter Sessions, make full use of the psychiatric reports Ormsby would obtain, try to get the case in front of a reasonable judge and hope for the best.

Because of insufficient briefing I scared hell out of Ormsby on a flight with Australian Air Photos. Prior to take-off I explained about the necessity for tight turns over the city while a building site was being photographed; it was made clear that these would be safe, but I forgot to mention sideslipping. The first time I dropped about four hundred feet sideways toward the structure, there seemed to be a lot of shouting going on somewhere in the aircraft. Filling the viewfinder frame with my subject, and getting off three rapid shots, kept me too busy to be distracted by such noise. Uncrossing the controls and applying full power to regain lost height in a steep climb, I turned toward Ormsby to find out what all the racket was about. By then he'd partially recovered from his fright; he merely looked pale and ceased creating a din. My nonchalant remark that we'd just done a sideslip for some close-up shots brought a tense reply; Ormsby quickly informed me that the surest way of keeping out of jail, short of getting us both killed, was to ensure that nothing happened to my attorney. There were more slips, and a very tall building inconveniently close to the site further unsettled Ormsby's nerves. Safely back on the ground, he remarked that he wasn't sure the psychiatrists would be exaggerating if they claimed in court that I needed treatment rather than punishment.

The first doctor I saw, in pursuit of the psychiatric reports, I didn't particularly like. He did a lot of court work and, according to Ormsby, judges tended to respect his opinions. After talking to the man for a few minutes, I wondered if a lot of his appearances mightn't have been for the prosecution. The doctor's general questions were easily managed, because all I wanted to establish was an old pattern of instability, followed by self-rehabilitation after settling into an occupation that suited my nature. Going into the legal aspect, I explained that after many years I was being called upon to pay for those old counterfeiting offences. Without hesitation I said I'd do away with myself quickly rather than rot to slow destruction in the penitentiary. All this was written down, but it was privileged, so I had no fear of its reaching the wrong quarters and leading to cancellation of bail.

A remark by the psychiatrist made me think that Ormsby had chosen the wrong consultant. When I told him about the offence being so old that it was outlawed in the country against which I'd really offended, he expressed his disapproval of statutes of limitations allowing people to escape the consequences of past misdeeds. Rather than argue and give the impression of a smarty who'd use the law to dodge just punishment, I let the remark pass. Though the man was prosecution-oriented, no harm could come of it, since his report was destined for Ormsby's desk and not directly for the court. I was pretty certain that it would end up in the wastepaper basket, and we'd have to find someone who wasn't such a law-and-order man.

Several days later Ormsby showed me what the doctor had written, and the report was a complete about-face. In a couple of pages the man said I was a cyclothymic, possessed intelligence and ability, appeared to have accomplished self-rehabilitation, was enough of an individualist to have done an England–Australia flight by single-engine aircraft, and finally would commit suicide if sentenced to lengthy imprisonment, which, in any case, would serve no useful purpose. Ormsby thought this material had impact and could influence a judge to settle on a more charitable basis and not just on the strict merits of the case.

Something similar from another eminent specialist would give us a second barrel to our gun. Armed with two such reports Ormsby hoped to negotiate a deal with the prosecution, where I'd plead guilty to a couple of lesser charges and the rest would be dropped. Then there'd only remain the problem of getting my case in front of the right judge. Another favourable report was arranged, but the prosecutor's office wouldn't give an inch. At the time it seemed worth risking a short sentence and then continuing with Australian Air Photos in preference to becoming a fugitive.

Months passed with nothing more exciting than approaches from people who wanted me to print money for them, or set up plants they themselves could operate. Most were turned down in a way not likely to offend those capable of applying pressure. Saying I was frequently followed by police was sufficient to discourage these individuals, though there was a man to whom I did listen. He was a friend of someone I'd known for years and was interested in fake money, not as something rushed through while I was out on bail but as a long-term proposition. What made his deal interesting was that it would be carried out someplace else, and most important, he could obtain for me an Australian passport under a different name. It would come from

322

the passport office, with somebody else's documentation but my picture, and the job would only take a month or six weeks to organize.

Since even last-minute dealing with the prosecution seemed remote, and quiet departure might be the only solution, I was greatly interested in the talk about passports. Levelling with the man because I felt he was not somebody to be tampered with, I explained that if moves by my lawyers were successful I'd rather not enter into another counterfeit deal. Apart from trying to talk me into changing my mind, the fellow applied no pressure; he said the proposition would remain open if I had second thoughts, or if it became necessary for me to escape the country.

Ormsby having assured me that the case would be called for trial within the next five or six months, I felt safe in promising the man a definite answer later. I made the mistake of not realizing that even lawyers can be dreadfully wrong. Not three weeks were to pass before I was to find that the passport offer should have been snapped up the instant it was made.

14 Treat or punish   casing Camden
airport   Romeo Charlie Alpha, do you
read?   antics over Sydney   pep pills and police
to the rescue.

THE SIEGE OF SYDNEY

A registered letter I nearly set aside as a tax notice informed me in cold officialese that my period of liberty was about over. In twelve days I was to surrender myself, and stand trial on the charges listed on the page. As they stared me in the face, those offences looked like a lifetime in jail. A final sentence advised that if represented I should inform counsel, so he also could be present at court.

My first coherent thought was that somehow I'd have to get the trial postponed—at least for a few weeks. As the case had lain dormant for nearly a year, with little being heard, Ormsby thought we still had plenty of time. There'd be little chance of getting away now, unless Ormsby came up with something legal. To escape from the country in the next few days I'd have to abandon just about everything, which wasn't important any more, but there was the passport problem. Any request to the American Consulate for a fresh passport to replace the one held by the police would be inviting arrest. The contact who'd offered me one made it clear that it would take at least a month, and I didn't like my chances of using it after failing to turn up for trial.

For the moment all that made sense was to see Ormsby. He phoned to enquire if the prosecution would agree to an adjournment, and was told they'd consider no such thing. Their witnesses, including the Secret Service man on his second trip from America, would be assembled on the due date, and they were ready to go to trial.

324

Ormsby's early-warning connection on the other side had let him down badly. Though I was frantic, Ormsby remained calm and suggested the only way to delay trial would be for me to get sick enough to be certified medically unfit. Otherwise, he could only come up with a wild suggestion that I crash the airplane and land in hospital. Ormsby then remembered the psychiatric reports, and thought they might be useful in a special hearing on a motion for adjournment.

Five days later we were in a nearly empty courtroom, facing a stern-visaged judge. Apart from a couple of people who looked like press, the only others present were my counsel, the psychiatrist, and a prosecutor who appeared confident; the latter seemed to be relishing the prospect of chopping our application to pieces. For the little time it lasted, my side of the hearing sounded as if it were going well. The barrister led the psychiatrist through various details of my mental condition, scoring the point that I should undergo treatment before being subjected to the ordeal of a trial. At that stage the judge looked impressed, but the prosecution hadn't yet been heard.

Before making my psychiatrist go to water, the prosecutor stressed the importance of the trial proceeding as scheduled. At length he explained the inconvenience of a delay, and then went on to demolish my expensive psychiatrist. Pulling my witness apart was so easy for the prosecutor that I felt like calling out to remind the doctor which side was paying his bill. As well as he had made my case when led by my counsel, he now did the same for the other side. Under cross-examination the fellow agreed that my condition wouldn't improve with a trial hanging over my head, so no further damage would be done by getting it over quickly. At that juncture my case was totally destroyed. The prosecutor wore a look of great self-satisfaction while the judge gave his ruling.

For the first time since getting out on bail, I had suicidal thoughts. Then the idea occurred that, if this was necessary, it shouldn't be done in a way to allow the authorities to mark my case as closed. If nothing was found they'd never know for sure what happened, and prosecution mentalities would never rest easy if there was the slightest indication I'd escaped punishment. With so few days left before trial, I was at an all-time low.

Something began to shape up in my mind that made the

prospect of losing out the hard way less appalling. Ormsby's idea of an airplane crash could be carried further, hitting the authorities with some publicity a lot less favourable than they'd get from a trial. A flight out to sea until my fuel was gone, with radio calls to let them know what was happening, should really toss them. They'd be silly enough to send the navy on an expensive search, and if I put out false information they could spend days looking in the wrong places. If nothing was found floating in the sea, they might think I'd turned landwards, put down in some remote place and gone into hiding.

Thinking more rationally, and deciding that I really didn't want to be finished with life just yet, I figured something like that could be pulled off. Law-enforcement mentalities wouldn't allow the officials to drop a thing like this. They'd have to know for certain that I wasn't putting something over, and avoiding punishment. As bad losers, the authorities wouldn't like the little package I was mentally concocting for them. Cheating the detective sergeant out of his moment of glory in front of a court full of people was something I could relish.

Before developing those plans, I called on the man with the proposition for setting me up elsewhere. In more detail his proposal was that I go to a country not friendly with the United States, to make American money on a grand scale. Before my situation had become desperate, it sounded like going to a neutral place and printing the stuff for a group that would float it where they could, but now the ramifications were different and I'd have to accept the idea of never leaving that country. Had I accepted the offer in the first place, I could have quietly left Australia using a newly arranged passport, but that was out now because a passport couldn't be obtained in the remaining days and my description would be circulated to all points of exit. With time running out, the fellow could only put me into hiding until a particular ship arrived in port, and I'd be smuggled aboard.

The man explained that this was a firm offer from certain people who were aware how well he knew me and accepted his word that I could be trusted. For long I'd known that my acquaintance had peculiar political connections, without realizing they were so strong. Leaving the office, I wangled a few days to think things over.

For the remainder of that day I tried not to think that

326

whatever I did, my lease on any sort of life I was used to was running out. It was hard to avoid thoughts of being finished with it all in a week, or committing myself to one of those drab Communist countries. Until the evening papers came out, I was in my own private stew over what would be best. To prevent emotional scenes I planned to say nothing about the day's happenings, but now it was out for those close to me to read. The story made it very clear that my bid to delay almost immediate trial had failed. All along I'd been maintaining the illusion that everything was under control. That night after I'd done my lying, telling both girlfriend and wife that there was a sure-fire legal move still to come, I went alone to my apartment to do some heavy thinking. For a long time in the late-night silence I thought about going to a Communist country; my conscience could be squared by blaming the Australian Government's obsession with punishment, but still I didn't like the idea.

Thinking about a one-way flight, and the consternation I could cause with radio transmissions, I was struck by an inspiration. Suddenly there was a way out, with my survival practically assured; this was so good that I jumped up and headed straight for the pill bottle. What I needed was publicity that would cry out how I would be destroyed by strict inter-pretation of the law. Up till this moment I'd been too blind to see the means staring me in the face each time I went to the airport. Instead of going meekly to the slaughter, or disap-pearing to where I didn't want to go, I could put up a real fight. Handled the right way, I should be able to win public opinion in a most dramatic manner. My plan would have all those in power wishing me dead and gone, but they'd have to act with the public looking on. It seemed a sure bet that they'd make some sort of deal rather than allow this to happen. They were pretty well hardened to quiet self-destruction in their institutions, but now I'd discover how they liked it with the public as an audience.

To bring this off I'd have to spend a few hours circling the city in my airplane, before heading out to sea if necessary. A fair few radio transmissions could be sent while I was beyond physical reach, and I'd make sure they were picked up by the right people. Publicity could be arranged so that news media on the ground would blaze the story, while in the air I attracted attention

327

buzzing tall buildings. The message to the public would be that unless I was given a reasonable deal by the authorities, I'd fly out to where I could never be found. The idea was germinating fast now, and I could almost see the furore it would cause. With radio stations interrupting their programmes, people would rush into the streets to see the aircraft flown by a "crazed pilot" threatening a suicidal flight unless his demands were met. Among the crowds would be many hoping to see a crash staged in the city. My guess on mob psychology—leaving out those wanting something gory—was that when the story spread the public would not align themselves with authority; Australians are great champions of the underdog, and display a sporting tendency to support anyone battling against odds.

An operation of this sort could hardly fail to capture public imagination. Officialdom would have to affirm publicly the principle that punishment transcends the right to life, or else give in to my fairly reasonable demands. I figured the masses would be sympathetic to someone who was not dodging a showdown with authority, or running away with his tail between his legs. Instead I'd be fighting the law in the sky above their biggest city rather than in a courtroom. My mind was racing ahead on thoughts of officialdom's mental processes. A delicate matter was the sort of demand I could make, without backing authority into a corner from which there was no face-saving solution. Allowance would have to be made for the fact that no normal official would tolerate the thought of publicly giving in to the demands of a law-breaker. My requests—they'd be requests rather than demands—would be such that the opposition could compromise without appearing to be in abject surrender. The primary request over the aircraft radio would be withdrawal of the charges, to allow me to resume a normal life. That might stick in the officials' throats no matter how many people were involved, but there'd be room for compromise.

If I expressed willingness to spend a little time in a psychiatric institution, all concerned might save face. It would look as if I needed treatment rather than punishment, and in their wisdom the authorities could publicly see to it that I received what was required. Another possible proposition was that they allow me a month to wind up my affairs and get out of the country. The mental angle, however, seemed best. Most important would be

328

that I make widely known my intention of harming nobody other than myself, or I'd lose public support. The morbid could look expectantly for an airplane crash, but I'd make it very clear to the media and authorities that under no circumstance would I come down in the city. I would repeat continually my intention of heading seaward, when fuel reached a certain level. This would strengthen my position, since I'd see to it that there was no privacy in communications with the authorities.

Next was the particular official to whom all this was to be directed. The one man in a position to give meaningful undertakings would be the Commissioner of Police, so there was really no choice. From what I'd read of the chief, there was no suggestion that he was at all vindictive. He was also said to favour good publicity, and this might be a chance for him to inspire some. Since the Commissioner might need guidance in the crisis I planned for him, it could be worth while having someone representing my side in close contact. Ormsby would be perfect, but I didn't think lawyer-to-client privileges would cover this if he had prior knowledge. So that he wouldn't be guilty of compounding a law breach by not informing the authorities in time to stop the flight, he'd have to be involved after I was airborne.

A letter instructing him to negotiate with the Commissioner on my behalf could be hand-delivered at the right time. Acting as a public-spirited officer of the court, Ormsby would be duty-bound to aid the chief in preventing the situation from deteriorating. The officials would have to regard the flight as potentially dangerous, because in my "demented" state I could unintentionally crash in the city. As someone acquainted with me, besides being my legal representative, Ormsby's suggestions should carry weight. The Commissioner would also be handed a letter about the time my airplane came within hearing range. My request in writing should indicate to the chief that this was a well-reasoned action born of true desperation and not to be considered lightly. Also it might reduce the risk of his weaseling out, by being "unavailable".

Publicity could be tricky to organize, because I'd have to tip my hand to a few people in advance and risk a leak. In exchange for an exclusive inside story I planned to bring in a major newspaper on my side. The editor I had in mind was a man I knew slightly. His paper controlled some radio stations, which if first on the air could set the tone for others to follow. Sympathetic treatment from those stations would quickly get the right message to the public. Knowing in advance what was going to happen, the editor could plant photographers where they'd get early shots of my aircraft. With general background information supplied beforehand, the paper could have an edition on the streets while I was still in the air. Fully loaded with fuel I'd be able to carry on my antics over Sydney for more than five hours, without cutting into the reserve for what might finally have to be done. For his own protection the editor could also be supplied with a hand-delivered letter; as a law-abiding type he'd inform the police of an operation already under way, then start rolling his story.

There would have to be some major untruths, since otherwise certain people would feel morally bound to denounce me to the authorities. One lie would be that, in case of failure with the officials, I might land at a remote spot far up the coast, in preference to a seaward flight.

Planning kept me up all night, but by first daylight I felt I'd covered each detail. My flight would take place two days later, with the first low passes over the city when the roads were jammed with traffic. No faked-up flight plan would be filed, since I'd only need a radio clearance for a country destination to get into the air.

At take-off time my wife would be standing by with the three letters in the foyer of a city hotel. To prevent the disaster of her delivering the letters while I might be delayed on the ground, she'd await a phone-call from a trusted friend who lived near the airport. Advised that I was airborne she'd hit the newspaper first, then Ormsby, and finally the Commissioner of Police. That order of priorities was established in case she should be detained at the police chief's office; if not held there, she would return to Ormsby's office to give him moral support and be available to the press. A weak link might be Ormsby's failure to arrive at his office at the usual time; to make sure this didn't happen, I'd tell him about something very important requiring his availability first thing that morning. He'd pump like hell to know what it was all about, so I'd have to stall while getting his promise to be there. Back-up in case of communication breakdown would be my girlfriend, who had an apartment on a hillside overlooking the city. By the time I passed over her place the letters would be delivered, if all was normal. Her part would be to phone anonymously the various people and verbally give the message, after sighting my aircraft.

Radio silence after take-off would be broken over the outer edge of Sydney, when I'd advise approach control that I was penetrating their zone on a direct heading for the city at fifteen hundred feet. Faced with an unauthorized entry, Air Traffic Control would be thrown into confusion. On this transmission I'd tell them only that an important message would follow. Five minutes later, from half-way into the city, I'd again call Sydney Approach, this time asking them to contact the Commissioner of Police. From that moment on, things would have to be played by ear. Waiting for a response, I'd be over the city creating all possible disturbance. Flying low over city streets crowded with workbound motorists, who would already be hearing the story on their car radios, I'd probably cause great traffic jams. If my runs were really low and noisy, I should be able to tie the city into a tangle, making the authorities realize that they were dealing with somebody who meant business. By the time I had the streets packed with people, Ormsby and the Police Commissioner should be discussing ways of persuading me to come down.

Recruiting the needed people took some selling. Both girlfriend and wife agreed to play their parts when I admitted I was backed into a corner. First to be involved was the newspaper editor. He needed no reminder of the newsworthiness of my arrest and court appearances. At the start of our talk I promised the man an exclusive on a story that would make earlier stuff seem tame. He reacted keenly. Before elaborating on the offer, I extracted promises of secrecy and sympathetic handling. Knowing that any leak could mean no story at all, the editor promised me everything. If I could pull this off, he said, I could count on covering page one, two and three; the edition, with pictures, would be on the street while I was still circling the city.

An appointment with a reporter and photographer was set up, away from the newspaper office. Pictures were taken, and a story worked up containing everything short of an admission that the paper had advance notification. A suggestion was made by the editor that I fly under the Sydney Harbour Bridge. This I agreed to do if conditions were right at the time, so along with

331

photographers stationed at other points there'd be a couple in a tug on the harbour. The radio frequency I'd use would be monitored, so my "requests" to the authorities should reach the public within minutes. Finally I had to give a solemn undertaking that no other paper would be let in on this, and that my suicide threats would be no more than bluff.

My friend with the proposition to go to another country was kept dangling, while arrangements for the flight went ahead. He might come in handy if the authorities wouldn't cave in. My latest plan in that event was to crash-land in a remote clearing too small for any shadowing aircraft, and as a hunted fugitive try to make my way by night to the fellow's house; though I'd be red hot, there seemed little chance of his turning me away.

Walking early next morning toward where I'd left the airplane tied down outside its hangar, I saw that something had gone badly wrong. My aircraft was an object of interest to a small group of men, and at least two had the appearance of law; parked squarely in front, to block any possible move, was an airport truck. They spotted me about the time I saw them. Instinct told me to beat a retreat, but that could look like an admission of guilt and lead to arrest. Bluff seemed my only hope. Luckily I'd taken some amphetamine before starting out, so my nerves were under enough control to allow me to talk convincingly. As the distance between us narrowed, I thought that my position mightn't be hopeless. What they'd heard was rumour and couldn't be proved. I'd have to wait for them to talk first, before I denied anything. Holding my camera case (the editor had requested pictures of the happening), I could insist that I was purely carrying on my normal business as an aerial photographer.

Silence was broken by a man who looked very official. All he said, politely, was that he'd been instructed to ask me not to fly my aircraft. Apparently this would be a low-key encounter, if I didn't push my luck. Acting dumb and asking why such a request should be made, my mind flew into top gear. There'd been a leak, but these people were acting as if they weren't quite sure of their ground. No more sense could I get than a repeat of the "request" not to fly, but I didn't think much of my chance of getting their truck moved out of the way if I insisted. Realizing that these were relatively toothless Commonwealth cops, acting on Department of Civil Aviation instructions, I thought the situation might somehow be salvaged. If the D.C.A. didn't feel strong enough to have me picked up, it could be that they weren't very sure of their source. Possibly I could convince them that whatever they'd heard was ridiculously untrue. Wasting no more time, I walked from the aircraft in the general direction of the briefing office. Safely clear of that bunch, I detoured to the parked car containing a reporter and photographer covering my take-off. How the editor intended explaining airport coverage of something he wasn't supposed to know about ahead of time was no concern of mine, but his men were present and I had to tell them that for now the operation appeared to be blown sky-high. Even in my nearly stunned state, I was able to say with some confidence that the job would still be done between now and trial-day.

Then I stopped at a phone, to disassemble the rest of the operation. I told my girlfriend there'd been a technical problem, and the flight would be put off a day or two. She sounded relieved, as if hoping I might come to my senses and not do the thing at all. My wife, who thought this would be the call setting her in motion, was simply told there'd been a leak and she could take the letters home. She was so upset that I quickly told her I'd find some way of pulling it off.

Going into the briefing office, I thought there probably wasn't much I could say to effect removal of the guard from my airplane, but there might be a chance to lay the groundwork for putting over the stunt another way.

Nobody in the place could or would tell me why I wasn't to fly, and the only suggestion was that I call the Chief of Operations. Waiting for a connection, I thought that if the authorities offered to drop all charges, I'd still be disappointed at not going through with this flight. I was so keyed up, after all the preparation and pills, that the prospect of such a challenge to authority was almost irresistible. Tying up one of the world's great cities for hours, as a blow against those wanting to destroy me, appealed to me so strongly that it just wasn't possible to forget the idea. My flight would be done even if it meant stealing an airplane, or getting one by some trick. The officials were going to get the performance I'd planned for them. No civil aviation people could block my fight for survival, just because it would upset them to have me floating around.

Quite calmly I told the operations chief that on arrival to carry out a photographic assignment I'd found my airplane under guard, and perhaps he could give me some explanation. The start of the man's well-prepared speech covered his department's feeling that, in view of psychiatric evidence at my recent court appearance, I shouldn't fly until cleared by their own examiner. This was difficult to argue against, though I tried. My stand was that what happened in court was only a lawyer's trick, and now I was being forced to let down a customer. What came next was incisive, and pulled the rug from under me. The chief said that when he heard of plans for a low flight over the city, with newspaper photographers staked out, he had to put a guard on my aircraft. I suggested it should be acceptable if I were to hire an airplane with pilot and be flown over my job. He countered that the department would "prefer" I did not fly at all or even approach an aircraft until all was cleared. Hanging up, I savoured the thought of that man's reaction when eventually he heard I was in the air—on a grand scale. Nothing he said suggested knowledge of a plot to hold the government to ransom, so there'd be a surprise in store.

The editor's great concern was whether my flight could still be staged. He was sure the leak hadn't come from within his organization, but he wavered when I mentioned the photographers. I promised the operation would go on, but security would need to be very tight. My other airplane had long since been cannibalized for spare parts, and was too close to the guarded one, but I'd have four days to arrange something.

The editor sounded sceptical, even as I tried to convince him that too much depended on this for me to let it slip by default. I explained that through my aviation connections I'd get some sort of aircraft. Not wanting to lose a story for which he'd developed considerable enthusiasm, the editor was willing to accept my terms on how things should be done. I insisted that nobody else within the paper should know the stunt was still planned. Final notification of time of flight would be late the night before; nobody but me would know which of several country airports was to be used as a point of departure. Staff were not to be advised of any impending news beat, but if the editor happened to have reporters and photographers to send immediately to the predetermined locations it would be helpful.

Though the editor would have eight or ten hours' advance warning, he was not to act on estimated times. Nothing must roll until he received a phone-call from a woman, informing him that the flight was in the air tracking toward Sydney. Letters could be dispensed with, it was agreed, because his word about the call should satisfy the authorities. A point raised by the editor was picking the right day for my flight. The stunt wouldn't succeed if done at the weekend, so that left only a Friday—or the Monday morning when my trial should be commencing. Since any half-cocked move, such as indiscreet haste in trying to obtain an airplane, would kill the operation, I opted for the Monday. That meant cutting things so fine that I'd be in the air at the actual time I should be walking through the courthouse door. All going well, the newsman would be contacted at his home the night before.

I began to worry about the state cops picking me up on the excuse that I mightn't be available for trial. That sent me running to Ormsby, to tell him what had been happening. Not wanting to compromise him, I said nothing about lining up another airplane and still doing the flight. My fear of arrest before trial was eased when he said it wouldn't happen, because I hadn't breached the conditions of my bail.

Later I was in another office, delaying still further my final decision on the overseas trip. My excuse this time was that I would need a few days to clear my business affairs. This could take up to and past trial day, which the man didn't like very much. Before leaving, I was given a number to call if still at large after trial time. A car would be sent to pick me up from wherever I might be.

My girlfriend and her daughter were genuinely upset when I told them there'd been a minor leak. Passing it off as suspicion rather than anything really definite, I said that the exercise was still on.

When I reached my wife's place her boyfriend was there, and I brought him into the picture. He wanted to help, by accompanying me to the airport early next morning when there wouldn't be many people around. If the situation looked right, he'd overpower the guard while I took off. As an ex-Foreign-Legion man who'd seen a lot of action, this was the sort of thing to appeal to him. I had to explain that violence would spoil my case, but still he was willing to help me steal an airplane. Unfortunately, he had never learnt to fly, so he couldn't hire an aircraft and hand it over to me at an outlying field.

Next morning, while it was still half dark, I checked to see just how seriously the officials regarded their brief. From a distance, through binoculars, I saw my airplane, and two guards lounging against the airport truck. I watched for a long time, until two others came to relieve the original pair. It was fairly obvious that my airplane was being watched twenty-four hours a day, to prevent a night operation. The authorities didn't want publicity over an "insane" pilot, about whom they'd been warned, getting into the air. These precautions showed how apprehensive they were, so however I obtained another aircraft it wouldn't be safe to be seen around any airport in the Sydney region. If they even guessed the extent of my plan, it would be worth their while to guard every field within striking distance. When I was safely in jail, they could release the story of how their vigilance had saved the city from hours of terror.

Different airplane owners came into mind, and I discarded all but one: a man who owned a similar aircraft to mine, whom I wasn't afraid to approach. At his house that night I could sense that he'd heard something. Airports are great centres of gossip, so this was to be expected, but I hoped he hadn't picked up too much. Boring straight in, I asked if I could hire or borrow his airplane. Without hesitation he said yes, then stopped to think for a minute. Apologizing for talking about my private affairs, the man said he knew of some problem with the D.C.A. and hoped whatever I planned wouldn't get him into trouble. Like others who knew me he was aware of my problems with the law over counterfeiting, so that was of no immediate concern. There was no concealing the fact that I wanted the airplane for some very special purpose, but before I could give a plausible tale I had to find out how much the man already knew. After a round of verbal sparring I ascertained that he knew my airplane was under guard, and my licence suspended, but he had no idea what lay behind the official moves.

We reached a point where I could get the aircraft, as long as the owner was convinced it wouldn't be used for an illegal purpose. What I planned was probably legal, except for minor aviation breaches. No government would ever have thought to

336

pass laws against people taking wing in airplanes and requesting immunity from criminal prosecution. My friend could overlook the fact that I wasn't supposed to fly, but otherwise he was suspicious and not prepared to accept too much at face value. I admitted the use of the aircraft, in some kind of publicity stunt, would probably save me from going to jail, but I just didn't know what to say next. He came to my rescue with the suggestion that my obvious intent was to drop leaflets on the city, to sway public opinion. I was annoyed with myself for not thinking of that cover first.

Now I had to make sure that he didn't take seriously anyone who might tell him the true story. Since I couldn't put him into isolation, my only protection was to suggest there might be wild rumours around the airport. I went on to explain that this project was harmless enough to have the backing of prominent people in the fields of law and journalism. With the introductory bit over and done with, it was time to discuss secrecy. To maintain this all-important secrecy, he'd have to fly to another airport and leave the aircraft there, with full tanks.

His airplane was inside the hangar where mine was parked, so there'd be no hope of his not noticing the men on guard. My idea was that, by timing the move correctly, he mightn't be exposed to them for too long. Sunday afternoon, when many private owners flew to blow the cobwebs away, seemed the best time. Something I didn't like was his airplane being the same make as mine, an old-fashioned type that tended to attract attention. A guard might put two and two together, and ask questions. To prevent panic if it happened, I had to mention the possibility.

Final arrangements were that on Sunday afternoon my very good friend would fly from Bankstown airport to Camden, about thirty-five miles out of Sydney. There he'd fill all tanks, giving an endurance of better than five hours, and secure the airplane in the open where I could get at it easily next morning. My role would be to take him from Camden back to Bankstown. Before and even after that pick-up I had plenty of reason to think the situation was hopelessly lost.

Half an hour past the time the airplane should have landed, I began to feel sick with worry. From a safe vantage point I was checking all arrivals at Camden, through my binoculars. When an hour dragged by with no sighting of the right airplane, I began to imagine all sorts of possibilities. Here I was, completely dependent on someone who had no stake in the venture. A change of mind perhaps accounted for the man's non-arrival. Or had he been questioned and suckered into admitting he was lending me his airplane. He was probably driving over, at this moment, to deliver the bad news. More time passed, and I felt helplessly desperate.

About eighteen hours remained before I was due in court, so it was probably too late even to steal an airplane. Too many people using this field knew me, and that ruled out the possibility of searching in daylight for something with full tanks I might "borrow". After dark there might be a remote chance of readying an aircraft for early-morning take-off, if there was no watchman. With two hours of daylight left, it looked as if I'd have to say good-bye to my wife and girlfriend, and take that trip out of the country.

Then an aircraft loomed on a downwind leg for landing, and I could see that it wasn't modern. With my glasses pointed the right way, I recognized it as the airplane I'd waited for so agonizingly. I felt relieved and certain that my worries about an airplane for next morning were over.

Quite some time later the man came toward where I was parked, looking very distressed. He spoke first, to the effect that he wasn't sure he wanted to go through with this. Before I could say more than how this would screw me up completely, he told me what had happened. The cops guarding my airplane took a lot of notice when he rolled a carbon copy out of the hangar. They questioned him on whether he knew me, where he was headed, and so on; they refrained from asking straight out if he'd made any kind of deal with me. My friend admitted he knew a pilot who kept an airplane like his in the same hangar. He said we didn't meet often, because most of his flying was done at weekends. No more was my name mentioned, but still there was the question of destination. The simple answer was that he intended flying to a distant country town, for an overnight visit. That neatly covered failure of the airplane to return at the end of the day. It left open a possible check of the aircraft's supposed destination, but that wouldn't be too easy since the place had no Air Traffic Control.

All this I heard without interrupting, because it seemed wise to

338

let the fellow blow off steam before getting down to what was really frightening. Although the airplane was fuelled up and ready for departure, the owner now had serious doubts about me. The very real determination of someone to prevent my flight caused him to wonder if there mightn't be a lot more to this than I cared to admit. The man was picking inconsistencies in my story about a simple publicity stunt, and I could only let fly a torrent of words, amounting to the simple fact that my straightforward flight would produce the desired results.

By the time I dropped my friend outside Bankstown, I had "bought" his airplane—the only way to end a lengthy discussion that was getting nowhere. I suggested that if he was worried all that much over getting into trouble for helping me, there was a simple solution: either for real, or as a paper transaction based on a holding deposit subject to flight test, I'd buy the aircraft. Though he wasn't anxious to sell, the idea hit home. Parked off the road we wrote the deal, and the fellow was satisfied that whatever I might do was now none of his business. To make it legal, a bill of sale was drawn up and I handed over a cheque for fifty dollars, which was all my friend would take. Neither he nor I considered the aircraft sold, despite documentation to the effect that it was—subject to payment of balance within seven days, and passing of such flight tests as I saw fit. How the testing would be carried out was up to me, though I did promise not to bend the man's airplane.

Then I learned of yet another complication. My own airplane had long ago been equipped with a suitable radio, but this one had only a crude device with few channels. The Sydney Control Zone ones were entirely missing, so my communications with the Commissioner of Police would have to be relayed via Bankstown Tower. To the Air Traffic Control of that secondary airport would fall the task of notifying Sydney that I was coming, also the setting-up of whatever lines might be needed by either side.

Another worry was that with so much time on their hands guarding my aircraft, the Commonwealth cops might start thinking. Having taken the trouble to question the owner of a similar airplane, they might have the state police check the field where it should land. Failure to locate it could only direct suspicion my way. It shouldn't take the civil aviation people long to learn that the airplane was sitting on the ground at a minor airport close to Sydney. There seemed quite a chance of a guard on the airplane by my planned departure time of eight next morning.

The only way I could now see of pulling off the job was by first crack of daylight take-off. Though early departure would mean wasted time before the city was busy enough to get tangled by my performance, I'd still be in the air when the court opened. By practising maximum fuel economy, I'd probably get close to six hours out of the airplane.

With the operation degenerating into a last-minute act of desperation, I had to dispense with all but the bare essentials. There'd be no letters and my wife could make the phone-calls, with back-up from my girlfriend's daughter. Ormsby would be left to pick up the news on the radio. Once airborne, I'd have to play things pretty much by ear, without really knowing the strength of my ground support. About all I could count on would be the newspaper man and his facilities.

Late that night my girlfriend and her daughter went through a second briefing. Another flight lunch was prepared, along with a thermos full of coffee, which would go well with the pills I'd have to take, after being up all night. As premature calls couldn't be risked, they were to look out for the aircraft from first daylight on. To make sure my girlfriend's daughter didn't phone the editor, or try to reach the police chief, after sighting some distant airliner, I promised a couple of roof-level passes down the valley in front of their apartment. They weren't to know that my wife would make similar calls—if she and her boyfriend got away from the airport without running into trouble.

I phoned the editor at his home, to tell him the flight was definitely on in the morning. He'd receive a call after I was airborne, I explained before pleading with him not to act beforehand. On the chance that he trusted his organization more than I did, I fed him false flight details. Departure would be from a field about a hundred miles north of Sydney, I told him, and a quite different type of aircraft would be used. If there was a leak, cops would be sent to the wrong field to watch for the wrong aircraft. To make sure there were no slip-ups, the editor thought he should plant a man or two on the roof of the newspaper building; my arrival over the city was to be announced by giving the place a low buzz.

340

Departure for Camden airport was from my wife's place, early enough for an hour of darkness to check for guards. My wife was to remain in the car outside the airport.

Half-way to Camden the effect of sleepless nights caught up with me, and I began to feel that all this wasn't much use. Something would have to go wrong at the last moment. I pulled off the road and took a couple of pep pills, and within minutes the effect of these and moral support from my wife had me ready for action.

When we arrived, the boyfriend and I walked quietly through the darkness. Close to the hangars, but hidden from where the airplane was tied down, we stopped and listened for any kind of sound. Apart from truck noises on a distant highway nothing could be heard, so we moved slowly on trying not to crunch gravel underfoot. After what seemed an eternity of slow motion we reached the corner of a building, around which I hoped to find an unguarded airplane.

While my physical back-up remained out of sight, I poked my head into the open, to see only the faint outlines of several airplanes. There were no people or ground vehicles to be seen, so I moved silently clear of my doubtful shelter. Without using any kind of light, it was just possible to locate the right airplane and ascertain that nothing blocked its access to the taxiway. Before returning to where the boyfriend stood ready to spring to my aid, I fumbled around in the dark and slipped all the tie-down lines.

Back at the car the three of us waited until it was nearly time for the first traces of daylight. Then we repositioned ourselves inside the airport gate. If any car that didn't look right appeared on the scene I was to hop out and disappear, while the boyfriend mildly bumped it with my heap. In the argument that was likely to follow, with an accompaniment from my wife, I'd sneak up to the aircraft and take off in whatever light was available.

Eventually there was sufficient light and I didn't dare postpone the event any longer, so we all walked to where the airplane stood. Visual inspection showed main and cabin tanks full. I climbed aboard and studied the cockpit layout, to locate things needed for starting the engine. Though the aircraft was similar to mine, items such as fuel selector and battery master switch were situated differently. After these were sorted out, I stowed the camera (the editor still wanted his pictures) and my

341

flight lunch along with the coffee flask.

I signalled readiness to start the engine. With my wife and her boyfriend safely clear, I pressed the starter switch, hoping to Christ I wouldn't be grinding away on a weak battery while a carload of law drove up to block my taxi-path. On its second compression stroke the engine caught with a roar, but my nerves were in no shape to hang around making noise while it warmed up. As soon as the r.p.m. indicator steadied on a thousand, I answered the waves of my wife and her friend, released the brakes and let the airplane roll. Past the hangars I went, fearful that some vehicle might dart out to cut me off. Then in the crisp light of dawn there was nothing ahead by the runway intersection. As the place had no Air Traffic Control, there was no one to notice my movement toward the end of the runway. Lined up for take-off I did the normal cockpit checks, then poured on the coal. With plenty of lift in the morning air I was off the ground quickly, and through the three-hundred-foot level over the far end of the runway. Interrupting my climb, I put the nose down, after turning toward where my wife and her boyfriend were standing. At less than two hundred feet their tiny figures weren't long in sight, though there was time to dip a wing before resuming my climb.

I was now occupied with flight procedures, leaving less time to think of what might lie ahead. After reaching a thousand feet, there was the switch from main to long-range tank. As usual with these arrangements this one had no fuel gauge, so I made a note of the time. When a certain amount of time had passed, all buzzing and other low-level work would have to be done on the main tank. The other one would be allowed to run dry when, for ease of radio communication, I went to higher levels. Because I might need maximum endurance I'd have to plan on running the cabin tank right out, subjecting myself to the usual power-off drop. Next came adjustment of throttle and mixture, for best fuel economy.

By the time those details were organized, the clear ground below was covered by a thin sheet of fog, which would burn off when hit by the sun. With nothing solid in sight I had to set a compass course for the outlying town of Parramatta, just outside the Sydney Control Zone, where I'd make my first radio call. Meanwhile there was time to take another pill, relax and light a cigarette.

My operation mightn't be perfect, I thought while fiddling with the radio, and it could lack polish—but the best efforts of the authorities had failed to keep me on the ground. Short of engine failure they had no way of getting me into court at the scheduled time—or at any other if all went to plan. Even if they went berserk and sent the Air Force up, which they wouldn't, there'd be no way of getting me down once I got among the city's tall buildings.

No voices could be heard on any of the radio's few channels, and I had the horrible thought that I mightn't be able to transmit my "requests". Before realizing it was too early for traffic on these frequencies, I had a wild idea of trying to drop notes onto the newspaper building roof. Then I caught a static-loaded carrier wave, and hoped everything would be all right; only when I made my first call, over Parramatta in about five minutes, would I know for certain.

Barely had I finished another cigarette when the ground fog became patchy. Then the outer reaches of Parramatta were sliding underneath, so I switched to the Bankstown Tower frequency. That facility would be open for business, though it was still a bit early for any in or outbound traffic. No voices came over, so I'd probably be their first customer for the day—and one to remember for a long time.

When downtown Parramatta came visual through medium haze, it was time to press the microphone button and start talking. My first words were solely to establish contact, so keeping traces of stress out of my voice wasn't too difficult. After saying, "Bankstown Tower this is Romeo Charlie Alpha—do you read", there was enough silence to twist my insides. Time stretched right out of proportion before the headphones finally crackled out, "Romeo Charlie Alpha—Bankstown—reading you strength five."

This prepared them for something routine, like reporting inbound. Now I was ready to inform Bankstown that what I had in mind was slightly different. Trying to keep my voice as calm as though I only wanted terminal information, I began talking. After repeating the aircraft call-sign as per custom I went on to say, "I am entering the Sydney Control Zone without clearance—tracking via the Parramatta River to the central city area below one five zero zero feet. Would you please inform Sydney as I do not have their frequency."

That transmission was startling enough to bring instant reply, and my nerves were so keyed up I had to go on talking. With barely a pause I continued, "This aircraft is being flown by Robert Baudin, who would normally be flying Sierra Echo Delta. The reason I am flying this aircraft instead of my own is that mine is under guard by Commonwealth police. I request that you contact the Commissioner of Police, as I will have a message for him later." I couldn't resist adding, "You could advise the police guarding Sierra Echo Delta that since I am already airborne in another aircraft, there is no further need for them to watch mine. Perhaps they'd like to go home." Following a brief delay a strained voice replied, "Stand by, Romeo Charlie Alpha, we will call you back."

Having delivered myself of those words, my nerves began jumping all over the place. That terse reply sounded like an anticlimax, though I could well imagine the feverish activity it would trigger off on the ground. My intentions, except for the bit about the cops, had been stated too clearly for this not to be treated as an emergency. Sydney Approach would already be in the picture, tracking me on their radar. Traffic in and out of the main airport would be kept well clear of Romeo Charlie Alpha. With a minimum of fuss Air Traffic Control would gear its operation to the premise that a large part of the control zone was unavailable to other aircraft.

I was headed downstream, toward a murky bank of smog. Beyond that mess Sydney should show up fairly clearly, with improvement as the morning wore on. Over the city I'd pay Air Traffic Control the courtesy of defining the limits of my operation, so they'd be able to direct their airliners in and out with the least possible trouble. That information would be relayed in a later transmission, after I'd assessed visibility conditions.

A voice in the earphones made me jerk. After saying my call-sign, it asked me to report my present position. No emotion accompanied those words, and the call seemed almost unreal. As a delayed reply to what I'd put on the air, I was getting nothing more than the impersonal voice typical of all air traffic controllers. Emerging from the smog ahead was a bridge about

344

five miles before the city. They'd have me on radar, so why in hell ask where I was. Possibly they were trying to work out the state of my mind, I decided. Hoping to sound untroubled, I reported approaching Gladesville Bridge, two and a half miles upstream from Sydney. Soon after my position report the city began to shape up in the murk ahead. First a cluster of tall buildings appeared above the lower haze layers, and then there was the immense iron framework of Sydney Harbour Bridge; this was the structure I was to fly under for the benefit of the editor, if conditions permitted. Finally I was clear of the smog bank, with all ahead looking bright and clean in the early-morning sunlight.

A wide circle a thousand feet above central Sydney revealed a little early traffic. Looking down at it, I made another radio call. Because I didn't think enough time had elapsed for lines of ground communication to be set up, this was only a brief one. Primarily it was a request for Bankstown to inform Sydney Air Traffic Control that I was in my operating area and would proceed no farther south than the lower end of the city, so as not to interfere with their traffic. I added that I would shortly have a message for referral to other authority.

Suddenly I realized that my slightly sick feeling was the result of not eating since leaving for the airport all those hours before. Continuing my wide orbit, I ate some of the flight lunch and had a cup of coffee. I felt better, but to feel on top of the world I needed another one of those pills—and a piss. I had to look for something to do it in, and the only thing in the airplane was the Thermos top; not wanting to discharge corrosive liquid on the floor of somebody else's aircraft, I loosened my seat belt, edged forward and managed to cut off before the cup overflowed. In getting rid of the contents my judgement went awry. Sideslipping to create an outgoing draught, as is customary when casting stomach contents over the side, my knee nudged the stick just as I emptied the cup. The incoming blast picked up the piss and slammed it back into my face. Overcorrecting the other way brought reverse airflow, so now, instead of the body waste feeling warm as when it first hit, my face turned freezing cold; like a bucket of ice water, it snapped me out of the languid state I'd settled into while eating.

Wiping the cold wetness from my face, I started a dive toward my girlfriend's place. Above a ridge overlooking the building I crossed the controls for a steep angle of slip. Headed directly toward some open parkland down a valley, I applied full power as the airplane came level with her hillside apartment. That noisy blast brought no visible results because I was gone too quickly, but next time my girlfriend and her daughter were out on their balcony; one flapped an outsize towel, and the other jumped up and down waving excitedly. To make sure they definitely knew it was the right aircraft I made a third pass, and this time some of the other balconies were occupied—by people who appeared to have tumbled straight out of bed.

Back to a thousand feet, where the radio would work better, I prepared to transmit the full story. Opening in the stylized way of a normal call, I went on to say, "Would you inform the Commissioner of Police that it is my intention to remain in the city area until such time as my fuel runs low or I have received certain assurances from him. If I do not have an undertaking from the Commissioner that charges against me will be withdrawn by the time my fuel is down to one hour, I intend to fly out to sea until it is exhausted. I have a supply of sleeping-pills which will be taken when clear of the coast, if I do not receive a satisfactory reply to my requests.

"Also I wish to make clear that I do not threaten to crash the airplane into the city, or any other place where it could harm persons or property. If my request is granted I will land after receiving proper assurance, but in no circumstance will I put down at an airport without this. I can accept going out to sea as an alternative to rotting in jail, so I'd like to make clear from the start that I will not settle for anything less than the terms I suggest."

All that came out with less strain than I expected. I closed with no more than: "Did you copy, Bankstown—and will you convey to the proper authorities?" Quickly came the answer, "Copied your transmission, Romeo Charlie Alpha, and will pass it on."

Three men waved at me from about fifty feet below, when I passed over the newspaper building. It seemed unlikely they'd waited for phone-calls before getting up there, and a minute later over the harbour I was certain that the editor had jumped the gun. Lying dead in the water near the Harbour Bridge was a tug, with men on deck holding what could only be cameras. Where others might be planted didn't matter, because these fellows were

346

in position to get good shots whether or not I flew under the bridge. I wondered if there'd been a further leak, sending guards to the distant field.

The last pill seemed to be knocking out all remaining tension. What had happened so far was only the beginning of something that could last for hours. When they were ready down below, I thought smugly, they'd call back and I'd reply. Throttling back, I put the airplane into a steep spiralling descent; it was exhilarating. To people below unfamiliar with flying I'd appear out of control and spinning straight toward the ground. Levelling off with a sudden application of power low down over a wide city street, I had the impression of hearing my own racket bouncing back. I'd do more of this later, when there'd be lots of people around to appreciate my effort.

Trying to go under the Harbour Bridge for the benefit of the photographers very nearly landed me in trouble. They had opportunities for shots when I buzzed the area around their boat, before moving off to let down really low over the water in an attempt to give them something special. Some buildings on a point of land served as a reference for judging height, but when they were gone it was difficult to define what lay ahead. A dirty windscreen that was no problem with contrast subjects such as buildings made it hard to see just where air ended and water began. The harbour surface was like a smooth sheet of black glass in the morning light, and I couldn't estimate whether it was five or fifty feet below. Also the pills seemed to be affecting my perception of depth.

What lay outside the aircraft was now too far away for precise height-finding, and I was over the better-lit part of the harbour. Much of the surface around the bridge was in shadow, with the sun still at a low angle. The situation did not look too good. Fast approaching in the gloom was the bridge's underside, lacking detail through my windscreen. It was difficult to estimate just how high I could go, without risk of scraping some part of the structure. Had there been some wind-raised ripples on the water, I might have been able to guess my height within twenty feet, but instead there was only limpid flatness appearing to stand still under the aircraft.

Almost too late I decided it wasn't worth the risk. In the rapidly shortening time left to break off, I made up my mind that

347

fulfilling the commission would probably give them one-in-a-lifetime shots of an airplane making a mighty splash. Thinking out loud, "Fuck those bastards and their pictures", I poured on full power and started a climbing turn toward the only way out. So late was my decision that, even after the airplane began lifting away, I thought I'd have to throttle back, turn again toward the darkness under the bridge, and hope to get through without flying into the water. I soon realized that I'd diverted too far from my original heading to do that, without slamming into some building near the bridge approach. In one direction only was there hope of climbing into the clear. To do it, I'd have to achieve sufficient height quickly to pass over the huge hull of the P & O liner *Canberra*, tied to a wharf in my line of flight. Any turn away from the ship would put me on a collision heading with buildings much higher. My only way out was to aim for the low part forward of the superstructure, and hope to get across without clipping anything. So high did that ship loom that I realized, with sudden fright, just how close to the water I'd been.

Buildings on shore beyond the liner weren't high, but the ground under them rose. Struggling to get farther away from the water, I saw how dangerously late I'd left my change of mind. If I cleared the ship, it would be a hard uphill climb to a ridge several streets back. With the throttle all the way in, the airplane just didn't seem to climb as it should. It was gaining height, but that great white hull ahead was assuming massive proportions. Coming closer, I thought I'd clear the main part of the ship, but wondered about masts and wires. Pulling harder on the stick would involve a less efficient angle of attack and cause mushing, so I had to resist that temptation. A slight S turn provided the needed bit of extra run. Only when it would have been too late to do anything but brace myself for impact was I sure I'd get over the ship.

Climbing hard, I crossed the main deck forward of the bridge, and would definitely clear buildings in the immediate foreground. Behind them the ground went up fairly fast, so I wasn't yet confident. Some of the time I seemed to be fighting a losing battle with the rooftops, but finally I reached where I could see downhill on the far side of the ridge. To the left of where I cleared the high ground was a building of about twenty storeys—the airplane passed it around the tenth-floor level.

348

With that experience behind me, something suddenly registered. Passing a mass of apartment buildings on the way down to skim the water, I had the impression of people on balconies. Noise on descent wouldn't have attracted them, so the presence of such numbers could only mean one thing—that they'd heard about me on the radio. Wondering what sensational news flashes were being broadcast made me realize I should have brought a transistor radio; but for that lack of foresight I'd know as much as the public about what I was doing. Thinking of radios, it dawned on me that nothing had crackled through my earphones for quite a while. After my transmission to let the authorities know what I wanted, there'd only been a few calls between the tower and other aircraft; these dwindled when Bankstown Tower informed all traffic that until further notice this frequency would not be available for arrivals or departures. The channel was definitely set aside for communications to and from my airplane, but nothing was coming.

Since nobody wanted to talk to me, I decided to climb to where they'd hear me loud and clear and say something. Then I could go back down and give the city a buzz. This time I deliberately sounded emotional as I repeated my requests. Labouring the point that I wouldn't crash into the city served the purpose of making the authorities think I might be fighting temptation to do that very thing. Pausing to let that sink in, I continued, "My proposition is that I will land if guaranteed that all charges are withdrawn, and I am subjected to no further court appearances. If that is not acceptable, I suggest the following alternative: that I be allowed one month to wind up my business and leave the country."

My first intensive buzzing was around the office-building area, close to where the Commissioner had his headquarters. As on my frightening climb from the water I was barely above rooftop level of lower structures, but there was a difference: the airplane had plenty of speed, was responsive and clearing well. Slight stick pressure quickly lifted me above medium-height buildings in my way; tall ones of four or five hundred feet didn't lend themselves to such tactics, so I simply threaded my way around them. Judging where to break off a run and go into a steep turn or fast climb, to avoid boring into something, didn't allow me much chance to observe what was happening in the streets. Climbing to a respectable five hundred feet, for a respite from the strain of rooftop dodging, enabled me to see what I was achieving. Quite a few cars were pulled up, with people standing beside them looking skywards. I was creating some confusion, but it was still fairly small-scale. When workbound mobs were pouring into the city, I figured I'd succeed in really snarling up the works. For the present it didn't seem worth tiring myself to play to such a restricted audience. At a safe height I'd use the remaining fuel in the long-range tank by flying until the engine quit. I could then work off the full gauge-equipped tank when the crowds were thick. Too much of the kind of flying I'd just been doing could lead to a mistake in judgement, at a height where there'd be no margin for error.

Passing level with the upper bridge girders on a climb over the harbour, I noticed a lot of little figures on the walkway below. Ahead on land I could see that I hadn't lost my balcony spectators, but this bunch half-way across the harbour was new and rated a closer look. Coming out of a steep turn down level with the bridge deck, I saw that these people weren't just out for their morning exercise: all appeared to be standing still. Among that crowd would be some who hoped to see me crash, so I decided to give them a thrill. From higher up I began a manoeuvre intended to make those unfamiliar with flying think they were about to witness a prang, uncomfortably close to where they stood. Anyone with knowledge of aircraft-handling techniques would see the sham of what I was doing.

Throttling back, I crossed aileron and rudder before the airplane got very close to the bridge. Increased crossing of the controls as the aircraft came closer altered my flight path to where there was no risk of contact, but it wouldn't look that way from below. This had to be done with a certain amount of caution, so there was no opportunity to see if any ducked for cover as I slipped past and away. Resisting temptation to repeat the performance, I climbed to kill time, using the fuel left in the long-range tank. I hoped there might be word over the radio.

It seemed strange to sight a large aircraft about three miles away, apparently inbound for Sydney. Up to now, the Air Traffic Control had been keeping everything well clear. The other airplane was around my height, running parallel with the coast near the harbour entrance. Looking at it, I thought the controllers must be pretty sure I'd stay close to the centre of town. While I was thinking that Air Traffic Control was bold to use airspace I'd unofficially reserved for myself, a move took place that made me change my mind. Instead of continuing toward Sydney airport, the aircraft made a tight turn, to head back the way it had come. At the other coastal extremity I'd resumed, it turned again. On its next run along the line it was so obviously patrolling, I flew close enough to identify it as a Department of Civil Aviation aircraft and not something belonging to the Air Force as I'd begun to suspect. There was no way of knowing how long I'd been shadowed by that aircraft. I hadn't seen it from down among the city buildings, or when I was performing my antics for the people on the Harbour Bridge. The airplane must have taken up station along the coast on account of my remarks about flying out to sea. This was my first indication of anybody taking that threat seriously.

A look in other directions revealed no additional air traffic, but something was definitely happening on the harbour. As my eyes followed the run of water toward the sea, and the patrolling aircraft, I saw a number of boats churning up wakes as they sped in that direction. They weren't so far below that I couldn't see what sort of craft they were. All had the official look of water police, customs or such, and appeared as if they were in a race to be first out of port. Flying in endless circles, I gleaned some indication of what the authorities were doing, but still there was nothing in the earphones. It was up to my imagination to assess what strategy the officials were using. Probably they hoped to crack me by only acknowledging my calls, while at the same time deploying their forces to cover other possibilities. If that was the way they wanted to play things, I thought, it might be necessary to find out just how long they'd put up with an airplane running low on fuel over their city.

Somebody other than the police, I was sure, had conceived this as a contest of nerves. With civil aviation heavily involved, it wasn't difficult to guess who was organizing emergency plans. The airplane between my position and the sea made no effort to be inconspicuous, and was probably impressing me that I couldn't go anywhere without being followed. I thought of putting out a call to the effect that I understood the psychology of their tactics and it wouldn't work, so we might as well negotiate.

351

That could sound too sane and calculating, and spoil the effect of my earlier aerial misbehaviour. No message was sent. For this to work, I should act as if not caring too much whether I emerged dead or alive. Calling my bluff would then seem a danger to the city below.

The shadowing airplane and all those boats could be a public display of official competence, in case something went wrong. Also, they might hope I'd await a reply until my fuel was down to where I couldn't fly beyond range of their little armada. Then they'd be credited for both a rescue and a capture, while as a loser I'd be beyond the scope of public interest. If my nerve went and I landed without scoring my point, I'd be ratshit to everyone and dealt with as such by the court. The authorities would have the last word, in the form of a good story about their carefully calculated precautions.

Having that big airplane so close almost eliminated any chance of escaping up the coast, to land at some remote place. Its crew could radio my moves, and the police would surround wherever I landed. While I was trying to think of some way of losing the government airplane if I didn't get satisfaction, my engine quit. Although I'd climbed to my present height to allow this to happen without danger, I had since forgotten the matter. It was like something exploding in my guts when the noise in front stopped. Instinctively I pushed the stick forward so the airplane would glide rather than stall, and then had to think for a few seconds about how to get the engine firing again. I was so deeply engrossed in other thoughts that it was difficult to cope with the immediate present.

Since I'd been dragging the tail on an economical throttle setting when the engine finished draining the cabin tank, I began losing height fast. To pick up safe gliding speed, I had to drop a couple hundred feet, before exerting any back pressure on the stick. When finally my mind caught up to what I was doing by reflex action, I reached for the fuel selector handle. My hand fell to the place where it was in my own airplane, but nothing was there. So much time was lost in clumsy fumbling that, even after locating and turning the selector, I wondered if the engine would pick up before the airplane sank dangerously low.

For a long time I heard nothing but the whooshing sound of wind. I tried frantically to think of reasons why my engine wouldn't start, and what steps might be taken, before worrying too much over lost height. The horrifying sight of city buildings rushing up toward the aircraft suddenly made me realize how fast the altimeter was unwinding. With everything below getting bigger by the second, the engine almost unexpectedly returned to life. Already going steeply downhill to keep the propeller windmilling, I let the airplane accelerate too rapidly with its newfound power. A firm pull on the stick prevented my getting so close to the buildings that I couldn't effect a recovery before it was too late.

The cut-out and my slow reaction brought me down to around six hundred feet. One way or another, the officials would probably learn that I'd already used up a tank of gas. About two and a half hours remained in the other tank, and I could be pretty certain that they'd have checked on the aircraft's total endurance.

The situation grew too static, so I thought a premature move toward the coast might stir a little action. Coming out of my circle, I took up a heading away from the city. Before I could cover more than a couple of miles the big aircraft caught on to my move, and broke from its run along the coast. A tight turn put it on bearing to intercept my track, if I held my present heading. Holding my course I continued seaward, while the other airplane positioned itself just beyond the coastline. Like a dolphin playing in front of a ship, but farther ahead, it carried out a series of turns in the airspace I was approaching. Not wanting to appear easily bluffed, I made a slight turn and flew parallel with the coast. This could give the impression that I was confused, and didn't know what to do next. At a slight risk of still being headed off, I swung around in a very wide arc. After working my way back to the protection of tall city buildings I turned for a look, to see the other airplane again on its coastal patrol. During my trip away from town I took little notice of the boats, which had begun to spread out beyond the harbour entrance.

From above I observed activity that deserved further study. Down the harbour a short way was the Navy Yard, and something very unusual seemed suddenly to be happening where previously both a destroyer and an aircraft carrier had been quietly berthed. Dropping down for a close look, I sensed that current naval goings-on were related to my flight. In the time I'd been out of visual range, the sleek Australian destroyer had released all its lines and was now moving stern first toward open water. So urgent was the ship's mission that in clearing the wharf her propellers churned up great clouds of harbour mud. She lined up in the channel and had her engines to what must have been full forward in less time than it took me to fly a complete circle. When I came nearly overhead, the ship already had steerage way. Tightening my turn, I cut back for a close look at this splendid naval spectacle, to see the destroyer beginning to make a good bow-wave with her after-section well down. She was headed for regions where the big airplane lurked, so I contented myself with watching her wake spread far and wide astern.

During my long-ago first pass over the city an American destroyer had been starting her slow run toward the open sea. As the U.S. ship receded into the distance, I had thoughts of following her beyond the territorial limit, ditching alongside and asking for sanctuary as an American citizen. I dropped the idea like a hot potato, when I realized that loud protests from the Australian authorities would cause the Americans to hand me over rather than risk an international argument.

I turned again toward the Navy Yard, to see what else might be going on down there. After what I'd just seen, the navy could no longer be dismissed as a sleeping monster. Instinctively I held to a more respectful distance, and most noticeable from my position of respect was activity on the carrier's flight-deck. No move to put to sea was being made by the lumbering monster, but it appeared her deck was preparing hurriedly for a landing. Launching of anything seemed too remote to consider, and no fast military aircraft would land on a motionless carrier in the close quarters of the harbour. The only airplane they could possibly be clearing to receive would have to be mine! The naval authorities must have thought they should provide facility for an emergency landing close to where I might run out of fuel. By sending a destroyer with half my cruising speed out to sea well in advance, and readying a landing-place in the harbour, the navy seemed to be covering all angles.

The thought occurred to me that of all situations where a government would spare no effort to save a life, mine must rate top priority. Punishment was involved, so there could be no restraint on any resource. Apart from a revenge motive, I could only imagine the navy being sent out for publicity purposes. That kind of thinking led nowhere, so I put the punishment people out of mind. By its show of sea and air power, the government was demonstrating how seriously it took my threats. Failure to communicate a counter-offer to my proposal suggested that they were hoping I'd weaken; if that was the case, they still had plenty of time to do a rethink. They would probably push me to the limit of my nerves first, and then suggest a landing on the carrier when the fuel situation was critical. That would only be likely if they were foolish enough to leave me circling the city past the point of safe return to the airport. Having popped more pills, and thought about dying by inches over a period of years in jail, my resolve was to see this all the way through. Either they'd give me what I wanted, or there'd be no future beyond my final power loss.

I'd neglected the city for a while and decided I should again fly low to let the public know I still existed. Also there were films to be handed to the newspaper, if things worked out. Before diving on the city I did a medium-level circuit, letting off a ten-exposure roll out the open window. Working a Koni-Omega, the easiest box bigger than 35 mm because it only needs pumping with one hand and shutter release with a finger of the other, I took shots from all angles. From high enough not to have to worry about flying into anything, I did the run with my knees gripping the stick and both hands free for the camera. Still at a safe height I reloaded and put on a telephoto lens, hoping to get some editor-pleasing crowd scenes while beating up a few city streets.

I went down in a spinlike spiral, with a pull-out to run full throttle below rooftop level along one of the city's major streets. Tall buildings at the end forced me to do a sharp pull-up, before nosing back down to work over another. Choosing only busy streets, I gave the crowds five minutes of low flying before deciding that they were ready to have their pictures taken. Out of my mind went all other considerations, because now I was practising what I liked to think of as a profession. Steadying the airplane in a turn with my knees, and making sure I didn't risk ramming some building while looking out the side through the viewfinder, I got off a couple of exposures that would be good if there was no camera shake. For scenes highlighting the aircraft's effect on city traffic and crowds, I let off extra frames. At such close proximity fast-moving things can come out fuzzy, so I had to photograph out of fairly tight turns with a little sideslip.

After each burst I had hurriedly to forget the camera, and get back to the aircraft's controls. Using methods developed over the years, I steadied my scenes in the viewfinder during the instant of taking. So stimulating was this job that I nearly finished the roll, before remembering the reason for these photos and feeling a little sick. I thought about the people on the bridge, and how the editor might appreciate a close-in picture; it was shot at nearly deck level, before I put the camera back in its case without bothering to remove the second roll. With a little co-operation from the authorities, the paper would have a good supply of "actual photos taken from the aircraft as it terrorized the city".

Before climbing back to a fuel-saving level I had a close look at the courthouse, where I was expected to lay my neck on the line. Out of sight beneath the hideous building was a labyrinth of dungeonlike cages. For the last couple of hours of my flight, transfer vans from the penitentiary would have been filling them with individuals who'd lost their freedom and their futures. They'd be milling around and talking nervously, as they awaited their turns to be led through holes in the floors of different courtrooms. When I still had half an hour to fly beyond reach of any authority, a few would already have learned their fate. Unless some cop had told them, they wouldn't know that one of their kind was flying around outside the coop defying all takers for as long as a gas-guzzling engine would keep going.

With an hour and a half to go before things became critical, I levelled off at a safe cruising height, and my long silent radio came to life. "Romeo Charlie Alpha, this is Bankstown. Do you read?" the metallic voice said in a strained manner. After I acknowledged, the voice came back with "We've been trying to reach you for some time. Would you please remain at an altitude where you can receive our calls? We relay the following communication from the Police Commissioner. If you land, the court will give every consideration to your case." That was all, and there wasn't a mention of what form the "consideration" might take. After the few seconds of building myself up to high expectations, this was such a let-down that at first I couldn't even answer. The Commissioner must take me for a fool, I thought. What the man was stated to have said didn't mean a damned thing.

356

Before pressing the switch to reply, I tried to decide whether that call was an opener for further negotiation, but could reach no conclusion. Since the Commissioner had waited this long to come up with this reply, he mightn't soften up for real discussion until my flight became dangerous. Speaking closely into the mike I said, "Bankstown—Romeo Charlie Alpha—request you inform Commissioner that his offer is not acceptable. My terms, which I will repeat if necessary, remain as stated in earlier communication." Bankstown acknowledged my rejection by saying it would be passed on, and again asked me to maintain height. In a defiant mood I said I'd stay up if I wasn't busy doing other things, and if I was difficult to reach they could just keep trying.

Two more low runs along city streets were made, as a gesture of rejection. Then I climbed back to where the radio would pick up calls. When nothing came after ten minutes I took a couple more pills. For the first time since take-off I felt a real sense of failure, and it was hitting hard. In a little more than an hour the engine would quit again. When that happened, my only way out would be to point the airplane straight down and bore into the harbour at maximum speed. Whoever had power to give the right answer didn't appear to be coming around. At last I was becoming aware that my earlier thinking was only wishful. They just weren't responding as I'd hoped. Their sea and air preparations were real enough, but there'd been absolutely no indication that they'd ever deal with me directly. The Commissioner's single message had to be considered as resolving absolutely nothing.

Looking down on the city where I'd earned a top reputation as an aerial photographer, I realized how impossible it would be to surrender all that in exchange for prison. Though Sydney was less than two thousand feet below, it was beginning to look remote. I felt that my last connection with the place was already severed. The streets were jammed with cars and tiny specks representing people, but none of that was important any more. On all counts I'd lost, so with my fuel down to an estimated fifty minutes there was no point in doing anything beyond circling around until the engine quit. I'd made some impact on the city as planned, and still had time to go down and stir things again, but since the operation had apparently failed, there wasn't any reason to do so.

This late in the game I would not call and ask for

consideration. They'd been given plenty of time to throw me something, so I wasn't inclined to compromise now. I'd accept such a face-saving offer as a little time in a psychiatric place, but I wouldn't call first and risk the humiliation of a contemptuous turn-down.

Now my gas was down to forty minutes, perhaps somewhat less on official calculations. Flying aimlessly in a large circle, I was gazing toward the horizon and waiting for time to pass. This seemed a good time to take more pills, so I wouldn't be frightened when the engine stopped. It was important that my nerve didn't go when it came time to push the stick forward and head straight for the water. I thought of the night ditching off Singapore, though in that situation survival had been all important. It was from about this height—and even now I could remember the eternity spent working the controls all the way down—but this time the water sparkled in brilliant sunlight. My approach would need to be fast, to shorten any terror. An unpleasant thought was pulling the wings off, in a panicky too-late attempt at recovery.

My circles were becoming sloppy, and I couldn't summon the concentration necessary to make them neat. When I thought about the people below, I no longer felt part of them. I had no wish now to fly down low where I could be seen from close up. The masses had been great when I was trying to manipulate them against the authorities, but I didn't need them as witnesses to my defeat.

Ten more minutes passed, and I had the thought that there'd been no instructions from the officials about the aircraft carrier. They should have come through with word about it by now, so probably the deck clearing was ordered by the ship's captain. If the authorities planned on my using it, they wouldn't surely have waited this long to give me a briefing. Very likely the captain acted on his own initiative, hoping that in an emergency I'd use his floating airport. This was idle thinking to pass time, because that avenue of escape did not exist in my calculations.

I was waiting now for the engine to stop and was not bothering to fly the airplane. Left pretty much to itself, except for an occasional nudge on stick or rudder when its behaviour became too outrageous, the aircraft wallowed around like something half dead. No longer was I holding to a definite circle, and corrections were only made when I seemed to be drifting away from the

358

water.

For two or three seconds before my call-sign came over the radio I had a feeling something was coming. Probably there'd been some noise on the carrier wave that hadn't fully registered. When Bankstown asked if I read, I confirmed, trying not to sound anxious. I didn't want to build up hope, in case this was just another empty call. If it had been, I decided that there would be no further transmission from this aircraft.

Then came "Romeo Charlie Alpha—we relay the following message. Your conditions are agreed to and you may land. Confirm that you are tracking to Bankstown." This came as such a shock that for an instant I was stunned, and didn't know whether to believe what I'd just heard. In spite of a feeling that this was unreal and didn't really relate to me, I was suddenly overcome by a tremendous sense of elation. Quickly I pushed the throttle forward so the airplane would fly instead of wallow, checked the fuel gauge to see if there was a chance of reaching Bankstown, and started talking into the microphone. With indecent haste, and before communicating more than my call-sign, I whipped the airplane around onto the shortest possible heading toward Bankstown. Struggling to maintain a steady voice, I confirmed that I was on track.

In my excitement I pushed the throttle too far forward. The airplane flew magnificently, while using fuel at such a rate that I'd be unlikely to reach Bankstown. Power was eased off to an economical setting, before something in the back of my mind came to the front. My reprieve should be checked, in case it was phrased in some sneaky way that would nullify the whole thing. So little time had passed since setting course that almost as part of the original communication I asked for clarification. After giving my call-sign I said, "I understand that conditions stated in earlier transmission are acceptable and I can land without threat of arrest. Is that correct?" "That is correct, Romeo Charlie Alpha," came the answer without hesitation. Following acknowledgement, I nearly added that I hoped my fuel would last the distance. I'd have to hope too that later on others wouldn't put a different interpretation on just what had been said, because quite possibly the only record I'd ever have would be that stamped indelibly on my mind.

In the interest of air safety I should have been sent the much shorter distance to Sydney airport. Having heard what I just did, I wouldn't tempt fate by reopening communication. Navigational instructions weren't to be queried, even if they might involve me in a crash landing somewhere short of Bankstown. Passing abeam the main airport I expected a call to inform me of its availability, if I had a fuel problem. Nothing came, and I felt I'd rather press on than have further discussion with authority. Anxiously I studied the gauge as Sydney airport slid farther away. Without feeling any real fear, I wondered if all this would end with my having to pull off some sort of crash landing in the midst of trees and houses.

With the crash possibility very real, I was spared having to think too much about what might happen when I had finally to face the authorities. As a temporary diversion, the question of whether I'd reach the airport was almost welcome.

Realizing that I'd probably walk away from a controlled crash, I couldn't help wondering how my newly promised immunity would be implemented. On close examination this gift of life revealed a few minor flaws. Clearest of all was that I wouldn't be popular with the police or any other authority. They'd have to honour their promise, but I could see other factors emerging. Cops would be on hand to greet me at Bankstown—if my fuel stretched that far. They'd never allow me to walk away on the strength of a promise extracted minutes before under conditions amounting to blackmail. There'd probably have to be a release procedure, and Ormsby's assistance could be needed from the instant I stepped out of the airplane. In the time it might take for him to learn where the police had taken me, I could get quite a battering.

Half-way between Sydney and Bankstown my thoughts were interrupted by a call. This time it was a terse, "Romeo Charlie Alpha, this is Bankstown. Will you confirm that there is no other person aboard that aircraft." Nothing further was said after I "confirmed", and they left me to wonder why the question was asked. All I could imagine was that an imaginative official thought I had someone from a newspaper on board, and the whole thing was a big con job. If they could catch me out on something like that, they'd have an excuse for cancelling any promise. Somebody's fond hope must have been dashed, when I said I was alone.

Five miles from Bankstown the gauge hovered on zero, with an occasional surge to indicate something sloshing around the bottom of the tank. Since passing abeam Sydney airport I'd been eyeballing every piece of open land bigger than a tennis court, though I already knew there was nothing really usable. Some places were big enough for initial touchdown, but I'd have to rely on buildings or trees to brush off a lot of ground speed.

Bankstown airport was in clear sight now, and it was time to call for landing instructions I might never use. Rather than go through that formality just yet, I decided to wait until things looked more certain. Meanwhile there were thoughts about bracing myself for a rapid slowdown, after putting the wheels onto some sort of ground. If badly caught out on space when the power went, I'd sideslip in and rely on the crumpling of the airplane for deceleration. Though it would be a shame to do that to a perfectly good aircraft, I'd at least stand a good chance of being around to enjoy my new freedom.

Since setting course I'd allowed the airplane to gradually lose height, gaining speed for fuel consumed. Below a thousand feet and still descending, I had to force myself to crack on more power. From about three miles away, with the gauge no longer bouncing, I called Bankstown Tower and was told to use the one one runway. Seconds later they added that I'd have the airport to myself, and could land any way I chose. Finally I came within gliding range and turned downwind for the one one, ready to break and land across the field if I had a power loss. My close-in approach brought me almost directly over the airport's cluster of buildings and roads, and below was a startling sight.

Cars jammed the roads, mobs of people were gathered round the tarmac area, and at choice vantage points were what appeared to be mobile television units. The law and a few newspaper people were about all I expected. In front of that crowd I'd have to do a good landing, handicapped by bad depth perception from taking too many pills. It would be humiliating to bounce off the runway and hop like a kangaroo in front of them. This aircraft needed to be three-pointed onto the ground, with the stick well back at the right instant, and the thought of television coverage was almost too much. Had there been an out-of-sight runway I'd have made for that.

Though a "turning base" call wasn't needed at an airport

361

closed to all other traffic, I still made one. Stupidly I added, "I've not slept for the last couple of nights, and could have trouble with my landing." Then I was too busy with landing preparation to think any more about how I would perform. Not once as I set the elevator trim, lowered flaps and lined up with the runway did I give a thought to being stung on pills or appearing incompetent in front of press and public.

Over the beginning of the runway I was a little too high for my flare-out, unless I wanted to risk a bounce. After sinking a few more feet it seemed time to bring the nose up, cutting off my view of the runway ahead. Looking out the side to get an exact idea of remaining height I saw the hangars clearly—and masses of people standing near them. All that mattered now was that I was doing a landing, and I liked my landings to be smooth. What lay outside the airplane was of interest only to the extent that it indicated when to chop remaining power, before easing the stick gently back toward my belly. All must have been done correctly, because after a few seconds of floating clear my wheels sank onto the runway, to stay there without bouncing off.

Flaps were brought up while the airplane was still rolling. As it slowed to a stop, I couldn't think of much beyond being relieved that somehow I'd managed an acceptable landing. Taxi instructions, in a startlingly clear voice with the engine idling, were vague, as though the man in the tower didn't know where I should be sent. All he said was that I could use any taxiway. At any instant I expected police cars to bear down, with cops dragging me out of the airplane in range of the television cameras, but it didn't happen. The taxiway I was on led to the tarmac area, where crowds were held behind a fence. Right now, my biggest worry was being taken into custody in front of all those people. Around to the right of the control tower, missing the thickest crowd, was the way to the hangar where my own aircraft and this one were kept. I headed in that direction, expecting at any time to be signalled to a parking spot where I'd be publicly arrested. No ground or radio signal came, and now I was clear of the tarmac on a taxiway blocked from public view by hangars.

Approaching where I'd turn between two sets of hangars, and have finally to face up to officialdom, I was quite calm and relaxed. If it weren't for the pill effect, I realized, this was where my nerves would break. While I faced almost certain rough

362

treatment, I wasn't even capable of feeling fear. At the end of whatever bad time I was given, there'd have to be freedom. Rounding the corner of the hangar, I had a sudden view of what looked like utter chaos. Most of the mob from the tarmac area seemed to have come running to the fence separating the space in front of the hangar from the access road. With nobody attempting to stop them, some carrying heavy photographic equipment were scrambling over the barrier. In the middle of all that was where I'd stop, shut off the engine and climb out of the airplane.

Trying to act as if none of this existed, I taxied slowly, prepared to stop the engine if anybody came too close to the propeller. By concentrating on not clipping anything with my wings, I was able to regard these people as no more than background. In front of the cavernous open hangar, no more than the length of the airplane from the fence, I came to a dead stop. Holding the brake tight on one wheel I applied power, pivoted around to where my tail faced the fence, then got ready to shut down. With the thickest crowd comfortably out of sight behind me, I started the motions of bringing the engine to a stop. A defensive reaction against getting out in front of people who might think I was insane caused me to perform all actions with exaggerated slowness. Since they could stare with contempt I wanted to act aloof, and conclude my flight with some dignity.

Slight revving of the engine, followed by mixture out to full lean, brought the propeller to a stop. I made no move to open the door, and those inside the fence came only a little closer. Nobody seemed willing to be first to walk right up to the cabin door. In sudden silence, after all those hours, things seemed so unreal that I was able to look toward different parts of the airplane quite oblivious of bystanders. Above all, I was aware of a high-pitched ringing sound in my head.

Very deliberately I went through the motions of shutting down, then double-checked to make sure nothing was overlooked. Though there'd be little left in the tank, I moved the fuel selector to the off position. As if it could only be removed in the correct manner, I carefully lifted off the headset and hung it on its hook. This acted as a signal for those inside the fence to move closer.

Two well-dressed gentlemen detached themselves from the

rest, and came to within a couple of feet of the door. They waited while my eyes roved round the cockpit making sure everything really was shut off. Only then was I ready to leave the aircraft. Releasing the latch slowly, to suggest that I was ready for those who wished to speak to me, I pushed the door slightly outwards. As I moved toward the half-open door, the two men came closer. Apparently sensing that I wanted to muster dignity in front of the spectators, they carried out their end accordingly. Instead of loudly ordering me out, one of them said they were there at the Commissioner's request, to provide me with transportation to the court. After replying that I quite understood, I climbed down to the ground. I turned and reached back into the airplane to bring out my camera case.

15

What a stunt!   peace in a police car   man of a
myriad misdeeds   courtroom tenterhooks
judgement from a lofty perch
trapdoor exit.

MOMENT OF TRUTH

Mention of "transportation to the court" nearly caused me to
protest, but this seemed neither the time nor the place. Saying
that I shouldn't have to go to court might be provocative, and
create a scene in front of the audience. Also the trip might be for
nothing more sinister than having the charges officially withdrawn. As I walked from the aircraft, one of the officers reached
for my camera case, saying, "I'll carry that if you like."

Photographers and reporters crowded in as I was led to an
unmarked police car. Questions were still coming through the
open window as the car moved away, through standstill traffic
that held us to a crawl even beyond the airport gate. The whole
scene made me think my story must have received considerable
coverage, but of more immediate concern was the direction the
police car was taking.

A direct road led from the airport to Bankstown Police Station,
also on to Sydney and the criminal courts. This wasn't for us, and
after turning in a different direction the driver said something
about dodging the press. No longer could I see any press to be
dodged. Anxiously I wondered if "instructions" mentioned
earlier weren't really for me to be held incommunicado at some
out-of-the-way place. Another turn, and more talk about not
being followed by reporters, made me think something was very
wrong. Next came the terrifying thought that these cops had
orders to make sure I spoke to nobody about my understanding of
promises that came over the air. For a minute I had visions of

being dragged into court without getting a chance to mention the matter. Then I realized that others would have listened in on my air-to-ground communications, so there should be plenty of verification.

Finally the cops quit turning and headed for Bankstown Police Station, where I'd definitely be beyond reach of uninvited reporters. During the ride a metallic voice repeatedly came over the car's radio, informing all units including boats that "the aircraft had landed".

At the station I was taken straight upstairs, to a detectives' squad room. The place was jammed with police, all very friendly, and nobody seemed ready to treat me as a prisoner. It seemed clear that the cops knew I'd been promised something, though there was recurring talk of my having to go to court.

Had Ormsby been there, I might have worked up enough nerve to try walking out of the room. Without him, my sense of discretion, or cowardice, strongly told me not to remind these police that I considered myself to have an official promise of freedom. Convinced of my rights, I just hoped it couldn't be too long before I could make contact with either Ormsby or the barrister. Right now it seemed best to tag along with events—not act as though I felt good about backing anybody into a corner— and leave details of my release to those able to negotiate at high level.

My name was called out, and working their way toward me through the mass of cops were Ormsby and the barrister. Both began firing questions, without worrying about being overheard. They were anxious to learn as much as possible while the police remained in a mood to let us talk. Along with the news that sent him rushing to Bankstown, Ormsby had heard about some sort of promise; he wanted full details.

After explaining my "requests" and being left in the air until my fuel was almost gone, I gave an account of the transmission. As well, I told about my further call for confirmation. A sharp question from the barrister established the fact that at no time had I spoken directly to anybody other than air traffic con-trollers. Some quick talk between the lawyers ensued. They discussed the fine points of just how binding any promise of consideration would be. It was suggested that since no high official had personally come on the air, it might be difficult to

366

establish responsibility. Then the barrister suddenly remembered being told by a reporter that the government broadcasting service had taped all communications between my aircraft and Bankstown. While they talked about obtaining a copy by subpoena if necessary, a large figure bearing an infuriated expression barged into the room.

Even in his fury the big detective had sense enough to exercise restraint when challenged by two lawyers. Answering Ormsby's demand to know what was going on, the cop said that he was arresting me for stealing the airplane. This suggested that the officer thought I might be safely clear on the real charges. Ormsby's reply was that I'd borrowed the aircraft. Letting me slip the bill of sale for the plane to Ormsby, the detective blew any remote chance of charging me with theft. When the sergeant maintained that my use of the airplane for a purpose other than testing constituted fraud, I had the impression that he might already have threatened the owner. The detective backed off slightly when Ormsby said that a fraud charge would never stick. For the moment the situation appeared to be resolved, but then the cop announced that he was arresting me for violating air-traffic rules. The barrister quickly countered by saying that such a charge would be a matter for the civil aviation authorities.

The sergeant walked away. That gave me an opportunity to ask Ormsby why he was so hot under the collar, when none of the other police was behaving that way. Ormsby explained that as officer in charge of the case he'd probably been hoping to wind it up with a conviction. With great assurance Ormsby said that he'd cool down in a little while.

Expecting to be searched somewhere along the line, I handed Ormsby my first roll of film, which, together with the one still in the camera, was to be given to the news editor. While I talked about it, a young cop pulled my close-up crowd shots out of the camera, straight into daylight. When it was all spoiled, the officer looked smug, as if he'd destroyed something useful to the defence. I complained that my best pictures had been ruined. Ormsby told me to shut up. He suggested the police might not be happy about my taking photos of the excitement I'd created.

The lawyers informed me I'd probably have to go to court. I kept insisting that, according to what I'd heard on the aircraft's radio, I shouldn't go anywhere. I was surprised at not feeling sick with worry during the discussion, and then I realized that my pills were still working well. My thinking didn't seem to be affected, though by now my emotional senses were pretty well blunted. Detached from blind panic I could argue with my lawyers and direct them to contact someone high up; one of them replied in no uncertain terms that they were perfectly capable of taking the right steps.

From wherever he'd been, the detective reappeared, saying he was ready to take me into town. To protect me, Ormsby accompanied me in the police car. It was during the fifteen-mile drive that peace was made with the detective sergeant.

As an opener, Ormsby said that he believed there had been a firm commitment from high up. The cop expressed doubt about anybody being able to interfere with the Justice Department. The way he spat out "anybody" indicated little respect for some official above him. As far as the cop was concerned this was his case, I was his prisoner, and nobody had the power to deprive him of the privilege. Implied in all this was the detective's supreme moment of triumph, when just before sentencing he'd stand up in court and deliver his own thoughts about the prisoner.

Approaching downtown Sydney, the sergeant spoke to me in a friendly manner. First he made the profound observation that I must have been saving fuel toward the end of my flight, because he'd noticed from the ground that I was flying slowly and dragging my tail. Newspaper placards proclaiming, "Crazed pilot buzzes city", brought the friendly remark that I'd created quite a stir. This new attitude raised false hopes that somehow I'd be able to avoid an actual court appearance.

Entering the courthouse through the front door, and not the prisoners' entrance, raised further hope. I was taken straight into a courtroom, but there weren't any signs of readiness for a slightly delayed trial. Only a few people stood around as if waiting for something to happen, and there was no judge behind the bench. When I entered, there was confusion and a number of busy little conferences rapidly took place. The dock gate was shut behind me; then Ormsby, the barrister and the detective went into a huddle with a man I thought must be the prosecutor. A shuffle at the far end of the room put a sudden stop to all discussion. While everybody stood in silence a gavel was banged, and the judge

368

climbed into his lofty perch. His distant face looked more human than that of the much closer prosecutor. Confronted by these trappings, I still felt more like a bystander than the subject of immediate events. The idea occurred that I should be in a frenzy of terror. Instead, it all seemed unreal and I wasn't terribly frightened. None of this was important because I'd been given an assurance, and sooner or later these people would have to accept that fact. When I mentioned it to Ormsby as he paused near the dock, he rather sharply told me not to bother him about such things now.

Court didn't really seem to be in session, until my barrister stood up to speak. What he had to say was very much to the point. All he wanted was a lengthy adjournment, because in the present climate of hysteria it would be difficult to empanel an unbiased jury; he gave an impressive demonstration of courtroom histrionics. Fully wound up, he shouted that with newspapers emblazoning my story for all including prospective jurors to see, and radio stations beaming it out every few minutes, it would be impossible to hold a fair trial. Not a word was said about official assurances, and this oversight I could not understand.

My barrister's last sentence triggered off a tirade from the prosecutor. Any hysteria or publicity, he said, was invited by the defendant. It was inconceivable that the accused should benefit from his actions, or that the trial should be postponed for such reasons. If those reasons weren't enough, he maintained that the Crown had gone to great trouble to assemble its witnesses, including a Secret Service agent from America. This was followed by more scathing remarks about my criminal conduct in creating the present state of affairs. Then without giving a ruling on the delay request, the judge announced recess until after lunch.

After the formality of all standing in silence while the judge departed, Ormsby said he'd see me down below in the cells. A trapdoor was raised from the floor, and I was herded down through it and along an ancient stone corridor to a large cell already occupied by a dozen or more prisoners. Most were too worried about their own fate to be interested in the doings of others, though there were remarks about a crazy pilot flying around the city when he should have been in court. None was aware that I was the individual concerned.

A lunch better than anything dished up at the penitentiary was brought around, along with cups of tea. Mine was handed to a prisoner with a voracious appetite. The tea I drank, and it seemed to reactivate the drugs in my system. When Ormsby and the barrister turned up, I was in a talkative mood. The three of us were taken to a private cell for our conference. Getting straight to the point, Ormsby said there didn't appear to be much chance of my being released as a result of any assurance I might have extracted. I was still shouting my protests when the barrister said they could probably reach a compromise. In a voice breaking with emotion, I bellowed out that most likely they'd get me ten years instead of twenty.

I told my lawyers that I had no intention of even trying to serve a long sentence. Speaking as a pair, Ormsby and the barrister told me to calm down, because things weren't nearly as bad as they looked. They had things to do, and would see me again in a little while. Back in the holding cell I started to feel better, but then realized it could only be the pills at work. Half an hour later I was called out again, to face an almost jubilant pair of legal advisers.

Suspicious of the breezy way they were behaving, I tried to brace myself for a shock. When the barrister said five years, I could only shout that I'd never last the distance. Telling me to shut up and let him finish, the lawyer went on to say that it looked as though I'd get five years with a non-parole period of twelve months. Things looked brighter as the thought that I could live through twelve months flashed through my mind. Both lawyers apparently expected me to be jumping with joy, which inwardly I was. I knew that, assuming good behaviour and no record of violence, the non-parole period represented the length of time actually to be served. Ormsby did all the talking, because the barrister probably didn't want to sing his own praise. All that remained was for me to go back up the trapdoor and face the court.

After the lawyers departed, my feelings ran from elation to depression. The latter wasn't critical, because at last things would be settled—and without my destruction. Failure to gain release didn't mean that my flight was a flop; the lawyers and I believed it had created the right climate. As a result of the morning's performance I was facing only a year in jail. With that logic, I could consider my "terror flight over Sydney" ninety per cent successful.

Pleading guilty waived any official commitment, though I was gaining most of the benefit of that forced assurance in a way that was face-saving all around. Those who might be a trifle upset over the flight should cool down by the time a year had passed. Right now I was glad to be in this cell, and not on a one-way trip out of the country. Warming my feelings to those ill-used lawyers, I realized that they were putting my interests above their own. If I'd not pleaded guilty, mine would have been the sort of trial where my eminent barrister could have shown up brilliantly in well-publicized jousts with the judge. Ormsby's briefing would have been equally masterful, and yet both were willing to forgo all this rather than place my future in jeopardy. They knew I was financial enough to stand a long and to them profitable trial, but still pressed me to accept a way out that would quickly sever their connection with the case.

After a long wait a cop came to the cell door, saying they were ready for me upstairs. All others connected with the case were seated in the courtroom, when I made my entrance through the hole in the floor. Ormsby and the barrister were at the bar table, not even glancing my way as they carried on some quiet discussion. Across from them sat the prosecutor, with somebody who seemed to be assisting him. Neither of those two looked happy at the turn of events. How the judge appeared at this juncture I wasn't to know, because my eyes simply didn't want to reach as high as his face.

Something I hadn't noticed before was the way all of the courtroom trappings were labelled. Little signs reading "Judge", "Jury", and "Jail Recorder" struck me as unnecessary and rather grim reminders. The bailiff's announcement started proceedings, and soon I was on my feet pleading guilty to one charge after another. The list took so long to get through that somewhere past a possible sentence of fifty years I lost count. I couldn't help thinking, at this stage, of the prosecutor. Finally I pleaded guilty to the last of my offences against Her Majesty's Government.

The bailiff indicated that I was to be seated. A glance from the judge let the prosecutor know that it was time for him to address the court. With an edge of bitterness, the prosecutor merely said

371

that the defendant's plea would satisfy the terms of the indictment. This was taken by my counsel as indication that the opposition had nothing further to say. Rising as his opponent sat down, my barrister started to make a speech.

Enumerating my many virtues, the lawyer began with my work as an aerial photographer. After praising this to high heaven, he mentioned various government departments that used my service. When that subject had been exhausted, he laboured away at the fact that my life had been beyond reproach in the years since I'd made counterfeit money. Terms like "counterfeit" and "years" made me shudder, because they didn't seem altogether appropriate right now. Then the barrister said that for someone of my temperament prison could be destructive, as would be indicated by psychiatric reports available for the court's inspection. While the judge studied the two reports at length, my barrister thoughtfully refrained from talking. His Lordship read what the psychiatrists had to say and cogitated in silence.

But there were others who'd not yet been heard. Behind the "Jail Recorder" label a dried-out individual stood up, to impart to the court some very important information. Waiting for silence, he started to read out my recorded past misdeeds. Most of my long-ago arrests in America hadn't gone into F.B.I. records, so their weight of numbers could not be brought to bear. What the jail recorder's sheet lacked in length, he made up in emphasis, with a pause between each item. It was announced for all to hear and take note that in 1936 the prisoner in the dock had been jailed for five days in New York State, for illegally riding a train. Then, after a pause for effect, it was stated that two years later in Vancouver, Washington, I'd been sentenced to a couple of days in jail for peddling without a licence. So serious did this sound that I remembered with gratitude how a city court judge all those years ago made a charge—that could have been "swindling"— into the most minor of offences.

Then there was the little arrest in Sacramento, California, when just off a freight train I'd been caught in the act of biting a citizen. The alert detective put the charge down as "mooching", and so it was labelled in F.B.I. archives. The term now led to consternation, as it was read out half a lifetime later in a court on the other side of the world. Nobody knew what "mooching" was, least of all the jail recorder. Confronted with unfamiliar "legal terminology" he hesitated, waiting for somebody more knowledgeable to enlighten the court on just what the accused had done in far-away Sacramento.

The strange word was repeated by different people in the court, the judge looking as puzzled as anyone else. For a moment I expected to be called upon to make the embarrassing explanation that the offence in question was panhandling. A word from somebody let the jail recorder know that it wasn't vital for the court to learn the exact nature of this charge, because the only penalty listed was a "floater". Again His Lordship appeared curious about American expressions. My barrister filled the breach by saying that in his understanding, based on earlier discussion with the defendant, a "floater" was a sentence suspended on condition the offender left town.

At last it was time for the jail recorder's dreaded *pièce de résistance*. In fine voice for this entry on his list the recorder read out stark facts of a sentence served in McNeil Island Federal Penitentiary, for offences relating to forged ration tickets. While that resounded through the court, I could only look down at the trapdoor. Finally, the man mentioned three minor charges concerning illegal betting in Sydney. Satisfied that he'd done his best, the jail recorder sat down, and I braced myself for whatever might come. My only hope was that the barrister would be allowed to say a few more good things about me, before sentence was passed.

Going through my mind was the notion that someone should be telling the court about those old offences not being really serious, if viewed in the context of their time. Still there was no signal for me to stand up, so I waited to see what else could possibly happen before the blow fell. Hoping it would be something to steer the judge's thoughts away from what he'd just heard, I felt as if the trapdoor had dropped from under me when the bailiff called out the name of the detective sergeant. With things supposedly cut and dried, I didn't expect that officer to be called. Then he entered the witness box, presumably to make comments that must surely settle my fate. After a little prompting, the detective began to recite what I thought was a nicely prepared speech. He spoke about my more recent activities, but there was no mention of the flight. He could,

373

however, have dispensed with a quote from the head of the government money-printing department, in which that person supposedly claimed that some of my work was better than similar produced by his men. It was intended, I imagine, as a tribute to my skill, though I thought the court was not the best place to bring it up. I hoped the judge would regard it as evidence of a long-dead craftsmanship.

The witness's next words undid any minor damage. He stated that as a result of his investigation he was quite certain that I'd not engaged in activity related to counterfeit money for a number of years, and that I was now highly regarded as an aerial photographer. The detective said that with my capabilities I could have made a success of almost anything—and then stepped down from the box.

With all eyes in the court now focused on me, I didn't need the bailiff's signal to indicate that this was the end of the line. Standing stiffly upright, I heard myself sentenced separately to five years' hard labour on every charge but one. For some reason that offence carried only a four-year penalty. Then the judge said that all sentences would be served concurrently, meaning that unless he had something else to say I'd do five years. His Lordship added that he was setting a non-parole period of twelve months, and recommended that my sentence be served on a prison farm rather than in the penitentiary.

That marked the end of the court proceedings, so all those others who'd been privileged to remain seated now stood up. I went back down through the hole in the floor, thinking thank Christ the suspense was over, and twelve months wasn't for ever. Behind me, the trapdoor closed with a thud.

EPILOGUE

Twelve months stretched to fifteen, when following on-time parole approval the relevant papers were "misplaced" instead of being forwarded by the court office to Commonwealth Attorney General for final signature. Much chasing around by Ormsby eventually straightened this out. Though I never so much as pretended to follow any religious faith, prison chaplain Reverend Brand provided untiring assistance in gaining final release.

Sentence was served at a state penitentiary rather than a prison farm. Jail officials informed me that they and not the judge had last say as to where the term would be served. Possibly this was some official's way of "getting even" for my performance over Sydney, or the earlier cigarette-dropping flight.

On arrival at the penitentiary note was taken of certain skills I possessed, which resulted in job assignment to the institution's well-equipped print-shop. For several months this irony passed unnoticed in higher quarters, then some branch of authority "woke up". The remainder of my term was served in the library.

After discharge, Australian Air Photos was reactivated and I was again employed by State Government departments, with the past forgotten. At first it was necessary to carry a licensed pilot, who flew as a passenger, because there were still matters to be straightened out with the Department of Civil Aviation. Despite highly vocal opinions of legal advisers and others, my pilot's licence was restored following clearance by a D.C.A.-appointed psychiatrist. One of the first passengers to be carried on a photographic flight was the Reverend Brand.

With clients not serviced during the period I was "unavailable", Australian Air Photos again flourished. The old Auster from Singapore, after shedding part of its fuselage fabric in flight, was finally replaced by a modern Cessna.

On the occasion of the opening of the Sydney Opera House by

Her Majesty Queen Elizabeth II an exception was made to the rule prohibiting civil aircraft flying over royalty. One airplane was permitted to fly overhead for photographic purposes during the Queen's actual presence. That aircraft was the shiny Australian Air Photos Cessna, piloted by myself, and a large number of pictures were taken for the Public Works Department. On parole when that event took place, I was technically "serving a sentence outside the walls", so this would have to be the first ever occasion when the Queen was overflown by a time-serving prisoner from one of Her Majesty's penal institutions. It is extremely doubtful whether any official was aware of this when approval for that flight was granted.

Looking back on years of excitement, and then examining the lives of contemporaries who opted for conformity, leaves me with few regrets.

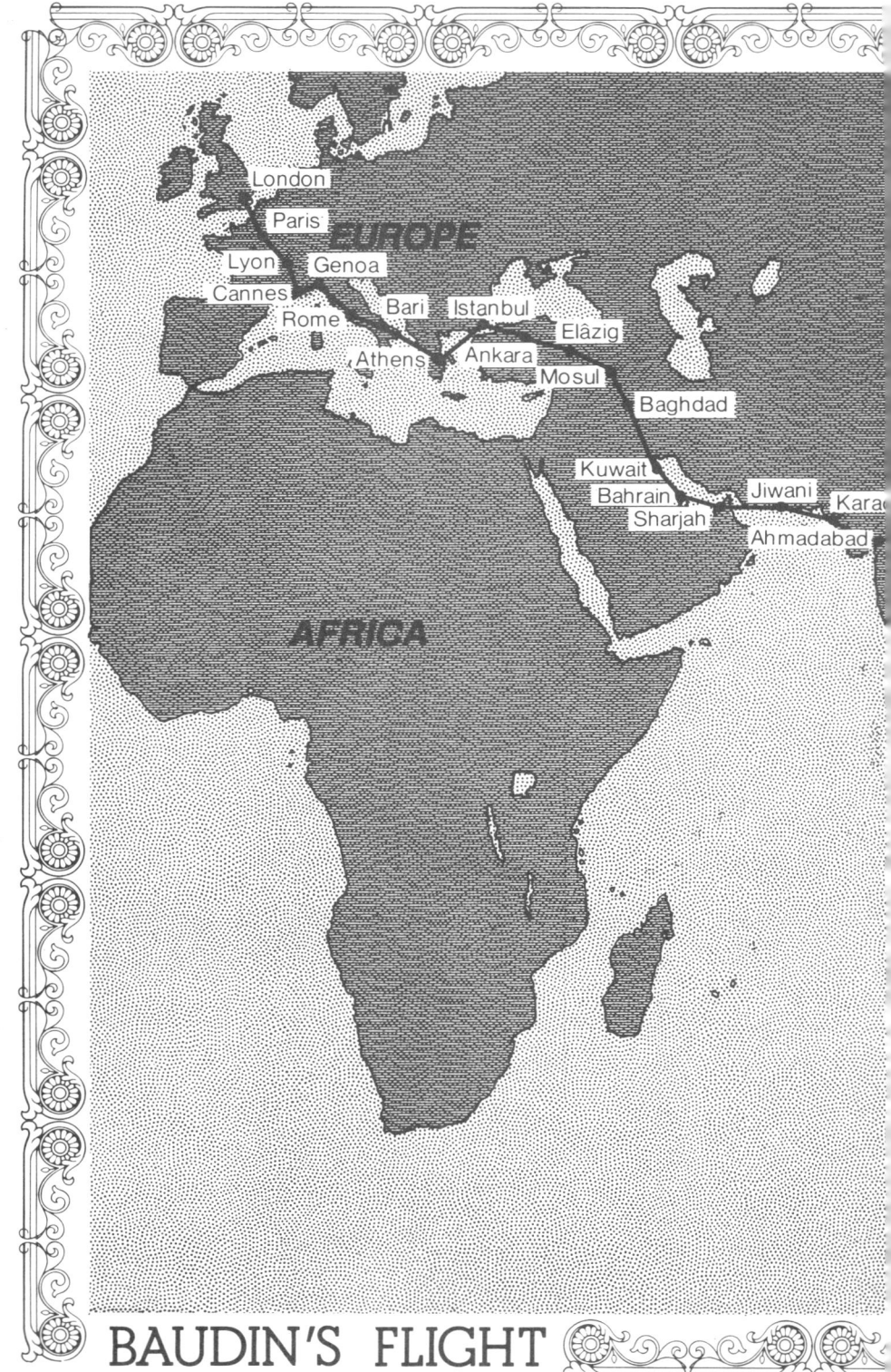

London
Paris
EUROPE
Lyon
Genoa
Cannes
Bari
Istanbul
Rome
Elâzig
Athens
Ankara
Mosul
Baghdad
Kuwait
Jiwani
Bahrain
Kara
Sharjah
Ahmadabad

AFRICA

BAUDIN'S FLIGHT